Sister Kenny

The Woman Who Challenged the Doctors

*The University of Minnesota Press
acknowledges with gratitude the
financial assistance provided by
the Elmer L. and Eleanor J. Andersen Foundation
for the preparation of the manuscript*

SISTER KENNY

The Woman Who Challenged the Doctors

by
Victor Cohn

THE UNIVERSITY OF MINNESOTA PRESS, MINNEAPOLIS

Printed in the United States of America
at Napco Graphic Arts, Inc., New Berlin, Wisconsin
Published in Canada by Burns & MacEachern Limited,
Don Mills, Ontario

Library of Congress Catalog Card Number 75-15401

ISBN 0-8166-0755-9

Second printing, 1976

For Marcella, who did so much

Contents

Sister Kenny

The Woman Who Challenged the Doctors

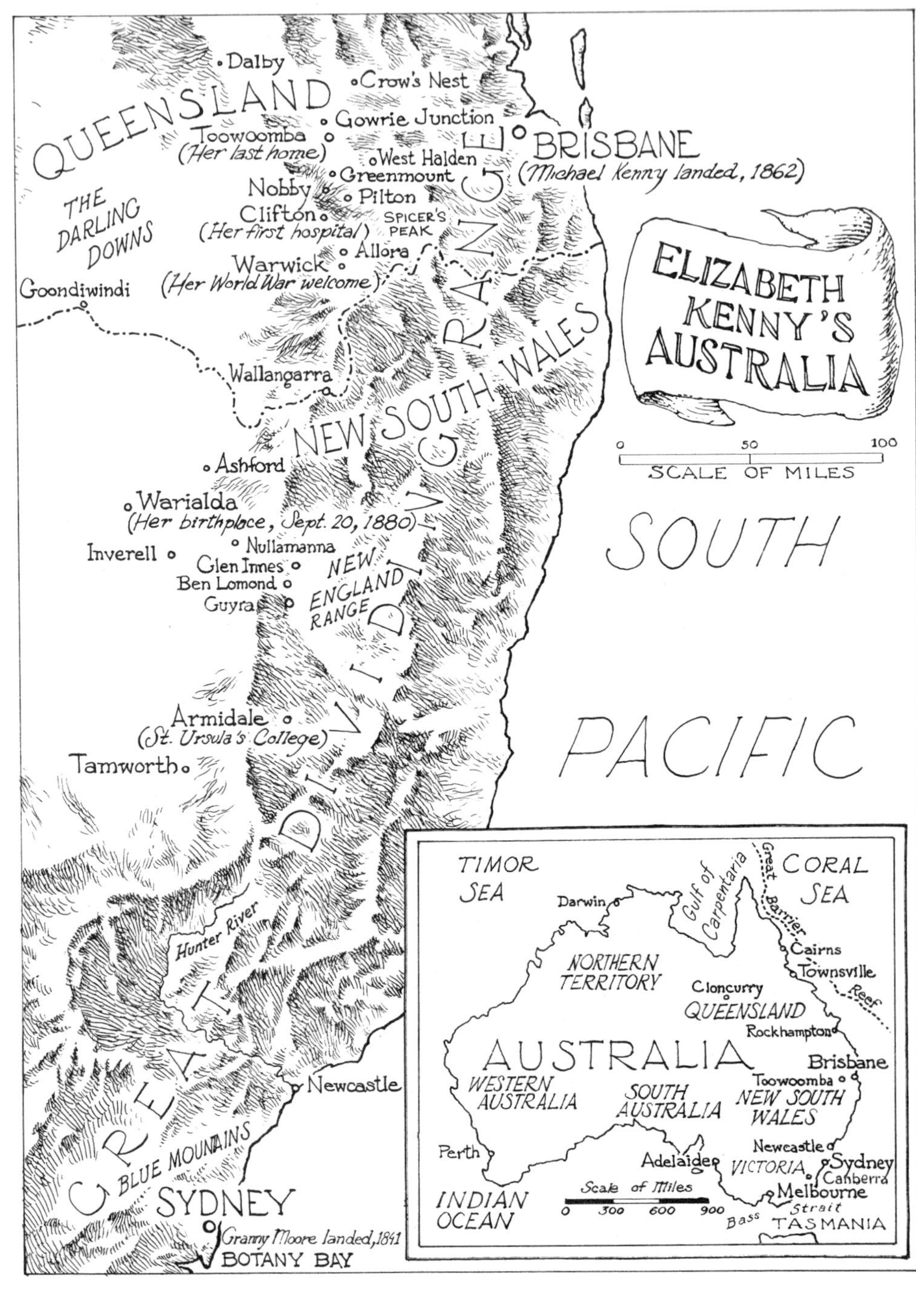

ELIZABETH KENNY'S AUSTRALIA
QUEENSLAND
Dalby
Crow's Nest
Gowrie Junction
Toowoomba
(Her last home)
West Halden
BRISBANE
(Michael Kenny landed, 1862)
Greenmount
Nobby
Pilton
Clifton
(Her first hospital)
SPICER'S PEAK
THE DARLING DOWNS
Allora
Warwick
(Her World War welcome)
Goondiwindi
Wallangarra
NEW SOUTH WALES
Ashford
Warialda
(Her birthplace, Sept. 20, 1880)
Nullamanna
Inverell
Glen Innes
Ben Lomond
Guyra
NEW ENGLAND RANGE
GREAT DIVIDING RANGE
Armidale
(St. Ursula's College)
Tamworth
Hunter River
Newcastle
BLUE MOUNTAINS
SYDNEY
Granny Moore landed, 1841
BOTANY BAY
0 50 100
SCALE OF MILES
SOUTH PACIFIC
TIMOR SEA
Darwin
Gulf of Carpentaria
Great Barrier Reef
CORAL SEA
Cairns
Townsville
NORTHERN TERRITORY
Cloncurry
QUEENSLAND
Rockhampton
AUSTRALIA
Brisbane
Toowoomba
WESTERN AUSTRALIA
SOUTH AUSTRALIA
NEW SOUTH WALES
Newcastle
Perth
Adelaide
VICTORIA
Sydney
Canberra
Melbourne
Scale of Miles
0 300 600 900
INDIAN OCEAN
Bass Strait
TASMANIA

Introduction

A Nurse's Revolution

ON APRIL 14, 1940, a woman named Elizabeth Kenny stepped onto a pier in San Francisco. An independent-minded bush nurse from Australia, she was determined to shake up the doctors. She wanted to make them reverse their surely wrongheaded treatment of one of the most dreaded diseases of all time: poliomyelitis. She wanted to show that their "paralyzed" children could walk.

It was late in her life. She had lost her battle in her own country. On some days her legs ached and on some her hope sagged. She was a crusader, however. At the age of fifty-nine, half sick at heart yet stubborn as youth, she had sailed to America to try again.

Within five years, she succeeded. She relived the classic story of Upstart versus Authority and reminded the world that the learned establishment is not always right. A person with her roots in the turn of the century, she became ever contemporary, in her own way a questioner like a Kepler or a Freud, a rebel whose life casts light on all times.

Elizabeth Kenny's one-woman revolution helped start modern medical rehabilitation. She taught doctors to substitute optimistic activity for the immobilization of polio victims in plaster casts for weeks and months, one of the most painful and harmful treatments ever practiced. By this achievement, she prevented a vast amount of crippling in the years before the Salk and Sabin vaccines. Even more important, she helped turn medicine toward a new aggressive approach to all injury.

A strapping woman with a flamboyant way and a sometimes flip, sometimes cutting tongue, she also caught the country's imagination. She became a heroine with her name in lights on Broadway, and for ten successive years American women, polled by Dr. Gallup, named her one of the women they most admired, second each year only to Eleanor Roosevelt. In 1952, shortly before her death, she was named first.

In a way, women were cheering a new and rousing fighter for female equality. Elizabeth Kenny was born in 1880, when Florence Nightingale was still alive and fighting male disdain. In Elizabeth's youth, Susan B. Anthony and her suffragists were parading and agitating for the vote. Carry Nation was chopping up saloons, and the first few daring women were emerging in skin-tight bathing costumes. In far-off Australia, young Elizabeth heard the challenge, and in the esteem of midtwentieth-century American women, Dr. Gallup discovered, she led Helen Keller, Margaret Sanger, Clare Booth Luce, Grandma Moses, Shirley Temple, and, in Elizabeth Kenny's last year, even Mrs. Roosevelt.

Who was this old-new woman who so suddenly captured America? A rare and independent soul, she had spent much of her life as a self-appointed country nurse, her only pay often a fresh-cured ham or a "thank you." She had also been an inventor, a businesswoman, and no mean politician. She was called "Sister," but she was not a nun; "Sister" in British countries is a head nurse's title.

As a young, self-made nurse she had hit on some new ideas about polio treatment and encountered what to her seemed to be medicine's blindness. She had politely, then impolitely, then brutally been told she was wrong. She had run out of youth, and by 1940 no one was listening to her in Australia. So she sailed to America.

She went first to New York and Chicago, where doctors considered her a "screwball." She then went to the Mayo Clinic at Rochester, Minnesota, with some Australian letters of introduction. The staff there listened, but Rochester had no polio cases, so she was sent to the nearby Twin Cities: Minneapolis and St. Paul. She arrived in mid-May, feeling defeated, expecting to stay a few days.

She stayed for a decade, and she worked almost day and night well into her sixties. During one polio epidemic she worked eighteen hours a day. For here in Midwest America, in the springtime of 1940, she had found a few doctors who were interested and who let her demonstrate on some patients. Partly because neither he nor anyone else could quite understand what she was talking about, one invited her to spend some days in his home. This was Dr. Miland E. Knapp, a specialist in physical medicine and a man described by his friends as "the most patient soul that ever lived." He listened and watched her and said she should be allowed to show what she could do.[1]

Another Minneapolis doctor, an orthopedist, Dr. John Pohl, asked her to see one of his patients. Pohl had been hostile at first. For she said stiff, sore, tight muscles, muscles in "spasm," were causing most polio crippling. Pohl had studied with the best authorities at Harvard and in London. Polio, he had always been taught, killed nerve cells and left affected muscles sagging. These "weak" muscles were supposedly pulled out of place by opposing strong ones; therefore they must be kept straight by immobilization in splints or casts. To this view, she said, "No, I see only tight, shortened muscles, in spasm—your splints and casts are illogical; throw them out." She applied her soon-to-be famous hot packs to relieve spasm and tightness. Then she quickly began a program of muscle reeducation. Her patients' arms and legs, Pohl noted, did not seem to atrophy and become shrunken and sticklike. As he remembers it:

> The more she talked, the more it seemed she made sense. Before she came, our city hospital was just crowded with polio. And treatment, in plain language, was just no damned good. If you could have visited the hospital, you would have seen little kids lying stiff and rigid, crying with pain, even though —as she saw—they were not necessarily paralyzed. We'd take children to the operating room in those days, straighten them out under anesthetic, and put them in plaster casts. When they woke up, they screamed. The next day they still cried from the pain. That was the accepted and universal treatment virtually all over the world. I saw it in Boston and New York City and London. She said, "That's all wrong."[2]

Still skeptical, Pohl took her to the home of a lawyer whose eighteen-year-old son had been stricken by polio in September 1939. His back, stomach, both legs, and one arm had been paralyzed. He had received the best treatment available and had even been a patient at the famed polio treatment center at Warm Springs, Georgia. She found him in his bed, encased in a stiff body corset, an arm splint, and two long steel leg braces. He had been told he would have to wear braces for the rest of his life. "There is some woman here from Australia," Pohl informed the young man's parents. "I don't know if she has anything, but he won't walk again and it's worth the try."

His father had to carry the youth down the stairs. At first Sister Kenny could not even force him into a sitting position. But she believed that many of his muscles were still alive and "in spasm," and he went back to the hospital where she treated him. "Ordinarily," recalls Henry Haverstock, Jr., "no one bothers to think how his muscles operate, but she started out to train each one of mine to perform its proper function, and showed me exactly what it does. Miss Kenny would ask me to concentrate while she moved a limb, and after a lot of training I could move it myself. One boy she treated said he learned so much he could be a muscle dancer."[3]

Before long she gave Henry two short hand crutches, and a witness reported: "The doctors and nurses almost fell out the windows when he came walking out of his room." Henry entered college in the spring of 1942 and walked up and down stairs, and in time he became a lawyer.[4]

Pohl's skepticism melted, and so did that of many other Minnesota doctors who came in close contact with Sister Kenny. Dr. Wallace Cole and Dr. Knapp issued an optimistic report on Kenny method results, and medical men all over the country started to watch what was happening. Astonishingly, in December 1941 the Medical Advisory Committee of the National Foundation for Infantile Paralysis publicly endorsed her new treatment, and a simultaneous editorial in the *Journal of the American Medical Association* approved its principles.[5]

What followed had few precedents in medical history. There began a dramatic shift to her methods; one contemporary authority described it as the "banishment of artificial encasements for hundreds of victims in hundreds of hospitals." "Sister Kenny has dropped a bombshell," said Dr. Edward L. Compere, a Northwestern University professor, and Dr. Philip Lewin, a leading Chicago orthopedist, reported in late 1942 that "the swing-over from the orthodox to the Kenny treatment is practically complete. Continuous rigid splinting is not only on its way out, it is out." By 1947 the National Foundation sold for scrap thousands of splints once kept on hand for great epidemics. Some years had passed without call for them.[6]

The awareness of this suddenly burst on the nation. Like Einstein or Shirley Temple or Marilyn Monroe, Sister Kenny caught on. She had arrived at a time when polio epidemic after polio epidemic, the stricken President Franklin D. Roosevelt, and massive publicity had all made the nation poliomyelitis conscious. The antipolio March of Dimes, inspired by F. D. R., was just three years old. There was a new gala, nationwide observance, the President's Birthday Ball, to collect funds.

Summer was polio season, and every summer the little-understood disease was headline news. Some years the headlines were bigger than the problem, pumped up by press agentry and near-panic. But in most years there was far more behind the news than publicity: a real scourge, the leading crippler of children, causing justifiable fright in millions of parents. The time was ripe for the dramatic appearance of an underdog who appealed to parents with the simple message, I can help your children.

Here then was such a woman, also one with an absorbing background of lone nursing in the Australian outback. To women, she was a woman who spelled success in the male world at a time when women held only a thin beachhead. Few women before or since have so stirred Americans. For ten years she was followed, interviewed, and photographed for countless newspaper stories and magazine articles. The *Saturday Evening Post* profiled her, and the *Reader's Digest* canonized her. This "healer from nowhere," she was called, and this "angel from the outback." When she visited Washington in 1944, the *Washington Times Herald* reported: "More than a thousand parents of crippled and cured children surged into the room, packed the mezzanine and overflowed into the corridors, even into the lobby while police tried vainly to hold them in check. . . . 'It's like watching a miracle,' a policeman whispered hoarsely. 'You can't keep them back.' "[7]

Hollywood made a romantic movie, *Sister Kenny.* At its world premiere in New York in 1946, news stories reported: "Traffic in Times Square was a mad mixup as some 20,000-odd people jammed in for a close look. . . . Extra squads of policemen were unable to keep the crowd under control. Twine barriers broke under the pressure. . . . There was a major uproar when Sister Kenny arrived. . . . Jams of crowds nearly threw her off balance as barriers went down, and the platform from which she had just spoken was shoved out of position."[8]

Her honeymoon with the doctors was brief. Despite the great general change in the treatment of polio, she demanded even more change, in many cases justifiably, in some not. The controversy became bitter, and soon heat on both sides consumed reason. The public, however, remained on her side. To attack her was to attack a national phenomenon.

She was commonly called amazing by friends and foes. She was actually more amazing than anyone knew. Although often termed "a medical wizard," she had received practically no formal education, medical or otherwise, except for some scattered years of bush and backwoods school and lessons at her mother's knee. She had made of herself a sort of bluff neighborhood angel of mercy on horseback. She never became a formally trained nurse, a fact that even her worst enemies in the United States never uncovered. Ignoring the deficiency, she had flouted ordinary rules to become an army nurse or "sister" with the hard-fighting Aussie troops of World War I.

When she treated her first case of polio in a slab hut under an Australian gum tree, she did not even know it was polio. When she first started working extensively with polio patients in the midthirties, she possessed some stubborn ideas and had noted some important things, but she still possessed little true physiological information. Her best medical friends in Australia testify to this. In fact, in those years they laughed at her. Within five years, she flabbergasted them. She listened and learned from her medical critics; she imitated them, profited by her mistakes, and soaked up knowledge until in 1939 the same doctors who in 1935 had called her ignorant and uncouth were amazed to see her handle patients with consummate skill.

She herself yielded up only snippets of the story. The author's pursuit of her path in the United States and Australia unearthed almost no one who knew more than one bit or another. Even those who knew just a part, however, would say: "Imagine the audacity of this really crude country girl with almost no background, who became obsessed with the idea that she could do something that the doctors couldn't. And did it." And then moved through life with the air of a duchess, half-cloaking the uncertainty of a self-trained outback nurse.

Asking older doctors about her could still stir a controversy two decades after her death. When I began to try to answer the question What did she contribute? I was myself skeptical because many doctors derided her. I talked to authorities in the United States, Britain, and Australia, and I took doctor after doctor point by point and year by year over the history of polio treatment. I found wide agreement among the specialists who knew most about the disease that she did lead them to change their treatment, and she did relieve suffering. It is given to few people, scientifically trained or not, to overturn a system of medicine, and the generous and knowing give her this credit.

In 1943 Dr. Wallace H. Cole, then head of the Department of Orthopedics at the University of Minnesota and a most conservative and cautious man, wrote:

> Unfortunately, there are members of our profession who do not remember how some of the great advances in medical science came about. . . . It is pertinent to quote Oliver Wendell Holmes, who stated that medicine learned "from a Jesuit how to cure agues, from a friar how to cut for stone, from a soldier how to treat gout, from a sailor how to keep off scurvy, from a postmaster how to sound the Eustachian tube, from a dairy maid how to prevent smallpox, and from an old market woman how to catch the itch-insect." In all humility, I suggest that the following be added: "and from an Australian nurse how to treat infantile paralysis."[9]

To a fellow nurse, who judged her just as a nurse, she emanated "poise, strength and enormous reserve." "Her hands are remarkable," this witness wrote in a professional journal. "They are full of healing. You wonder, as you watch them in fascinated absorption, if they are the result of 32 years of bringing healing to people, or if they were always strong and supple and magnetic. . . . I watched them as she sat on [a] stage before more than 3,000 eager nurses. . . . Her hands were at peace in her lap. Yet in [training films] those busy hands were commanding. A single finger would be raised in command, and the patient would make prodigious efforts to make his muscles comply." One physician who observed her said: "I can't get anything out of her writing or out of her lectures, but when she's at the bedside she's another Osler."[10]

She was more than a healer, however. She was as human a human being as has lived. She exulted. She sulked. She coveted. She aimed and she failed. She laughed and wept and prayed and lied. She was a sincere humanitarian and a self-seeker. She was shoddy, and she was as true as a saint. And she had style, like a torero or a great prizefighter. She had style and fire.

"Sister Kenny?" says one person who knew her. "Good heavens! She could be a saint one minute while treating a child, and two minutes later turn to a doctor and blister him." She disagreed once with a paper by Dr. Joseph Moldaver of Columbia University. She dismissed it by saying he had enjoyed the benefit of meeting her only once, when they talked for half an hour, "and it usually takes clever doctors about three days to understand what I am talking about." When Dr. Philip M. Stimson of Cornell Medical College made a statement that she did not like—he called her treatment "widely accepted" as the best physical therapy, but this was not broad enough for her—she retorted: "Dr. Stimson knows nothing about the early treatment of polio except what I taught him, and there is still quite a bit he doesn't know."[11] In these ways, she could be her own worst enemy. All her life she made terrible enemies as well as devoted followers. Simply to condemn her for this or only find it amusing, however, is to fail to understand her. There was much tragedy within her: only deep wounds make deep scars.

She covered them with a heroic calm and bearing that earned her, even from friends, nicknames like "the Duchess" and "the Queen." "She was the Queen Mary in full steam when she came charging into a room," said one. "She had the power of a tiger, the nickname which stuck to her over the years," said a writer in Sydney. An Australian doctor said: "I used to call her 'my old dreadnaught.' She always loved to fight. She would sail in with all guns firing." She had the appearance to go with the role. She had an ample form, often deployed under a broad, sweeping hat. "Look, Mum, there goes Mae West," a small boy exclaimed during her Brisbane days (the latter half of the thirties). She was, in her prime, erect, overpowering, and positive—five feet, eight inches tall, about 170 solid pounds. She had large, open brown eyes and a direct gaze that could turn to sharp steel. In her American years, she had wavy gray hair, later white, cut short. She had a strong, jutting jaw.

Grim and lonely, difficult to talk to much of the time, firm as a rock in some ways, flighty and unpredictable in others, she was often at odds with even her co-workers. Yet her few close friends saw an entirely different woman. "She looked like an M-4 tank," contributes actress Rosalind Russell, a friend who insisted on making the film *Sister Kenny*. "But her eyes were the loneliest and loveliest I have ever looked into. They almost talked, they were so eloquent."

Like an actress, she had stage presence. She dominated a room, stage, or ward. She often arrived at a meeting a little late, after everyone else was seated. Everyone usually stood as she sailed slowly to her place. One advertising man who saw her several times said, "She carried her own pedestal." Even on such occasions, however, she was detached, still shut up in her own private world. "She grew thorns, like a rosebush," said Dudley Nichols, the screenwriter. "She had to protect herself." When slighted or attacked, she was quick to hit back—by telegram, press statement, long-distance telephone, overseas cable, and all other means of communication. "She knows every muscle and bone in the human body," one interviewer observed, "and there isn't a meek one in her own."

She frequently credited this to the Gael in her. She was by descent mainly Irish, "75 percent Irish, 25 percent Scotch for some balance," she liked to say. She was also an Australian. An Englishman and an Australian, she would say, once walked down the street, "the Englishman as if he owned it, the Australian as if he didn't give a damn who owned it." There was often a good dose of humor in her bite; she could be unbearably pompous one moment and puncture pomposity, her own or somebody else's, the next. She would be tough with someone, then turn and wink. She landed at the Madrid airport in 1946 and was greeted with roses by eight doctors. "It is very gratifying," she said, "to receive flowers from doctors while I am still here to smell them."[12]

She was never fully satisfied with her life, at the end of her career or any other time. "Oh, Minnie," she told a cousin when she was young, "I don't always want to stay in Australia!" She got away from Australia, all right, and in a way she conquered the world.

"A great life is a thing of beauty," maintains André Maurois. Millions still remember Sister Kenny's life warmly. To them, she represented their feelings about polio and suffering. Perhaps if she was a great person, it was because she wore the anguish of many. Or perhaps her character gave her a degree of greatness. Her willingness to do battle with anyone, anytime. Her ability (to paraphrase the words of a biographer of Pasteur) to rise triumphant from the ashes of her own mistakes. Her possession of what a man who wrote to the *Minneapolis Star* after her death called "a magnificent sense of contempt for the word defeat." The average among us breathe youthful fires and cool as we age and harden into old, average patterns. She never gave up.

How can we explain this woman who was called both a fraud and a medical genius, a cheap quack and an unhappy martyr, a raging old tiger and a merciful angel?

1

Australia

ELIZABETH KENNY was born in 1880 in the village of Warialda ("place of wild honey") in the new, still raw nation-continent of Australia. Australia was "a young whale just ready to blow" in the words of British traveler Anthony Trollope. It was a mixture of the frontier country of sheepmen, stockmen, bushrangers, and adventurers, and the folk and folkways of the British Isles.

Australia's *Mayflowers* had landed less than 100 years before: cramped ships carrying Britain's unwanted convicts and their guards. The convicts were cutthroats, highwaymen, pickpockets, and footpads—and Irish rebels and starved Britons caught poaching a partridge, their sentence "transportation" for life.

They were soon joined by free immigrants, including Elizabeth Kenny's Irish forebears. Ireland to the Kennys and their kith and kin in Australia long remained a place close-felt in talk and mood, in Celtic gloom and Celtic dreams, leavened by the new Australian freedom and zest. Australia was another America in its distance from the Old Country and its fierce independence; yet it was as different from America as Ireland was from England.

Ireland had been anger—anger and frustration that drove out millions, who were restless to burst on the world. The Irish of the nineteenth century were largely ragged potato-eaters living in stone or mud cabins. Shoeless and cold, they and their young worked twelve to eighteen hours a day in peat bogs and fields. One European traveler described them as "slaves," worse off than Russia's serfs.[1] Famine was common. In 1845, 1846, and "black '47," fungus destroyed their potatoes, while the landlords relentlessly exported the land's plentiful corn, wheat, and barley. The people lost their plots and their cottages, and the roads came alive with wandering families—little groups carrying coffins, children who looked like skeletons, and tottering men and women, their eyes hollow.

Meanwhile the English landlords wore fine cloaks and tall hats, and rode in gilded carriages. They also tried to suppress the local religion. The people replied with insurrection and murder. The American and French revolutions gave them hope, which turned to bitterness. Treason trials and soldiers with portable gallows kept a snug lid on their fury.

Still a poet wrote "Erin, the tear and the smile in thine eye." When they had a few potatoes and some ale, these same people rollicked and danced, played at cudgels, and smiled or cried at the telling of old tales. Fairs, weddings, christenings, and funerals, said a visitor, commonly produced scenes of tumult and fighting "such as may be expected among a rude people addicted to spirituous liquors."

The priests took up war against that. In 1838 one Father Matthew, a suave, early-day Billy Graham, started a temperance crusade which swept the land, and every place he went thousands signed the pledge. In 1844 at the Kilkenny fair, which was probably attended by members of the family Kenny, a visitor was told, "You'll not see such fun, ma'am, now, as you would have seen before the days of Father Matthew. Then we had a power of bloody noses, broken bones and fine work for the police."[2]

No wonder a visiting Scotsman once said, "Ah, it's a heaven of a place, but a devil of a people." A good many Scots remained, nonetheless, and some helped calm the future Kenny genes. One such, Richard Pearson, settled in about 1790 in County Donegal on Ireland's windswept northwest shoulder. He won himself his own land, but years later, aging, he guaranteed a loan to a friend and lost all but enough to buy assisted passage to Australia. In 1841 Richard and his wife bravely boarded the vessel *Cadet* along with two daughters and their own new families. Daughter Elizabeth's husband, "Big Jim" Moore, was a giant of a sea captain, at least six feet, four inches tall. Elizabeth, twenty-three, blonde, blue-eyed, and beautiful, was to be Elizabeth Kenny's maternal grandmother.[3]

The Irish Kennys lived in southerly County Kilkenny, among gentle hills and dales, high plateaus, and a green valley, caressed by the silvery River Nore. Spring flowers, blossoming hedges, and the song of the lark in the fields fed the Irish sense of beauty, and fairies, it was said, leaped in and out of the hedges. The Kilkennyman had an unmatched reputation for independence. "The contentious Irish from County Kilkenny," a saying went. "If you say it's a good morning, they'll say it's a bad one." And an eyewitness of the time wrote, "Though every peasant in the Emerald Isle knows that he belongs to the 'lower order' (for his teachers and landlords are fond of telling him so), the Kilkenny rustic, by his self-possessed manner in presence of his superior, says, 'I am also a man.' "[4]

Kilkenny had its name from Saint Canice, who founded a church at Kilkenny City in the sixth century. The family name, "Kenny," had a different origin, being Gaelic for "sprung from fire." The cottage of Henry and Julia Kenny stood in a fertile bit of the Nore valley called Toorbeg, where blooming roses and trees surrounded their thatched roof and white walls. Their son Michael—first of ten children, future emigrant to Australia, father-to-be of Sister Kenny—was born there in 1834. A fortunate boy, he was able to go to a Catholic "hedge school" run by his father's brother Patrick. Hedge schools had just been made legal; until then, courageous masters like Patrick had often run them behind hedges or at other hidden sites. Michael also went to a new government school for a time; he may briefly have studied for the priesthood as well.

When he was eighteen or nineteen, his mother took him to hear the temperance crusader Father Matthew. Caught young, he took the pledge. Six feet tall, auburn-haired, red-complexioned, he helped till the land, reached age twenty-seven, and wondered about the future. During 1845 to 1850 alone, a million and a half of the unhappy Irish had sailed away, and another half a million had died.

One day in 1862 the perplexed Michael took a walk to visit cousins. One had a ticket to Australia but was unable to use it. Michael's face flushed and his eyes shone, and he said, "I'll go." His mother and father listened later and agreed. They agreed and they wept. Such a journey could mean death by drowning or illness. In almost every case it meant separation for life.

The September wind blew at the quayside on the day appointed for Michael Kenny's departure. On ship and shore fathers held babies aloft for a last look at relations; mothers and sisters wailed and fainted, and patriots waved the green flag with its harp. Henry and Julia took their last look at their firstborn, the wind filled the white sails, and the heavily laden sailing ship *Conway* set off for the 15,000-mile voyage.

Sailing to Australia 100 years ago was like sailing to the moon. Big Jim Moore and Elizabeth were a weary eight months making the voyage. The same journey took the more fortunate Michael Kenny fourteen weeks.

The manner of travel was the same: tall-masted ship, setting out with white canvas and brightly painted figurehead down the long coast of Africa. A sharp change in course to the east around the Cape of Good Hope. Then, canvas turned weather-beaten and gray, more than 5,000 miles out of sight of land across the Indian Ocean to landfall on south Australia and a final leg beneath the continent to the east coast and its cities.

The Irishmen who had never before been more than a few miles from home saw familiar stars turned upside down in southern heavens and lost the Big Dipper but found the Southern Cross. Their food was aging salt pork and biscuit hard as rock, soon infested by weevils. There was some singing and dancing, but death and disease were more often the rule. An 1852 surgeon's diary read:

> July 15th—5th day. Nearly all very seasick. . . .
> July 21st—11th day. Ship rolling much in the night. Single women frightened. . . . All the leeches are dead.
> July 22nd—12th day. With few exceptions and the measles all well and happy. Danced almost every evening.
> July 27th—17th day. McG's child died 1½ A.M. Had been sinking all evening. Child buried at 10 A.M.

Entries continued: "blown out of our course," "terrific gale lasting 48 hours," tropic heat, high seas soaking bedding, eight births, twenty-six deaths and funerals, quarrels, measles, diarrhea, "all anxious to reach their destination," landing on 99th day.[5]

The Moores' unlucky vessel was becalmed, ran short of drinking water, had a fire on board, and ran onto a reef off Africa. The passengers were lowered in boatswain's chairs to pitching boats, and they and the ship separately managed to reach Capetown, where repairs took two months. The vessel finally reached Port Jackson—Sydney Harbor—in August 1841.

It was Australian winter then, temperature in the seventies, bright sun and blue sky, stiff winds churning the waves. The master set his course toward what seemed to be unbroken cliffs, but then steered through a great mile-wide opening between two rocky headlands. These were the North and South Heads, the spectacular gate to the city of Sydney.

Inside them, the sea waters stilled, and the sea-weary immigrants stared at a harbor reaching inland for miles. They sailed past a thousand bays and coves with hilly forests of cedars and gray green gum trees—eucalyptuses—growing down to white sand. Flocks of white cockatoos whirled and gleamed. After the endless Pacific, the travelers were beholding a scene which inspired Trollope to write: "It is so inexpressibly lovely that it makes a man ask himself whether it would not be worth his while to move his household gods to the eastern coast of Australia, in order that he might look at it as long as he can look at anything."[6]

The Moores sailed past a fort with brass cannons. They passed Pinchgut Island, where unruly convicts were still dumped without food, although forced transportation to this territory, New South Wales, had just ended. Next, thickets of masts signaled Sydney, a crude, young London. Wool ships crowded its approaching quays, and whalers made the air two miles around reek with blubber. The long-delayed immigrant ship finally alongshore, the newcomers saw a steep, hilly city, a city of high, wooden fronts and dirty gutters, descending to the harbor along narrow streets.

Wax-moustachioed dandies drove their carriages along the bustling waterfront, taking their young ladies on afternoon spins. Far more interesting to the immigrants, however, were several bearded men on horseback, jumping dirty gutters and waving slouch hats. These were Australia's "squatters," a new sunbaked kind of squirearchy. Land kings and wool kings, expatriate English quality, and unwashed landgrabbers—their quarry today was labor: the raw immigrant or "new chum," the prospective station hand or "jackaroo," Big Jim Moore.

The Moores alighted from their vessel and sat on a log; a squatter promptly rode up and asked, "Looking for work?" Moore or his new employer hired a bullock dray to carry Elizabeth's blue china plates, decorated with Asiatic pheasants, and other possessions, and these immigrants said a quick good-bye to crowded Sydney.

From a dusty track, they rapidly began seeing the real Australia: the bush or endless forest of gum trees, growing well apart to let in air and sun. Gums keep their leaves and change their bark, so the bark hung in shreds and the steadfast leaves gave off a sharp, pungent odor. The new chums set out wearing thick Irish woolens but soon packed them away;

they turned raw with sunburn and then browned. Their skins toughened against sandflies and mosquitoes. After the damp Irish winters, they began to relish the warmth and clean light of the southern days.

The Moores' destination was the Hunter River Valley in the Great Dividing Range that separates Australia's eastern coast from its fertile tablelands. In the sight of these blue mountains, Elizabeth Moore bore her first daughter, Mary. Jim Moore soon began farming for himself to the north—in New England, "high country," "snow country" in low, warm Australia. At Inverell, at the foot of the New England highlands, the Moores first took up their own land. Years passed—two decades.[7]

Put ashore at Brisbane in December 1862 after a mere ninety-eight days of smooth sailing, Michael Kenny saw a city not unlike early Sydney: winding, dusty streets, slab buildings, bullock teams, bewhiskered bushmen in broad hats. But Brisbane was a smaller and more agricultural place. A stockyard stood in the middle of the city, and stockmen led mobs of cattle through the streets.

Like young Jim Moore, young Michael headed inland. He worked his way down from tropical Queensland to New South Wales. He became a jackaroo, herding cattle. He watched herds of sheep for days on end, sleeping in a watch box to guard against dingoes, Australian wild dogs. He moved from job to job, mixing with shearers, stockmen, bullockies, and boundary riders. These tender new chums had to cut tracks, clear land, fell timber, bore water holes, build fences, and shear. Many a young man from crowded Ireland or England now rode alone day after day with a water bag, a billy can to boil his tea, and the rest of his possessions wrapped in a blanket. Not all lasted. The survivors became hard, rough men in flannel shirts, moleskin pants, and big-brimmed hats to keep off the sun.

Educated Michael Kenny was not overly fond of such work, but he survived. He had a mannerly way even while doing hard labor and a good touch with animals, especially with horses. He began to be known as a bit of a veterinary. One day he was called to Jim Moore's to purge one of the horses. In this way the sober redhead met the Moores' tall daughter Mary. He had reached thirty-seven and she was twenty-eight; it was time for both to be wed. They warmed to each other, taking little account of their difference in religion—he was Roman Catholic, she, Church of England. But there were few priests or preachers around, often none for months, to enforce doctrine. On May 30, 1872, Michael and Mary were married.

He took her to a new homestead on the same New England tablelands. He became a dam contractor and construction foreman; the dams were little digs in the hillsides to hold rainwater. He tried tin mining. He wielded a pick, then was a supervisor for a time. Everything he did lasted only for a time. "My father was a wanderer," his fourth-born, daughter Julia, was to testify. Michael and his family were never to starve in this land of steak, eggs, and pineapple, but he would never enrich himself. His good manners remained. "He didn't do very well, but he was a fine gentleman," an old farmer remembers. One relative thought he would have made a good millionaire.

The first Australian Kenny, daughter Rachel, and the first son, Henry, were born at Inverell; then came a first Elizabeth, who died of bronchial pneumonia; Julia was born next at a new homesite at Bannockburn.

The family moved again, farther west, to what Julia late in life remembered as "a beautiful country" of gum trees and bees, into a shingle and wood house "beautifully comfortable, with every room lined with calico and paper, and an old wide fireplace, a fireplace built with stones, not narrow like your little American fireplaces." This country was also harder country. Its long grass bent low in the wind, and the tops of its high, stiff gum trees nodded too. To vex the farmer, there were granite outcroppings and many gullies and ridges. Summer temperatures ran up to 110 or 115 degrees. Rose-breasted galah parrots flew from the trees, and blue gray mountaintops dotted the eastern horizon. It was still high land, 1,500 feet above sea level, part of the New England Range's northwestern slopes.

The nearby town was Warialda, an agricultural township or village. A coach came through daily. False fronts and corrugated iron roofs adorned three hotels. Old stockades from the convict days were still standing.

Michael Kenny's place was five or six miles out of town. On September 20, 1880, either there or at a friend's house in the township, another daughter was born. Three weeks later the Kennys decked her in ribbons and took her to the wooden slab Church of England. She was solemnly sprinkled from a graven stone font, and the vicar wrote in the baptismal register: "Number 496. . . . Child's Christian Name, Elizabeth; Parents' Christian Names, Michael and Mary. . . . Abode, Kelly's Gully, Warialda; Quality or Profession, Selector"—or homesteader, again only for a time.[8]

2

Elizabeth

ELIZABETH, like her father, was a wanderer. She walked when she was nine months old, and soon her mother or sister had to tie her to a stump to keep her from roaming. When she was four or five she climbed on the stump, put her arms out, and tried to fly. She fell, and that taught her for a time.

Elizabeth and Julia, only three years apart, soon wandered together about the Kenny clearings, bothering the chickens and cattle. Then they ventured into the bush to peer at wistful-looking koalas, mobs of kangaroos and their pouch-young, the joeys, and goanna lizards that grew to six feet in length. When a leathery goanna came near the house, the girls screamed; these creatures gobbled both chickens and eggs. At least once young Elizabeth saw an aboriginal corroboree: signal smokes and a gathering of the tribe for night fires and dances. The tribal blacks appeared once a year on their long-distance walkabouts, and Elizabeth might spy them gathering wild berries and grubs, and spearing goannas or tender doe kangaroos.[1]

The abos wandered, Elizabeth wandered, and Michael Kenny kept wandering. More young Kennys were born. Spring Vale, Inverell, Bannockburn, Warialda, Wallangarra, Ashford, Nullamanna—the Kennys kept on the move. "Get along for yourself and no nonsense," busy Mary Kenny frequently had to tell her growing family. The girls' own children were dolls, usually dressed-up bottles or rags. One doll developed pneumonia, a hard case. Elizabeth got a hospital going. "She was a born nurse from the time she put poultices on those dolls," one sister said years later.

Something more than a game, doll-nursing came naturally in this age when diphtheria, pneumonia, scarlet fever, and smallpox took some members of every family. "You'd go to the graveyard"—the recollection of a Kenny neighbor—"and you'd see a common tombstone where three children died one day and a fourth the next. My father died when I was five and our only family outings were to visit the cemetery. The horse knew the way."[2]

Julia and Elizabeth caught diphtheria and were in bed for three months, while the struggling Mary boiled eucalyptus leaves until steam dripped from the rafters, so that the girls might breathe the fumes. Bush Australians largely had to be their own doctors; they applied goanna oil, dugong lard, and Perry Davis's Patent Pain-Killer for ailments major and minor. Another Kenny baby, James, died of pneumonia. For years the family believed they had left him uncovered too much; it was a day when mothers heaped blankets on babies summer and winter. Mary also blamed her vanity—"I boasted about him, I admired him too much."

Julia, often called "Judie," was soon mother's help. A new, little Mary was the quiet child. Her twin Margaret, or "Maggie" or "Meg," was the mischief. Elizabeth was the bushman. At the age of six, she was "living on horseback," she said later.[3] By seven or eight, she could saddle her own animal and help round up the cows. By eight, she rode cows, calves, horses, anything; sidesaddle, man's saddle, bareback, any way. A frock stayed clean on her only a few hours, and her mother called her "tomboy."

She was rarely called Elizabeth. Her family almost always called her either "Liza" or "Eliza." Both displeased her. "Don't call me Liza!" she would command. The family never stopped until she was grown; later she learned to take it quite calmly. She was also sometimes called Bessie by Irish cousins. That was all right with her.

The Kenny houses, like most bush houses, were built just off the ground on "stringybark" sleepers—long poles with crossbeams—and atop them a wood floor. Snakes liked to nap among the sleepers, a cool place in summer, a warm one in winter. If there was a crack in the floor, a snake sometimes poked its head up. Liza learned to observe quietly. When she was eight, a poisonous death adder confronted her in the bush. She stood her ground, lifted a stick, and walloped it; then she carried it home and dropped it at her mother's feet. It came to life and wiggled away.

Schooling was haphazard. She was never to get a great deal of it: six years at most, possibly less. She left no real record and memories are imprecise. At Nullamanna, it is certain, Julia went to school in a tent. Then a roughhewn timber building was built, and Elizabeth at least started there. Often no school existed, and parents had to be teachers. Michael, who had learned mathematics from his Uncle Paddy and had dabbled in engineering and construction, gave the arithmetic lessons. He also knew Latin. The brunt of the teaching fell to Elizabeth's mother, however. Tall and straight, a fine stamp of a woman by all accounts, Mary Kenny spoke out in a clear, sometimes commanding tone and gave the children their reading and writing. As a girl, it was said, she had enjoyed "a tutor from Oxford"; her English was uncommonly fine for pioneer days. She was bright, and the lonely bush life gave her time to read. She had an incredible memory and quoted Goethe, Sir Walter Scott, Shakespeare, and the Bible.

The Bible and religion were an unquestioned part of learning, and Mary told each child, "You are a child of God." But she seldom stressed that they were Protestants. Michael always remained a Roman Catholic, though he was never famous for observing the forms. Mary remained Church of England, and the children were all baptized Protestant, the sect depending on which preacher rode by. Young Elizabeth was thus christened Church of England, and her brothers and sisters, Methodist and Presbyterian. "I never heard a religious argument in our house," the adult Elizabeth remembered.[4]

For an hour each day, mostly in the evening, Mary would gather her children around her knee and recite Shakespeare or classics or read from scripture. "Even today," said Elizabeth a half century later, "I can hear my mother's beautiful voice" and remember how "we would weep, we would sigh, we would lament" as she "took us to all the countries of the earth," with romantic ballad, Bret Harte, knights, ladies, soldiery, *The Lady of the Lake*, and *Hiawatha*.[5]

The family circle also sang Irish ballads: "The Rose of Tralee" and "the minstrel boy to the wars has gone." Or for the Scotch connections, "Loch Lomond." Michael Kenny lost his brogue but often told tales of the old country. Sometimes the whole family would make an evening of writing letters to the Kennys back "home."

Storytelling swagmen, vagabonds who "waltzed" a pack, their "Matilda," often appeared at the threshold. They added outback stories and yarns lasting half the night about Ned Kelly and Australia's other bushrangers—bandits who sprang from a bitter class of farmers squeezed from their lands by wealthy squatters. Bushrangers were this young nation's Robin Hoods. The slim, dark-haired Ned Kelly had been sentenced to hang in 1880 (Elizabeth Kenny's birth year) at age twenty-six. "I will see you where I go," he audaciously told the judge, then went to the gallows, where he calmly observed, "Such is life." Eleven days later the judge died, Kelly sympathizers rejoiced, and a bush poet wrote:[6]

> And so they took Ned Kelly and hanged him in the jail,
> For he fought single-handed although in iron mail*
> And no man single-handed can hope to break the bars;
> It's a thousand like Ned Kelly who'll hoist the Flag of Stars.

All this the traveling swaggies told the new chums and jackaroos, the struggling selectors and young Australians, including Elizabeth Kenny, a quiet, thinking one.

The Kennys moved to some of New England's highest country, a series of high ridges that the settlers called the Ben Lomond Range. There were mile-high peaks here and winter bite. Rainbows rose from the mist over blue gray foothills, gum forests climbed the slopes, and sheep grazed in mountain meadows among vast fields of daisies and grass. Green weeping willows lined the creek beds, and the lands beyond were bright golden, drenched in sun.

The nearby township was Guyra. It was well populated with Kenny kin: Moores and Pearsons and their big families, mostly better off than the Kennys. One of the Moores helped Michael put up a bark cottage on a piece of Moore land, a hut made of big, shaggy bark sheets from the stringybark tree. Two rooms at best, it was the typical bush dwelling, built either of bark or rough slabs of timber hewed out with an adz and laid one on the other with chinks in between; a roof of great chunks of bark, like pieces of elephant hide; and a mud or stone chimney. The interior was typically graced by bullock-hide carpets and sapling furniture, with a sheet of bark, perhaps, for a door and a bootlace for a latch. In the least of the Kenny houses, there would still be one or two small windows with curtains; Mary Kenny, poor or poorer, was the lace curtain type.

Mary hung her copper kettle over the hearth. She cooked in the fireplace, brewed tea there in a crusted black kettle, baked bread in a camp oven hanging from a hook, and hung bacon in the chimney to smoke. The Kennys had their tea at the fireplace. They grilled their steaks there. In

* Home-made armor.

winter, when the snow occasionally drifted against the logs, they drew up closer to the fire and warmed their hands on their tea mugs.

Feeding and clothing the family took much sewing and scheming, at a time when some of the Moores had maids, as well as iron roofs hauled from Sydney and seven-room houses instead of two-room bark cottages. Mary never complained. She made clothes, planted flowers and vegetables, and always kept a little orchard when she could. The whole family sowed wheat by hand, ground it, plowed with a single-furrow plow, watered the cows, churned butter, and carted extra milk to the cheese-maker's. Energetic Liza smashed pumpkins with an ax and threw them to the pigs. All the girls gathered wild strawberries for the table and wild flowers to brighten the home. In spring they gathered tender new eucalyptus leaves, fresh-looking and fragrant. In summer Mary whitewashed the hearth with pipe clay from the creek, covered it with baskets of flowers, and then did the cooking outdoors.

Michael, by now red-bearded Mick Kenny in his fifties, farmed at this and still another Guyra homesite. He was quiet, dreamy, and gentlemanly, but he was no businessman or farmer. Mary called him "Michael" and treated him with respect, but she tightened her lips and lifted her chin an inch and, in her forties, became the rock. She became almost impossible to sway, especially when Michael had another notion and she thought her children's welfare was at stake. She developed a stately manner, and sometimes the relatives called her "Queen Mary." Elizabeth grew up in a matriarchy.

On daughter Elizabeth, Mary put a set of woolen drawers, a knit comforter, a long dress, a white pinafore, high-buttoned boots, and black stockings, and sent her to school. It was a white, one-room school with a tin roof, and there was a bell on a white post in the schoolyard. The pupils filed outdoors one day and posed for a photograph: fifty-four boys and girls ranging from squinting six-year-olds to big, gawky girls beginning to fill grown-up dresses. In a back row, on a box, stood Elizabeth, fairly tall, stocky, round-cheeked, dark hair combed down in bangs over her forehead, and eyes ahead.

Photograph taken, the pupils filed back to their schoolroom to parse verbs, decipher fractions, and practice a graceful, looped handwriting on lap slates. In her writing exercises, Elizabeth copied out such sentences as "He was a big, quiet, zealous fellow and just in his dealings with others."

For misbehavers there was formal punishment. For example, from the 1893 *Punishment Book* of the nearby Ben Venue School: "Name, Michael McNamarra . . . Age, Yrs. 8 . . . Nature of Offense, Lying . . . Instrument of Punishment, 2 slaps, cane." Liza's teacher, Mr. Surtees, was gentlemanly when it came to punishment, in contrast to one of his successors, Mr. Leggo. "Leggo used to bash a lot," according to one of Elizabeth's cousins. "No, I don't remember Liza ever getting the cane. Surtees didn't give the girls the cane too much. He used to threaten to send them home. And with a mother like I had and like Liza had, it would have been a terrible thing! The little girls, six or seven, he used to make them walk up and down with one hand in his coat pocket, while he'd say, 'Oh, the disgrace of having to walk up and down with the school master.' They'd howl with the disgrace. This would be when he would be in a fairly good humor. Otherwise he might smack them."

Liza and her cousins met each morning and walked to school together. In winter they ran along frosty paths, and in spring they chattered as they skipped through fields of bluebells and honeysuckles. "Liza had a vivid imagination, she was a terror to romance," say the cousins. "Such tarradiddles she'd tell, such awful tales! . . . All the same, if you understood her, you sifted it out and you liked her. She was always that way, you know, all her life. She should have written tales." The poor cousin, "she liked to make out she was of some importance."

She spent more and more time alone. She was reserved, quiet, dignified—a little overdignified; she corrected people. At home she read by the fireplace, her head in her book. When it came time to wash the dishes, she disappeared in the bush. Buried deep in tall grass, she read in the fields on sunny days. Then she ran to the paddock, saddled a horse, and helped find the cattle. Or she galloped into the bush to meander. She broke out on high meadows or raced down a grassy slope at a gallop to look down on pieces of silver, the farmers' round stock dams holding the mountain water.

On a late afternoon she would ride down to a clump of willows along a blue stream, the long shadows of girl and horse falling a quarter-mile across the field. The bright sun painted the yellow fields and green willows and tall eucalyptus trees with Van Gogh colors, and the girl, alone, exaggerating to no one, was more herself than she was with her family, or her cousins, or her fifty-three schoolmates at the state school.

The days in the highlands darkened, and the winters brought rains, at first welcomed, then endured, then damned. During one period there was no sun for three months. Elsewhere in Australia, men were dying of heat and thirst in what Australians called "the dry." But in the Kennys' highlands there were three perverse years in the wet, until meadows became marshes and clover fields turned to bogs. Cattle died in winter frosts, and sheep perished of foot rot and fluke. The hopes of good men were shattered, and they grew older and changed.

All Australia was growing older. "It was not a land of easy meadows and green savannahs," one Australian wrote. "It was an ancient land which had drawn its resources more and more into itself"; it had to be forced to surrender its riches.[7] The eager had continued to flock to the southern continent, lured by British and Irish land agents' signs, "Sail to a land of milk and honey!" They came and sweltered; bush fires burned their grass, crops, and fences; tropic monsoons flooded creeks, and black flies, sand flies, mosquitoes, and flying ants swarmed in armies. Food became scarce. Tea leaves were used, reused, then boiled to shreds in a third try.

In the years of Elizabeth's adolescence, both man and nature, it seemed, had gone "crook," meaning sick, bad, or rotten. In a time to be remembered as Australia's "Gray Nineties," defeated selectors joined shearers, miners, seamen, and wharfies in strikes and lockouts; financial panic closed banks, and by mid-1893 wool had dropped to a ridiculous seven pence a pound. Striking shearers desperately burned woolsheds; but courts, police, and soldiers broke the strikes, and workmen gradually turned to politics, combining as "Labour." The year 1894 was the first of nine consecutive years of terrible drought over most of the island continent, while water from the Kennys' flooded highlands ran into the sea.

Under such pressures, men sometimes turned on each other: it was by no means unusual in the highlands to nobble an unfriendly neighbor's horse with a bullet or to poison it. More often, however, the beleaguered Australians drew together, and "Mate" or "Hey, Matey" became their usual greeting, regardless of class. "Mateship," a bitter realism, and irreverence toward authority created a new Australian character; the once submissive immigrant who had tugged his cap to his betters might now toss a curt "Kiss me foot!" at any boss who demanded too much.

The new immigrants had become physically tough, quick of muscle, tanned and lean, spare with words, and hard-bitten. The wet, the dry, the bush fires, floods, howling winds, tropic monsoons, and a sun that curled everything it struck, these along with outraged blacks with spears, bushrangers with guns, fulminating diseases, and terrifying loneliness had eliminated many and had left a daring and damn-all brand of survivor. When an Australian chose you as mate, he walloped you on the back. When he chose to ignore you, you could freeze in the chill. In his relationship with Australia there grew love and hate. It was in such a culture that Liza Kenny was budding.

One day in the winter of 1892–93, Michael Kenny, his beard flecked with gray, and Mary, wearing a choke-collared dress with a skirt like a tent, herded their family onto a northbound train. Into the wooden coach climbed Elizabeth, a gawky twelve-year-old. She put her nose to the window, and the hopeful clan deserted New South Wales for the sunnier north, the semitropical plains of southern Queensland.[8] Wheat and barley grew there, sheep and cattle grazed, and nowhere were prospects more favorable than in this area—an Australian Montana called the Darling Downs, a country of rich black soil and, until government land division had begun a few years before, of sheep runs covering miles. In the 1840s one Darling Downs squatter had "owned" a sheep and cattle station larger than England and Wales.

The train rattled north. The weather grew warmer. The houses were blistered wooden dwellings raised on stilts to discourage white ants and to help ventilate the inhabitants. Deep, open verandas circled many of these homes. The sun was brighter, the hat brims were wider, and the Queenslanders drawled in a leisurely way.

The Kennys' destination was Headington Hill, which had been one of the grandest sheep stations; it had just been divided among landless selectors. Michael worked, and the Kennys lived there; then they moved to a place called Gowrie Junction, where Kenny looked after stock and teams. Their typical neighbor was the new selector or "cow cocky" (so called because he raised a few cows and chased cockatoos off his wheat and maize). Cockies and wage men like Michael Kenny cleared the land, felled the trees, and grubbed out stumps and roots with pick and ax.

Elizabeth helped with the cows, then walked or rode a horse three miles to a Wetalla school. Wetalla was the end of her education. But it was by no means to be the end in her recollections. She would say for *Who's Who in America* in the 1940s that she was "privately educated," as well as a graduate of "St. Ursula's College, Australia, 1902"; she would tell a secretary that her mother had sent her to this convent school to make a lady of her. Later there were several St. Ursulas in Australia, girls' secondary schools operated by Ursuline nuns. In 1902, however, the only one was at Armidale, twenty-eight miles south of Guyra. She was to be known quite fondly there, but she was never a student. For *Who's Who in Australia*, she reported only: "Educated, Guyra, NSW."[9]

Her limited schooling was by no means unusual. There were only six classes or grades at Wetalla. Fifth class was "scholarship," the last year of most pupils' schooling, and either the fifth or sixth class was the end of hers. She was by now a bright young devil of a thing in some ways, always climbing trees and skylarking. But she still read and read; "I'd sit on a rock," she told a friend once, "and I'd dream of great things."

One day at Headington Hill—at age thirteen—she leaped onto a horse without examining the saddle girths and began galloping. The saddle slipped, and she was thrown. The startled horse stood on her skirt, and when she tried to move him, she found that her wrist was broken. Shaken and in pain, she nonetheless tethered the horse to a tree with one hand and then started home. But when her brothers and sisters spotted her on foot, she began bawling in shock. Sensible Mary Kenny applied padding and a sling, and gave the order: "Put her in her best frock." She was to be taken to Toowoomba, a thriving business and market town on the rim of the Range, to a doctor.

None of the Kenny family had ever enjoyed the attention of a doctor of medicine before. Now that one was necessary, it would be the best, Dr. McDonnell. Aeneas John McDonnell was about thirty, short and wiry, a brash young surgeon with blue eyes, fast fingers, and a black-brown handlebar moustache. Born in Australia, he was an honor graduate of Sydney University Medical School, first house surgeon of Toowoomba General Hospital, and sometime traveler and student at the clinics of Johns Hopkins and Vienna. From age twenty-three he had been extremely deaf. He had a primitive hearing aid but hated wearing it, so everyone had to scream at him. Many men in such a circumstance would have given up active practice for teaching or administrative work. McDonnell merely shouted "Speak up," developed a peppery manner, and became *the* doctor in Toowoomba.

With horse and buggy, Michael Kenny drove the injured Liza the rough forty miles, while Mary sat beside her. Down broad, tree-lined Margaret Street, the main avenue, they hurried the girl to McDonnell's surgery, alongside his house. Hours had passed; her wrist was badly swollen. The stern surgeon swiftly cut the sleeve of the precious frock, examined her swollen arm, and set the bone. "She has to stay in Toowoomba awhile!" he almost barked; he was accustomed to country folk balking. The Kennys merely asked, "At a hotel or the hospital?" Mc-

Donnell's manner softened. "I like the girl, and my wife will like her. I'd like to have her stay with us for a few days."

Liza looked uncertain. "Will you stay here," the doctor asked, "and I'll take you for drives with my team?" In the days that followed, she and Dr. McDonnell indeed rode together and talked.[10]

The McDonnell home was the finest in which Liza Kenny had slept, a house with an upstairs and downstairs, a library, and a parlor with delicate china, pottery, and lace antimacassars. The bush girl came home wide-eyed.

♦♦

The Kennys owned a fine but untamed stallion named Satan. No one could ride him, and Mary insisted that he be sold; but Michael, asserting himself, said, "No." The argument threatened family peace. Liza stepped out to the barn one day, mounted the beast, and rode him bareback, using only a bridle.

Michael saw her and shouted: "Get off that horse!"

"Very well, Father," she shouted back. "But who's going to ride him?" She stayed on.[11]

Michael finally made his last move, putting in his name for a piece of crown property on the spur of a knob grandly called "Rocky Mountain" or, by some, "Rockfield," which was more accurate. He got his eighty acres, made a payment, and the Kennys moved into a new house with an orchard and vineyard. Mary planted roses, lilacs, and two fragrant pepperina trees. The orchard provided them apples, apricots, quinces, and mulberries, and, in the words of an old farmer, "They weathered the storms of drought, floods and God knows what else."

Skinny brother Willie teased the cows and rode bareback, yet was considered frail. At eleven, he would often tire on the way to school, and the older children would carry him piggyback. Liza, age eighteen, brooded. She hitched a ride to Toowoomba to ask her friend Dr. McDonnell "What can we do about Willie?" "Sometimes nature can be helped," he told her. He prescribed calisthenics, and Liza supervised them.

Willie or Liza also found a magazine with an ad: "Build your muscles!" The course was endorsed by P. T. Barnum's protégé the great Sandow, who had biceps like grapefruit, as his photograph showed. They saved pennies to send for his course, then set up pulleys in the barn for the exercises.

Dr. McDonnell gave Liza a lecture on muscle structure and loaned her a textbook. She studied it ferociously and returned to bombard him with questions. At an age when other girls were fretting over new frills, she rigged up a wooden man with pulleys and strings to show Willie how his muscles worked. She also sat in McDonnell's study and pored over his anatomical skeleton. McDonnell, quietly laughing but intrigued, gave her some colored ribbons to represent muscles. She spent hours fitting them on the skeleton in the positions shown by his anatomy books and copying out muscle lists. After three years, she wrote later, "I was able to trace muscles from their origin and insertion and had gained a fair knowledge of their function."[12]

For his part, Willie developed like a junior Sandow and, like Sandow, could isolate his principal muscles by voluntary contraction. He ran, boxed, pole-vaulted, and broke horses. His biceps, like Sandow's, looked like grapefruit. He pounded little sister Maggie until she turned black and blue.

♦♦♦

In the evenings the family sat on the cool veranda and sniffed Mary's roses. If it was still light, Rachel and Julia sewed; they were taking in sewing to help the family. Their mother made them new dresses and underclothes. Liza, for her part, played the piano: the first piece she mastered was "The Storm."

The adolescent Kenny girls were all attractive. Trollope's description of Australian girls is apt. "As a rule they are very pretty, having delicate sweet complexions and fine forms. They grow quickly and are women two years earlier in life than are our girls."

The oldest, Rachel, was tall and quiet, with hair like corn tassels. Julia, who was beautiful, was the next, slim and tall with a roselike complexion and chestnut hair. Of the twins, Mary was a dark lovely; and slight, winsome Maggie, or Meg, had the haunting kind of delicate, though not perfect, features, that once won her a belle-of-the-ball contest.

And Liza? "She was best looking of all, I think," says one sister. She was tall and by turn-of-the-century standards she had a good figure, for she was big-boned, with large shoulders, a full chest and hips, and long legs. Big, stately women were the vogue, and those who weren't big put on several voluminous petticoats, flounced, ruffled blouses, and padded hairpieces to make them look more like the period's ample pinup girls.

She also had wavy hair, long black curls, and a regular, handsome face with dark eyes. But she seldom fussed over her looks, and sometimes she gave her sisters her prettiest things. While her sisters discussed young men, she helped drive the stock into the paddocks. She ignored admirers and dutifully helped her subdued father.

When she was twenty-one, Australia was shriveled by the Great Drought of 1902. During eighteen dry months, fields turned brown, then black, then bare. Much of the stock died, and the Kennys had to labor to keep a few milkers alive. Farmers would struggle to lift a collapsed cow onto her feet; a downed cow was a dead one. In desperation, they stood their cattle between shafts and fed them by hand—wild thistles or wild prickly pear, scalded to burn off the thorns, or straw chaff mixed with molasses if they could get it. They and the cattle drank stagnant water, green with scum, from a tank by the side of the house.

Liza in this crisis worked with the men. But she didn't like this brand of labor. Ambitious and intelligent, exposed to Toowoomba, McDonnell, and science, she saw no attraction either in the life that country boys offered or the life that most country women led. "I was healthy and strong," she later said, "and I was not given to fainting." She took an increasing interest in unwomanly things, roamed the outdoors, and grew strong in a day when, she recalled, it was "rude to be healthy," and one was not ladylike "unless she could faint at will or be subject to what was politely called 'the vapors,'" and "lose consciousness at the sight of a drop of blood or a mouse."[13]

It was an age of primness, yet dying primness. A growing number of women were fighting for equal rights, equal votes, equal opportunity for jobs in places better than sweatshops, and a single standard of morality. The stormy Australian singer Nellie Melba was capturing the imagination of Europe, America, and Australia. Melba was lusty and independent, a hard-swearing dinkum Aussie, and her tempests won her as much fame as her singing did. She gave an independently inclined Australian maid a fiery symbol.

Whatever else Elizabeth had on her mind when she reached her twenties in this age of the bloomer and Melba, it was not settling down to boiling prickly pear or lifting cows into cartshafts. Muff before her, long skirt behind, back straight, and eyes ahead, she was ready to advance into the twentieth century.

3

Womanhood

SHE DONNED a garden of a hat with a brim six inches wide. To go to a Sunday school basket picnic, she dressed all in violet. She pinned her hat to her hair, grabbed a stick for field hockey, and joined other young people in a carefree outing, with cakes and chicken spread on a cloth, shirt-sleeved young men lounging and joking, and a few girls boldly poking five inches of black-clad ankle from beneath voluminous skirts. She tried that a bit, but nothing came of it.

As for occupation, she taught Sunday school without pay; like her mother, she could remember the Bible from Genesis to Revelation. She taught piano a little. She tried domestic work. She was "a sort of governess" for the Presbyterian minister's family; she worked for other families as a lady help, a housekeeper. She didn't like that. She reached twenty-seven without husband or career.

Old Granny Moore, once young Elizabeth Moore, still lived in New South Wales, a white-haired, fragile woman of eighty-nine. A widow of character and gentility, she wore a black jacket and lace collar, a black ribbon around her neck, and she looked you straight in the eye. She also smoked Yankee twist tobacco in a clay pipe. She fell ill in late 1907; Liza volunteered to visit her. Her aging father raised one objection. There was another outlaw horse in the paddock, Black Punch, who refused to let anyone but Liza catch him.[1] Liza delegated this task to brother Willie and then set off on what she called "the long journey" to Granny Moore's town of Guyra. The distance was only 214 miles, but the Darling Downs was still a closed world for most of its dwellers. There was no passable road to Brisbane, and few Queenslanders ever saw Melbourne or Sydney.

Liza spent a few weeks with Granny Moore, heard about the days of the new chums, and inspected the blue plates decorated with Asiatic pheasants that had been carried from Ireland. She also met her many cousins. One, Minnie Moore Bell, had a baby son, and another baby was expected. Liza decided to stay with her for a while. Anything seemed more exciting than going home.[2]

She also began to help at Jim Bell's bakeshop. Children came in for confections; their clothes were shabby; times here were still bad. The area was mostly potato and cattle country, and only scattered sheep grazed where today there are thousands. The potatoes were growing, but the local market was glutted. Guyra was no marketing center; it was not much more than an old hotel, two stores, and a blacksmith.

A hard-hit young farm couple came to her grandmother's one Sunday. The wife was expecting, and they were disconsolate. Liza knew that Queensland needed their produce, and she told them she thought she could sell their potatoes. She wrote seventeen letters that night to Queensland firms. Two days later Granny Moore's front door shook to the banging of a messenger boy. Liza received seventeen telegraphed orders. Her young farmer alone could not possibly fill them.

She dauntlessly called a meeting of neighborhood farmers. Haltingly (so she later described her manner, although witnesses deny this) she presented the situation. Questions poured in, the main one being "How do we bloody well know these companies are good for the cash?" But the banker established that her buyers were sound, and she became a middleman in earnest, a commission agent dealing in Guyra Blues, Satisfactions, and other potatoes, as well as oats, onions, and general produce. She regularly hitched up Jim Bell's bakery cart to visit her farmers and had their potatoes put on the rail by the wagonload. She proved to be a great talker, the locals recall. And she took it as a personal insult whenever the market dropped.

She stayed with the Bells almost two years. She sewed clothes for cousins' babies and played the "Wedding March" at their weddings. She was willing to help anyone anytime, although she still hated housework. If she had to do any, she paused often to recite poetry.

She was keeping company, it was said, or thought she was, some insist, with Reg McAllister, the chemist. Reg was a young bachelor who came to the Bells' for dinner sometimes, but it was "never any romance," as Minnie remembers it. Still, another connection has it that "when Liza was staying with old Granny Moore once, Liza was out in the kitchen with McAllister, spooning and paloodling. Granny just went and stood there in her nightdress. McAllister got up and bolted. Oh dear, Liza was burning!"

Obviously nothing came of her relationship with McAllister, but she sold Guyra produce by the hundreds of tons and earned what she called "a goodly sum" in commissions. Three produce merchants came to town to buy potatoes in competition. She scurried out to the farmers and bought more potatoes than all three of them together. "She's wiped up the floor with them," the men at the hotel—the pub—laughed.[3]

They also laughed at her, however. Her role won her no thanks from the established middlemen, who had been too dense to think of new markets. When she walked down the main street, some of the young people began turning their heads away. She soon realized why. "I had stooped to do a thing a woman was not supposed to do, and therefore was supposed not to be quite a nice refined girl." A proper young woman did not think of worldly affairs, "in fact, she was supposed to depend entirely on her male relations."

Even some members of the Kenny family said that she would be better off staying home. She was approaching thirty, an age when most single women donned shawls and gloomy head coverings. "It was a terrible calamity when I went out to make my own living," she said later. "I was supposed to get married like the rest to justify my existence."[4]

"I'm going to travel, Al," she assured cousin Alicent Woodward. "One day I'm going to go to America." And she told Minnie Bell, "It's better to be a lion for a day than a sheep all your life." But how did a little-educated woman who was approaching spinsterhood become a lion? At best, there were few independent courses for a female: teaching, sewing, and menial labor. Anything that appealed to her required an education.

Yet she was more prepared than she knew. She had arrived in Guyra an immature country girl. She had ventured and profited there, put her hand to mature work, blushed with praise, and burned with criticism; in all these ways she had grown. She was riper in mind and body, more impatient for life.

♦♦

She listened to Sunday preachments on the heathen at the Union Church, and when her produce-selling brought her snubs, "I felt strangely apart and lonely, and I then and there made up my mind I would become a missionary and go away to India." Years later in America she once laughed about this and said: "Oh, I had a religious fit when I was young."[5]

She broached the idea in all seriousness, however, to Dr. McDonnell, and he told her that a missionary must know nursing. The thought seemed natural enough to her. Her mother had always been a woman who "helped" by nursing sick neighbors and sometimes delivering babies. Back in Guyra, a Nurse Sutherland operated a simple maternity home. Liza offered to help her, to spend afternoons caring for her patients, just for the experience. When someone in the district had a baby, she began to go out and look after the new mother and child. Nurse Sutherland told her that she had a bent for the work. For the next few years she worked with Nurse Sutherland or went off on her own in New South Wales or Queensland, at times no one knew just where.

She went vacationing one such time on a friend's station in the hilly borderland of the Darling Downs, in the foothills of the Great Dividing Range. A woman became sick nearby, and Liza volunteered to go to her. The house was three miles away in a valley hemmed in by sharp hills and ravines, country too rough for a horse. She said she would walk. Her hostess and a daughter went along to start her off.

The sun was setting fast; it was soon dark. The trio walked for hours, it seemed, mainly downslope, dislodging stones and hearing them splash into a creek below. They reached level ground, and Liza thought she could find her own way. "Stay on the left bank of the creek," her friends told her.

The silence was intense; the chuckle of a possum and the calls of night birds seemed weird. Suddenly she found herself on a narrow tongue of ground with water on both sides. An arm of the creek had looped sharply and, in the blackness, confused her. She climbed a hill to see where she was. The moon was just rising, and she could then see the perplexing creek winding and up-creek the white, corrugated-iron roof that she wanted. "Standing alone" she wrote later, "looking out on the dark foliage of the eucalyptus trees, I felt like earth's only inhabitant."

She scrambled down and at the bottom, exhausted, found her way blocked by a tall, wire-mesh fence. She was about to shout "cooeee" for help when she heard footsteps and a deep voice. It was a man, a big, broad man, "very tall, very handsome," a new owner of nearby land. He couldn't find a gate either, but, an unhesitant Australian, he pulled out a fence pole, knocked down some fencing, and helped Liza across.

They went on to the house together. It was early spring, probably September. The yellow wattle was in full bloom, and its scent made the air heady. That night she abandoned the idea of missionary work among heathen or Hindus and decided that her own Australia needed her.

She called this man "Dan" when she wrote about him years afterward. She saw him often. He proposed and she said she would marry him as soon as she could finish her preparations for nursing. Time passed—two years, three years. He wanted her to give up this "nonsense." Twice in one month he said it was time they were married. She was attracted; it was not his fine home or his herds, she said, only he, "big and bronzed . . . as stubborn as I."

They had a date for the annual picnic races and a dance at the woolshed. He arrived driving a pair of bay horses and a new buggy. She adjusted the blue sash on her white lawn dress and tossed a cape over her shoulders. She was ready to leave when a boy rode up, panting. His father was away driving cattle, and his mother was about to have a baby prematurely.

Dan objected, saying that surely someone else could help. She said there was no one else, and his jaw hardened; but he offered to drive her there.

No, she said, the fastest way was by saddle through the forest.

He exploded. "Decide now whether you are to be married to me or your vocation!" She tried not to cry, turned away, and said, "I have to change my dress." She heard his buggy wheels bounce down the road.

She rode off, and "the birds seemed to have ceased their singing," she would remember. The baby was born out in the bush before the next dawn, with Liza assisting.[6]

Some of the passages above were set down by Martha Ostenso, the novelist who more than thirty years after these events worked with Elizabeth Kenny on her autobiography and interviewed her to try to fill in its vast gaps. Some parts were included by Miss Ostenso just as an older Liza wrote them.

When the autobiography was published, some of Sister Kenny's former neighbors voiced doubt about Dan's existence. Her sisters were assuring yet vague on the subject, and none had ever met him. In her late years, she herself at times said conflicting things.

When Ostenso questioned her, however, "she balked a little but then opened up. There were tears in her eyes. And there were regrets, you could tell it. His name was really David, but she didn't want to use that. She said he used to sing the 'Londonderry Air'—'Danny Boy'—so we called him 'Dan.' "

"I spent the following three years preparing myself," she said in her autobiography, "won my certificate and was ready for the field." For *Who's Who in Australia,* she wrote in the 1940s: "Graduated as nurse, 1911." All the evidence, however, indicates that her only training was what she could pick up here and there, and her only "certificate" was a dream.[7]

She certainly learned some things with Nurse Sutherland at Guyra. Back in Queensland, she usually told people she had trained "in New South Wales"; in New South Wales, however, she said it was someplace else. After her long Guyra stay, "She took her potato money and went off to study nursing. No, she didn't have training here." This was all Minnie Bell knew.

"She did learn nursing and midwifery from Miss Sutherland," her sister Julia maintains. "And I know she did a lot of obstetrics training, working with a doctor at Armidale." Liza herself recorded no such details. She merely wrote that Dr. McDonnell often told her she would be a splendid nurse, so "I forthwith entered a private hospital and began my training."

Her usual answer in later life to interviewers who wanted to know more was: "What do my early years matter? It is my work that counts!" In 1951, pressed, she said, "I was trained at the Scotia Private Hospital in Sydney. It has long ago ceased to exist." Another time she said, "It burned down long ago." No one has been able to find any evidence of such a hospital or nursing, convalescent, or rest home.

In 1914 a Mrs. Catherine Caskey was a patient of Nurse Kenny's, and Liza told her: "I wanted to be a nurse, but the training was too expensive, so I went slum nursing in Sydney for a while with a friend. We had to pay £45, but the training for an ordinary nurse was much dearer. On an obstetrics case, the first thing we'd have to do, sometimes, was get the mother out of a drunken stupor. When the baby was born, the family might produce an old frying pan to wash him in."

There were indeed slum nursing services in Sydney, although none has been able to find Elizabeth Kenny's name in its records. Both New South Wales and Queensland authorities say that she was never a registered or certified nurse on their rolls, though registration started in New South Wales in 1906 and in Queensland in 1912. In both cases, women who had been nursing for some time were "blanketed in"—registered without examination. She never applied, and she joined no nurses' associations.

How then did young Liza really become a respectably uniformed nurse? One solid piece of evidence is that the attending doctor at Nurse Sutherland's "hospital" was a Dr. John Solomon Harris, short, Jewish, rather stiff but always willing to do a kindness or favor. By reliable report, he gave Liza a letter saying she had done satisfactory work for him; in fact, he "certified" it. Then she grandly commissioned a Mr. King, Guyra's tailor, to make her a nurse's outfit.

A red silk nightingale, a little cape named for Florence Nightingale, covered her shoulders and was worn beneath a longer cape of dark velvet that flowed softly around her. Under the capes she wore a snow-white uniform with a white belt and on her head a dark velvet nurse's cap with a stiff crown. She put on this outfit, held her shoulders back, and showed up at home as Nurse Kenny.

4

Bush Nurse

SHE MOUNTED a horse in the year 1911 and rode into the Never Never. She was a bush nurse, self-anointed, not on the roll of any government or nursing society. She did not bother to apply for a formal job for which she had no "qualifications." Ambitious and restless, she saw a place for herself, and she saddled up.

There were few doctors in the neighborhood; they were far apart and overtaxed, and the country roads that could reach them were rough wagon trails, if that. On such a rain-sodden dirt track, traveling a mile by horse and buggy could take an hour. The first motorcars on the Darling Downs were just appearing; they were still curiosities. Of one thing there were many: the sick. A certificate? Some people knew the Kennys' wandering daughter really didn't have one; the rest had no idea what a certificate was. A postmaster in the district had performed emergency surgery with a jackknife. Given this sort of need, a nurse of any kind was a gift.

Liza's usual base was the Kenny house, but out in the bush she often slept in a shack. A farmer, his wife ailing or ready for childbirth, would come for her in a horse and sulky. Or he would send a son galloping, and she would saddle up. Or her brother would saddle her horse while she dressed, and then she rode. She rode in the country around Greenmount, Felton, Pilton, Clifton, West Halden, Back Plains, King's Creek, and Mount Saddletop. She rode across the inland plains of the Downs—flat land for miles, shining gold or silver with tall grasses high as wheat. She rode on the hilly, rolling land near the Range, up and down through quiet sunshine. In the high hills, she would smell the sharp aroma of the mountain eucalyptus trees. Then she would pass an unbelievably quiet pool, with rose and yellow water lilies and a few wild ducks. As she watched, a fine rain might start, making little circles in the water.

She rode in winter with a kerchief around her face and her felt hat pulled down past her eyebrows. She rode on days when the wind blew like bally-ho—some said bally-hell—and dirt and stone flew like buckshot. She spent days and often nights in the saddle and sometimes walked long distances. In the wet, she forded rushing streams, then dismounted to help her horse pick its way through deep mud. But it was most often dry and hot, baking hot, and the earth felt like live coals. Still, she had never been happier. "I loved it. I loved the wild rides," she said. "I loved racing toward a lonely house."

She delivered babies. She learned to shoo the older children down to the creek for a game while their mother was in labor. Then, as she said once in her grandiloquent nineteenth-century language, "How joyous would be the song in my heart, having launched another frail barque on life's sea." The barques could not have been too frail. Liza delivered them in huts with dirt floors and in sapling beds covered with wool bags; she delivered one baby on a bullock wagon. She also tended colic, broken legs, and split skulls. She often sat up all night fighting pneumonia, a disease that was a nightmare in a day without miracle drugs.

She stopped at one crude hut to help a mother have her baby. Waiting that night, she slept on two chairs. The baby eventually came. The next morning the other children came in with eggs, saying, "We got them out of Peter's coffin." Peter, it seemed, was another child, gravely sick in bed but alive. Liza tried to hush the youngsters, but their father said, "It's all right. We've already made three coffins for Peter, and he's outgrown them." She stayed on, and Peter got worse and had to be taken to the hospital in Toowoomba. "Well," the father said, "we'll just carry him in the coffin." Peter eventually died, and the parents and children accepted it as bush life.

She once found a group of men working, "and one died," she remembered, "and nobody could say a prayer. So they danced around his grave singing, 'For he's a jolly good fellow.'" Another time she reached a house in black darkness; she had to light matches to find an ailing woman and a note from a doctor. The note ordered poultices; Liza boiled a pumpkin to make them. All night she stumbled around, applying the hot pumpkin, fetching water, trying to find her way. In the morning the patient's husband marched out of the barn, where he had gone for a quiet night's sleep.

Liza tended such patients, washed family clothes, scrubbed floors, boiled bed linen, and wiped noses. "When we went into a home," she remembered, "we didn't take over the patient, we took over the whole family. We knew what sickness and accident meant to these remote people, and we wanted them to lean on us. And they did." One day she encountered a hobbling abo chief. Half of one leg was missing. She arranged for a peg leg to be fitted. His tribe then renamed him "Chief Waddy Mundooee"—"Chief Wood Foot" or "Clubfoot"—and the name, advertising for Nurse Kenny, was engraved on a great half-moon of brass hanging from his neck.

She never asked a fee. Sometimes she got a modest one, often not. Often the payment was a present—a leg of mutton, a rooster, or a cut of beef, brought around later when a beast was slaughtered. One day she was resting in her bush shack when she saw something bobbing up and down in the distance. As it bobbed nearer, she saw that it was a man carrying an armchair on his back. He was a grateful patient, or the relative of a patient, bringing a gift.

She had found herself a life here or the beginning of one. The sun above Queensland was a hot disc in a deep, endless blue sky, and she rode under it, almost satisfied.[1]

On a June morning in 1911, Australian early winter, the sun low, a fresh touch to the air, a young stockman rode up to the Kenny house. He pulled up to the two pepperina trees; he was tired and tense, almost tongue-tied, but he choked out his message. Liza was needed at the McNeil hut ten miles away.

The sun was already beginning to set when she approached the young Irish immigrant's bark-roofed slab hut, under the boughs of a towering eucalyptus. Something was wrong. There were no shouting McNeil children to meet her, only McNeil, a giant, waiting to help her swing out of the saddle.

"Thank God, you've come."

"What's wrong?"

"Amy—I don't know—but she's in awful pain."[2]

The nurse ran into the long, low hut. Mrs. McNeil grabbed Liza's hand and pulled her to a cot. Amy, two years old, blonde, lay there unable to move. Her golden hair was awry on the bedclothes, her eyes were filled with terror, her body was twisted beneath the coverings. Liza had known her before as a gay child, if shy. Now she was whimpering. One knee was drawn toward her chin, and her foot was pointed downward, with its heel twisted. One of her arms lay on her chest, elbow bent. The nurse cautiously tried straightening the arm and leg. The child screeched. "What is it?" the mother asked. Liza had no answer—she felt beaten. She kneeled and prayed.

She also knew she must send a telegram for medical advice. She studied the girl. Mounting her horse, Thunderbolt, she galloped like ballyhell several miles, then she wrote out a message to the doctor she knew best.

"How long before there'll be an answer?" she asked the telegraph operator.

"Three, perhaps four hours."

She waited much longer into the night. While she waited, another disturbed father came looking for her; he lived four miles from the McNeils. A son, ten, and a daughter, four, could neither stand nor walk. Liza could only promise to see them as soon as she could. She waited outside the telegrapher's shack watching the stars. Finally the operator called her. The message was bleak: "Infantile paralysis. No known treatment. Do the best you can with the symptoms presenting themselves. Aeneas J. McDonnell."

To the untrained young nurse, the message was devastating. She walked outside, put her hand on her horse's warm neck, "and I whispered the words my mother had taught me: 'I shall lift up my eyes to the hills from whence my strength cometh.'" And she thought she heard her mother's voice responding, "I can of my own strength do nothing."

That seemed to compose her. Five miles, perhaps more, she rode into a night wind that carried the harsh bite of winter. She had barely heard of infantile paralysis. It had never been seen in her area or, if it had been seen, it had not been recognized as infantile paralysis. She thought merely of the "symptoms presenting themselves" and of what she knew about muscles from her days of exercise with brother Willie.

Mrs. McNeil was still at the bedside. Amy was in agony, her twisted leg obviously causing the torture. To Liza its affected muscles looked shortened and tightened—contracted. She breathed deeply. The contraction must be overcome. There was one resource, heat. She knew heat relaxed.

> I ran into the kitchen, where a wood fire burned on the stove, filled a frying pan with salt and then put it over the fire, then poured the salt into a

bag. The bag I placed carefully on the deformed leg. . . . The child moaned, and I knew the pain was no better than before. The next thing I tried was a linseed poultice. . . . Again I realized that I had utterly failed. . . .

Maybe moist heat was the answer. There was a blanket on the bed—a heavy one of soft Australian wool and, almost in desperation, I seized it and tore it into strips. On the stove was a kettle of boiling water. I put the strips of wool in a basin and poured boiling water over them and wrung every drop of water out. . . . Gently I wrapped the hot, damp cloth around the tortured limbs and in a moment the child stopped whimpering.[3]

With a few more applications Amy's eyes closed, and, Liza would write, sleep, "nature's soft nurse," took over. Later in the night, however, Amy woke up in fear and sobbed out a plea both tragic and comic: "I want them rags that wells my legs!"

Much of the rest of the night the kettle boiled, and the McNeils and Nurse Kenny soaked the strips of wool in a basin, wrung them out to prevent burning the skin, and applied them. The sharp smells of hot, wet wool and wood smoke filled their nostrils; the work kept them from collapsing. The child's blue eyes remained closed. She slept, and finally Liza too slept a little. The next morning she put on more hot "foments" or "fomentations," as she called them, and then—completely ignorant of textbook warnings—she very gently began trying to move the child's leg back into normal patterns. The sight would have chilled eminent infantile paralysis authorities thousands of miles away.

She went on to the house where the brother and sister were stricken. Their symptoms were the same. Within less than a week the inexperienced, self-appointed nurse found herself with a polio epidemic on her hands, affecting six of the twenty children in the thinly settled district. She rode from child to child, heating wool strips and putting them on painful arms and legs, sleeping when she could, eating when somebody put food before her.

Within a few days in each case, pain subsided, and she could begin to try to teach the child to move his limbs again. At first the affected limbs were limp and helpless, and the nurse patiently moved them herself through their normal paths, telling the child to "try to remember" how to move them. Gradually strength began returning. Gradually all six children recovered without paralysis and were again running into the bush.

In late August, the beginning of spring, a girl, twelve, was sick. "Keep the sun over your right shoulder until you come to a stock route," Liza was directed. A thunderstorm broke on her. She hopped off her horse, peeled off her clothes, popped them under her saddle, and put the clothes and saddle under a waterproof blanket. Then, atop a stump, the tall, tan nurse sat on the bundle and enjoyed a shower. Soon she could dry herself in the sun. She later recommended this style of bathing to all who are not shy before birds and koala bears.

She arrived at the girl's house to find her suffering severe abdominal pain. The nurse suspected appendicitis and longed for a messenger to alert a doctor. There was a stock road not far away, so she climbed a tall tree stump and lustily bellowed "Coo-ee-ee" three times. She soon heard a soft clap-clap of hands. She was petrified, for she knew it for the handclapping of the lubras, the aboriginal women, at a corroboree, a solemn assemblage with ritual drama performed by natives painted like skeletons. Only evil, it was said, could come from interrupting them.

She hurried into the house, bolted the door, and returned to her patient. Besides abdominal pains, the girl now had infantile paralysis symptoms. But if Liza put on her hot foments and the child really had appendicitis, it might cause a ruptured appendix. How could she get a message out? The girl's dog growled: someone was coming. There was a clear *tap*-step-*tap*-step outdoors, each footstep followed by the tap of a wooden peg. Chief Waddy Mundooee.

There stood friendly, naked Waddy, with his wood leg and shining brass breastplate, his ribs and cheekbones painted a skeletal white and feathers stuck to self-inflicted ritual gashes in the calf of his good leg and his thighs. He wore a string around his waist to support an inadequately long collection of possum tails and was accompanied by a similarly painted retinue.

"Whitefeller Mary in trouble?" he asked.

She wrote another telegram to Dr. McDonnell, Waddy designated a messenger, Liza covered him with a red tablecloth, and he mounted her horse for his trip to the telegraph shack. Dr. McDonnell replied that the abdominal muscles were often affected in infantile paralysis, so she followed her previous course.

Almost a year passed before she next saw McDonnell. He was an important man now, the handlebar-moustached senior surgeon at Toowoomba General Hospital and a member of the Queensland Medical Board. He also owned one of the first motorcars on the Downs: in a high-crowned motoring cap and a long, double-breasted cloak, he drove for miles on roads like washboards. "It was nothing," observed the *Toowoomba Chronicle* on his death at age seventy-five, "for him to hire a special train in order to go out on a case, sometimes as far as Cooyar, Chinchilla and Goondiwindi."[4]

Liza Kenny was a minor personage in such a life. Still, McDonnell thought well of her. She was, after all, an unusual young woman. He happily greeted her now when she showed up at his surgery on elegant Margaret Street, and he smiled at her splendid uniform with the velvet cap. She flushed. To her, Dr. Aeneas John McDonnell was professor, counselor, idol, and friend, a man as important to her as her father and more important than any "Dan."

On the surface, he was peppery and to the point. He didn't make small talk. "What about those polio cases?"

"There were more—worse than the first lot. But they're all well now."

"Splendid!" he said. "How badly are the children crippled?"

"Why, they're not crippled. They're entirely normal."

"Do you mean to tell me they recovered?" He was shouting a little. People had to raise their voices so he could hear them, and he habitually shouted back.

"Why, of course!"

He looked at her skeptically and went to a file for her telegrams. "These read like severe cases, some of them already in the paralytic stage. Good heavens, nurse, such cases don't just recover as completely as that!"

"But they're all right. Should they be otherwise?"

"What did you do?"

"I used what I had—water, heat, blankets and my own hands. The children recovered."

McDonnell calmed down a little and took her to Toowoomba Hospital. On a white bed lay a small boy, a recent poliomyelitis victim, undergoing immobilization treatment. Both his legs had been strapped onto splints, but he was still in pain.

"Here is a new case," McDonnell told her. "Now show us what you did."

His young country woman stepped forward. Patiently she removed the splints and the bandages that held them. She asked for hot water and a blanket, cut the blanket into sections, heated the strips and began packing them around the boy's limbs. As the strips cooled, she replaced them, and the child seemed to be getting more comfortable. Doctor and nurses watched with intense curiosity and strong disbelief. Later she told them how the stricken muscles looked to her—"in spasm," contracting in pain, suddenly and involuntarily. To ease this, she used the moist heat. Then when the pain was relieved, she was able to begin reteaching movements that she told him were "forgotten."

"Elizabeth," McDonnell said, "you have treated those youngsters for symptoms exactly the opposite of the symptoms recognized by orthodox medical men."

"You told me to do the best I could with the symptoms that presented themselves," she answered.

"Yes, I know."

He showed her the books in his library; they said nothing about spasmodic or contracting muscles. Some said that in the acute stage of polio, muscles were weak, flaccid, loose, and sagging, and were pulled out of shape by adjoining normal muscles. Therefore they must be held straight by splints. Then, even though dead, they might remain straight, to be supported in future years by steel braces so the patient could move and walk.

"But they don't say anything here about *spasm*. And that's what I saw and treated!"

McDonnell took a long look at her. She later wrote once that he said, "Your heart will be broken and your spirit will be crushed, for medicine is not kind to its reformers. But the day will come, if you have the courage . . . when your work will be recognized, and the great cities of the earth shall gladly welcome you."

Such overripe phraseology was not McDonnell's but her own, though that could have been the gist of his message. On another occasion she said he simply told her, "You have the eyes of youth. Keep it up." And: "You have knocked our theories into a cocked hat, but your treatment works, and that's all that counts." And finally some practical but bad advice: "Go ahead with your ideas, but whatever you do, don't fight with the medical profession. Because if you do, you won't make any progress."

McDonnell did not seize on her new methods himself or follow them up. He did not take her into the Toowoomba Hospital to give therapy; he left any polio treatment to accepted doctors and theories. Polio was not yet a common problem, and he was busy with many things. He knew that she had seen only a handful of cases, that no medical man had confirmed her results, and that it was entirely possible that she had seen light cases which did not resemble these in Toowoomba Hospital. He indicated things like this to some colleagues. But he was certainly open-minded enough to have advised her to "keep it up."

"For the birth of something new, there has to be a happening," says Maurois in his *Life of Sir Alexander Fleming.* "Newton saw an apple fall; James Watt watched a kettle boil; Roentgen fogged some photographic plates. And these people knew enough to translate ordinary happenings into something new. . . ."

Two things seem clear. Nurse Kenny saw muscles contracting in pain and perceived cause and effect. She discovered that heat, properly applied, could not only relieve the pain but also relieve the contraction. A modern doctor would call her use of heat and exercise "physical medicine and rehabilitation." These things are taught in medical schools now. Her reasons for using them, she later said, were ignorance of the then-prevailing medical treatment plus common sense. "Do the best you can," McDonnell had told her, and she had used heat, the remedy that every mother uses on pain.

A number of her detractors contended later that she must have seen or heard about early medical writings that advocated varying degrees of heat and exercise in polio. There were indeed such works. But most were ignored. Dr. Bernard Roth in Great Britain in 1884 advocated early and vigorous treatment including warm baths, massage, passive stretching, muscle reeducation, and therapeutic exercise. In 1905 Dr. Ivar Wickman in Sweden urged "active physical treatment" including hot packs, passive and active movements, and electrical stimulation—an early medical fad later abandoned in most of the world. Others wrote along similar lines.[5]

Among the most important writings of the era were those of Dr. Robert W. Lovett of Boston, who in 1921 helped treat the polio-stricken Franklin D. Roosevelt.* Lovett as early as 1908 recommended warm baths, gentle massage, and cautious encouragement of the use of the muscles. But he was far more cautious than Roth had been in the 1880s. The point he stressed most was the need for immobilization to prevent contractures, and he warned that permanent damage to muscle would result from the kind of early and vigorous "over-treatment" that Liza, uninformed, attempted. All these physicians, except, perhaps, the thoroughly forgotten Dr. Roth, were far more hesitant than she to use passive and active exercise early in the course of the disease. "The general regimen of the day," in medical language, "consisted first of immobilizing the affected limb or limbs in splints," and there was deep and general fear of damaging "fragile," polio-stricken muscles by premature motion or exercise.[6]

* The treatment was ineffective. Roosevelt did not receive modern physical therapy early in his disease.

In short, those who early and vigorously advocated the use of physical methods did not prevail, and there is no evidence that Liza Kenny knew anything about them. "Nothing makes me madder," she once wrote, "than for someone to say that I invented the hot packs. Mrs. Noah used them on her husband on the ark." Still other detractors in the 1940s said she would have used splints had they been available in the bush. She replied hotly that "I would have given the standard treatment in a minute if I had known about it. I would have been out tearing the bark off the trees to make splints."[7]

One more intriguing footnote: In 1955, in what was still the small marketing city of Toowoomba, Dr. Alexander Horn was interviewed in his surgery on the subject of Elizabeth Kenny. A little Scottish doctor of about seventy, he sat on an old carved chair at his rolltop desk in a small circle of light, surrounded by antique medical apparatus, sucking on a pipe, and peering through half-moon glasses. A bolt of lightning would not have moved him an inch.

"I started here in 1908," he said. "I know the Kennys, and I knew Elizabeth Kenny. I brought her sisters' babies into the world. When I first met Elizabeth she was a bush nurse, a country nurse. And I'll tell you this. When she met her first case of polio she did in fact appeal to Dr. McDonnell. Then she asked me. I said, 'Well, we haven't had a great deal of experience with polio in this territory, but I'll tell you what they used to tell us in medical school in Scotland.' It's a manual thing that any sensible mother can do. In Scotland, they used stupes made with the old, dark-colored blankets. It relieved the pain and it warmed up the cold limbs. I told her to use those hot stupes right from the beginning." (A medical dictionary defines "stupe" as "a cloth, sponge or the like, for external application, charged with hot water, wrung out nearly dry." The word is well known, if archaic.)

"And I do remember telling her," Dr. Horn continued, "that after the coldness went out of the limbs, she should try to reeducate the child back to natural movements. I can see Sir Alexander Ogston saying that so plainly to us at Aberdeen University. So it wasn't McDonnell at all who put her onto that, it was myself." But just when did he tell this to Liza Kenny? "Well, she used to visit me when she wasn't well—that would have been in the '20s." But her first polio cases were in 1911. "Look, I'm not so sure she didn't come to see me before the war. I do remember that she asked me about a patient." Who was the patient? "I'm not so sure." Then he reflected. "I'm sure it was the Cregan girl—I fancy it would have been that girl that I attended. But I really can't remember. Things fade a bit, you know."

"The Cregan girl" was a spastic, not a polio patient, whom Liza cared for in the 1920s. Still, Dr. Horn's story shows how commonly heat was used as a remedy in a time when doctors had little to offer but pink pills and kind words, and mothers and country women did as much doctoring as the doctors.[8]

Liza wanted to get ahead. She spotted an empty house in the Darling Downs hamlet of Clifton, bought or rented it, and opened a "hospital." It was much like Nurse Sutherland's maternity hospital in Guyra, one of a myriad of semiprofessional cottage hospitals in a day when professional hospitals were few.

It was an old, one-story, wooden house with a false gable, painted a creamy color called "stone." The site was the north end of Norman Street, which was not so much a street as a wagon road, with here or there a house or a business. Liza's was the last dwelling before the race track, where there were races only now and again; most of the time the track was a campground for swaggies. The town of Clifton consisted principally of the track, a pub, Provan's Store, a produce business, a draper's shop, the rail station, and, most recently, a dentist and a doctor. Liza named her new establishment "St. Canice's," for Michael Kenny's County Kilkenny. She dressed all in white—white frock, starched apron, and flowing headdress—and awaited her patients.[9]

A child with diphtheria was carried in. A hired man lost an arm in a chaff cutter and was rushed there. She nursed a bad gallstone case "and it came out all right," people said. The storekeeper's wife was there for "weeks and weeks" with neuritis. She even admitted emergency surgical cases, though she had only makeshift operating space. The choice in such a pinch was either Liza's hospital or Toowoomba; the ride to Toowoomba could have spelled doom to some who survived at St. Canice's.

There were often as many as four or five maternity cases in her hospital. The baby was delivered in the mother's bedroom. The doctor was not always on hand, but Liza was there, starched and proud. She began to become well known as "clever, mark my word!" "She's not afraid to tackle anything," the townspeople said. "She'll have a go at it." Often she had to act on her own, without a doctor's advice.

It was a day when "the doctor" was sometimes very good and sometimes hopelessly bad. She had not been in Clifton long when one practitioner wanted to operate on a child for appendicitis. "Doctor," she said, "I believe that diagnosis is wrong."

"Who are you to say?" he challenged her.

"I'm sorry, this is my hospital," she answered, and she refused to prepare for the operation. She was not quite as sure as she sounded; if the child died because no surgery was performed, it could ruin her. But to her the child did not look perilously ill, and she had decided this doctor was incompetent. She believed the child could stand the train trip to Toowoomba, to be placed in the hands of the nonpareil Dr. McDonnell; this is the course that was followed. The child did not have appendicitis.

She needed a helper. She drove to nearby Nobby in a borrowed horse and sulky and asked Mrs. Donahue if she could spare one of her girls. Mrs. Donahue volunteered Eileen, fourteen. Eileen cleaned and cooked, but she stayed only eight months. When Steven Martin had to have some fingers amputated by a Dr. Hammond, poor Eileen was to help; but when Hammond sawed a finger off, the girl fainted. "Well, she won't make a nurse," Liza commented.

Catherine Caskey's boy Willie died at the hospital, and Liza, trying to comfort her, told her, "There is another link to heaven now." Later Mrs. Caskey's son Allen, aged two, was ill with what the doctor called a stomach inflammation. "The doctor had given him up," the boy's mother remembers, "and they were praying for him in the church. But Elizabeth told me, 'Look, Catherine, I'll give him an enema if you approve.' It was such a simple thing, but after it was done he improved so quickly, he began to look around and gained consciousness."

Mrs. Caskey told the nurse, "The doctor didn't tell you to do that."

"I do a lot on my own ideas," Liza answered.

Talking with the mothers one night, she said, "If I can run this hospital for two or three years, I think I can do very well anyplace, because this is such a responsibility." Another night, however, several patients were sitting with Nurse Kenny, chattering, and she suddenly said, "To tell you the truth, I'd rather be Mrs. Caskey, married to a farmer, than anyone else."

Four or five bachelors lived across the road from her hospital. She would call on them sometimes when a swaggie whom she had fed declined to move on. Some of the young men, with Una and Irene Clairingbould, the postmaster's daughters, and Mr. Dodd, the young Methodist parson, would often sit in her parlor, chat, and play the piano, and Liza would lean on the settee and sing and laugh.

There was a good deal of talk of a serious romance between Liza and Dr. Hammond, a reserved man in his thirties, tall and dark. She would meet him at the door in midmorning after his home visits and show him the mothers and babies and the other patients. Then they would stand and talk and joke on the steps a long while. At times because of the nature of their work she spent hours alone with him. Years later she told a nephew that she was asked "by someone" in Clifton to marry him.

She might well have dreamed there of marriage. But she also dreamed of the world. Late one night—some say the night before he went off to World War I—Dr. Hammond suddenly married his housekeeper, and Liza borrowed the ring for her.

She continued some country nursing when called. She rode from Clifton to Allora every Monday to help give the chloroform while a Dr. Sapsford did his operations. She also saw more polio cases. She went visiting in the town of West Holden in the spring; on her birthday she gave the neighborhood children a picnic. During the footraces, she noticed that something was wrong with a girl of nine who had always been a swift runner. Now Mary Lucy was lagging. Liza put her on a table. "As I ran my hands over her strong little body, something struck me. . . . There was an odd condition." The child said she was fine. The next day she was still cheerful enough; but the day after Liza was called to her bedside, "and I had the answer. That condition I had noted in Mary's muscular system was the first symptom" of polio. Not from textbooks—she had begun to read textbooks skeptically—but with her eyes and her hands, Liza was learning.

In 1913 Michael Kenny, the Irish emigrant of the 1860s, died at age seventy-eight. Liza's mother sold the farm, lived at the hospital a few months, then bought a little house outside the village of Nobby, separated from its lone street and sprinkle of stores by a mile-long stretch of field. Mary Kenny was not quite at ease, however. She read the Toowoomba newspaper, and knew what was going on in the world; she often said, "Liza, there's going to be war."

5

War Nurse

THE YEAR WAS 1914, and Australia went to war. Bands played, drums rolled, and excited Aussies stood on roofs to watch war pageants with banners that cried: "St. George for England!" In 1914 the word "home" still meant the United Kingdom to most Australians, though few had ever seen it. It was "home" or "the old country" that was in peril, then, when the assassin shot the archduke and Europe exploded, and the popular political leader was he who pledged that Australia would defend the empire "to our last man and our last shilling."[1] The defense began at home. Britain declared war on August 4. The next day the German merchantman *Pfalz* tried to escape Sydney Harbor, and Australians fired the Southern Hemisphere's first shot to prevent it. Soon C. J. Dennis, the Australian bush poet, wrote:

Fellers of Australier,
  Blokes an' coves an' coots,
Shift yer bloody carcases,
  Move yer bloody boots,
Gird yer bloody loins up,
  Git yer bloody gun,
Set the bloody enermy
  An' watch the bugger run.

Get a bloody move on,
  Have some bloody sense,
Learn the bloody art of
  Self debloodyfence.

Fellers of Australier,
  Cobbers, chaps, an' mates,
Hear the bloody enermy
  Kickin' at the gates!
Blow the bloody bugle,
  Beat the bloody drum,
Upper-cut and out the cow
  To kingdom bloody come![2]

Before the end of the war, 416,000 cobbers, chaps, and mates, all volunteers, had put on uniforms topped by slouch hats with an impertinent roll. Lean and sinewy, accustomed to sun and outdoors, they were, in the view of poet John Masefield, "the finest body of young men ever brought together in modern times. For physical beauty and nobility of bearing they surpassed any men I have ever seen." No one of course dared call them "beautiful" to their faces.

Among this tough force was Liza's young brother Willie, now "Bill," six feet tall, properly lean and sinewy, and mostly silent. In baggy uniform and plumed digger hat, rifleman Kenny posed for a photograph before sailing, a buddy on each side, arms entwined. He stood a head above one friend, a half a head above the other. This first client of Liza's muscular miracles had become a boxer and pole-vaulter, with a chin like a bulldozer. On November 1, 1914, the first convoy of the Australian Imperial Force embarked, steaming under the flag of the thirteen-year-old Commonwealth of Australia: blue field, Union Jack in the corner, five stars of the Southern Cross on the fly. Among the troops was Bill's Second Light Horse Regiment.

The convoy's ultimate destination was the Black Sea peninsula of Gallipoli, where heavily Anzac (Australia and New Zealand) British forces were trying to take the Straits of Dardanelles and open a supply route to imperial Russia. The eight-month-long attempt proved a disaster, in part owing to lack of British Army support, despite the pleas of the campaign's architect, First Lord of the Admiralty Winston Churchill. In the face of Turkish machine guns, the bloodied Anzacs had to dig into trenches on their thin beachhead. "What are you *doing*?" one Aussie would sardonically call to another. "Digging, digging, always bloody well digging" became a standard reply, and these troops and Australians generally became known as "diggers."[3] Digging, shrapnel, sniping, and death further hardened the hard Aussies. Gallipoli, it is often said, made a nation of Australia.

Brother Bill fought at Anzac Beach and Shrapnel Gully—diggers' wry names—and ultimately the *Toowoomba Chronicle* ran a photograph of

Pvt. William Harold Kenny, "referred to in the cables respecting the immortal Anzac landing . . . as 'The Big Queenslander' who 'tossed a Turk right over his shoulder on a bayonet.' . . . His mother is in receipt of advices from the Base Records, Melbourne, intimating to her that the French Republic has bestowed the Medaille Militaire on her son, in recognition of his distinguished service. . . . Pvt. Kenny is a well-known athlete and a splendid specimen."[4] Kenny and fellow Anzacs fought until December 1915, then withdrew. The debarkation lasted a final precarious month, with Bill a member of a demolition party and one of the last men to leave.

Maybe Willie's joining, or the new Australian patriotism, or her itchy foot decided Liza. Early in 1915 she sold her hospital and made a visit to the dependable Dr. McDonnell, who wrote her some testimonials, stating for all to read that she was a capable nurse. So armed, she took a train to Brisbane and bought passage for London on the P. and O. liner *Medina*, still sailing and carrying some civilians, despite the hostilities.

Her intention was to join the Australian Army Nursing Service. The ordinary practice, as she and McDonnell must have known, was for a nurse to join in Australia after presenting credentials or certificates showing hospital service and training. Liza did not have them, so she simply boarded the *Medina* and sailed through the Suez Canal and the Mediterranean to England.

Among her fellow passengers was a well-bred, well-educated young widow, Alice Perrott. Mrs. Perrott had been brought up on a cattle station in the north; she was on her way to England to join a daughter in school. She noticed Liza the first day out: a tall, tidy figure in a brown linen dress, skirt down to her ankles, white nurse's apron, and velvet cape. Liza told her about her "credentials"—in point of fact, her letters—from Dr. McDonnell, and together they watched the sea and the sky.[5]

They landed in Britain in spring. Liza found a bed at a nurses' club, and the next day (she wrote twenty-five years later) she reported "as directed" to a General Williams, who ordered her to France for special duty, after which she was to help take the first Australian Gallipoli casualties back home. Mrs. Perrott tells the story rather differently. By her account, Liza took her recommendations in hand and went first to a senior officer in the Australian Army Medical Corps, Colonel Thomas Dunhill.

"Are all your family as splendid looking as you?" he asked.

"No," she said, "I'm the only weed."

They tried her out for a month, according to Mrs. Perrott. "They sent her to a military hospital, and she proved herself. They accepted her, and they put her in an Army nurse's uniform." Her appointment certificate in the Army Nursing Service attests only that she was "Appointed to the A.I.F." on May 30, 1915. Army records (according to F. R. Sinclair, secretary, Department of the Army, Commonwealth of Australia) add only that "the nature of the qualifications possessed by her prior to enlistment are shown on her attestation papers as 'Medical, Surgical and Obstetrical Nurse.' This is Sister Kenny's own statement, and it is not substantiated by documentary evidence. Army records do not indicate whether her training was formal or informal before she entered the Army." Paradoxically, Mr. Sinclair goes on to say: "An applicant for enlistment in the Australian Army Nursing Service during the 1914–1918 war was required to be registered as a nurse in a State or Territory of Australia, after having passed the prescribed nursing examinations." Which Elizabeth Kenny had not.[6]

Army nurses at places Liza worked were soon watching her. Her methods were just a little different, they told each other. Original. And she never mentioned her training, a favorite topic of nurses. One nurse, then submatron of Southall Australian Military Hospital in England, says, "There was some mystery about how she got there. She did not enter the way the rest of us did."

The mystery does not seem very deep. Liza's testimonial-providing friend, Dr. McDonnell, was a member of the Queensland State Medical Board, a captain in the uniform of the Army Medical Corps, and an important adviser to Australian nurses: a member of the council of the recently organized Australasian Trained Nurses' Association and Toowoomba examiner for the Queensland Nurses' Registration Board. His signature on either a formal "credential" or a plain, handwritten letter would have been golden. In Britain the severely wounded were being returned from Gallipoli by the shipful. There was a shortage of nurses of any description. The outlook was for a long, hard war against so far victorious foes. As one Australian hospital official has put it, "The 1915 Army wouldn't have argued whether she was a bloody trained nurse or not!"

As for Liza, she merely carried herself straight and serene in her new drab gray outfit with red shoulder tabs and a cape with red lining. She was thirty-four, though she had set down her age on army papers as a more youthful-sounding thirty-one. She was now legally and officially Staff Nurse Kenny; as for training, she watched and she learned.

The Allies stemmed the early German advances across Belgium and France. The Second Battle of Ypres was fought in April and May 1915, ending in stalemate and leaving western Belgium and northeastern France a maze of muddy trenches, which would become a battleground for three and a half years. Casualties were appalling. Liza found herself pressed into service with a British Red Cross unit. She lived in a tent, slept on the ground, and cared for soldiers and refugees in France and Belgium. She dressed the wounds of Albert, king of the Belgians, when he was struck by shrapnel. He had walked unescorted into the dressing tent. "How dare you come in here! What's your name?" she challenged. "Albert of Belgium," he said. Meek for a change, she ministered to him.

Shells bursting, the fighting at its height, she was assigned to a hospital in a convent near Ypres Gate. With an English nurse, she attended a soldier there. The explosions came closer, but they went on with their work. Then a shell tore through the ward and burst into fragments. Struck in the leg, knocked down, she stared in a daze at her companion, dead, holding their dead patient's foot in her hand. Liza fainted. A fragment of shell had passed through her left knee, and several bits of shrapnel had riddled her leg. She awoke in the shattered convent to find herself being cared for by quietly comforting nuns. She asked for a mirror and found that her hair had started to gray.

The wound was slight, but the experience and the awakening by the hovering nuns renewed an old attraction to her father's religion, richer and more emotional than outback Protestantism. In Australia after the war, Liza told a friend, "I took the Catholic faith in France but never practiced it." That she was frightened and merely prayed with the nuns is more likely. In any case, the shrapnel won her a quick return to London and a furlough. Her three weeks were nearly up before she could walk easily. On a bright afternoon, she and a fellow nurse went strolling in Kensington Gardens. In relaxed civilian garb, they chattered under the chestnut trees and waved when they saw three Aussies, early Gallipoli casualties, wearing the emu plumes of the Light Horse Regiments. One was ineptly trying to adjust another's arm bandage.

The nurses repaired the dressing and learned that the diggers were overdue in Surrey. Wicked London had snatched their last shilling, and their train was to leave in half an hour. The nurses were out of money too, but Liza's friend reminded her that it was the last day she could stay out of uniform and a secondhand store a few streets away bought used clothing. Liza told the horseless Light Horsemen to wait, undressed, and sat behind a screen while her companion took the men her thirty-five shillings and picked up more clothes for her.

Two years later Liza received a letter from one of the trio. It contained seventy shillings and the message: "We should have written you thanks before this time, but after our holiday we got rather messed up over in France. The other two boys got it, so it don't hurt any more. Seems to me I ought to send you this, because although they are dead, I know they would want you to have the money."

On another leave, she crossed the Irish Sea and stayed at the Kenny family cottage in Toorbeg where her father grew up. She walked under Kenny trees and slept in a bedroom with a bowl of blue flowers in the window. Later she fliply wrote of the place as "the paternal potato patch in Kilkenny." But she also told how an old man, her father's boyhood friend, gave her an ancient Celtic greeting meaning "a thousand welcomes to Ireland to Michael's daughter." She also saw reapers still using hand sickles, women binding sheaves, and beggar women visiting the kitchens seeking food. Ireland was yet Ireland.

One day she heard Uncle Martin Kenny, her father's brother, say he was taking some cattle to the fair. "I'll go along!" she volunteered. Uncle Martin was painfully silent and then said, "The women of this house do not attend fairs, my daughter." The Kilkenny Fair was still too raucous for females, so Liza quietly went back to the war.

Embarkation date was October 8 for her new assignment as nurse on the first ship to sail to Australia with Gallipoli casualties. The Gallipoli result was already plain: bitter and expensive defeat. A brass band greeted the disabled, just the same. Doctors and nurses were taken aboard a luxurious White Star liner, deposited in plush cabins, but cautioned not to unpack. It was a maneuver to fool any scouts for the U-boats: at midnight all were aroused and walked on long stretches of slippery piers. Then the medical crew and 600 sick and wounded were loaded on a sagging old sea hag named the *Suevic*. A former immigrant ship, she had once split in two on a rock, but both bow and stern had survived to be enlarged and rejoined. Now she was to serve as a "dark ship": no lighted hospital vessel exempt from attack, but a converted merchantman with combatant passengers and a gun on the stern in addition to the wounded and the merchant crew. As such, she was fair game for submarines and traveled without lights.

The ship sailed. The desperately scarce gun and four gunners were dropped at Dakar to be transferred to a ship returning to European waters, and the gray old *Suevic* wore her way across the Indian Ocean. The four-week voyage passed, and—as told in a Sydney newspaper in 1935—"The story ran through the ship of a soldier shot through the shoulders and completely paralyzed in both arms, who, through some treatment by a sister, had been able to carry off his pack at Melbourne, and who actually came back to the ship to tell his mates that he had reenlisted." The nursing sister was Liza. She had just worked on reeducating his muscles.[7]

The worn transport moved unannounced into Melbourne docks. The few onlookers were too deeply affected even to cheer; these were the first war-wounded that Australians had seen. The ship steamed on to Sydney. Liza took a train to Brisbane, then to the Downs. She arrived at Nobby at midnight, unexpected. A night porter took her luggage, and she walked the mile home by bright moonlight. An old watchdog failed to recognize her; his barking awoke her mother, and Nurse Kenny shouted, "It's me, Mother, Liza!"

The war nurse visited Toowoomba and Dr. McDonnell. "She's a fine woman and doing a lot of good," he crowed a bit to the matron—chief nurse—at Toowoomba Hospital. The town of Warwick, south of Nobby and Clifton, gave her an official welcome, arranged by the Red Cross and a committee of prominent women. Tall and self-possessed in her gray and white uniform, she climbed off the train there, the first Queensland nurse to return from the battlefront. "We were a long way from the war, and we were overcome with the idea of looking at a person who was actually fighting. We were thrilled to the marrow," one woman recalls. The citizens presented Liza with red roses, and she spoke, "but without any great conceit. She didn't give you the impression she was the only woman that was nursing."[8]

Back in Brisbane, she served at more military hospitals, then was assigned to the new Number One Sea Transport Section of the Australian Imperial Force. She returned to Britain in late November on the troopship A. 32; she sailed back to Australia with some of the first digger casualties from France. For the next three years she would serve mainly on troopships. Northward voyaging was gay and cheerful, with men full of zest and self-confidence. Homeward-bound, injured and listless men in hospital blues or pajamas played endless card games—crown and anchor and housey-housey. In December 1916, she was promoted from "staff nurse" to the rank of "sister" (equivalent to first lieutenant), which entitled her to two smart pips on her shoulder tabs and gave her the title she was to use tenaciously for the rest of her life.

The years passed—1916, 1917, 1918—she plied back and forth on the *Orestes*, *Marathon*, *Thermistocles*, and the *Suevic* again. She was always well known on board. Once some soldiers were target-shooting at a biscuit tin hanging on a string at the stern. They dared the nurses to try it, and the women shouted for Ken, the bush nurse. Liza had never used a revolver but said in sheer bravado, "The string would be a better mark." She raised the weapon uncertainly and with one shot cut the string. She airily declined to try ever again.

Neither nurses nor wounded diggers let the war overwhelm them. The dark ships usually touched at ports like Freetown in Sierra Leone and Durban, South Africa, and she watched the men go ashore seeking "adventure." They lubricated their adventure with whiskey, and Freetown authorities finally closed that city to troops. Heading ashore at Capetown, the members of one amputee force left their new legs behind so they could move faster on crutches. The ship arrived in Australia with twelve more artificial legs than returned soldiers.

On another trip a three-day storm sank three ships of Liza's convoy off Africa. Her own ship was reported lost, and when she arrived in London she found she could not get paid. When a senior officer asked her what was the matter, she lightly told him, "I'm dead." Back at sea, submarine scares often sent the nurses to boat stations. Once a puzzled officer found them there in their formal, red-lined capes, rocking with laughter. One of Liza's nursing shipmates had filled her arms with the garments, by army order to be worn "on all occasions." "This *is* an occasion," the young woman said. "We are about to be sunk."

Such was the war. One night Liza could not find a patient. She wrapped a flashlight in red flannel and brown paper; in less than ten seconds she found him under a bed, but she had to talk herself out of being confined to the brig for violating the blackout. On another darkened ship, she went to the infirmary for some medicine. She was reaching for it when she saw a demented soldier with a knife. He had escaped from the mental ward; she was trapped. "Oh, Johnny," she told him, "I don't think that knife will do the job. You see, I have a very tough neck." She persuaded him to let her sharpen his knife, and she went for help.

America entered the war. Sister Kenny, her companions, and 1,700 fresh Aussie troops were aboard the first Australian transport to take the Panama Canal route to Britain. Many of the Australians went ashore at the canal, but Liza was confined aboard, caring for cases of meningitis. One victim had just been buried at sea. Contagious epidemic meningitis—brain inflammation—had become an added horror of the war and in the First Sea Transport Section, Liza's charge.

On some crowded voyages her contagious patients were kept on the open boat deck under canvas in all weather to try to keep the disease from spreading. At other times, they were confined deep in a dim hold. The conscientious nurse often remained almost around the clock with the men, some delirious, some paralyzed, some dying. When action threatened, she had to take them to their own open and exposed raft, instead of to a comparatively sheltered lifeboat. Sometimes "Ken," two orderlies, and the patients had to sit on the uncomfortable raft for hours. She just laughed about any possibility of floating on the sea on that uncertain platform while the sharks nibbled. After all, she said, if the ship really sank, the raft would be sucked along with it, "and I would never know whether or not my toes had tempted a shark."

Remembering her 1911 polio cases, she started to watch her meningitis patients closely as they passed through an acute stage and began to recover. All too often they remained paralyzed and deformed. Nursing to her still meant "take charge": she began exercising the affected limbs, sometimes successfully, it seemed, and somtimes not. Her knowledge of the disease and its effects was only vague. The medical officers on board had no better rehabilitative ideas, however, and she persisted. "She was trying to work out a method," another nurse who worked alongside her reports. "She used to make the men think about their muscles, to get them walking."

An Australian doctor who discussed these patients with her after the war points out that "there was no penicillin then, and both the extent of crippling and death rate were high. Sometimes the death rate was 70 percent. The doctors and nurses were very busy. They ordinarily didn't take a great deal of notice of their patients' postures, but let them lie any way they liked. A lot of the men when they got better were then seriously disabled, twisted in various ways as a result of neglect rather than permanent nerve damage. Sister Kenny worked long and hard to change her patients' postures into normal positions at regular intervals. So her patients, when they did get better, got much better, with upright limbs and flexible arms."[9]

Nurse Ella Morphett served with her much of this time. "Kenny," she says, "had great ideas of her ability. She'd be quite certain that if nobody else could do something, she could." At the least, she would try. She was not afraid to give any doctor her opinion, and when she had a patient, the patient was everything. The wounded liked her for this, yet she was not one who laughed and joked with them much. Instead, she could sit on deck alone for hours, gazing into space. One officer saw her sitting this way and asked, "Are you in trouble? You look so unutterably sad." But Nurse Morphett chided her later: "He doesn't know you as well as I do, Kenny. You knew you were attracting attention, and you were just posing."

Still, according to Miss Morphett, "she *was* a good nurse. Oh yes, definitely. There was no nonsense about her, and she had a remarkable influence over her patients. She could talk to them and give them confidence. And she had *beautiful* hands with long, slender fingers, the most beautiful nursing hands I've ever seen." She also was a good sailor. She volunteered more than once for duty again at the front; she was told that many nurses could work ashore, but few could work on rough seas.

On some trips back to Australia, Liza couldn't get home but was disembarked to accompany Queensland wounded by rail, often through her old district. She would telegraph ahead then, and her mother and sister Maggie would stand on the railroad platform waving. The engineer, briefed by the wounded, would sometimes wink at the rules and stop to let the nurse hug her mother, while diggers leaned out the windows and cheered. "If the flaming engineer *won't* stop," her patients once informed her, "we'll just pull the emergency chain and stop the flaming train." When even that didn't work, her mother nonetheless waved as the train passed, and the soldiers cheered all the louder. "Ah," Sister Kenny would tell her friends back on the ship, "it was beautiful."

Five Australian divisions fought in France. With the British in 1917, they battered the Hindenburg Line, and in fall 1918 they helped smash it. At Fromelles, Passchendaele, Ypres, Villers-Bretonneux, Mont St. Quentin, they were called some of the most effective shock troops the world has seen. In one battle, a digger was carrying a wounded comrade on his back across No Man's Land. Rifle fire and machine-gun bullets were spraying the earth all around them. " 'Ere," cried the victim, "what about turning around and walking backwards for a spell. You're getting the V.C., but I'm getting all the flamin' bullets."[10]

Throughout the bloodshed, these sardonic men filled their water billies and made tea, blandly using their tin hats as kettles. In the ruins of Ypres, they stood in careless circles tossing pennies in the Australian gambling game of two-up. They also made "Waltzing Matilda" an Australian anthem. Beneath all their swagger, however, the war had become anything but a song. Nearly 40 percent of all Australian males between the ages of eighteen and forty-four volunteered; 329,000 went overseas; two out of three were casualties. In a population just reaching five million, 60,000 died. Australia lost more men in action than the United States in these years when the words "Western Front" meant the ultimate in death and destruction.

Bill Kenny saw action in France from July 1916 to April 1918. He was wounded three times and was again mentioned in dispatches; the Distinguished Conduct Medal was added to his decorations. He was still tall and rangy and liked to joke, but his hair had thinned and turned gray, Liza found, when they managed to meet in London. "I've seen too many good fellows hanging on the barbed wire," he told her.

In London, she learned to wait out raids by cigar-shaped Zeppelins and, later, big Gotha bombers, forerunners of the World War II bomber fleets. Throughout the 1917–18 London winter, every moonlit night was a night of the crackle of A-A guns, falling shrapnel, and bombs. Liza put on a tin hat, crouched against a wall, and prayed. It was small destruction compared with the raids of World War II; but death from the skies was unfamiliar to her, and sometimes she felt it was the end of the world.

Between voyages, she mainly served in military hospitals. In early 1917 she was at Harefield, an Australian convalescent hospital west of London, a mere makeshift of wooden huts, each housing thirty men: the amputees, the gassed, the victims of bullets, shells, grenades, bombs, and shrapnel. Off duty, Liza and roommate Pattie Kirton huddled together to make tea. They had to huddle; their tiny room was unheated. They wore woolies and kept moving.

The war became ever bloodier. Near Liverpool, her ship narrowly escaped being torpedoed. The vessel *Mindie* of the same convoy was sunk. No ship dared stop to pick up survivors, and all on board the *Mindie*, 800 men and nurses, were lost. Docked at Liverpool, Liza had to turn away when she saw clusters of women asking about their seamen sons and husbands. Another time, two ships of her convoy were torpedoed and lost. On still another occasion, a live mine came awash on the deck of her ship. She accumulated more time in the danger zones than any other nurse. For three years, she once said, she accompanied

Australia's bravest, who would become killers, would be killed, or would come home as misfits. Often, however, she heard the men say it was well "worth the price" to assure peace.

The war touched minds as well as bodies. In October 1918 she had what she described as a "strange and almost unbelievable experience."

> My ship was plowing south. . . . Three men lay close to death in the crowded wards below when I went off duty. . . . Perhaps I was asleep. I don't know. I remember insistent fingers touching my shoulder, plucking at my sleeve. I opened my eyes. . . . In the doorway stood the figure of a child. She was dressed in the garb of a nun. . . .
>
> "I'm overwrought," I thought. "This is nonsense. There's no child aboard ship—certainly no child dressed as this one was." So I turned my face to the wall. A moment passed. Again the plucking at my sleeve—again the pleading face in the doorway. I sat up and the child vanished. My common sense told me that what I needed was sleep, that overwork had brought with it hallucinations. But instead of lying down again I rose and groped my way down the dark passageway to the ward. . . .
>
> As I came through the door I heard a voice whispering, "Padre. Mother." The nurse lay unconscious on the floor. She had fainted from exhaustion and seasickness. One of the men was gasping out those two words, "Padre. Mother!" I ran to his bedside and bent low. In his right hand he clutched a small bag. I took it from him, knowing what he wished. In it was his identification disk which said he was a Catholic. At once I called an orderly and sent for the priest, the "Padre." There was nothing else I could do. Before dawn he was dead. . . .
>
> It was not until I reached Australia that there was any sort of explanation. I sent a tiny package containing the few pitiful possessions of the dead soldier to his mother and presently there came a reply. "Thank you, my dear," she wrote. "He was our only child and we had hoped to have him back and well again. We had one other child, a little girl of thirteen. But she died two years ago."
>
> All right. Call it a dream, or a hallucination. But as Hamlet said: "There are more things in heaven and earth, Horatio, than are dreamt of in your philosophy."[11]

Liza's dark, curly hair, like her brother's, became heavily streaked with gray. Her eyes became a shade colder, her jaw more prominent. Any innocence was gone, but her look was still open. Her figure was fuller but still handsome. In flowing white headdress, she posed for one photograph in which she was the picture of mercy and near beauty, and for another in which she looked belligerently ready to take on the world.

It was rumored in later years that she had met Dan at times in London. It was also said that she had a shipboard romance with a man named Brown. A British army officer from Kenya told her friend Mrs. Perrott, "Oh, she's fine. She's splendid." But nothing came of any of it. "She just wouldn't acknowledge any admirer," according to Mrs. Perrott. Once on board ship, a flowery chap told the nurse, "Ah, those beautiful black eyes of yours with that faraway look, from gazing over the sea." She replied, "Yes, like two burned holes in a blanket."

Roy Pickering, one of the young men who had helped chase the swaggies away from her hospital in Clifton, was wounded in France. With 1,000 others, he was sent home on the *Suevic*. He walked on deck, and the first person he saw was Sister Kenny. She had become "one of the silent type," he found, "but she had a great name as a nurse." On some voyages, it seemed, she mixed with everyone on the ship, and on others she was as reserved as a stranger.

The 1918 flu epidemic raged; it killed twenty million people all over the world. On her ship in October, doctors and nurses paraded all hands past a fumigating chamber every day, so they could inhale steam impregnated with a formaldehyde solution. The heroic measure was useless; men continued dying, and most of the nurses got sick. Liza and one companion were left to look after 500 ill and wounded. They made night rounds in bitter sea cold, and more than once worked more than twenty-four hours. Liza's legs, still peppered with shrapnel, throbbed with pain.

The flu let up a bit. On November 11 the ship was still at sea when the news came of the armistice. Excited Sister Kenny was one of the first to hear it. "The war is over!" she shouted to a group playing cards on deck. The men did not answer, and she repeated her news. Finally one turned and said, "Is it, Sister?" Then he turned back to his companions and asked: "Housey-housey, who'll have a card?"

Within a few days, crewmen were removing the dark-lights. Sister Kenny had served on the first dark ship to Australia and now on the last, traveling altogether about 200,000 miles. Exhausted, she was given a month's furlough to go home and rest, and then she was named head nurse at Enoggera Military Hospital on Brisbane's outskirts. Although it was scarce, she blackmailed the authorities into providing the hospital with vital equipment—otherwise, she told them, soldiers' deaths might be blamed on neglect. She also obtained Red Cross delicacies and cricket gear for her charges. Many of the cricketers were amputees, yet they were not without resources. The "wingies" did the running for the "stumpies," and the "stumpies" did the batting for the "wingies." A crowd watched, and the patients' friends provided afternoon tea.

She was still tired and began suffering faint spells. She said nothing, and when an attack came, she just stood for a few minutes until it passed. She was opening her mail one morning when an unusually severe seizure occurred. Doctor, now Colonel, Aeneas McDonnell happened to be entering her office for a visit. He ordered an examination, and the verdict was acute myocarditis or inflammation of the muscular wall of the heart. She was examined by a medical board, pronounced 100 percent unfit, and discharged in January 1919 with a pension.

A viral infection may produce such a condition, and a patient may recover completely. In 1919, however, she, her friends, and her family thought that her days were numbered, and so did her doctors. Hospitalized for a time, she overheard one physician say that she had a few months perhaps, not more. Another said she had six months.

Her morale was at a low point. Then she got out of bed one morning, put on her clothes, and when her nurses asked what she was doing, she said with a shrug, "If I have only six months to live, I'd better get busy."

6

Inventor

SHE RETURNED to the little farmhouse outside Nobby. She limped in on two canes because her wounded leg was acting up. She sank into bed, but then a tired doctor from Clifton came by. The flu had descended, two funerals had just been held; an isolation hospital was to be opened, would she run it? He didn't have to ask twice. She rose and took charge of the makeshift facility in the Clifton Show Pavilion, where prize sheep and cattle were normally promenaded. She tied on a gauze mask and marshaled fresh bed sheets, tarpaulins for ground cover, and cheery flowers from the gardens of Mary Kenny and friends. The First Sea Transport Section's Sister Kenny soon had things running militarily.

The flu virus gradually disappeared. Only one of her patients, a young mother, died. Liza climbed back into bed. It was summertime, and summer heat and a million thoughts made rest impossible. She traveled to the cooler New South Wales highlands, collapsed there, and spent another three months in a hospital. Then she returned to Queensland where Dr. McDonnell—shouting, "Good God, Elizabeth!"—ordered her to bed in his own surgical hospital.

McDonnell and two colleagues examined her. They retreated into the hall; their voices carried. "She is coming to the end of her last journey," one of the gloomy consultants pronounced. He gave her four months. Liza furiously climbed out of bed and was dressed when the doctors returned. "Gentlemen," she announced, "I'm off on a sea voyage, and I have to go to Brisbane to purchase some items." McDonnell just raised his sandy eyebrows and acknowledged that "she usually does know what is best."

She not only went to Brisbane but against medical advice took ocean passage for Europe. She had heard of a "great" specialist in Stuttgart, she explained. But perhaps she just wanted to return to her familiar element, the sea. She reached Dublin and had to spend another few weeks in a hospital there. At County Kilkenny, her Catholic kin urged her to visit Lourdes. She saw her Stuttgart specialist finally; he had no magic to offer. She tried six weeks at Lourdes, then set out for home. More than her allotted "four months" had passed. She was at least alive.[1]

She was still in and out of bed, "struggling for breath," she told all. But she was also eager to go back to work, and, army nursing record or not, she was not a certified, regular, employable nurse. Like many ex-warriors, she had a problem of postwar readjustment. She went back to neighborhood nursing, but her real salvation may have been a new medical challenge, one she later called the starting point of "my special life's work." The challenge came in a letter from one of her cousins in Guyra: "Remember Amelia Cregan? You dressed her for her wedding." Amelia and Will Cregan, the letter explained, had several children, and one was a six-year-old daughter with cerebral palsy who needed help. The Cregans had taken her to Sydney and Brisbane: no doctor could do anything for her. The difficult, untrained, spastic Daphne was making the Cregans' family life a misery. Would Liza be willing to take her for a while and try to "do something with her"?[2]

Still half-hobbling, Liza boarded a train for the Cregans' prosperous sheep and cattle station high in the New England Range. She found Daphne to be a blonde, blue-eyed child with a pink and white Irish complexion, a child "as beautiful as a rosebud." The girl could not even sit up straight, however; when she tried, she rolled over. Her movements were uncoordinated, her hands trembled. "I'll try to help her," Liza said. The child would live at Nobby, and the Cregans would pay for her keep.

First, Liza saw the Cregans' doctor, who sat like a rock when she told him the plan. "You have a colossal amount of cheek to give this child's parents any hope," he snapped.

"I've only told them I'll try," she protested.

"The best medical skill in Australia can do nothing," he insisted.

Liza began fuming. Sad little Daphne was present and listening, and, hearing the argument, she turned anxiously to Liza. Everyone had told her that the girl's intelligence was subnormal; Liza thought otherwise.

"Did you tell the doctor you'll make me better?" Daphne asked her later on a train back to Queensland.

"We'll have to work with God," Liza told her. "He's the Great Doctor, and sometimes he chooses people on earth to help him."

She stopped at Toowoomba to ask Dr. McDonnell's help too. "Will Cregan will gladly pay for anything anyplace," she assured him.

"I don't believe in robbing the rich any more than the poor," McDonnell barked back, possibly because he had something of a reputation for overcharging the rich. He too cautioned, "Don't raise her parents' hopes," but he was a little more positive: "Do as you would in infantile paralysis. Treat her as you think best for the symptoms you see."

Liza had already begun. At her mother's farm cottage, she put on an old housedress, filled a bathtub with warm water and salt, and lowered the girl into it to exercise her limbs. "Just sit back and rest, child," she said. "I'm going to teach your arms and legs to work when you tell them to." She put cold water in the tub to try to stimulate the muscles; she gave Daphne warm sulphur baths "to ease her pain"; then she carried her to a table and rubbed her arms and legs with the household goanna salve and olive oil. She did these things daily. For a while she tried bark splints on Daphne's legs and right arm to try to straighten them. "This is the way I treated the meningitis on board ship," she told her mother. "This is a very similar disease, and the treatment should be similar."

Her ignorance of much of medicine was flagrant, but the concentrated treatment and exercise began to help. The tremor in the little girl's hand became less, and soon she could pick up a light object and put it where Liza directed. "Am I doing right?" she asked. One red-letter day, she started to sit up at the dinner table, and she soon learned to feed herself and pass a spoon or the butter when asked. "She's improved," said Dr. McDonnell when he saw the girl again in Toowoomba. "Carry on."

Liza hurried back to Nobby, put Daphne in the tub, and made her use her fingers under water. She bought her a toy piano, and the girl, now seven, could soon play the scale, then simple tunes. She took her to Brisbane, bought her high surgical shoes, and had her fitted with braces to steady her legs. She taught her to stand, if unsteadily. Then she said, "Now come on, Daphne, you can walk over to me." Daphne walked a few steps and fell on her face. But gradually she did better. If one thing did not work, Liza tried another. She was almost endlessly patient and kind, as she undertook without textbook or guidance the difficult task of muscle education.

The Cregans were staunch Roman Catholics, and once a fortnight Liza dutifully took Daphne to the Catholic Good Samaritan Convent at Clifton to pray for the use of her hands. She prayed alongside her. She was never seen to take Catholic communion there, but down in New South Wales, when she periodically took Daphne home, some said they saw her both go to confession and take communion on at least one occasion, and the adult Daphne Cregan wrote, "She did tell me that the late Bishop Coleman baptized her." There is no confirmation of this in parish registers, and a district priest says, "I always understood that Sister Kenny was not Catholic, though she sometimes accompanied the Cregans to mass."[3] Liza's religion in fact continued strong and nondenominational. She probably would have prayed with Daphne no matter what her religion was.

After the first months with the child, Liza taught her mother to give the exercises and began going away often on other errands. She renewed her country nursing. In summer, she took the improving child to the Cregans' and spent much of the summer with her. A young doctor in the area was impressed and urged Liza to take Daphne to Dr. John Irvine Hunter, a brilliant investigator of muscle physiology at the University of Sydney. Liza did this. Hunter was impressed too and said the nurse eventually ought to demonstrate her methods to the medical profession.

"Work with the child a while longer," he told her. "Get her just a little further. Then I'll help you."

This was a new thought: teacher to doctors. She asked Dr. McDonnell about it in Toowoomba. He smiled but shook his head. By her account two decades later—his own language would have been far sparer and less sentimental—he lectured her: "Your ideas are opposed to all orthodox ideas. . . . You are succeeding where they have failed, but you will not be able to convince them for years. There is little ahead of you now but physical exhaustion and mental agony." He also reminded her of her bad heart and told her: "Weigh it all very carefully, at least."

He was, it seems, not enthusiastic. Was his pupil getting a bit too creative for him? The bright Dr. Hunter died before Liza and Daphne could see him again, so his suggestion that Liza could show her methodology to doctors came to nothing. But Daphne kept improving, and for three and a half years Liza continued to work with her until the spastic girl could walk with a stick, ride horseback, write letters, and, finally, go home to stay. To the ordinary onlooker, her new "walking" was only painful hobbling; to those who had known her before, it seemed miraculous.

Liza's country nursing was thriving too, and people still said, "She won't take a shilling." She took pride in making no-payment her usual rule. She had her war pension; she was steeped in the bush tradition of "helping"; maybe she feared running into new and stricter nursing regulations. It was still all right, however, to take a dressed fowl or jars of farm produce.

If she heard about a sick child someplace, she would pack a bag and go there. The Automobile Era had at last reached the Downs, and Liza, summoned, now sent for a neighbor with a "motorcar": a big, floppy-looking touring sedan, usually, with wire wheels and hard tires. By automobile then, if possible, by horse and sulky if not, she would be off in a dust cloud, a kerchief around her face. Or, increasingly, she would phone young Stan Kuhn who owned a motorcycle with a sidecar, and down the ruts they would bump. Everyone now addressed her as "Sister Kenny" or, simply, "Sister." Four rings in the night, the Kennys' party-line ring on the new wall phone with a crank, and she would be off. Infections, bronchitis, farm accidents, lost hands, crushed limbs. Burt Gillan had an arm taken off by a chaff cutter; Sister Kenny was the first help on the scene. A Kahn boy was "in a bad way"; a doctor called it indigestion, but she insisted that he go to Toowoomba, where the problem turned out to be kidney disease. She brought the Rooneys' twin boys into the world. They were a month premature; she wrapped them in a warm blanket and laid them near the wood stove. "She's spunky," said the people around Nobby, Clifton, Pilton Hills, Headington Hill, Greenmount, and Dalby.

There came a fling as a club woman. She organized and became first president of the Nobby chapter of a new, soon-Australia-wide Country Women's Association. She led her chapter in raising money for a pedal wireless set for an outback family. By the time of the Queensland CWA's 1926 Southern Division meeting in Toowoomba—a conclave of sun-tanned, rough-skinned country ladies in white silk and pink crepe de Chine—she was one of the group's leading figures.[4] She had begun to develop an air. Sometimes she wore her gray wartime uniform and red-lined cape for special events, but she really did not need it. She had begun bearing herself with her own kind of stiff, lofty dignity.

Old Mary Kenny became lonely. Liza heard of a red-haired, Brisbane-born girl of eight and a half from a broken home. Of Scotch and English descent, she was named Mary Stewart, and she was up for adoption or a foster home. Liza made the arrangements and on a Sunday in 1925 picked up the child. In April 1926 the independent-willed Liza formally adopted her, a rare and even daring step then for a single woman, and this girl became Mary Stewart-Kenny. Legally, Liza had a daughter, though the child remained companion to "Gran" while Liza gallivanted.[5]

A child, country nursing, country women—they filled the days, but they were not enough. She fussed restlessly about the Nobby place, having it painted, installing gaslighting, arranging for neighbors to plow and sow. Every few months she was off to Brisbane to see about getting an increase in her war pension or to New England to see relatives or to flirt with new ideas about marketing farm produce. She went to war nurses' reunions and zipped from town to town on Country Women's Association affairs.

In the evenings, restless, she read the *Toowoomba Chronicle*: there were naval disarmament conferences in London and Washington, and Scarface Al Capone and his gang were shooting up Chicago. An evolution trial boiled in Tennessee. She read by the new bottled gaslight, then wandered outdoors by the tall, turning windmill and red iron water tank, alongside the pigpen, to the orchard and fields. The nearest human noise or activity was an occasional laugh, audible even a mile away, from the hotel at Nobby.

She marched into Nobby in the morning to buy something, anything, at Brodie's Store. Nobby was made of rusty or galvanized iron, blistering, unpainted wood, dust, and weeds; it was a few stores and shacks tossed here and there. The tin-roofed rail shed now loaded more wheat than any other Downs station. But often loungers leaned against posts, hands in pockets, waiting for anything. They respected Liza in a way, but they also ridiculed her. "She thinks she's something," the hotel crowd scoffed. A hometown, it has been said, is where they wonder how you ever got as far as you did.

On a sunny early morning of May 1926, midautumn, summer harvest in, time for a new growing season, Liza's motorcycling friend Stanley Kuhn was out plowing. His little sister Sylvia, seven years old, sat behind him for the ride.

The field was too bumpy; she wanted to get off. Her dress caught, and she fell into the sharp spikes of a plow wheel. Stan heard three snaps—bones cracking. Sylvia's left thigh and right ankle were broken. A toe and the sole of her right foot were torn off, and another toe hung by a wisp. Stan jumped off the plow and picked the screaming girl off the bloody soil. He ran a half-mile with her to the house. "Get me Sister Kenny!" Sylvia's mother shrieked to the telephone operator. Stan was already on his Harley-Davidson, starting down the rough road. Within minutes, Liza was jumping into his sidecar.[6]

She found Sylvia lying numb; she quickly bandaged her bleeding foot, bound splints to her legs, and covered her to fight shock. The new Nobby motor ambulance had been called. It would be thirty miles to Toowoomba and a hospital. Liza thought of the hard ride ahead: she had seen soldiers die on jolting ambulance trips in Belgium. Sylvia was pale; she too might die. When the ambulance men came running in with their rolled-up canvas carrier, Liza said, "I would like to use my own stretcher."

She pointed to a big linen cupboard with heavy doors. "Take off one of those doors," she ordered. Sylvia was stretched out on it. Liza tied her down with strips of sheeting and tucked hot water bottles around her to reduce shock. The makeshift device was placed atop the ambulance drivers' canvas stretcher; then Sylvia, door, and stretcher were placed in the lorry.

Warm and relaxed, the girl fell asleep within a few miles. Down a muddy dirt road with deep ruts the ambulance bounced. Seven miles from Toowoomba, they met a car coming toward them, caught in the same ruts. The collision was head-on. Liza, sitting with Sylvia, hurt her shoulder, but thanks to the stretcher the child was unharmed. The offending driver, it turned out, was Sylvia's uncle. He helped get the mired ambulance out of the ruts, and it finished the trip to Aeneas McDonnell's St. Dennis's Private Hospital. Minus two toes, Sylvia emerged after six weeks to become a swimming and running winner at school the next summer.

"I think you saved your patient's life," a newly impressed McDonnell told Liza. A less injured boy had arrived in severe physical shock the same day after a similar ride. More complications had set in, and he died. "Elizabeth, you ought to get a patent for that stretcher," McDonnell suggested.

She wasted no time. She knew that too many injured were dying needlessly of pain, shock, and pneumonia, in effect shaken to death. She sat up late at night under the white, glaring gaslight and drew a rough sketch. Then she made a small model of bits of cloth and wood, with hairpins for springs. A friend's son built her a full-sized version. Liza stitched a length of olive green canvas for a canopy, then stretched the canopy over the framework of the new contraption. Young Mary Stewart-Kenny had to lie down in it to test it.

"What are you making?" friends demanded. Liza would reply only, "Wait and see," but to visiting sister Julia she admitted, "I'm trying out an invention."

Her completed invention had a firm plywood base to keep spine and back straight, and a series of straps to hold the patient in tight. It also had six coil springs; a firm mattress; a cowllike canopy on a collapsible framework; hot water containers in side pockets; and rubber-tired wheels to keep the patient off the ground. It was, in Liza's words, "light, durable and sterilisible." Altogether, it looked something like a rolling oxygen tent. She named it "the Sylvia Stretcher."

At a meeting of Country Women's Association executives, she offered to give it to the association as a money-raising scheme. "Money-raising be blowed. Sister Kenny has made this. Any gain should be hers, and we ought to help her," said her friend Mrs. Sterne, who had been secretary of the Warwick welcoming committee when World War Nurse Kenny was honored. The ladies fully agreed.

The stretcher was patented and a manufacturer found. Liza demonstrated the device at the Northern Darling Downs corner of the 1926 Brisbane Exhibition, and "the Governor-General (Lord Stonehaven)," the Brisbane newspapers noted, "viewed the demonstration and expressed appreciation of a very useful adjunct in minimising suffering." At the Brisbane headquarters of the Queensland Ambulance Transport Brigade, "a tangible tribute to the efficacy of the new device was immediately forthcoming by two orders being given." The newspapers of Sydney, Toowoomba, Clifton, and Warwick also took notice of the rolling wonder. It was clever, everyone agreed; it could be transported by open car, truck, ambulance, railroad car, aircraft, or horse-drawn dray, and it could be rolled right into a hospital.[7]

Yet total sales were only thirty after more than a year's effort. Her response was direct. As her nephew Jack Kenny later wrote, she set out selling stretchers "with the zeal of a prophet." She had been a plainly dressed country woman; now she blossomed in a fur-trimmed black velvet dress, a new, broad-brimmed hat, and a coat with a bushy fox collar, and she sailed into the headquarters of Elliott Bros. Ltd. of Sydney and Brisbane and negotiated a new contract for manufacture and sale. She herself drafted the proposed agreement granting her a minimum annual payment of £150 to £200 (between $750 and $1,000), a substantial amount in the late twenties in Australia. "Miss Kenny," objected a Mr. William Miles for the company, "I won't sign that!" So she went to two of the firm's directors, and, as Miles tells it, "They were a bit softer than I, and they signed it. She also told them Mr. Miles had spoken to her pretty harshly."

Brisbane nephew Jack, older brother Henry's son, helped her get publicity. The magazine *Country Life* ran an article about her titled "The Adventurous Life—Elizabeth Kenny—Nurse, Benefactress." "She did noble work in the Great War," the magazine said. Her now silver gray hair freshly marcelled, a string of pearls around her neck, she accosted doctors, ambulance men, and welfare organizations. The Country Women in Queensland and New South Wales adopted the stretcher as an official project, and CWA branches bought stretchers for their local ambulances. Some ambulance officials said her gadget was too complicated and costly. "The stretchers you use now are refinements of torture," she tossed back. "Ambulances in Australia should have the best equipment and no other." She also accused some of her opponents of collecting royalties on competing stretchers.

Dashing about, she often paused to visit Daphne, now a special student at St. Ursula's College for Girls, near the New England highlands. The pretty girl—fourteen when Liza first visited her at St. Ursula's—had improved greatly, though she was always to be sickly and severely handicapped. At St. Ursula's she took prizes in art, composition, and spelling, while visiting Sister Kenny watched triumphantly.

Every now and then, temporarily worn, Liza took to a bed for a few days. Once her salty Warwick friend, Mrs. Sterne, found her there after what Mrs. Sterne remembers as "the most dreadful heart attack." "I'll be all right," Liza told her, "as long as I lie here quietly." In the morning, she was "right as pie."

Newly confident, she sold some wartime nursing friends shares in "foreign rights" to the stretcher, then hopped a ship once more, and showed it in London, Paris, and Stockholm. She managed to sign agreements for distribution in Britain, Northern Ireland, the Crown Colonies, France, Germany, India, Ceylon, Siam, the Union of South Africa, China, North and South America, "and adjacent islands." It was time to go home.

She decided to return via America—her purpose, more stretcher selling. Despite the stack of sales agreements, her pocketbook was near empty. She borrowed money for the trip and (as reported by the press on her return) "had the gratification" of seeing an ambulance fitted with the Sylvia Stretcher "and equipment driven from New York to Kentucky" for use in the Sylvia Stretcherless hills.

She collected little or no additional cash. The Great Depression had begun. It started in 1928 in Australia and pinched off stretcher sales just when they were beginning to mount. By 1930, nonetheless, a Sydney newspaper found the device "in general use throughout Australia."[8] General, but still scattered, use. Many ambulance centers were finding it cumbersome. Elliott Bros. may never have manufactured more than 200, and foreign sales never became significant, although twenty were shipped to Siam.

She collected her guaranteed £150 to £200 a year, just the same. Elliott Bros. kept the Sylvia Stretcher in its catalog until 1943, and as recently as the midfifties the Queensland Ambulance Brigade still had several in use at country centers and found it had "many advantages" for the rough work it was made for.

One of Liza's Elliott Bros. director-friends—a Mr. Cohen, who had signed her annual guarantee—approached the firm's Mr. Miles one day in the thirties, when sales had dwindled to a few a year. "That was a fine thing you got me into," Cohen said.

"I didn't get you into it," Miles replied. "*I* didn't sign *anything*."

Cohen and Miles sighed. As for Liza, the guarantee plus her pension gave her enough money to live and travel on. She had gained some degree of financial security and more experience in living, selling, arguing, and cajoling.

8

Crusader

ONE DAY in February 1935, while adjoining columns told of hard times and despair, a headline in the *Sydney Morning Herald* read: "PARALYSIS. A New System of Treatment Presented to Nation. Doctors' Praise." The accompanying story told of the showing of a new film to a group of prominent medical men and government officials. Other movies in town that week included Eddie Cantor in *Kid Millions* and Claudette Colbert in *Cleopatra.* This film, however, was no entertainment but a medical movie exhibiting the work of one Sister Kenny.[1]

Elizabeth Kenny, single-minded, energetic, was bursting forth on Australia. Patients from South Australia and South Africa were traveling to see her. An important new friend, Mrs. Eleanor MacKinnon, world founder of the Junior Red Cross, arranged the screening and the attendance there of *her* friend, Commonwealth Health Minister William Morris (Billy) Hughes, who had been a fiery World War I prime minister. "To a layman," Hughes told the audience, "it looks like white magic to see paralyzed children able to walk and even run." The doctors present reserved comment, but Liza rose and (the important *Morning Herald* reported) "in a dramatic moment . . . announced her intention of presenting the fruits of her labor to the Commonwealth government 'for the good of humanity.' "

The Commonwealth of Australia, Hughes excepted, was not quick to accept. The good-hearted Mrs. MacKinnon had assembled four recently afflicted girls and one boy in a convalescent home in the hope that some Sydney hospital would admit them for Kenny polio treatment. None would. Townsville was too far by train for them: the obvious solution was an airplane. Mrs. MacKinnon set to work, and within a few days the *Sydney Daily Telegraph* was announcing that it would raise a public fund for the 1,200-mile hop, the longest ambulance flight yet proposed in Australia.

Sister Croll, one of Liza's nurses, came along on the aircraft to help care for the children. Two little girls were still in splints; they were carried aboard. Three of the children were placed on a makeshift bed on the floor, and the youngest was held by her grandmother. Sister Kenny in a black slicker and floppy black hat climbed aboard. It had been raining, but the rain stopped just in time, and the sky turned clear and starry. Teary parents on the ground waved good-bye, and at 3 A.M. the roaring, trimotored Fokker took off.

The trip took nine and three-quarter noisy, vibrating hours, as well as three fueling stops. All three girls on the floor became airsick, but the plane arrived at 3:30 P.M. The flight was pronounced a success, all Australia read of it, and the children received Kenny care. "Cripples Must Leave the State to Be Cured" Sydney's *Labour Daily* complained in a headline.[2]

The new Brisbane clinic was humming. Liza induced a Townsville friend, Dr. Jean Rountree, to become medical superintendent, and in the first year nearly 400 patients were accepted for daily or weekly treatment, about four-fifths of them polio victims, and the rest cerebral palsied. Liza dressed her nurses in her favorite sky blue, with flowing head-veils. Bulky yellow ambulances with red Maltese crosses on the side pulled in and out with the patients, calling for them and depositing them at their homes. Attendants in gray motor coats and peaked caps carried children in and out.

Brisbane was a busy, rushing city, a sprawling subtropic capital with flaming red royal poinciana trees and many old, colonialstyle frame buildings with white-painted scroll work and iron balconies. It had a seafaring waterfront on the Brisbane River, twenty miles from the ocean. The river wound through the city like the Seine, between grassy banks. The two-story Kenny Clinic occupied one of the white-latticed and balconied colonial structures. The government had painted the interior in

Liza's blue; it had equipped and installed treatment tables, exercise steps, baths, and blue curtains to her design. She still accepted no fees, but she lived in a comfortable suite and was cared for by a private secretary, a cook, and a housekeeper. She took this in stride: like her father, she would have made a good millionaire.

She also worked. To gauge the results of her treatment correctly and fairly, she told the health minister, she should be allowed to treat polio from its onset. "Upon advice received," she was informed, the minister could not allow this. This meant she had to treat the chronics again. She and Dr. Rountree examined 500 applicants in the first twelve months. She now turned away nearly 100 because they were beyond help. Yet she still accepted too many of the untreatable. Her Townsville associate, Dr. Guinane, says: "I think her kindness was a bit of a handicap, because she wouldn't refuse any kiddie treatment." Some of it was kindness; some, error; some, ego.

To combat the charge that any good results were owing to her own personality, she began to do almost no regular treatment herself, leaving it all to her nurse-therapists. She still gave special attention to difficult problems, but mainly she taught and demonstrated. No magic touch or magnetism is needed, she lectured, but rather "intense cooperation between the therapist and child" and thorough concentration.[3] Even though many of the patients were severely crippled, this method produced a number of successes.

She and Cilento, by now Sir Raphael, still had words. He announced one day that she had apparently been offered a "better opportunity" in New South Wales and would go there. She denied it: "As far as I am concerned, I am nobody's servant. I am going where I like, when I like." Cilento briefly gained Health Minister Hanlon's ear, and Chuter "by direction" had to inform Liza that her services were no longer needed in Townsville at least, though if she wished to visit she would be extended the "courtesy" of consultation. As successor, Cilento wired young Sister Leila Cooper: "SISTER KENNY'S CONNECTION . . . HAS BEEN TERMINATED STOP YOU HAVE BEEN APPOINTED NURSE IN CHARGE." When Leila, age twenty-one, got the telegram she was shocked. "I had led a very sheltered life. I was afraid Sister Kenny was going to murder me."

Protest meetings in Townsville backed Liza, and Queensland's Parliament was peppered by telegrams supporting her. At the same time Cilento, pressing further, wrote Hanlon a memo suggesting: (1) registration of the names of all children with paralysis; (2) appointment of a new committee to evaluate all polio treatments; and (3) continued treatment at Townsville and Brisbane under *his* control. But Chuter too had been seeking Hanlon's ear, and the minister threw Cilento a mere bone, his paralysis registry. Tough, redheaded Chuter was from then on the ministry's real power.[4]

Some of Cilento's criticisms of Liza's treatment were well founded. But he was also making two errors. He was failing to discern her method's potential and failing to see the wide horizons of modern rehabilitation. He maintained in one critique that "it must not be overlooked," that the object of treatment was saving government pension money by remaking patients into citizens who could earn a living; short of this, he doubted whether it was worth transforming a physically low-grade pensioner into a high-grade one.[5] In sharp contrast, Liza wrote: "The treatment is not considered finished until the patient can walk reasonably well, feed and dress himself, speak, write, and use his hands well," and if it is not possible to make all patients wage earners, they should still be trained "so that as far as their personal needs are concerned, they are rendered independent."[6] This is the very essence of modern rehabilitation: at the least to restore dignity. She was one of the rare voices saying it.

She retained her authority at both Townsville and Brisbane.

Several inquisitive and respectable medical men poked their noses into the Brisbane clinic. They included her old Toowoomba mentor, Aeneas McDonnell. Most seemed friendly. Floating on air, she asked some to serve on a medical board, to visit regularly, and ultimately to issue an assessment. With commendable honesty, she described the clinics as "experimental" and said only medical evaluation could finally determine their worth.

One of the board members suggested that the group ought to have government status. She quickly agreed. Charles Chuter agreed too. In the *Queensland Government Gazette* of October 26, 1935, Premier Forgan Smith named eight doctors, including McDonnell, a Royal Commission to investigate "the Elizabeth Kenny method of treating infantile paralysis, spastic paralysis, and birth palsy, and to compare the results of the Kenny method and the results of orthodox treatment."

The ongoing study was quickly outstripped by the establishment of new Kenny clinics. In December one was opened at the Royal North Shore Hospital, Sydney. The Royal North Shore was—no coincidence—in William Morris Hughes's constituency. In January 1936 a clinic was opened at Catholic St. Vincent's Hospital in Toowoomba, with government equipment and staff. By October 1936 there were more than 600 Kenny patients at Brisbane, Townsville, Toowoomba, and Sydney, with three full-time medical officers and forty-eight attendants, more than forty of them trained nurses. There were patients from London and China, and there were 600 more on the waiting lists.

Success made Liza an increasingly zealous crusader and prophet. "The movement now must be regarded as of national importance and indeed may go farther," she said. If a crusade were needed, she would lead one, and the role she would henceforth play would be a sort of turn-of-the-century combination of Emmeline Pankhurst, Sarah Bernhardt, and Joan of Arc. One night her village of Nobby gave her a ball in its tin-roofed "School of Arts," a combination cinema palace and town hall. She appeared all in white, a formal and rigid figure, with several of her nurses.

Most of the time she ignored outer trappings and wore militantly plain gunmetal stockings, solid black shoes, and often a cream-colored suit, a Brisbane addition. She was greatly taken with that creamy suit and had one like it made again and again. If she needed dresses, she would phone a shop and have several sent to her. On the hottest day, oblivious to the weather, she might charge down the street in one of her old black velvet dresses, head bare, hair uncombed. "You don't look proper," her staff would tell her. So, soon, she never went out without adding a big hat. Still, she was not without grace. She posed for a photograph in the *Australian Women's Weekly*. Her nearly white hair was carefully set. She wore pearls and a fine lace collar on one of her better velvets. She showed poise, strength, and determination. The headline said: "A new Australian Florence Nightingale."[7]

She did not make friends easily and spent years with most of her nurses before calling them by their first names. Yet all of them regarded her as "kindhearted, though she *might not* always give you that impression." Always quietly, she diverted personal gifts to her patients and paid their rail fares. "What do I want of money?" she told one friend. "I've got all I can eat." And of someone else: "He'll never prosper—he never casts his bread upon the waters. He never gives, only takes."[8] She crowed about her polio treatment but not about her good deeds.

She was family-proud. No Kenny could do any wrong. She brought her sister Julia's daughters Mary and Bessie Farquharson and cousin Minnie Bell's son Bill to Brisbane to become polio therapists. She treated all her trainees more or less as her nieces: no fingernail polish and she would indeed call a girl's father if she suspected her of late hours. For relaxation, she took tea, read, chatted, and took more tea. James Michener once calculated that Australians take tea seven times daily: "In bed at seven, breakfast at eight; morning at ten; lunch at one; afternoon at four; dinner at seven, nightcap at ten." She also liked bush picnics: steaks grilled over fragrant eucalyptus twigs and tea from a billycan. She no longer walked much. She developed a blood clot in her bad leg at one point and often used a cane.

She had a soft voice except when she was angry; then it either got louder or ominously softer, and she soon found herself arguing more and more. Australian doctors, conservative, British-drilled, abhorring publicity, read headlines like "Ex-AIF Nurse's Cures of Infantile Paralysis," and scoffed, "Cures indeed!" Medical men who later came to admire her testify that "she'd see a child who'd lost everything in one arm, and tell his parents *and him* he'd soon have the use of it. . . . She'd see a badly paralyzed girl and say, 'I'll have you dancing in three months,' and I believe she really believed it." She constantly antagonized her child-patients' former doctors by telling the parents she could have done better.[9]

The new Royal Commission visited the Brisbane clinic twice a week. Shortly after its visits began, a mother brought in an eleven-month-old baby, affected with polio only a few weeks. Liza wanted access to a hospital bed to care for it and hopefully phoned a commission member. He told her, she claimed, that doctors were not about to be taught by a nurse. Another doctor close to the commission said she would not get a royal sniff at any early case. She called this "a great blow." Still, she had encouraged the study in full knowledge that she would have mainly chronic patients.

At the outset, moreover, the commissioners asked her to estimate treatment results in any cases she chose. She did so in six, forecasting several "100 percent" recoveries—a crippled boy would be able to assist his father in farm work, a girl would be able to sew—and she signed her predictions. "They were all terrible," attests Dr. Jarvis Nye, one commissioner who subsequently became a supporter. "At the end of twelve months poor old Kenny's evaluations were completely hopeless."

Her champion, Dr. McDonnell, "Old Mac" now to young colleagues, took all this in as one of the commissioners. "Through the years," she always maintained, "one doctor always supported me—Dr. Aeneas McDonnell." She said that on one of her visits to Toowoomba, in fact, he urged her, "You'll never get any place wearing kid gloves. You'll have to take off the kid gloves and put on boxing gloves." But he was sometimes disgusted with her too. He was well into his seventies; he had become testier. He had a nickname, often a little obscene, for everyone he disliked: he habitually referred to Queensland Premier Forgan Smith, who was against organized medicine, as "Foreskin Smith."

McDonnell was also beginning to ail, and his mind was slowing. He could state a kind opinion of someone one day, a harsh one the next. "That bitch Kenny," he more than once told a colleague; then he was at his most charming when he visited her a few days later. He was "definitely very keen on her but he often thought she exaggerated," one of his fellow commissioners recalls. On the one hand, it seems obvious, he took pride in his bush-nursing protégée; on the other, he squirmed at seeing her clash with his medical colleagues. He began to absent himself from the commission's visits and went off to Japan on a tour.[10]

In June 1936, a British Medical Association (New South Wales Branch) committee issued a cool evaluation of her Sydney clinic. In reply she said: "Look at the harm your treatment has done!" Official nurses' groups joined the attack on her, charging—true enough—that she was never formally trained and had no registration certificate. Health Minister Hanlon finally told them that if they continued, he would take legislative steps to register her himself.

She got 99 percent cooperation from Hanlon and Chuter, but she wanted 100 percent. Irritated, she would call the health minister ten times a day or plant herself outside his office until he would see her. "Shut down and think a bit more," Chuter would sometimes tell her. Then she would sulk a while and complain that "no one will help me."

Hanlon pointed out to her once that as the beneficiary of more financial support than any Australian government had yet given any single rehabilitation program she had certain obligations, such as patience and tact. She was outraged and demanded "independence." Or else, she declared, she would drop the whole effort and close the Brisbane clinic. Hanlon told her it was the government's clinic, not hers, and it would remain open anyway, with its staff. The argument raged for a few days. Then she quietly said, "I'm going to ring up Mr. Hanlon and tell him I want to see him and settle this." She and Hanlon quickly came to a sensible agreement: she would run the clinic, and she would also do certain things the government's way. "It was the first time to my knowledge that she compromised," says her nephew Jack Kenny. Not many days later, however, she was calling Hanlon to demand something new.

When she had a major problem or faced some new assault, she often sat and thought for hours behind a closed door at the clinic or at brother Henry's. Then she suddenly sprang to a telephone or a taxi to resume battle. She began to relish controversies with "the doctors" and to confound them. A hardheaded, one-armed young public health man, Dr. Abraham Fryberg, succeeded Jean Rountree as medical superintendent at the Brisbane clinic. He was skeptical of her methods at first, and she and he had "ding-dong rows," her nurses recall. Fryberg nicknamed her "the Tiger." She liked that.

She battled with men, mainly, and enjoyed it. In no other country did Man have Woman more under his thumb than in muscular Australia. "Men! I don't want anything to do with them," she often fumed. And: "I won't let any man boss me."[11] Then she would sally forth into man's world to do battle.

Later she would once more fall into despair and tell her secretary, Mrs. McCrae, "I'll close the clinic tomorrow." The secretary, a diplomatic, young widow, would sit with her until midnight and talk. For a while she harbored a delusion that someone—"quacks," medical enemies—wanted to "steal" her method. She told the *Australian Women's Weekly* that she couldn't describe the treatment in an article because quacks might exploit it. She posted a list of rules for her Brisbane staff. "No member," went Rule Number 10, "shall divulge to anyone the whole or any part of the Sister Kenny method of treatment."[12] She never really adhered to this; she was well aware that anything in medicine stands or falls on its trial and acceptance by the medical profession.

She feared that the skepticism of the medical men, the baleful looks from some of the royal commissioners, were poisoning her nurse-trainees. Behind her back, she knew, her nurses sometimes discussed her lack of "training." She brooded over this, but she always came back.

For her these were still transitional years. She went to Sydney to spend some time at the new Kenny Clinic at the Royal North Shore Hospital. She had picked her people well. A lively physiotherapist, Betty Shuter, joined the staff because she remembered her own desultory polio training at the university there: "When there were infantile paralysis patients, you just looked at them and said, 'That's too bad.' "

There was a great deal of good work done at "the Shore," according to Miss Shuter. "She always said she wasn't God, but that she could at least make useful citizens. And she did! But Kenny would fight with her own shadow when she got antagonistic." She would tell the staff to do something, "then later look at us with a straight face and say she never said such a thing." Some of the staff got a little black notebook, wrote down the things she told them to do, and made her sign them. Then later they would produce this and say, "That's peculiar, here's your signature."

Dr. Henley Harrison, her first medical superintendent in Sydney, had done graduate work in London, Edinburgh, and Vienna. He was just starting his practice and was taking an advanced course in anatomy. She gave him the impression at first that she had had years of experience. "But she hadn't," he soon found out. "She didn't know how to pick the cases she could help, and her knowledge of anatomy was limited." She thus failed on many patients. Occasionally Harrison corrected her, and she didn't like that. But she began to defer to him, "for information, you might say, and she usually wouldn't make the same mistake again. She learned very fast." Harrison resigned to launch his own practice; but she often phoned him when in Sydney, and he found that "she was undoubtedly becoming an authority on polio."

His story was common. Charles Chuter introduced her to Dr. Herbert J. Wilkinson, dean of the new faculty of medicine as well as professor of anatomy at the University of Queensland. His specialties were neuroanatomy and candor. When he taught at the University of Adelaide, he admitted, "If I had been asked about polio I would have replied that it affects anterior horn cells in the spinal cord, and if they are destroyed nothing can replace them, and nothing can help." He had recently been doing some research of his own, however, on the innervation of muscle. He now believed the picture in polio might be far more complex, offering more hope that nerve and muscle cells could remain intact to be restimulated. He thought "the potentiality of the nervous system with its 10,000 million neurons is extraordinary and has been far from exploited."[13]

He agreed therefore to see this nursing sister and her work. A conservative man in his midthirties, methodical and correct, he was disappointed at first in her work and her ways. But he kept coming around. One day she phoned him; she had a new patient, a boy of fifteen who had received five months of orthodox treatment at a country hospital, then some weeks of treatment in Sydney: splinting plus daily physiotherapy under leading orthopedists. Yet he could not turn his arm or hand (loss of pronation and supination). His arm was fixed at a sharp and grotesque upward angle, the angle at which it had been splinted. Wilkinson and some other medical visitors accepted her invitation to examine him.

Three days later she summoned them again. "Turn your hand over," she told the boy. "Turn it back." And he did, to Wilkinson's vast surprise. Ultimately the youth could hold his arm at his side normally and to a large extent use it. Wilkinson began to think she indeed had something. He invited her to his laboratory, and she stared while muscles were dissected; she examined and fingered them while he lectured to her. He guided her to various books. She read them but soaked up most of her knowledge by listening. According to Wilkinson, she was mainly gaining a good working knowledge of surface anatomy, that is, of the muscles that can be indicated from the surface, including those principally affected by polio. If she identified a muscle incorrectly, he would correct her, and she never forgot it.

He also admonished that there was no such thing as a 100 percent cure and that she should forget the expression. He told her why her treatment was healthy for tissues: how exercise and warmth improve blood circulation and nutrition. "The nervous system," he told her, "is a wonderful coordinating mechanism. If one part is destroyed or upset, the whole body is affected. If you have a large telephone exchange, hundreds of millions of wires and connections, and someone drops a bomb, you can imagine the disorder. In the human body these parts cannot be replaced. The person affected has to learn control with what's left." This was what she was doing by her muscle reeducation.

He also told her that he regarded badly incoordinated muscles as one of the most troublesome results of polio, and that "the problem is to get the patient to recover smooth control." This concept of incoordination was by no means new in medicine, but she made it hers too; and Wilkinson thought she learned it from him. He considered original what he terms "her very wonderful idea" that if you put a muscle in a splint, it begins to forget that it ever existed—a phenomenon she labeled "alienation."

In 1937 she published her first textbook, written mainly in 1934 and 1935 with the help of young Dr. Guinane up in Townsville. It already lagged far behind the state of her treatment. She did not mention hot packs, though she was using them. She did not mention at least one symptom, spasm, that she considered vital. The book "was edited by a very clever young medical man," she explained later, thus hinting that any omissions were Guinane's. He had in fact improved the book. It remained amateurish, but the more scientific points, as she acknowledged in its foreword, were his.

She was still groping, but she had all her antennae out. A Sydney doctor made some sharp statements to her one day. A few days later he heard her blandly repeat them as though they were her own, and he turned to his colleagues and said, "She is an old fox, isn't she?" Several Brisbane and Sydney doctors testify that "she used to give demonstrations to groups of six or seven medical men, and if one made a brilliant observation today, she would make it tomorrow. . . . She absorbed everything. She had a mind like blotting paper . . . and the more failures she had, the better she got."[14] All of it became Kenny treatment.

Her Townsville friends decided to strike back at her critics. The city council named a Sister Kenny Memorial Committee, and a town meeting decided on a "Sister Kenny Playground," to be financed by a popular appeal. As part of the appeal, she was given a civic reception. "Sister Kenny Honored; Theatre Royal Packed; Her Noble Work Acclaimed," the *Townsville Bulletin* said.

There were 800 persons seated in the theater, and no one knew how many were standing. The West Side Past Scholars' Band played several numbers, and Mayor Alderman J. S. M. Gill presided. She finally spoke, looking down at the first rows occupied by her patients and former patients. One young lady was now a tennis instructor. This moved Liza very much; she had a hard time starting her address. Then she devoted much of it to giving credit to others: "You may think that I am something out of the box. There are other people as well as I. I direct and they do it." By this time practically everybody was teary, and all rose to sing Liza an old Scotch song:

> Better lov'd ye canna be,
> Will ye na come back again?[15]

She told a Brisbane friend at about the same time, "If I had a sixpence for every mistake I made, I'd be a millionaire."[16] But she rarely admitted that to the doctors.

She had accepted a spastic baby from Britain for treatment; the wealthy parents offered to send her to London to establish a clinic. She packed and sailed in April 1937 with two of her therapists, one of them her niece Mary Farquharson. In London she was introduced to several prominent doctors. She was not surprised when none wanted to have anything to do with her: her book had just been reviewed dismally in the *British Medical Journal*.[17]

She relaxed for a time, and her father's nephew Michael, a revenue officer in the London office of the high commissioner for Ireland, came visiting. A long-legged bachelor in black suit and black shoes, grave and overserious with a scholar's knowledge of Gaelic, he called Mary "Moira." He managed to get Liza and Mary invitations to a Buckingham Palace garden party, the first given by the new King George VI and Queen Elizabeth, with their pretty Princesses Elizabeth and Margaret Rose. An Australian correspondent cabled that a proud Sister Kenny was "smartly gowned in black, relieved with flesh pink touches and hat to match."

She returned to her rooms each day to confess failure in getting British support for a clinic. Then Queensland's agent-general in London got her an appointment at London County Hall with the medical officer of health, Sir Frederick Menzies. He listened to her story, and, pleasant surprise, said he was willing to attach a Kenny unit to one of the London county hospitals where it could be properly observed.

A Dr. Topping was assigned to help find her an equally willing hospital director. That was harder. At length Topping wearily suggested trying the Queen Mary's Hospital for Children at Carshalton, an hour from central London. This was the county council's star children's hospital, opened in 1909 to bring "the sick poor of the Metropolis out of the workhouses and onto the breezy Downs of Surrey." It had become an 840-bed, long-stay children's center, a sprawling yet graceful collection of red-brick buildings surrounded by a large grounds, a kind of combination park and estate with beds of flowers, a haystack, and a long avenue leading to the central administration building. The avenue was lined with blossoming almond and cherry trees. As soon as she saw them, she was in heaven. She was granted two wards there in which to try her treatment, as well as her own bedroom and sitting room and three of the hospital's physical therapists, headed by their chief, Miss Amy Lindsey.

The British therapists were flabbergasted when they saw Liza removing heavy plaster body and leg casts and metal and leather frames. Yet they knew the results of conventional treatment were lamentable, and they were willing to see what she could do. The doctors were not so friendly. An assessing committee was named: highly placed London orthopedists, neurologists, and specialists in internal medicine. She greeted them with some of her more extravagant claims and even repeated that word "cure." She pointed to a badly deformed child she had removed from a frame and said, "Look what *you've* done to him." The doctors recoiled in shock.

Her Australian therapists began getting some good results, however. They and Liza removed leg braces and spinal supports from patients who supposedly "had to" have them, and gradually they began to walk better without them. Her hot and cold sprays greatly improved circulation, in a country where central heating was considered unhealthy and patients were often blue from poor circulation. She paid closer attention to patients' day-to-day progress than anyone had considered necessary. More and more the hospital's therapists were won over. They also felt that they understood her goals better than did the doctors, who never stayed long. Her section grew from two wards to three, including thirty fairly recent cases. "England is the home of justice and fair play," she told a friend.

A Dr. Schwartz phoned her from Paris: his daughter had come down with polio six weeks before; Paris doctors had said she would never walk again. Would Sister Kenny see her? Liza flew to Paris, examined the child, and consented to treat her. The girl was carried into the Carshalton hospital stiff with paralysis. She later walked.

Alexander Zielinski, governor of the University of Warsaw, read about Liza in a Czechoslovakian newspaper; he wrote asking her to come to see his daughter, who had suffered an attack of polio three years before. Liza refused, saying that she did not see much hope. He sent her a set of airline tickets anyway, and she agreed to go. She was joining the air age, and, as a result of her trip, thirteen-year-old Wieslawa Zielinski, right leg in a brace, was soon brought to Carshalton by her mother. The girl could not speak English at first, but she was quick and sensitive. Before long, her own report appeared in Warsaw.

> Carshalton, in June.
>
> I am one of the sick children treated by Sister Elizabeth Kenny. Besides the English children there are also patients from Italy, China, Germany and Australia. . . . There are 43 children in my department.
>
> Sister Elizabeth Kenny is greeted joyfully by all. . . . She talks to all of us, says a few kind words and smiles. She treats us all with sympathy and tenderness which can be seen in her eyes. . . . A little fair-haired boy, sitting on a stool, sees Sister Elizabeth entering the room and he shouts in his shrill little voice: "Hallo, Miss Kenny!" Sister Elizabeth answers with her charming smile, "Hello, Connie, how are you?" Gay, five-year-old Lennie, his head covered with copper-colored curls, is always in some trouble with the nurses, doctors or other children, and he yells to Sister Elizabeth for help—"Miss Kenny!"—while Sister Elizabeth puts things right with her usual patience. . . .
>
> Sister Elizabeth took over my case one month ago. . . . All my leg muscles are already much stronger, especially around my knee and in the foot. . . .[18]

So the tough Aussie nurse seemed to the Polish youngster. Less than two years later, Wieslawa and her parents were dead in the ruins of Warsaw University, dive-bombed and shelled by invading Germans.

All in all, the work at Carshalton encouraged Liza. She was ultimately sent thirty-four convalescents not long out of isolation, twenty-one polio patients who had had the disease longer, and eight cerebral palsy cases. Most of the "early" convalescents had been immobilized for a month or eight weeks; they were not quite the fresh patients she really wanted. Still, the British medical observers issued a preliminary statement saying that the method was new and might be of some value; they asked for more time and a larger committee.

She got word that her mother was sick. "Gran" Kenny at ninety-three had broken her arm, and it wasn't mending. The Queensland government arranged air transport, and Liza went home, leaving the Australians and five British therapists to treat the Carshalton patients. She had been told she could go by land plane or seaplane, and she chose the sea route: ten days in a heavy-bellied Cyclops flying boat, with takeoff from Southhampton Harbor, then overnight stops. Athens, Egypt, Palestine, Surabaya, Bali, and finally a change to a small Qantas—an Australian overseas airline—plane that "looked as if pinned together with safety pins." A long flight over the Sea of Timor, with seats removed and an extra petrol tank installed, and Australian landfall finally at dusk at Port Darwin.

She arrived at Nobby on a Sunday morning and found her mother weakly sitting up in a chair. At twilight she was carried back to bed, and everyone talked quietly by the bedside in flickering kerosene light: the old woman had scorned electricity. Suddenly Mary Kenny sat up in bed and in a deep, clear voice told an old bush story. Then she looked out her window and said, "See, Elizabeth, my garden is blooming!" She died a few weeks later. Liza's father had bequeathed his daughter Elizabeth her itchy feet, unfulfilled ambition, and style; her mother, the brains, humor, and determination to make something of them.

Liza now had a new responsibility, Mary Stewart-Kenny, her legally adopted daughter, companion to old Mary Kenny for twelve years. She had become what Aussies call a pearler, a good-looking young woman with red hair and creamy skin. But an innocent: she had almost never been out of Nobby; at twenty-one, she seemed more like seventeen. Liza decided she too would go into "the work" and took her to Brisbane to start training as a therapist.

A new clinic was established at Newcastle, New South Wales. The last days of 1937 marked the beginning of a widespread polio epidemic. Other cities too wanted clinics. Liza traveled and negotiated, beginning to feel sure of success.

9

Defeat

On New Year's Day 1938, she was in Melbourne. She had waited twenty-six months for the crucial report of the Queensland Royal Commission. The premier of Queensland was the first to inform her that it was out. He phoned her from Brisbane and said only that he was sending her a copy by special delivery.

It arrived the next morning—it damned her. A half an inch thick, 130 pages, all disapproving, it said that she had failed to make good on several of her claims. Of forty-seven cases studied, the majority "showed no effective improvement, a few were worse and a few improved." Those who became deformed would not have done so under orthodox treatment. Established treatment was better, and immobilization, with no movement whatsoever for three weeks, was still essential. Her abandonment of it was "a grievous error," certain to lead to "a harvest of spinal deformities." Her numerous treatments were unnecessary; her early muscle treatment could not possibly minimize paralysis.

The report gave her mild credit for drawing attention to the plight of crippled children and called the organization of her clinics admirable. But it said the action to establish them had been largely political, the return to the people had been disproportionately small, and the money could have been better spent on existing orthopedic departments and vocational training. Among her spastic paralysis (cerebral palsy) patients, some children "did improve very much," but her treatment differed from the usual only in quantity: a trained masseuse could do as well "if given the same opportunity." The report admitted only obliquely the general lack of any such opportunity by calling for greater government and voluntary efforts for the crippled. Of the commissioners, only Dr. McDonnell did not sign; "owing to ill health," it was stated, he had been unable to take part for more than twelve months.[1]

She read the report at a Melbourne hospital while waiting to make new Kenny treatment arrangements. She had opened it eagerly; her reactions as she read were horror and humiliation. A doctor came in to look for her. She sat like a stone, "so depressed," she wrote, "that I refused to proceed." The doctor angrily told her, "It's a great pity you aren't as big mentally as you are physically."

She did not know how to reply; she wanted to run. She answered wildly. She could no longer leave the defenseless undefended. If the doctors would not care about the crippled, she would. Then she finished out the day, after a fashion.

The newspapers almost immediately had the story. "Produce the deformed cases!" she was demanding. "I would esteem it a favor if the Queensland government would give me the names. . . . I could present 100 cases which are grossly deformed as a result of the orthodox treatment. . . . If the commission can produce one patient to whom I promised a cure, I shall cease to associate myself with the work."

Commission members replied that they had her signature on her claims. "What about that?" reporters asked.

"Ah," she said. "I am so weary of untruths."[2]

"Our report was fair," maintains Dr. Jarvis Nye, who saw her do better work later. "At that time she had shown us nothing new. She had promised to get results which were completely fantastic and impossible." Yet the commissioners were right and wrong. They correctly described what they had seen, but they overoptimistically assessed the results of orthodox treatment. They presented an idealized version of it: immobilization relieved frequently by cautious exercise, which was in fact often slighted. They described current practice as a brief, careful period of splinting followed by reeducation and physical therapy. Lengthy oversplinting and little reeducation were in fact the rule. Elsewhere in the report, they admitted that a large proportion of practitioners "have been, and perhaps still are, inadequately acquainted" with proper methods. They also held that the aim of treating the crippled must be not merely a modest increase in muscle function but rather enabling the sufferer to earn a living. Lesser results, to them, were a waste of public money.

It was true enough that she could not restore the muscles of most of the chronic paralytics; objective testing often showed little or no change in muscle strength. But several of her patients were nonetheless leading more active, useful lives, if only more useful to themselves and to their families. This was true in some cases because they believed they were better and therefore tried harder. It was true in others because of skilled therapy. Liza's Sydney therapist, Betty Shuter, tells of a seventeen-year-old named Philip Jones, from a town near the Victoria border. "He came in completely paralyzed. We treated him, and from the waist up he recovered very well, but he got nothing back in his legs, only a little in his left foot. After two years of treatment, he was able to walk with sticks, but without braces. It was a matter of balancing and walking from the hips and will power. He showed what can be done even when you have no power in your legs, when you prevent deformities and leave patients limber and supple."

Such patients truly were living again, and several *were* earning their living. The orthodox doctors were right: she had been crude and unknowing. They were wrong, for her results outclassed theirs.

The governments of Queensland, New South Wales, and Victoria, Australia's three largest states, supported her. Labour was in office in Queensland. She too came from plain people, and the Labour leaders had their own troubles with the medical men. Besides, weren't parents voters? "Mothers Are Satisfied," said one Brisbane headline, over a letter from Mrs. U. Woodward of Eumundi who had a child at a Kenny clinic: "I have seen results that would make one's heart ache, and I say, 'Good luck to Sister Kenny.' . . . This is a matter for the mothers, and they should make their voices heard." The Sydney *Truth* printed two photographs of an eleven-year-old Kenny patient: one showed him cheerfully holding aloft his discarded irons, the long hip-length braces "in which he spent four pain-wracked years"; the other displayed him playing cricket.

"The government is satisfied," Health Minister Hanlon announced in Queensland. The clinics at Brisbane, Toowoomba, and Townsville would stay open, and new ones were being organized at Cairns, north of Townsville, and Rockhampton, chief port for central Queensland. In Sydney, the premier of New South Wales said that the state government had established the Sydney and Newcastle clinics and intended to maintain them. As for the state of Victoria, the prospective proprietor of a clinic in Melbourne, its government was likewise in no way influenced by this "sad blow to the people of Queensland whose children had benefited."

On January 10, four days after publication of the Queensland study, a new Sydney doctors' committee released a more favorable set of findings, though the committee urged a one- or two-year study using scientific controls. Liza knew, however, that she was still far from gaining medical acceptance and that without it any treatment would die, no matter how many mothers wrote letters. Whether or not she had fully realized it before, she was aware now that treating new cases, cases where she could have full effect, was her only hope.

It was polio season in Melbourne, a time of fright. Because of this, authorities compromised: she could have a section of twenty-two beds at a Children's Hospital branch and treat patients as soon as they came out of the acute ward, *if* parents asked for her. Several Melbourne doctors promptly met in secret to discuss the measures they firmly believed would be necessary to combat their patients' deformities after Liza and her therapists removed their casts.[3]

As for Liza, she labored. She worked alongside the Melbourne therapists for three months. She made consistent use of hot packs, muscle exercise, and education. Then she had to return briefly to Britain: a medical report was being prepared there too.

Eight clinics now operating in Australia, troubles left behind for a bit, she sank back and slept on the airplane, to land in London eight days after takeoff.

The British doctors' committee met there, and she spoke to these striped-trousered Harley Street specialists and representatives of the famous London hospitals, St. Thomas's, St. Bart's, Great Ormonde Street Children's, and King's College. The Queensland commission had not waited for a fair test of the treatment of acute cases, she told them. The main damage in polio was *not* caused by paralysis—her listeners' eyebrows rose collectively—but by muscle spasm. Spasm? "This is a new one on us," the chairman broke in.

When she tried to explain, the chairman looked at her politely, then turned to gaze out the window. His fellows followed suit. "There was a window for each of them," she remembered, and she inspected "the creases in the backs of their trousers." This was the last time she saw the committee. They carefully made sure that they revisited Queen Mary's Hospital at Carshalton when she was absent.

She still felt encouraged about the results there, especially with patients who were treated soon enough. The observation time allotted by the London County Council was over, however, and her Australian therapists had to leave. Amy Lindsey's permanent physiotherapy staff was to continue treating convalescents by the Kenny method, she was told, but she did not believe even that much would last. She boarded a ship again. It was August 1938, and one day the passengers heard the disheartening news of the Munich pact. She reached Melbourne, nervous and wary. A news report said that the British committee's report was out and had thoroughly condemned her. She cabled London and learned that was false. Soon the British report arrived.[4] Again she swiftly turned pages.

Almost the first thing she read was a slap: "Miss Kenny has claimed . . . complete recovery in all recent cases . . . she has personally treated from the commencement. . . . [If] Miss Kenny claims to be able to cure poliomyelitis completely . . . such a claim is in no way substantiated." Perhaps old exaggerations were coming home to roost.

She read on. Her hot foments and hydrotherapy were of value, it was conceded. Likewise, the very concentration and intensity of her treatment were commendable. Her emphasis on early movement and exercise? "Harmless but of unproved value." The report was a mixed bag. Almost at the end came the reaction to her revolutionary avoidance of immobilization: apart from contractures of the Achilles tendon in a few cases, which were overcome later, "we have seen the development of no contractures while the patients were recumbent and well supervised, nor have we found . . . delay [in return] of power. . . . We think, therefore, that it must be admitted that Miss Kenny's method of keeping limbs in a neutral position without splints when in bed is not harmful." In short, a group of observers had finally agreed that her refusal to splint had not caused the deformities and disaster that orthopedists had predicted.

For some hours this hardly sank in. Her first reaction was deep depression. At best, the report seemed halfhearted to her. All that evening and into the night she read and reread—this report, that report, her book, her manuscripts. Was the effort worth the agony? She looked at her clock. It was nearly dawn. She stepped onto a balcony into a morning wind. Two of her mother's maxims came to her. "He who angers you, conquers you." "The greater the fight, the greater the victory." There *was* a victory. The British had admitted that removing splints caused no harvest of disasters. She felt suddenly that "the lifting of the veil had started," that all she needed was *to get at the acute illness*, to see polio patients from the beginning of the disease.[5]

She kept demonstrating to anyone who would watch. A Melbourne medical statement was now issued. Two orthopedists found no stiffness, pain, or deformity in Kenny patients, though these problems were common in their own splinted cases.[6] She left Melbourne for Sydney carrying several copies of their judgment and the modestly favorable British ones in her voluminous black handbag, which was more a saddlebag or a briefcase than a purse and was over the years always packed with pertinent documents. Spotting a doctor, she would stop him and take an appropriate statement from her bag and see that he read it then and there. Most would just cough and say, "Interesting."

It was early 1939, the season of one of the worst droughts in Australian history. The temperature reached 114 degrees in the shade one day in Sydney, and fires burned in the bush, darkening the sky for great distances. She awoke after one hot, breathless night and picked up the newspaper. There was an item about her Newcastle clinic: a *modified* Kenny treatment was being given there, combining the best of the old method, including immobilization, with the best of the new. Moreover, the former Kenny Clinic was now renamed the Something-or-other Memorial Home. She dashed up to Newcastle and cornered her senior nurse, who informed her that she took directions only from the medical superintendent. Back in Sydney, she disassociated herself from the Newcastle hybrid.[7]

The friendly Melbourne statement that she had assiduously been carrying in her handbag was made public. It was soon counterbalanced by an adverse one from Newcastle. "I had the desolate feeling," she wrote, "of the world slipping away from under my feet." She was lonely and disconsolate, and felt that her life consisted of "storms and stress, misunderstanding and heartbreaks." She had been made acutely aware that, though her name might be attached to "Kenny" clinics, she had no real control over them when the matter was put to a test. The medical superintendents were responsible to their state governments, not to her.

She sat chin in hand by the hour and wallowed in self-pity, or, clutching her handbag, she went again from doctor to doctor, showing them the more favorable statements.

She concentrated on Brisbane once more. She resettled herself at the white-balconied Elizabeth Kenny Clinic on George Street and began phoning Charles Chuter, Health Minister Hanlon, Premier Forgan Smith, and the members of the now dormant Royal Commission. She wanted acute cases, she told them, *and* a hospital ward.[8]

She received a telegram informing her that two new patients from North Queensland were on the way and wanted her treatment. She again asked for hospital space and was refused. She then defied state law and medical custom, and turned one of her treatment rooms into a ward. "Put them in bed," she told her nurses when the stiff, sick patients arrived. "Take off their splints. Begin the hot foments." Whether or not she phoned Chuter beforehand is uncertain. She claimed later that she did not ask the health ministry's approval. But Chuter quickly knew what was happening. He, and undoubtedly the minister and very probably the premier, had decided to look the other way.

Officially, Chuter sent her a notice to dismiss the patients. She ignored it. Next, a father brought his fifteen-year-old girl to the clinic. He had just removed her from the hospital on his own; he was alarmed because the flesh on her legs was the color of dirty marble, and she had no motion at all except a flutter in one foot; she could barely even blink her eyelids. Liza called Chuter frantically. The girl seemed to be near death. The nurse did not want a fatality on her conscience.

"What should I do?" she asked.

"There's only one thing you can do," he said. "Take the kiddie in."

The girl's paralyzed legs could not be restored, but in two weeks she was sitting up in her bed knitting. In such ways, the number of bed patients at the clinic grew to ten. Most were admitted as at least subacute, still in the earlier stages of polio, still stiff and in pain, though past the first acute illness.

With the very first such patients, she also phoned Dr. Aubrey Pye, the superintendent of Brisbane General Hospital, and invited him to visit her new bootleg hospital with some of the hospital board. She also phoned the president of the Brisbane branch of the British Medical Association and other medical men. She urged them all to examine her new patients on admission, then check them at intervals. Some of the doctors she called did so, perhaps quietly urged on by Chuter. Some saw that she had removed splints and casts, and they used the familiar word "criminal." Her own then-part-time medical superintendent, Dr. Fryberg, at first thought the removal of the restraints unforgivable. "The splint restrains the mind more than it does the limb," she told him. "*You* put your arm up at a 45-degree angle and keep it there for two or three months and see what *you* can do with it."

Some of the doctors, including Fryberg, were gradually impressed. As for Chuter, he bided his time. Officially, he kept sending her stern notices to discharge the bed patients. She kept ignoring them, while he and she communicated unofficially. This could not go on indefinitely.

Under pressure, Chuter sent a new, stiffer discharge order. She answered that the patients could not be safely removed from hospital-type supervision, but that if they were shifted to Brisbane General Hospital she would happily supervise their treatment. All right, he wrote her back, please prepare a memorandum to that effect for the hospital board. The health ministry simultaneously requested that the board provide accommodations for patients desiring to be treated according to the Kenny method.

"It was my hour of triumph," Elizabeth Kenny later said. In the best of her black velvet dresses and a feathered hat, she marched into the lofty Brisbane Hospital for a conference with Superintendent Pye and the heads of departments. The meeting was memorable: everyone said yes to everything.

Remodeling was feverishly begun; paint and hot water were always essential when Liza triumphed. Several weeks later the red-and-yellow ambulances drew up on George Street to transfer her patients. Liza and Chuter sighed with relief: her defiance of authority had never become public; the entire Labour government could have been in trouble had some patient suffered a disaster.

At the hospital, Liza and her nurses were ready, the nurses in new sky blue uniforms and starched headdresses. She had nurses aplenty. At one point there were twenty-eight in service or training on George Street. The new Kenny quarters was ward seven, one of the oldest in the large, sprawling city institution, with its many separate buildings, pavilions, and small wooden structures marked "Post Office" or "Teas." The newest, most modern units were several-storied brick blocks; the older ones were low wooden buildings, and Liza was assigned one of these. As the patients were carried in, she ordered, "Fold up the walls." Her building had roll-up walls to admit Australian sun.

The nurses in blue and the stern-looking woman who led them were quickly the talk of the hospital. Several patients in the regular polio ward, or their parents, asked for transfers. Liza's friend Dr. Jean Rountree gave medical supervision. Patients in the acute stage, defined as three weeks in length, were kept in the regular isolation ward even if they selected Kenny treatment. Some of the Kenny nurses worked there, hot packing, running back and forth with the packs to a washtub and hand wringer, beginning gentle, passive exercises, while the conventional therapists stared. Isolation over, the Kenny patients were transferred to ward seven for further hot packing, increasingly concentrated exercise, reeducation, and, in some patients, hydrotherapy in individual bathtubs. Inquisitive, often apprehensive, doctors looked in; actually they were the more friendly ones, for others angrily refused to have anything to do with her. Parents visited, and Dr. Pye stopped by. The place was a beehive, with Liza, remembers one of her nurses, "buzzing in and out. We did almost all the treatment. She said we had to, or the doctors would say it was her magnetism or something. But she was the captain of the ship."

When a patient in the regular ward requested a transfer, she would appear there in white dress and long, white hospital coat, or maybe her cream-colored suit, to examine him and record his condition. With what she considered infinite patience, she would repeat to the non-Kenny technicians how pain and spasm caused stiffness, and stiffness, not paralysis, produced many of the contractions they saw. The orthodox therapists had always ignored stiffness; they worshipped "straightness." She inspected a boy named Tommy. His therapist proudly pointed out his straight trunk and limbs, as Liza tried vainly to flex them.

"Is he not beautifully straight?" his therapist asked.

"Yes," said Nurse Kenny, "he is straight, and there are several thousand lying peacefully out at Toowong just as straight." Toowong was the cemetery. "Tommy has just as much chance of recovering the use of his legs as they have."

Hoping to end such strife, she told Pye she wanted to work amicably with the medical staff. He arranged an evening meeting. Papers in hand, she was about to start speaking when the senior pediatrician rose and said he did not want any publicity about his being in her ward. The senior orthopedist said the same thing. Momentarily without answer, she started walking away. Pye prevailed on her to come back. She did and displayed a photograph of the severe muscle spasm that she believed had caused one girl's deformity. The photograph showed a marked prominence at the crest of the ilium (one of the large bones of the pelvis), indicating that spasm and tightness were pulling the pelvis upward and causing an apparent shortening of one leg.

"We treated her," Liza reported, "and within a few days the tightness and deformity disappeared." The girl's legs were now normal—the patient herself was paraded before the doctors.

The orthopedist came forth, pointed to the photograph and said, "That's an out-and-out fake." This broke up that amicable meeting.

Regular meetings continued, however. Skeptical or not, several doctors had said they were willing to listen, and they did. She prepared elaborate lectures, summoned patients, presented the pathology as she saw it, and, week by week, reported her results. The group of from six to ten men usually stood mute and impassive. After several weeks, she erupted. "You must all be good poker players. I would like to know whether you agree with what I have shown you." No orthopedic surgeon was present, so one doctor answered that they were not orthopedists and therefore were not able to judge. "You need only be chimney sweeps to see what I am showing you," she replied.

There were doctors who were becoming less doubtful, however. Some apparently severely affected children had now been treated from the acute period onward. They were apparently recovering. Of course, they *all* could have been spontaneous recoveries, the doctors said to each other. Still, there were not that many recoveries in their ward.

A boy of eight came to the hospital after three weeks of treatment in his hometown. Despite rigid splinting, Donald had developed severe bilateral foot-drop: both feet had fallen, toes down, to a sharp angle that no pressure could force back to normal. He could neither stand nor sit up. He was treated for two weeks in the standard ward, where he was further splinted; the orthodox diagnosis was that his leg muscles were paralyzed, and his normal, healthy foot muscles were pulling his feet down.

Summoned to examine him, Liza ordered the splints removed. A doctor warned that if she did not put them back, the deformity would get even worse. She looked at the clock. "It is now 15 minutes after 12 o'clock. If you come back tomorrow at the same time, you will see that this patient has no dropped feet."

Liza's therapists began applying hot packs to the tightened muscles, the muscles "in spasm" by her diagnosis, that were pulling on his heels and forcing his toes downward. In less than ten minutes the heat began relaxing the tightness.

The next day a group of skeptical doctors, including Superintendent Pye, entered her ward. Liza sent a nurse after Donald. She returned in alarm saying that his bed was empty. An orderly found the boy outside. He had never seen a trolley car before and had run down a grassy slope to look at one. A grinning Liza helped him onto a treatment table, and at her request he swung his feet in every direction.

"How long did it take you to restore function to the paralyzed muscles?" Dr. Pye asked.

"Just a few minutes," she said with a forgivable touch of triumph. "The muscles were not paralyzed. You have viewed this disease from the wrong angle all these years."[9]

An orthopedist who was present later spoke to Liza's friend Professor Wilkinson, who was also on the scene. The orthopedist told Wilkinson he had just returned from treatment centers abroad and had never seen such a thing. "It's fantastic!" he admitted. But some of the doctors who saw the incident turned and walked out, stubbornly sure that there was trickery or a previous misdiagnosis.

Liza mistrusted iron lungs—respirators—for cases where the breathing muscles were affected. A boy in a respirator was rolled into her ward. She stood over him all evening, watching nervously. At last she turned to a young resident doctor. "This is the first time I've ever done anything without a doctor's permission. But I want you to feel utterly relieved of all responsibility." Removing the child from the tanklike machine—"It was a heart-stopping moment," an observer says—she sat up all night, treating his affected muscles with hot packs. Muscle tightness relieved, the child regained normal control. "No orthopedist would have been able to get the same results," Wilkinson stated.

Her ward filled. She and her young women were treating some twenty-six patients, and the word began to get around that she might have something after all. The New South Wales Hospital Commission decided to send an observer and appointed Dr. Norman Little, a Sydney orthopedist.

"Why pick on me?" Little asked.

"Because you're the only orthopedist in Australia who hasn't blasted away at the Kenny method," he was told.

"How could I?" he said. "I haven't seen it."

In Brisbane, she had just admitted a sturdy, athletic boy two days after the onset of polio. He was in severe pain. He could not raise his head and could move only one leg slightly; the other was completely paralyzed. She told Little what she expected to do. She also lectured him about polio, and he was struck both by her knowledge and the gaps in it; like some others, he did not hesitate to correct her.

Eight weeks later he returned with two colleagues. She took them to the treatment room and, like a conjuror, withdrew a screen. There on a treatment table was the boy Little had seen earlier, now glowing and normal, every muscle functioning. "That happens sometimes," Little thought. Nonetheless, he was impressed by three things: her early treatment did not do any harm; her hot packs did relieve pain; and she had a treatment "as good as I'd seen any place in the world." Little, like various predecessors, was impressed by something else: "On my second visit, she had picked up word for word all the principles I'd set out on my first visit. It was *very* interesting." With men like Wilkinson and Little, she was beginning to win some medical friends of unimpeachable soundness.

Another such was the hospital's general superintendent, Dr. Aubrey David (Dick) Pye, M.B., Ch.M., Fellow of the Royal College of Surgeons (Edinburgh), Fellow of the Royal Australian College of Surgeons, a short, quick, direct man. He had seen her "ignorant," as he remembered it, 1933 demonstration at this same hospital. Now he began telling colleagues: "Remember how crude she was? She's now a shrewd and most competent observer—she doesn't miss a trick." He even found her to be human. The hospital needed to raise a good-sized fee to enter a nurse in a Brisbane queen contest. Much of the money was lacking. "Old Kenny," he says, "came to light with it."

Another medical specialist had been watching her for some time: Dr. Jarvis Nye, one of the most conscientious of the members of that thoroughly antagonistic Royal Commission, and one of two co-founders of the Brisbane Clinic, a medical group modeled on the Mayo Clinic. In late 1937, just as the commission was finishing its report, he saw a little girl who had been stricken with polio one month before. She had a paralyzed deltoid (the large shoulder muscle) and shoulder girdle, and her parents had decided to take her to Sister Kenny. A leading orthopedist asked Nye to prevent it, saying, "If this poor kid is not splinted, her arm and shoulder are going to be ruined!" The gentlemanly Nye felt he was helpless; the parents had made their decision. Three months later he saw the child again and was surprised to find that she had a perfectly normal deltoid. He realized that Kenny wasn't the quack he had believed her to be.

Liza phoned him from the hospital, saying that she was about to take over two patients who had been there for some months. She asked him to examine them with her, then look at them again in a fortnight. That seemed fair to him. He took a co-worker, surgeon Alan Lee. She showed them the patients; two weeks later the doctors returned and found her results to be "really amazing." Nye saw five or six similar cases. One boy, seventeen, was a patient some commission members had examined; an orthopedist had warned against removing his leg braces. He now came loping up the hospital stairs. Nye shook his head in astonishment. He felt that this strange nursing sister now knew more about muscle origin, insertion, and function than any of the doctors at the hospital, even if neither he nor his fellows could understand her lectures.

Brisbane, warm, lovely Brisbane, was beginning to look wonderful to her. The magnolia trees flowered, violet bougainvillea blossomed, and

Elizabeth Kenny. Age 31, the year 1911, when she made of herself a bush nurse and rode into the Never Never to deliver babies, treat illness, and invent a treatment for polio.*

* Photographs not credited are from the collection of the author.

1911: She donned a red "Nightingale" cape to become a nurse.

World War I: She (right) served at an army hospital in Britain.

An Australian army nurse, she was promoted in 1916 to the rank of "sister," which gave her two "pips" and the title she was to use for the rest of her life.

The little house near Nobby, the last family home, with windmill and water tank and little appeal to an ambitious woman.

Brother Bill: She helped build his physique until he had muscles like the Great Sandow—powerful enough to "toss a Turk over his shoulder" at Gallipoli.

164/1—Transport Stretcher, the "Sylvia" (Patent No. 3172). Illustration shows handles concealed for transport.

The "Sylvia" Stretcher is light, easily adjusted, and has many advantages over other stretchers. Comfortable to patient, and easily assembled. With mattress and pillow. Hood is erected in parts as desired. The "Sylvia" is the best community stretcher, and is recommended to communities by the Country Women's Association and Bush Nurses' Association.

1926: She had seen soldiers die in jolting ambulances, so she invented the ''Sylvia'' transport stretcher for rough Australian roads. Then she sold it ''with the zeal of a prophet.'' (1943 catalog of Elliott Bros. Ltd.)

1934: She established her first government polio clinic at Townsville in Australia's tropical north and told these nurses, ''All suggestions of helplessness must be combatted.''

April 14, 1940, news photo: She arrives in San Francisco "with what she claims is the most unorthodox and most effective treatment ever devised for infantile paralysis." (National Archives)

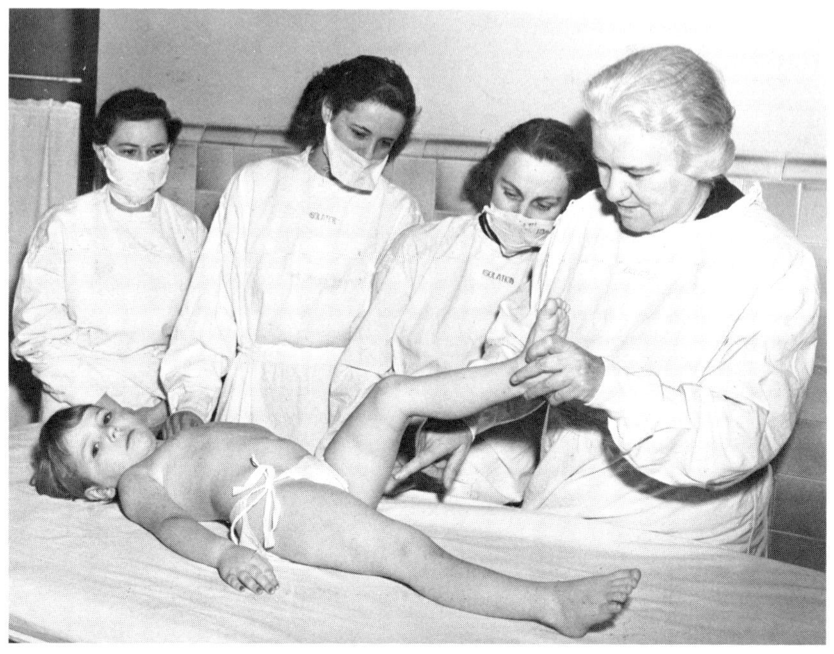

She taught Americans her treatment. ''See that. That is spasm. . . . Feel those tendons—tight as iron bands!'' (*Minneapolis Star*)

Minneapolis General Hospital gave her a ward, and she set nurses to wringing out hot packs to ease patients' pain. (*Minneapolis Tribune*)

TIMES-HERALD WASHINGTON, D. C. SATURDAY, MARCH 31, 1945

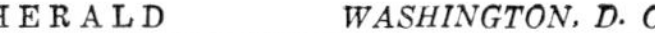

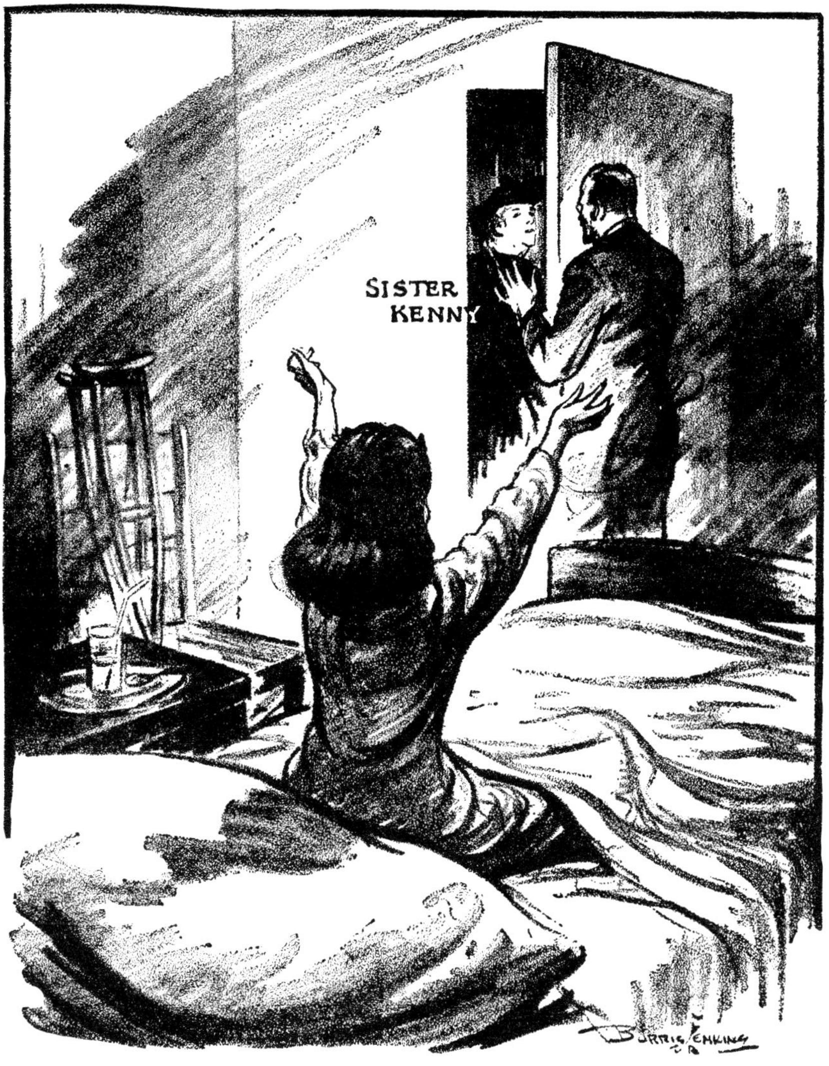

Don't Close That Door!

March 1945: The *Washington Times-Herald* pleaded with doctors to back her, as she threatened—once again—to depart. (*Washington Times-Herald*)

Screen star Rosalind Russell became a warm friend and fought to make the film *Sister Kenny*. (*Minneapolis Star*) On September 29, 1946, it opened at the RKO Palace (below) as 20,000 people jammed Times Square, breaking barriers to get near the famous nurse. (*Minneapolis Tribune*)

She and adopted daughter Mary met film star Cary Grant. (RKO Pictures)

In ornate dress and Aussie-style hat, she returned from Europe aboard the *Queen Elizabeth*.

The famed Yousuf Karsh made a portrait of her. He thought "faith shone through the fatigue" in her face. (Karsh, Ottawa)

August, 1951: Ill, her face a mask, she retired to Toowoomba on the rim of the Range and her old nursing territory. (International News Photos)

On November 30, 1952, she died, and the pupils of Nobby School lined the road to watch the old black hearse pass. (*Minneapolis Tribune*)

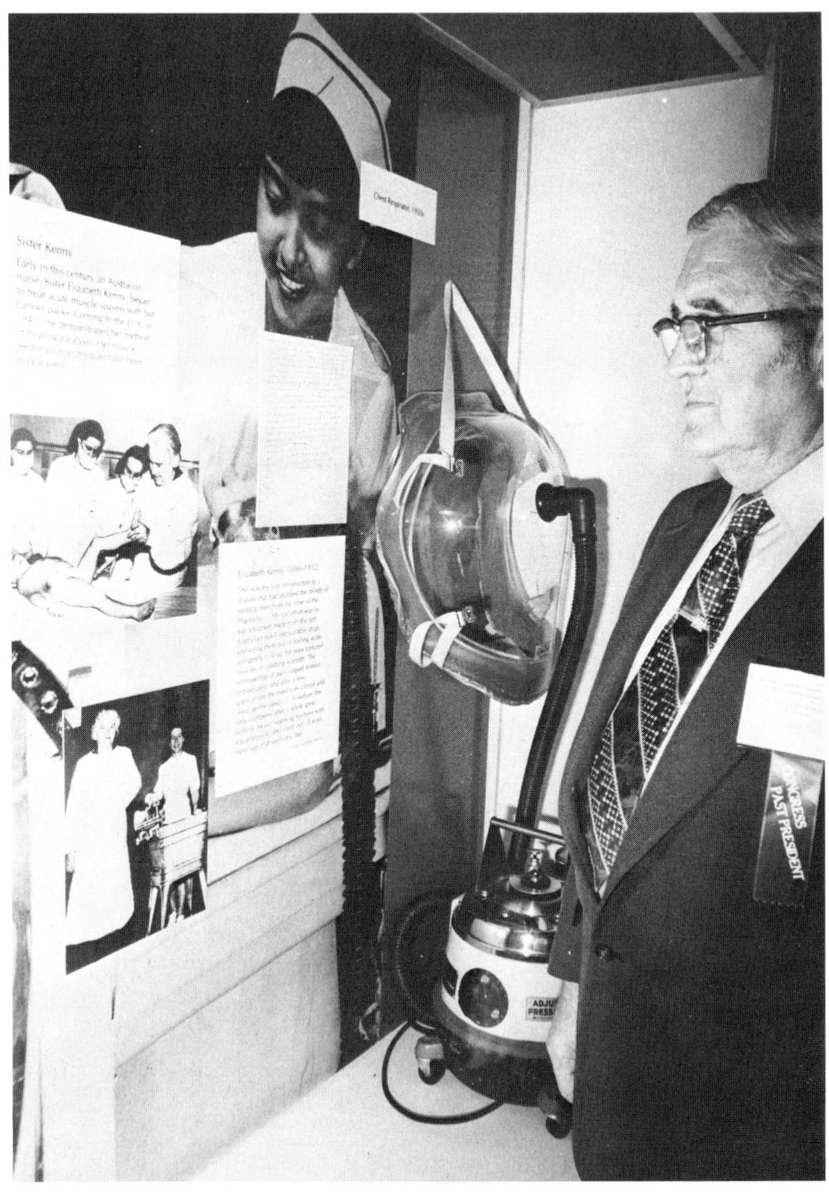

1974: Her co-worker Dr. Miland Knapp in Washington, as the Smithsonian Institution opened an exhibit on rehabilitation medicine—and honored Elizabeth Kenny as a pioneer. (Courtesy the Smithsonian Institution)

school girls in blue and white pinafores and straw hats with blue ribbons walked beneath the blossoms.

On August 10, 1939, Dr. Aeneas McDonnell, Old Mac, died of cancer in Toowoomba. She had visited him shortly before, and he had perked up for her. They did not discuss the Royal Commission report. On September 1, Germany invaded Poland, and World War II began. Britain and France declared war two days later. Pye telephoned to give her the news. She said she had just heard that the rest of the world was at war. "I've had it practically on my own for a number of years."

In November, five of her new supporters made a public declaration. Dr. Little, Dr. Alan Fletcher of Sydney, Dr. Alan Roberts of Newcastle, Professor Wilkinson, and her sometime medical aide, Dr. Abe Fryberg (who had become a state health official), said she had developed a satisfactory and commendable treatment for acute polio.[10] She was jubilant—at last she had the highest hopes that her method would win general adoption in Australia. It did not.

To the satisfaction of many doctors, she had shown that rigid, routine immobilization was unnecessary and had made a beginning at introducing immediate or early care. She had shown the value of moist heat. She had shown that in certain cases there could be recovery or improvement after two or more years. She had taken the crippled who had been neglected for years, shut in back rooms and hidden in shame, and given them hope. The old poliomyelitis treatment was being improved: some of the most stubborn immobilizers had gone back to their textbooks and had been reminded to pay more attention to movement. In short, she had at least started to wake the medical profession from its sleep over polio and disability. Yet none of it was enough.

Nye phoned every member of the Royal Commission to try to persuade them to confer again. None would have anything more to do with her. One called her "that lying old et cetera"; Nye replied that, "I'm not interested in her personality but her work." The commission's report stood to be quoted and requoted for years, and medicine as a whole in Australia would not acknowledge her. Most Australian doctors could only remember her earlier, cruder methods, and she still had treated only a handful of acute patients, not enough to win foreign recognition.

The war applied the finishing touch. Nurses and doctors were joining the army; the Kenny ward at Brisbane Hospital had to be closed for a time. Liza Kenny was not so much castigated as she was ignored, and her friendly doctors' new words were buried by war news. From the heights, she fell to the depths again, and she wrote of her bitterness and bewilderment at the silence that now greeted her phone calls, her appeals, and her compulsive offers to "give" Australia her treatment.

Nye called a meeting of six of her medical friends. There was only one place to send her, he said: America. They agreed; in the United States she might get a fresh hearing. The six—Nye, Pye, Fryberg, Lee, Wilkinson, and Dr. Felix Arden, pediatrician and medical superintendent of Brisbane Children's Hospital—signed a statement saying, "It is . . . our belief that she has made an important contribution." Then Nye went to his friend and patient William Forgan Smith, Queensland's premier. Nye told him the story and suggested that the government help her.

"Oh, so you want to get rid of her, do you?" Forgan Smith said.

"No," Nye answered.

"Oh well, send her."

To this shrewd Scotch migrant, the constant arguments in the press had become a political liability rather than an asset. The Queensland government had spent more than £50,000 on her clinics; he was glad to spend a few pounds more, dispatch this troublesome woman to another country, and get public credit for her "mission." He checked with Health Minister Hanlon, who agreed and then privately told a friend, "We're sending her to America. Bloody good riddance."

As for Liza, she morosely concluded that the door to success in Australia was barred to her. She announced that she had hoped to pass on her knowledge and take a less active role. Practically before the arrangements were made, however, she was planning her American journey.

Dr. Lee, one of the members of her self-appointed rescue committee, had just returned from Rochester, Minnesota, and the Mayo Clinic. He suggested sending her there. Nye and Arden knew Dr. Melvin Henderson, the Mayo orthopedic chief. They and Wilkinson wrote him. "I merely wish to assure you," Wilkinson said, "that I have met some medical men here in Australia who are competent to form an opinion and who, particularly from more recent observation of her work, are satisfied that Sister Kenny has made a definite contribution to the treatment of infantile paralysis and in fact has established it on a new basis." Practical Charles Chuter urged that a similar letter be sent to Basil O'Connor, head of the National Foundation for Infantile Paralysis. Forgan Smith cheerfully signed it, calling her a contributor to the cause of humanity who "does not seek personal gain."[11]

Before leaving, she returned to the Downs. For a few days she breathed the fresh breezes, fragrant with tall pines and pepperinas. The topknot pigeons flew among weeping willows, and a string of red cows shone golden in the afternoon sun, grazing among sharp-smelling gum trees. "I'm going to America," she told her Downs friends. "I've done all I can, and now it's up to science." She sounded discouraged, but a cousin remarked faithfully: "Ah, Liza will never stop at the bottom. She'll go on."[12]

Back in Brisbane, her George Street staff gave her a farewell luncheon, and Minister Hanlon, all smiles, put tickets for round-trip passage in her hands. The government's total contribution was £300 for the tickets. "I will return," she announced. "I have had so many knocks that I'm immune to them." Everyone cheered, and she and her adopted daughter, Mary, now a Kenny-trained therapist, climbed into a hired limousine with chauffeur and set off.[13]

Liza and Mary boarded their ship at Sydney. They tossed long rolls of colored paper to friends on shore as the vessel began moving. The streamers unrolled and broke as the ship made its way toward the Heads, the twin cliffs guarding the entrance to open sea. It was March 29, 1940. Like Australians Nellie Melba, Fighting Bob Fitzsimmons, Annette Kellerman, Sir Howard Florey, Sir George Hubert Wilkins, Sir David Bruce, Alan Moorehead, Judith Anderson, Percy Grainger, Sidney Nolan, Errol Flynn, Marjorie Lawrence, Merle Oberon, Joan Sutherland, Cyril Ritchard, and Germaine Greer, Liza Kenny left Australia, exported.

10

America

THE UNITED STATES in 1940 dreaded the capricious disease poliomyelitis. Australians feared it too, but the American concern was greater. There were far more cases, and there was a new social phenomenon, an American mass movement against the disease that one historian called "an exhibition of almost religious fervor."

The movement had begun with a historical accident. On the morning of Wednesday, August 11, 1921, the rising young politician, Franklin D. Roosevelt, had taken ill at his cherished Canadian summer home on Campobello Island in the Bay of Fundy, off Maine. "When I swung out of bed my left leg lagged," he said afterward, "but I managed to move about to shave. I tried to persuade myself that the trouble with my leg was muscular . . . but presently it refused to work, and then the other." Two weeks later Dr. Robert W. Lovett, a famous Boston polio specialist, confirmed the diagnosis: infantile paralysis. Lovett considered it a fairly mild attack and thought Roosevelt might recover completely, though he could not be sure. Sara Delano Roosevelt, FDR's mother, wrote her brother that the doctor "just came and said, 'This boy is going to get all right.' They went into his room, and I hear them all laughing, Eleanor in the lead."[1]

In mid-September, however, Franklin Roosevelt, still in pain, was taken to Presbyterian Hospital, New York City, where his record read: "Not improving." At his home, next, he learned to swing into a wheelchair by grasping a strap hung from the ceiling. By spring he hoped to be walking. In January, however, the muscles behind his knees began tightening, pulling his legs up like knife blades. His doctor put his legs into plaster casts and for two weeks tapped a wedge into each cast, a little deeper each day, to straighten the tendons.

In February, Roosevelt's legs were enclosed in fourteen-pound, hip-to-ankle steel braces. With his legs thus stiffened, he managed to get up on crutches and walk a little. At best, it was not really walking but a painful maneuvering with his hips. He was never to walk or stand without support. He refused to acknowledge this, however, and began exercising. Like Liza Kenny's brother Willie, he learned to identify his leg muscles by name and concentrate on them one by one.*

In 1924 an old banker friend, George Foster Peabody, wrote him about a spa he controlled at Warm Springs, Georgia. Roosevelt hurried down there, accompanied by Basil O'Connor, a brash young Wall Street lawyer, who was about to become his law partner. The business-minded O'Connor was more or less dragged along; to him the place was just a seedy, broken-down southern resort, "a big old hole."

FDR swam daily, however, and thought he was improving. Other paralyzed persons read that he was there, and they too came. He taught them exercises, and everyone began calling him "Dr. Roosevelt." Though O'Connor opposed it, Roosevelt bought the place and incorporated a nonprofit Warm Springs Foundation. Then in 1928 he was elected Democratic governor of New York. "Doc," he told O'Connor, "you'll have to run Warm Springs now." O'Connor, stuck, began to put the place on a sound financial basis, and both men began thinking of a nationwide antipolio effort.

Roosevelt was elected president in 1932, at the height of the depression. Millions of people looked on him as a savior and marveled at his conquest of his disability. To raise money, O'Connor and his advisers decided to go to these millions, for the hard times had dried up the previous source of most charity, the rich. At one meeting, some sort of new celebration was urged. "The president's birthday," responded Carl Byoir, the public relations genius. "A President's Birthday Ball held all over the country." The first nationally contributed money to fight polio was thus raised on the evening of January 30, 1934, to the strains of Guy Lombardo playing "Did You Ever See a Dream Walking?" and Eleanor

* John Gunther wrote that "Roosevelt's attack came in 1921. . . . Sister Kenny was unknown and her celebrated treatment . . . was of the future. . . . Had her methods been available at the time, his legs might have been saved." She never claimed this.

Roosevelt in satin dress and tiger-claw necklace singing "Happy Birthday."

Roosevelt meanwhile was becoming the most loved and most hated president since Lincoln. He and O'Connor were eager to separate the antipolio movement from his personality: in 1938 the National Foundation for Infantile Paralysis was established. The link to FDR lingered, however, because comedian Eddie Cantor attended another meeting and blurted out an irresistible suggestion: "We could ask people to send dimes directly to the president at the White House. We could call it the March of Dimes." The annual march and the associated campaign became the greatest such money-raising effort in history. It started with the collection of one million dollars, and in sixteen years, long past the day when dimes were sent to the White House, it reached a phenomenal sixty-six million dollars in a single year. Volunteers were participating all over the country, far more people than had ever joined to combat a disease.

They were raising the money that would lead to development of both the Salk and Sabin polio vaccines. Beyond this, they were creating that new American movement, the annual mass fund drive for health. Money-raising on this scale and the attendant hoopla have been praised and damned; but in the March of Dimes they reached their full growth, and polio, because of FDR, was the target.

The volunteers were not in the cause just for FDR, however; many detested him. The basic reason was the wrenching, nationwide alarm over poliomyelitis. In a more recent age of routine polio vaccination, even older Americans have to prod themselves to remember that only yesterday there was no more feared disease. In 1940, when Sister Kenny reached the United States, the disease and the fear were beginning their peak years.

The United States had suffered its first great polio epidemic in 1916, and the people responded with panic. The epidemiologists counted 28,767 cases that year, with more than 6,000 deaths; 2,407 persons died in New York City alone. Fright froze that giant city, thousands tried to flee, police halted them on train platforms and roads. Few New York hospitals would admit polio cases because they feared contagion; police had to break into apartments to take dead children from mothers. Authorities frantically tried to learn how the virus was transmitted. One newspaper seriously commented: "Cats and dogs carry disease, but what about doctors' beards?"

Terrible 1916 was followed by a short lull, but in the twenties and thirties polio became a regular part of summer and autumn. Other, more steadily occurring diseases—rheumatic heart disease, cerebral palsy, and tuberculosis—claimed as many or more child victims. Polio struck suddenly and mysteriously, however, in one part of the country one summer, in others the next. Once doctors learned to cope with breathing difficulties, the death rate dropped, but the crippling disease left lifetime victims. A large number of all the cases were almost certainly caused by other, related viruses; these cases were mistakenly included as "nonparalytic polio," inflating the statistics. Fright and awareness also brought scores of mild, once-unrecognized nonparalytic cases into hospitals.

Not only polio but also polio panic, then, became an annual scourge as year after year the number of cases mounted: 1940, 9,804 cases; 1943, 12,450; 1946, 25,698; 1949, 42,033; 1952, 57,879; 1955, 28,-985. Epidemics dominated the news, and newspapers and radio stations reported daily polio totals as they did baseball scores. Two doctors wrote as late as 1954, "There is literally no acute disease at the present day which causes so much apprehension and alarm in the patient and his relatives," and Dr. Howard Rusk in the *New York Times* found polio's story "one of tragedy filled with tension, fear and anxiety." *Life* called it "one of the most feared of diseases . . . capricious, unpredictable," and a *Saturday Evening Post* article read, "Polio—a word that strikes more terror in the hearts of parents than the atom bomb." Dr. John Paul said of one Los Angeles epidemic: "It was as if plague had invaded the city, and the place where cases were assembled and cared for was . . . shunned as a veritable pest house." A doctor at Los Angeles County Hospital wrote his wife: "People are hysterical, the interns, nurses and helpers are scared to death and have one or two cases among themselves each day. Fifty admissions every day—everyone strained and worried."[2]

Many doctors blamed the pitchmen of the new National Foundation for Infantile Paralysis and its clamorous March of Dimes for the terror. The foundation without question used every device of modern promotion, and its annual poster child, a cute youngster on braces or crutches, had the impact of a sledgehammer. The 1916 New York panic, however, needed no such aid. Minneapolis—to pick the city where Elizabeth Kenny was to settle—lived through several epidemics in the 1940s and 1950s; no city was subjected to more polio publicity, often with vast exaggeration. This undoubtedly had its ill effects. The publicity also spurred preparation, however, and neither in Minneapolis nor anyplace else was there ever as blind a panic as the one in unprepared New York in 1916.

Panicky or not, before the Salk vaccine was developed, Americans were as conscious of polio as of their heartbeats. They watched their children closely in polio season; they often kept them from beaches and gatherings; they called the doctor at the first sign of a stiff neck. The problem was by no means imaginary: polio was the cause of one-third of all crippling in children. Parents knew of neighbors' children or young adult friends who were in iron lungs or braces. Logically or illogically, they were afraid.

Such was the atmosphere on April 16, 1940, the day Liza landed in San Francisco, age fifty-nine, unwanted in Australia, pessimistic about American prospects.

The polio-conscious Americans had read about Sister Elizabeth Kenny's fantastic claims. Before she could get off the ship, she was accosted by the press. She stood by the rail to be photographed, clutching the sweeping black hat brim which topped her solid, expressive face with its belligerent chin. There was fight if not certainty in her eyes. She possessed the most unorthodox and most effective infantile paralysis treatment ever devised, she told the reporters. Yes, she was an Australian nurse. Her age? "Fifty-three."[3] "Never put your age down," she subsequently advised her adopted daugher Mary, now her companion.

The excited Mary gasped as their train crossed the continent. Her excitement infected Liza, who tossed off appropriate lines of her mother's poetry. In windy Chicago the pair had to race down the street, chasing Liza's aerodynamic hat.

In Denver, they saw polio patients in splints and casts. "Plaster prisons!" Liza jeered. In the United States, as in Australia, rest and immobilization were the common treatment. In some centers, the casts were removed once or twice a day after the acute period, and limbs were passively moved a bit. In others, even this timid motion was shunned, and young doctors were taught that if they disturbed the limb, they would lose all the good effects of the months of rest. Dr. Harvey Billig, a brilliant and original Los Angeles orthopedist, served at the Harvard Infantile Paralysis Commission Clinic in Boston, "and no loosening was done—none. The patients just lay there and developed contractions, and we just waited to see what surgery was indicated."

There were exceptions. For example, the pioneering physiotherapy team of Henry and Florence Kendall of Children's Hospital School, Baltimore, combined some heat, massage, and cautious reeducation with standard splints and supports. Still others in scattered institutions used limited amounts of heat and exercise. But the more common practice was long immobilization followed by a few hours of physical therapy a week, late in the disease, with the physical therapy used to attempt to overcome deformities rather than to prevent them. Orthopedists of the twenties and thirties, according to Dr. Sedgwick Mead of the Kaiser Foundation's Rehabilitation Center at Vallejo, California, not only "embalmed" patients in plaster for months; they also believed in the "extreme fragility" of affected muscles. Positively no vigorous exercise could be countenanced while muscles were fragile.[4]

There was medical dissatisfaction with this situation. "No specific treatment exists" for acute polio, and when there is an epidemic, "the helplessness remains," Dr. Kristian G. Hansson of Cornell Medical College wrote bleakly in 1939.[5] There was also medical disinterest. In 1926 Franklin Roosevelt wheeled himself around an American Orthopedic Association meeting in Atlanta, vainly seeking support for Warm Springs and polio rehabilitation. He found little concern (though eventually a committee was named to review a Warm Springs report). After all, polio treatment showed small result and was expensive beyond most patients' means. About all that could be done, most doctors felt, was a long period of essentially nothing, then perhaps surgery. In some cities as late as 1946, hospitals uniformly refused acute polio cases because they feared infection; after the acute phase was "treated" at home, a few would admit them. Even many county or public hospitals did this until the new polio foundation, doctors' committees, and public pressure jarred open their doors.[6]

In the United States as in Australia, many needlessly useless limbs and crippled bodies resulted. "Many patients who might have recovered completely were deformed," said Roland Berg, long the foundation's science editor.[7] Liza, seeing the indiscriminate splints and casts, knew that she had a colossal job ahead.

Liza and Mary arrived in New York City in rain and cold. Liza phoned the polio foundation and learned that its president, O'Connor, was in Warm Springs with President Roosevelt. She telephoned Dr. Kristian Hansson—she had his 1939 article—and he invited her to visit his hospital, where she talked to the staff. She aroused only a few sparks of interest. On May 1 she and Mary saw O'Connor. He listened for three hours, but she was told, finally, that the foundation conducted no research or treatment, that it merely made grants to institutions that did. "Let's pack our ports,"* Liza sighed, and the pair headed back to Chicago, where the American Medical Association had its headquarters.

* Portmanteaus or suitcases.

"She came in wearing that hat that made her look like Admiral Nelson. She *looked like* a screwball," remembers the AMA's principal spokesman of the day, the keen and loquacious Dr. Morris Fishbein. She was indeed an unsophisticated country woman in a shapeless black outfit. Her virtually white hair was brushed severely back and tied in a bun, and she wore no touch of cosmetics. Big and strong-looking, she stared at the Chicago doctors with her piercing eyes and talked of strange symptoms with the air of a messiah. They had never seen anything like her.

"I think we may as well go home," she told Mary.

"Oh, we can't," Mary answered. "We've got to stick it out. We've got to go to the Mayo Clinic."

Nothing could have kept Liza from delivering her Australian letters of recommendation to the great Rochester, Minnesota, institution, only a day's ride from Chicago. There her first interviewer was Dr. Melvin Henderson, founder of the clinic's orthopedic section. He was intrigued and sent her to Dr. Frank Krusen, who at forty-one was the country's leading teacher of the new discipline called physical medicine. He listened to Liza at intervals for two days and heard her address the clinic staff. When she said she could remedy foot-drop in twenty-four hours, he was certain there was something wrong with her. He also felt she would be impossible to work with. He told these things to Henderson. Still, he confessed, he was somewhat puzzled. After all, she had brought some good reports from Australia.

Henderson summoned Liza. Rochester was treating only a few polio patients, he pointed out. The place to go might be the Twin Cities, Minneapolis and St. Paul, ninety miles north. There had been something of an outbreak there in 1939; there were still many cases in the hospitals, and new ones might soon be appearing. He made arrangements for some key introductions.

"We can't stay long in Minneapolis," Liza told Mary. "Just a few days. We've got just enough money to get back to Australia."

Mid-May. The buds were late, just beginning to appear on the winter-bare Minnesota trees, though the grass, paled by winter snows, was starting to grow again. Fleecy clouds rode the sky, and robins spelled spring. Through rolling farmlands and fragrant, new-plowed fields the Australians rode a Jefferson bus to the Twin Cities, to be deposited in a cramped hotel room. Mary pushed her suitcase under her narrow bed and dropped like a rock.

"Tired of an eight-by-ten?" Liza asked. "We'll be going home soon."

Still, there was always tomorrow. At the Gillette State Hospital for Crippled Children the next day, Liza found the 1939 victims, aching and emaciated, strapped into their frames, splints, and casts. The day after, she met Dr. Wallace Cole, chief of orthopedics at the University of Minnesota Medical School and the man Henderson at Mayo had most wanted her to see. Cole was an independent, tough-minded professor at a growing, independent-minded school, and like some of his Twin Cities colleagues he was repelled by current treatment results.

For three days Liza demonstrated for Cole and Dr. George Williamson of St. Paul at three Twin Cities hospitals. At the St. Paul Children's Hospital she saw a two-year-old boy. One of his feet had dropped badly, toes down, heel up. His other foot was in the opposite position, extreme dorsiflexion, toes up, heel down. "These conditions are not caused by paralysis. They are caused by spasm," Liza said emphatically. The doctors, tolerant if confused, let Liza and Mary treat the boy, and within three days both deformities had been corrected.

She similarly aroused live but dormant muscles, stimulating them and dramatically making the muscle tendons stand out, in a boy with a stiff arm and deformed spine, immobilized for five months. In several cases, often within minutes, she demonstrated the existence of muscles that could respond to a proper summons, though for months they had remained unused.

"I think you'd better stick around for a while," Cole said. He drove her to the sprawling university on a high bluff of the Mississippi River where it cuts through Minneapolis and St. Paul as it flows down from the north. At 8 A.M., she was introduced to a group of staff and attending orthopedists and other faculty men. From her endless supply, she drew a sheaf of papers and reports. For more than an hour, in a deep, droning monotone that concealed her emotion, she recited reports and testimonials. Her audience fidgeted. What did she *do*?

She insisted on explaining to them that in polio the main problems were not caused by cell destruction and irreversible paralysis but by what she now was describing as three untreated conditions. The cardinal difficulty, she said, was the *spasm*: muscle tightness and shortening, causing pain, tenderness, and tenseness and pulling the opposite muscles from their normal position, thus distorting the skeleton. This caused a second symptom, *mental alienation*, a kind of pseudoparalysis in the opposing muscles, an inability to produce a movement even though nerve paths were intact. In effect, the patient had forgotten how to use the alienated muscle. Third, an affected patient involuntarily resorted to *incoordination* or jerky, ineffectual use of the wrong muscles, resulting in grotesque motion. If muscles in spasm were left untreated, their alienated opposites eventually atrophied, while those in spasm became hard, fibrous, and inelastic, pulling the skeleton into permanent deformities. If tight and alienated muscles were left in casts, she concluded, the stretching, immobilization, and unrelieved pain aggravated spasm and compounded the damage.

Her explanation was not in fact this clear or simple; it was murky and involved, and several of her terms—"spasm," "mental alienation," "mental awareness"—were peculiar. Some of the Minnesota listeners shrugged her off. One who did not was Dr. Miland Knapp, at thirty-five a patient yet highly progressive doctor, by training a surgeon, who headed the year-old Department of Physical Therapy in the medical school, so new it was not yet called "physical medicine." He felt he had to know more. She was no lecturer, he decided. Maybe her performance would be better.

"I have a patient I'd like you to see," he said, and drove her to St. Barnabas Hospital, near downtown Minneapolis. His patient was a boy named Jack Ruff, still under treatment eight months after a harsh polio attack. One leg was affected; he also had a paralyzed deltoid or shoulder muscle; his shoulder and arm were fixed hard and fast in an "airplane splint" that held the arm out like the wing of an aircraft. According to standard theory, his affected muscles were now limp, weak, and "flaccid," like old, saggy ropes.

Liza looked at the doctor and said, "What do you mean, flaccid paralysis? If you take that arm out of that contraption, you'll find it's so stiff you can't even force it to the boy's side."

Knapp removed the splint. The arm dropped a bit but still stood out like the broken wing of a bird.

"That is the result of untreated spasm," Liza said.

Jack's parents and Knapp accepted her offer to treat the boy. By the time snow fell again, he was outside shoveling. His affected arm was still weak, but he could use it and do the hard pushing with his strong arm. Within two years he was skating and bicycling.

On May 21, six days after Liza's arrival in Minneapolis, Dr. Williamson ordered the frames, splints, and casts removed from all his cases at Gillette and St. Paul Children's hospitals. Cole and Knapp agreed that further investigation was necessary.

"What would you need to stay?" Cole asked Liza.

"A bed and a meal a day," she replied.

Cole talked to Medical School Dean Harold S. Diehl, and Diehl phoned O'Connor. O'Connor promised support from March of Dimes funds. Knapp meantime asked Liza and Mary to stay at his home for several days while she explained her concepts to him. Knapp said later that "it took me two months to figure out what she was talking about." Meanwhile she visited more patients, with more cases, in Knapp's words, of "return of function in apparently paralyzed muscles after a few minutes of reeducation."

On May 28 Liza and Mary found an apartment on University Avenue, and with relief they unpacked their ports. Spring had at last arrived. Lilacs bloomed in profusion, robins hustled for worms, and pheasants strolled out of the brush along the river banks. "We had thought the green would never come," Mary remembers. "We were hungry for it."

The conversion of Minnesota doctors had only begun. Most remained skeptical, and one such was Dr. John Pohl. Pohl at thirty-six was a rising Minneapolis specialist and the attending orthopedist at the city hospital. He had trained at Harvard and Boston Children's Hospital and had been taught strict immobilization; Boston, in Dr. Kristian Hansson's words, was "the fountain of knowledge" of polio treatment. Pohl had a lanky frame and lean, Yankeelike visage, though he was actually of German ancestry. He was highly skeptical of the Kenny woman, but he was tired of hearing the crying of children in casts.

He had a patient just back from Warm Springs, Henry Haverstock, Jr., eighteen-year-old son of a prominent attorney. Henry had been struck by polio in 1939; he had received the usual treatment for five months, then been sent to Georgia, where he was given skilled standard physiotherapy for four more. He was also fitted there with two steel leg braces, a steel-and-canvas body corset, and an arm splint. Just returned to Minneapolis, he still had a curved spine, a paralyzed right leg, an all but paralyzed, useless left leg, a weak arm, and weak chest, back, and abdominal muscles. He had been told he would never be able to walk without braces, but he could not do even that. He was confined to his bed, where he could not be forced into a sitting position.

Uncertainly, Pohl took Liza to the Haverstocks, where she found Henry in his bedroom, propped up a bit. The senior Haverstock and Pohl carried him down the stairs and put him on the dining room table where the nurse examined him. "He is suffering principally from neglect of treatment of his true symptoms," she announced. Pohl, after some thought, moved the youth to Abbott Hospital, a specialists' center where he practiced, for Liza's care.

The first thing she did, naturally, was to discard young Henry's corset and braces. Two staff orthopedists promptly informed the administrator that if he continued to harbor "that quack from Australia," the hospital would be disgraced. But Liza and Mary continued, while the whole hospital watched. With heat, then movement, they relieved pain and tightness and began teaching Henry to use the muscles that real paralysis had not made useless. Within a week he could straighten one contracted leg. Before the end of the year he walked out of his room with a pair of hand crutches. His treatment continued for some time; his movement never became normal, but by spring 1942 he was able to start attending the University of Minnesota and he walked twenty-one flights of steps every day. With walking sticks and a good deal of courage, he ultimately became an actively practicing lawyer.

Henry's case made the reserved Pohl an evangelistic Kenny convert. It also attracted the attention of other doctors. Liza began lecturing repeatedly at the university and the city hospital. Cole and Knapp again conferred. Warm weather and possibly new polio cases were coming; both felt a thorough study should be made at a single site. Knapp suggested the city institution, the old gray-stone and yellow-brick Minneapolis General Hospital,* affiliated with the university and best equipped to treat acute patients.

Pohl headed the hospital's Infantile Paralysis Clinic, so it fell to him to take Liza before the Minneapolis Board of Public Welfare. This time she wore a hat with a plume of flowers sprouting from the crown, "quite out of style," a witness remembers, "yet on her it didn't look silly, it only added to her dignity." She arose, dipped into her briefcase, and began reading her unintelligible documents. Heeding Pohl, the board voted her space and equipment.

The season's first polio case did not appear until August. Her first March of Dimes maintenance check slow in coming, she and Mary sat in their cramped kitchenette much of the summer and made meals of bread, butter, and tea, alternated with economy-grade hamburger. Lunch and dinner invitations provided their only decent fare, and Liza told Mary that if she saw another hamburger, she would scream. The nurse finally got a $400 check in September and, after a few months more, a regular $65 monthly for rent, $23 for food, and nothing for luxuries. One reason for the delay was her irritation with red tape: asked to account for the first $400, she said curtly that she and her "niece" had spent it for winter coats; she considered that sufficient explanation.[8] She intro-

* Now Hennepin County Medical Center.

duced Mary as her "niece" or "ward" because she felt that Americans might not understand how she happened to have a daughter.

There were only a few new polio cases that year, but they were all she and Mary could handle. In October all the patients were moved to Station K at the city hospital, now to be called the Kenny ward. It was dowdy, but it was clean and ample and hers. Pohl, Cole, and their medical colleagues agreed to give the visitor pretty much a free hand. She could now use her latest and best knowledge on the new cases, with the help of a willing medical and nursing staff.

She put on a long white hospital gown stenciled "ISOLATION." She bent over a patient like a gardener over a plant. Her hands and wrists slightly arched, she ran a finger delicately over a stricken limb or moved the limb in smooth patterns.

She approached a bedside: a typical new patient, an eight-year-old blonde girl lying in rigid pain in the first, acute stage of polio, her contorted knees drawn up to her abdomen. "Now there," said the old battler, "we're going to help you." Her eyes softened, but her lips remained firm and her jaw set. A registered nurse at her side wrung pieces of wool blanketing through a portable wringer, a galvanized iron tub on legs, assembled to Sister Kenny's specifications. The assistant wrung each hot cloth twice, lifted it with a forceps, folded it double, then handed it to Liza.[9]

The girl's eyes were fixed on her. Working quickly, she covered affected part after affected part, wrapping sore muscles but leaving joints free wherever possible. "To maintain joint consciousness," she explained. "And so we can treat her. We don't even want her to *feel* immobilized."

The child whimpered. She could not even bear the touch of the bedclothes. "This girl is in acute spasm," Liza said. "We must apply fresh packs every fifteen minutes until the pain is relieved." It was done for two hours before the overweary girl fell asleep. "From now on you will pack her every two hours, twelve hours a day," Liza ordered.

When the girl awoke, she began the next step. "Now we will teach her mental awareness," she told the nurse-assistant. To the child: "Relax, honey. Think of nothing, and give me your leg." Delicately, to avoid aggravating pain and spasm, Liza put one hand under the girl's knee and the other under her heel. "Think of nothing," Liza repeated. "Think of a footless stocking without a leg."

Liza slowly raised the leg, bending hip and knee, until she reached a point where the girl barely winced. She then stopped, just short of causing pain. She moved the leg farther in this way each day, bending and straightening it in its customary arcs to achieve "tendon stimulation."

"At first it's like moving a dead leg," Liza told one of her new helpers. But after a full week of this therapy, all pain and soreness now gone as a result of regular application of hot packs, Liza at last felt a slight pull against her. This was the muscle tone, the spark that promised movement. Physiologically, she had aroused an involuntary, reflex movement, a proprioceptive reflex. These reflexes originate in nerve endings in the muscles, tendons, and joints, making them terminals that communicate with the brain to inform it of position and motion. This process provides much of a person's muscle sense.

All the treatment so far had employed only passive movements. For voluntary movement, movement the patient controlled, the girl would need the nerves of both the spinal cord and the higher brain centers. So now Liza stroked the area over the affected hip muscle, the hip flexor.

"This is your iliopsoas muscle," she said. "Don't try to move it, but *think* of it moving."

Liza repeatedly flexed and straightened the leg, while the child, tense and alert, concentrated. Again and again, Liza stroked and sometimes even slapped the area over the target muscle to make the girl aware of it.

"Now *you* do it," Liza said, continuing to stroke. "*Help* me move it." The stroking, the instructions, and the motion, she explained to her trainees, were all stimulation, aimed at her patient's tactile, auditory, and proprioceptive senses or reflexes.

The patient exhibited a slight trembling, a mere quiver. But it was a first result. As soon as she knew which muscles had latent life, Liza in this way began muscle reeducation, first by passive motion, then by active retraining of each muscle in its proper motion. Each day now this girl was placed on a treatment table, and Liza helped her flex her leg. Each day Liza asked for "one last try for today." Almost every day the girl was able to do a little more, while Liza watched meticulously to see that no muscles other than the one being trained that day were put into play. That would have been incoordination.

Cautiously, Liza stretched the little girl's tightened body structures, as her stiff joints audibly cracked. The child herself gradually learned to exercise and train both muscles permanently weakened by polio and normal muscles that had too long been inactive. All this and daily hot packing continued for three months—in some cases it was ten—until Liza was satisfied that all tightness and spasm were gone.

Then she said, "Now you have to learn to walk again, child." And: "It's got to be done right. We want you coordinated." For a few days the patient was allowed to try merely standing. Then she was taught each part of the complex act of walking, one movement at a time: "Bend your hip and knee—keep the other leg straight. Now straighten this one, put all your weight into it! Now bend the other leg." And continuing: "Stand up real straight. Look straight ahead. Keep those hips level! Now step, step, a little faster, come on. Now try again." Then: "That's better. Bend your knee. That's-a-girl."

Nurse Kenny treated a girl of ten, Rita Neville, whom she called one of the most severely affected patients she had ever seen. Rita was carried into the hospital completely paralyzed on one side; her head was pulled backward by her involved back, neck, and shoulder muscles, and she was unable to swallow. The diagnosis was bulbar polio, affecting the brain stem: her doctor had given her the conventional treatment for two days, while she grew worse. He then called Pohl, who advised that he turn her over to Sister Kenny. It took Pohl an hour to convince him to do so, and when he did, the reluctant physician also sent for a priest to administer extreme unction.

Liza listened to Rita breathe in shallow gasps and said she did not have a 5 percent chance for life, "but we'll see." She called for hot packs. In a few hours the girl's breathing became slightly easier. Liza stayed at her bedside for eight hours, hot packing her and instructing a special-duty nurse. The next day the treatment continued. Liza said that the odds had changed to 95 percent in Rita's favor.

The second morning the previously doubtful physician examined Rita, then sought out Liza to say: "You have taken me back to the Middle Ages. The day of miracles has not passed."

"It's not a miracle, doctor," she said. "It's simply understanding the symptoms of the disease."[10] Six years later, when the city was suffering the worst polio epidemic in its history to that date, Rita, age sixteen, spent her summer vacation as a volunteer in Kenny wards.

Liza Kenny on Station K at Minneapolis General Hospital treated both new patients and those who had first undergone days or weeks of immobilization without benefit, while their faces became stiff masks from their long pain and their limbs ached. "Feel those abdominals!" she would say indignantly on inspecting such a patient. "You can't use them to bend, can you? It's like trying to bend steel because your neck and back are so tight." Or: "Feel those tendons, tight as iron bands. See how that foot is turned in. That's tightness!"

She looked at her Minnesota patients with professional detachment;

she had learned to wear the mask of the trained practitioner. This was a mature American Elizabeth Kenny, with Nobby, Townsville, and Brisbane behind her. She had already made most of her mistakes; her experience went back to 1911. Here it all came together.

She shunned the word "cure" now, saying, "I do not claim that a complete cure for infantile paralysis has been established." She still hated to admit that polio victims often suffered nerve cell destruction, causing irreversible paralysis; yet she knew this condition existed, and at the insistence of her newest medical friends she faced up to it. She would do her utmost to arouse what she called "sleeping" reflexes, but if she failed, she knew there must be irreversible damage and she said so. Reeducation, it was true, might still help other muscles, and the patient might benefit; but she could not promise every patient the sun and the moon. She carefully used her eyes and touch as guides, then concentrated her care on the patients for whom she could do the most good.

She was still inventive. She saw that cold sheets irritated muscles in spasm, so she ordered that patients be tucked between blankets. She used footboards to keep bedclothes off sensitive toes and to keep feet at a right angle, maintaining standing reflexes. She called this "standing up in bed" and vehemently denied that it was anything like standard splinting. She still used her hot, then cold, spray baths to promote circulation in chronic cases. She ordered "the hardest beds in the world" to keep bodies straight.

She gave as much thought to psyches. She told her staff that the patients had to be happy or they would not cooperate. She winked and grinned, therefore, and genuinely enjoyed giving treatments, once acute pain subsided. "She does not baby her patients. She does not even baby the babies," one doctor noted. Yet her polio wards, once places of silence, became noisy and filled with laughter. Another medical observer said, "I have never seen a happier group in a polio ward in my life."[11] Elizabeth Kenny was to receive much credit for this accomplishment. All it took, actually, were children without pain and an optimistic therapist going from bed to bed joking.

The children worked for her. Their shouting quieted when she entered a room. The lines in her face relaxed. When she said hello to a child she smiled. But the smile soon disappeared, and she became a grave teacher. Or a conductor. "Now you can do this," she would say. "You *can* lift your foot." She spent hours with the children. One doctor thought she mesmerized them.

She addressed children simply and directly, however, never patronizing them, just telling them the truth about their illness in whatever language they could understand. "They must understand the facts," she said, "if they are to help the therapist help them." She would win a three-year-old girl's confidence by demonstrating exercises on her doll.

She sometimes handled children like a mother, lifting them to her breast and fondling them. She would stroke a tense child's hand, and his muscles would relax a little. "Her hand felt like a velvet glove," daughter Mary says. "No wonder so many people said she had the healing touch." And Dr. Pohl remembers that "she handled a limb like a fine watchmaker handling a watch. She instinctively seemed to know how to pick up a limb without causing a child pain. And children instinctively seemed to sense it." The children "got real love. . . . She ended any pretense and was never showy. . . . She was just natural, and they came to her like moths." So go many memories.

Yet, observes one of her nurses, she would habitually remember a child by the disability. A boy or girl was "always a trapezius or a deltoid to her," always a patient. Nothing brought a light into her eyes like a *sick* child, and the sicker the child, the greater the light. It was the sick child who needed *her*.

She hated polio, certainly. "Infantile paralysis is a damnable thing," she said. "It leaves a child neither dead nor alive."[12] Time after time she sat up all night with a patient. Yet even here her emotions remained mixed. Some of her nurses wondered whether she was interested mainly in saving the patient or in proving to a doctor that she could succeed where he had failed.

For whatever reasons, for all of them, probably, she worked eighteen hours a day, Sunday through Sunday, in these crucial months, taking advantage of the best medical facility and the most complete medical cooperation she had yet attained. She awoke at 4:30 A.M. in her dark little apartment, shook the sleep from her body, called a taxi, and was at a bedside by 5:30, to work until midnight. The next morning she would be on hand early again, her face still unawake, its lines deep. Then as day came and the children awoke and began shouting—"Good morning, Sister!"—she could throw off her weariness to grin back and start treatments.

She paused to drink her cold tea, ever cold by the time she drank it. "You know," one nurse told her, "we have a name for you—the Iron Horse."

"I came down with polio at a girl's camp," remembers a woman who was eighteen when she was treated by Elizabeth Kenny.[13] "And when I was told I was being taken to Sister Kenny, I thought I was going to a nun." But soon: "I thought I was bound to get well if she was taking care of me. She *was* stern. She was big. But her only interest was the patient. Here was this big, powerful woman, and she had the touch of a baby. Some of the doctors would try her procedures and practically kill us. One doctor came up to me and said, 'If I had you, you'd be in a complete body brace.' So I thought she was the greatest lady in the world."

11

Victory

SHE WAS TAUT, eager to prevail. Day after day, she donned a saggy, old print dress from the bargain rack in Brisbane and lectured to distinguished professors. Young interns and residents were astonished to see their chiefs quietly listening while, in the amazed words of one, "this *nurse* told *them* the score."

Minneapolis General Hospital was badly overcrowded, and she had to conduct some clinics and demonstrations on a stairway landing between elevators. The elevators discharged laundry and food carts, and interns and nurses on duty skipped up and down the stairs while she pressed on. "No, *no* splinting," she lectured. And: "If you want to learn what I have to teach, you must understand that the disease you are familiar with *does not exist.*" Questioned sharply—a standard practice in medicine—she would snap, "It's just as I say!"

Some such meetings broke up in ill feeling. Those doctors who returned, however, might see a patient who had been muscle-tested at zero before Kenny treatment, and she would present him and say: "You will see that he can now stand alone without support and doesn't buckle anywhere despite the fact that he has very little strength. So much for your muscle-testing." Impressed, one young Mayo Clinic doctor told his superiors that "the first acute case I saw demonstrated such severe spasm of the hamstrings in the right leg that on attempting to straighten the knee out, the tendons . . . stood out like a knife edge. It was impossible for the child to straighten the leg, and when forced to do so there were extreme pain and more severe spasm. Hot fomentations were applied and in three days the child's leg was out perfectly straight with no pain."

Liza and Mary treated twenty-six acute and subacute cases at Minneapolis General Hospital in 1940. Rochester's Dr. Henderson paid several visits and wrote Basil O'Connor: "Miss Kenny has the spirit of a crusader, but I believe she has something worthwhile to offer us." In December the university's Cole and Knapp wrote a first report. They were cautious, but said: "We think it is possible and appropriate to state definitely that these patients with acute infantile paralysis are much more comfortable and cheerful . . . than are those cases who are immobilized, and that we have seen absolutely no contractures . . . following this treatment. Even the most severely paralyzed patient has passively full range of motion in all his joints. No scoliosis or other spinal deformity has developed in these cases, and most of them are more limber than they were before the onset of the disease. . . . We believe that the paralysis is less severe than would be expected in nearly every case."

They added that "this method may well be the basis of the future treatment of infantile paralysis," and they submitted their conclusions to the *Journal of the American Medical Association.*[1]

People discovered that they had a medical messiah in their midst. The governor's wife entertained her, and she spoke on the radio. A nurse from "the wild bush," the newspapers termed her.[2]

Socialites began inviting Sister Kenny and "ward" Mary to dinner or tea. They were too busy with their patients most of the time, so they had to refuse and sustain life on gray hospital food. When they did accept an invitation, the rugged nurse was likely to blurt out, "I have to go home," as soon as dinner was finished. Mary then made up white lies to cover the embarrassment. Or when Mary managed to get Liza to a movie, she might again say, "Let's go." She had usually been struck by some thought about "the work" that she felt compelled to write down that instant.

Mary would sigh and tag along. Apple-cheeked, red-haired Mary, once bound to Nobby, was now deputy therapist, instructor, secretary, cook, maid, handservant, and daughter. She was still kept in strict tow: no dates, no "American" makeup. The young woman had sneaked on some lipstick on board ship from Australia; at age twenty-three, it was the first time she had used it. "Take it off!" Liza demanded. In Minneapolis, young men asked her for dates, but she was afraid to ask Liza for permission. Finally she cried to "Sister"—as she, just like everyone else, called Liza—"The nurses are saying I must have done something wrong because you won't trust me." "Sister" softened, and Mary began dating. But Liza insisted that there always had to be at least two couples on the date. Mary put on a little lipstick and even had her first drink.

Good results at the hospital had begun to mellow Liza. "Mary," she sighed, "if it just weren't so cold." The winter meant below-zero weather and deep snow and ice, which usually covered the ground from December to March. On Armistice Day, the area had its worst blizzard in fifty years. Liza donned a pair of black-buttoned gaiters, like a Church of England cleric's, to protect her lame leg. She should have chosen galoshes. After a patients' Christmas party on the afternoon of December 23, she went home to prepare dinner—Dr. Pohl was expected—and discovered there was no cream. She put on her gaiters and set out for the store; on the way back she slipped on the ice and broke her right wrist. In pain, she somehow got home, took a good look at her crooked, throbbing arm, and pulled it straight. Pohl arrived and decided she needed somewhat more skilled orthopedic attention. He took her to Abbott Hospital.

She warned him that she must have no anesthetic and yielded up the fact of her wartime "bad heart." Pohl got a heart man to look at her. "Hell," he told Pohl, "she's got a heart like an ox." He also told Liza that he could find nothing wrong with her heart. She gave him a queer look, said not a word, and meekly took the anesthetic.[3]

She hated being slowed down. "Why did it have to happen just when I was trying to show these thickheads and doubting Thomases?" she asked Mary. "Maybe the good Lord meant you to rest," Mary answered. One week after the accident, Nurse Kenny was back at General Hospital treating patients and balancing their stiff, rigid limbs on her own plaster cast.

She began pestering Drs. Cole, Pohl, and Knapp: when could she start teaching others? They did not really need prodding. She would begin special classes at the University of Minnesota as a guest instructor in spring. Pohl also persuaded several leading physical therapists to visit

Minneapolis; a group in mid-January 1941 included Alice Lou Plastridge of Georgia Warm Springs and Henry and Florence Kendall of Baltimore. The Kendalls combined early splinting with restrained exercise plus splinting in the convalescent period.

First, Liza lectured—mainly her "life history and the story of her success against great odds," the unpersuaded Kendalls would report to the National Foundation. She then described her concept of the disease and presented several patients. The Kendalls listened in strong disbelief. They returned the next morning, and Liza elaborated. Discussion followed.

As the Kendalls told it, Mrs. Kendall started by assuring Sister Kenny that she truly had a "contribution" to make in relief of spasm; as to other tenets, like no immobilizing, they *probably* would find in open-minded discussion that there were not as many differences between them as there appeared to be. This was not Liza's style. "Mrs. Kendall," she answered, "you say there is no difference between my treatment and yours, and I maintain they are entirely opposite." As Dr. Knapp, who was present, put it, "it was like trying to get an agreement between Winston Churchill and Hitler."

The Kendalls suggested that they defer discussion until Dr. Pohl and other doctors arrived. They pointed out that Dr. Pohl had invited them to observe the treatment. Liza said she didn't care what Pohl had done, she did not intend to show them any treatment. And they saw none. "Attended demonstrations Station K all day," Mary scribbled in her diary that night. "The least said, the better."

The Kendalls in their report strongly backed current methods and said no evaluation of the Kenny technique was possible without detailed statistical study. And because Sister Kenny forbade muscle-testing—they were its main advocates—they concluded that she should not be entrusted with teaching muscle action.[4] Liza's view of the Kendalls was equally unflattering. She reported that when they visited Station K, they predicted that one eight-year-old boy would develop a deformed foot within a few months because he had not been splinted. Liza's arm still in a cast, she concentrated on the boy for days, and there was no deformity.

Before long she turned over the therapy to Mary, so she could return to Australia. There was acute polio in Queensland, and she wanted to show her newly refined methods to her Australian therapists. She also wanted to show American skeptics that her results depended on no personal magnetism, that "Mary or any properly trained person can give the treatment as well as I can."

In Brisbane she found that new patients were still being given their choice of Kenny or conventional treatment. Most were choosing Kenny, but she thought that making distraught parents decide was "not in any way" in keeping with the dignity of the medical profession. She was further irked to find that the so-called non-Kenny treatment now included whatever "Kenny" they could recall from her lectures. She found patients with muscles still in active spasm being submerged in water, just because she had written in 1937, vaguely, to be sure, of bathtub treatment for chronic patients. Her protests were futile.[5]

She returned to the United States with two of her best technicians, Bill Bell, the son of her Guyra cousins, and Valerie Harvey, a wisp of a thing but a mighty nurse. Valerie's mother had met forceful Liza and had seen American gangster movies. "You can go to America," she told Valerie, "but two things I warn you never to do. Never go to Chicago, and *never* live with Sister Kenny."

Alice Lou Plastridge, expert Warm Springs polio therapist, made no report on the basis of the stormy January inspection. But with Liza off in Australia, she returned to observe Mary work. Then she wrote her report. Then and later, she characterized Liza as a woman with a mission who "raises your ire to the boiling point." Discussing the Warm Springs warm swimming pool therapy, for example, Liza had said, "You may as well fill up your puddles and make gardens of them." Her "pet trick," furthermore, was to march in two patients, one who was doing beautifully and another who was badly contracted. "She would show the two and say: 'This is the Kenny-treated case and that is the orthodox.' She would always pick out the most deformed patient for comparisons. Think of the psychological effect on the patient!"

Yet, Miss Plastridge concluded, Sister Kenny's antagonism was probably the result of the ridicule heaped on her for so long. "When she is in a friendly atmosphere and does not feel the need for 'fighting for her rights,' she has a fine sense of humor." She certainly was not a good lecturer or teacher; she was "neither scientific nor logical," although "she does know her anatomy." Whether or not her theories were scientifically sound, only time and further investigation could prove. "But the fact remains that she is getting such unusually good results that it does not seem possible that they could all be a matter of chance. One thing is certain. Her controversial theories have given a tremendous stimulation to further research in this field, and made many of us take serious stock of ourselves in the type of physical therapy we are doing."[6]

Liza soon returned to the United States to speak to the New York State Medical Society, a prime invitation. She was invited to make rounds at the New York Orthopedic Hospital. She found twenty-four patients in splints and casts; her icy reaction chilled most of the senior staff, but some of the young Turks were intrigued, and before long they started a Kenny treatment study.

Liza arrived in Minneapolis in May. Cole and Knapp's enthusiastic report appeared on June 7, 1941, in the *Journal of the American Medical Association.* Toned down somewhat by editor Fishbein, it was still a piece of medical fireworks, appearing as it did on the threshhold of a new polio season.

The University of Minnesota won a new National Foundation grant to study the Kenny treatment, with further maintenance funds for Liza and the Australian therapists. She was allocated a seventeen-bed ward at University Hospitals in addition to her Minneapolis General Hospital station. Polio incidence started rising in July. By August the outbreak was far worse, and both of the Kenny wards were filling up. She was being sent the worst of the entire state's cases, the hopeless and the terrible cases, she said later. They were the kind of cases any new treatment attracts. With poliomyelitis, this meant those patients most severely paralyzed, those in excruciating agony, and those whose paralysis was choking off their breath.

Dawn to dark again, running from hospital to hospital, treating, supervising, quarreling a little, and training. She fell into bed at eight one night and was quickly asleep. At ten the phone rang. Two sisters, fourteen and eighteen, hardly able to breathe, were en route by ambulance from a nearby town. The plan was to rush them into respirators. The iron lung had become a vital lifesaving tool in such cases, but Liza believed it was overused. Its use also hampered her treatment.

She hurried to the university and dozed on a duty officer's cot. The girls arrived at 5 A.M., one already blue from lack of breath. Liza asked the ward doctor if she could keep them out of the respirator for a few hours. He nodded. She wrapped hot packs around each girl's upper trunk and neck to relieve what she believed to be severe spasm of the intercostal and pectoral muscles and the diaphragm. She asked them to inhale to expand the thorax and exhale to contract the diaphragm, while she gently depressed their floating ribs. Her face calm, her eyes steady and convincing, she told them, "I am trying to restore the brain path. I'll help and you'll help." Their breathing improved as she kept up the intense treatment for hours, bending over them, touching, watching, placing the foments, and reteaching breathing. Their breathing became less labored, their color improved. Both lived and made good recoveries.

She took another patient, a ten-year-old boy, from a respirator where he had spent twenty-three hours a day. She had him breathing normally and eating well in a day. She treated a boy, eighteen, who had been in a respirator for three months. She also ordered that he be taken out. The doctors agreed but insisted he be kept near the iron lung "just in case." A few weeks later they phoned her. "He's dying," she was told. "We've put him back in." She rushed to the hospital and decided their diagnosis was right. But, she said, "If he's dying anyway, it won't hurt to take him out of the respirator again and let me work on him." He too recovered.[7]

"Spontaneous recoveries," some critics still scoffed. Some of her patients remained paralyzed, and some died. In speaking and lecturing, she still sometimes said erroneous, obviously unscientific things that made many doctors shake their heads. More and more, however, the doctors who saw her work were being won over.

At their peril, some had begun crusading. John Pohl, who was interested in discussing her ideas with his former professors, visited Harvard. "Oh, you're out there in Minneapolis. Say, what kind of damned fool is she?" one asked.[8]

Dr. Miland Knapp was invited to speak at a medical convention in Milwaukee. The invitation came from Dr. Robert Bennett of Warm Springs, who had been a trainee of Krusen's at Rochester. Expecting the worst reception, Knapp told Bennett that he had better order an ambulance to get him back home. "The ambulance is ordered," Bennett replied. Knapp got away with no bones broken and left some listeners interested.[9]

Liza wrote the polio foundation asking by what action, if any, they intended to introduce "the work" to the entire country. The organization's medical director, Dr. Don W. Gudakunst, replied that the subject would be considered by the group's Medical Advisory Committee in December. She wrote a short book called *The Treatment of Infantile Paralysis in the Acute Stage*. She neglected to have anyone edit it, and Gudakunst wrote an associate: "I don't wonder that you have had difficulty in obtaining any information from Elizabeth Kenny's book. I am of the opinion that it is one of the worst attempts to describe a technique that I have ever encountered." She herself later wrote that it "contained many things that were not scientific."[10]

She did better at raising money. More city funds were needed for her ward at General Hospital. A stalwart of the city welfare board was an energetic grain merchant named I. S. Joseph; fellow Jews called him "the city assessor" because he was always raising money for causes.

"I'm a businessman, not a doctor," he told her when she sought his support.

"You wouldn't have to be more than a tapeworm with one eye to see that my system of treating polio is superior," she retorted. That was one of her favorite themes. Joseph and his colleagues voted her all that she needed. A wealthy couple, the C. C. Webbers, asked how they could help, and they contributed a sum for nurses' scholarships. Eight young Americans began training under Liza and her Australian assistants, who were better teachers than she. Still, the new trainees agreed, she was a mine of information "once you could get it from her."

She also knew how to make them work independently. The new group had been in training for nearly six months when some visiting doctors arrived. She asked a few of the young women to demonstrate hot packing, and they added a few things she hadn't shown them.

"Well, that's the Americans," she said. "Show them a peach, and they'll grow a bigger one."

She turned to trainee Vivian Hannan, a strong and resourceful individual, and said, "Now you show them the treatment."

"I *can't*," Miss Hannan whispered.

"Yes, you can," said Liza. "You have to."

It was Hannan's final examination. From then on, she did the demonstrations for visitors.[11]

In the August 17, 1941, issue of the *American Weekly*, circulated to millions of homes with Hearst Sunday newspapers, Robert D. Potter, science editor, reported that "a new and revolutionary treatment for infantile paralysis is now being tested and demonstrated. In her quiet apartment near the University of Minnesota, I talked with this remarkable woman who someday may go down in medical history along with Madame Curie, Florence Nightingale, and Clara Barton."

And opening the lead article of the December 1941 *Reader's Digest*: "Dr. Aeneas John McDonnell, chief surgeon of Toowoomba General Hospital in Queensland, Australia, read a longish telegram . . . and shook his head sadly. Sister Elizabeth Kenny . . . needed advice in treating four children." Millions read these first major American journalistic reports on "this remarkable, strong-minded woman" with her "one-woman war," as the *Digest*'s Lois Mattox Miller described her.

But was the strong-minded woman right or wrong? The National Foundation for Infantile Paralysis was watching the treatment closely for an answer. The young, inexperienced organization had no official medical status. It was not a doctors' but a laymen's body. At a time when federal health spending was still small, it was nonetheless the nucleus of thought and support in polio care, research, and training. It had designated three on-the-spot observers of Sister Kenny: Drs. Cole and Knapp in the Twin Cities and Henderson in Rochester. In addition, the wary O'Connor had named a Minnesota subcommittee of three to advise his Committee on Research for the Prevention and Treatment of After-Effects; these three were Cole (Knapp acted as his deputy for a time), Krusen of Rochester, and Dr. Irvine McQuarrie, the University of Minnesota's noted chief of pediatrics. Krusen, when invited in early 1941, had written O'Connor that he would be glad to serve, but he was extremely dubious about Miss Kenny's claims. Fine, O'Connor answered, that particularly qualified him.[12]

By midyear, however, McQuarrie surprised Krusen by telling him, "If one of my children had polio, I would want him to have the Kenny treatment." On his travels, O'Connor was hearing similar statements. So were some of his principal advisers, in particular the American Medical Association's powerful Dr. Fishbein. One strenuously disagreed: a Chicago orthopedic surgeon, Dr. Philip W. Lewin. Short, chubby Phil Lewin looked like a bookkeeper for a grain warehouse, but he was a leading orthopedist and headed the Committee on After-Effects. In October, Cole and Knapp made a new and detailed medical report. Lewin went to Minneapolis to see for himself and was convinced. In November he put the subject before his committee, and, the record reads, "violent disagreement" broke out and no action could be taken. Lewin remembers it as "the hottest debate we'd ever had."[13]

Still, other glowing reports began reaching both committee members and Gudakunst. Unable to accept them, a few members resigned. Fishbein, Lewin, and O'Connor now agreed unofficially that Sister Kenny was substantially right and that some dramatic way of saying so was necessary to jolt orthopedists and change entrenched ways of treatment. They decided they would have to capture the attention of both doctors and the public.

On December 3, 1941, the Committee on After-Effects was recalled, and this time—better briefed—it agreed on a unanimous and highly favorable statement: "It is the opinion of this committee . . . after a study of a report of the workers at the University of Minnesota, that during the early stage of infantile paralysis, the length of time during which pain, tenderness and spasm are present is greatly reduced, and contractures caused by muscle shortening . . . are prevented by the Kenny method."* The American Medical Association simultaneously issued the text of an editorial to be published in the December 6 issue of its prestigious *Journal*, Dr. Fishbein's fief. The editorial vigorously approved the general principles of stimulating instead of immobilizing the muscles in the early stages of polio. There was no experimental evidence that Sister Kenny's treatment could revive degenerated nerve connections, the *Journal* emphasized, but past damage to polio patients may have been far worse than was necessary.

The medical association and the polio foundation both issued press releases. O'Connor and Fishbein spoke on the radio on a coast-to-coast hookup—this was a decade before television. The next day the foundation added that three independent groups of investigators had tended to confirm Liza's bush methods.[14]

Dr. Donald Young Solandt and his associates at the University of Toronto reported that completely immobilizing an animal's limb produced the same kind of muscle changes as nerve-cutting or nerve removal.

Dr. Harry M. Hines and associates at the State University of Iowa cut through rats' nerves to paralyze their leg muscles. They then put one group of rats on a treadmill to exercise several hours a day; they put a second group in a pool to swim; they immobilized the limbs of a third group in plaster casts and splints. Both active groups recovered more rapidly and completely than the rats who had rested.

Dr. Arthur Steindler and his associates at Iowa rechecked many of their former polio cases and indeed found that "contractures are not caused by the pull of unbalanced, powerful muscle (as is widely believed) but rather by pathological contracture" of immobilized muscles. The Iowa doctors could now see many of the symptoms she described, symptoms that doctors previously had missed. Steindler did not accept all of her symptoms or procedures; he continued to recommend some immobilization. But he admitted past mistakes and urged muscle retraining along her lines.

* The National Foundation report was coauthored by Dr. Herman N. Bundesen, the flamboyant but effective health commissioner of Chicago. Bundesen also crusaded against venereal disease and dirty restaurants and was known to reporters as "Herman the Vermin."

"SISTER KENNY WINS CRUSADE," said the *Minneapolis Star-Journal.* In winning the approval of the *Journal of the American Medical Association,* she had received "medicine's highest accolade." But the news of it drew "no hint of personal gratification" from Sister Kenny, the newspaper added.[15]

Liza had been alone in her apartment on the early evening of December 3. She was just back from the hospital, and she was hungry and worn. At 6:30 P.M. the phone rang. A reporter was calling to read the National Foundation and American Medical Association statements; he wanted to see her immediately. She said that the crucial thing just then was her dinner, and she would see the press afterward. "Aren't you excited?" he asked. She replied that she was indeed gratified, but that the day was gone "when I could feel any emotion over the publication of a fact that had been evident to me for almost half a lifetime."[16]

There were also a few minor irritations. The AMA editorial mistakenly referred to the use of "massage." "I do no massaging," she had to tell the gathering reporters. "The muscles of an infantile paralysis victim are in spasm, and to massage them would increase the spasm and lead to disaster. Please emphasize that—I do no massaging." In succeeding issues, the medical journal somewhat minimized any revolutionary element in the Kenny method, saying it simply elaborated well-recognized principles. This so infuriated her that in January she phoned the foundation's Dr. Gudakunst collect, threatening to make a lecture tour "exposing the medical profession of the United States." Gudakunst himself objected to such contentions; he wrote an AMA staff member: "Mister, let me say there is a revolutionary element. Hence the unwillingness and even the inability to appreciate just what she has."[17]

However, on that evening in December, her apartment jammed with reporters and cameramen from newspapers, press associations, and newsreels, she knew inner triumph. "It was my hour of victory," she admitted afterward. "My telephone kept ringing constantly. Calls came simultaneously from New York, Chicago and Minneapolis. Newspaper reporters began begging me for personal interviews and pictures. They wondered because I displayed no elation. But I was thinking of others who should be sharing in this triumph, my mother, for one."[18]

Outwardly she maintained the impassive calm she had learned to summon in the face of shattering rejection. "No, this is not unexpected. . . . I hope that now further research may bring forth a more perfect scheme." Inwardly, she danced on clouds. She had no diploma, no certificate, no R.N. or M.D., but now they all said she was right.

12

Revolution

WHAT HAPPENED next was a revolution almost unprecedented in medical history. All over the country, doctors and hospitals switched from splinting and inactivity to heat and activity.

It happened almost overnight. In 1939 the National Foundation had established a central stockpile of Toronto splints—light, shell-shaped immobilization splints—and Bradford frames in the basement of the Third District Courthouse in Manhattan, and by 1941 there were 10,000 such devices there, ready to be flown wherever doctors demanded them. The calls were heavy—4,297 splints had to be added to the stockpile that year. In 1942, after the pro-Kenny endorsements, the demands were far fewer. In 1943 they totaled three. Dust accumulated on the devices for five years, and in 1947 the foundation sold them as scrap. Even earlier, Joseph W. Savage, a foundation official, came across the plot of a Georgia farmer, who was using discarded Warm Springs polio splints as bean poles. He had them neatly pyramided, and beans grew on them profusely.[1]

The polio foundation largely fueled the Kenny revolution. "We are indebted to you for referring Miss Kenny to us," O'Connor wrote Queensland Premier Forgan Smith on February 24, 1942. O'Connor and Gudakunst, his medical director, hurried to Minneapolis to help the University of Minnesota start training courses financed by the March of Dimes for doctors, nurses, and physical therapists. Doctors got a six-day cram course, as did nurses learning to apply hot packs. Physical therapists or nurses who would serve as Kenny therapists studied for two to six months.

Gudakunst attended one of the first courses. So did Drs. Krusen from Rochester and Bennett from Warm Springs, and, in the months that followed, doctors, nurses, and physical therapists from all over the United States and Canada. "Infantile paralysis will lose its terror as the worst child-crippler just as fast as Kenny experts are turned out," columnist Albert Deutsch wrote rather overoptimistically in the New York newspaper *PM*.[2]

The university alone could not meet the demand, so the foundation arranged five additional training centers: Stanford and Northwestern universities, the University of Southern California, the D. T. Watson School of Physical Therapy in Pittsburgh, and Georgia Warm Springs. By October 1942, some 1,000 doctors, physical therapists, and nurses had taken the courses, and the demand was still unmet. Other training centers were started in New York City, Illinois, Indiana, and elsewhere, with trainees then becoming instructors. The University of Minnesota tripled and quadrupled the size of its classes; courses were started for army and navy doctors. By December 1943, this university alone had trained 358 doctors and 484 physical therapists and nurses; by mid-1944, 900 nurses and therapists had been trained.[3]

The revolution in fact pushed the polio foundation into a new field: medical education. It had to begin making basic training grants to increase the nation's supply of physical therapists, as well as of doctors and nurses trained in treating polio. The therapists turned out to be a vitally needed corps when the injuries of World War II finally made the medical world conscious of the need for rehabilitation. The federal government then took over these training programs.

The foundation also had to find the mountains of wool suddenly needed for the Kenny packs. Gudakunst suggested a national drive for old blankets; O'Connor hesitated to interfere with the many war drives. Bennett started using paper mill felts—discards from the processing of paper pulp—and in 1941 and 1942 the foundation begged 60,000 pounds of this absorbent wool wrapping, which they washed, cut, and packed, and then gave to hospitals.

The March of Dimes organization was reshaped in another way. It was already paying for the care of thousands of polio patients; in its first years it had become the first national body to say it would pay all the hospital and medical bills of anyone whose family could not afford them. Immobilization treatment had been simple and cheap; one nurse could watch many patients. The new Kenny method was far more complex, but it was what people wanted. "One of our main problems" has become "to appease mothers and fathers," a foundation consultant reported. The treatment bills went to new highs, demanding ever larger and more elaborate fund drives.

Polio was on the increase too: in 1942 there were 4,167 cases in the United States; in 1943 there would be 12,450; in 1944, 19,029. "The Kenny method revolutionized the treatment of acute poliomyelitis," a 1955 National Foundation historical summary concluded. "Patient care costs spiraled with its use. But above all there were the dramatic recoveries without deformity and the immeasurable gratitude of the crippled returned to a whole life."[4]

The following report appeared in *PM* on April 30, 1942: "A man-bite-dog scene was enacted at the Waldorf-Astoria. . . . Five hundred physicians, including some of the most eminent in the state, lent a respectful ear to a buxom, self-assured nurse."[5]

The occasion was the session on physical therapy at the annual meeting of the New York State Medical Society. In a Waldorf ballroom, Liza showed treatment movies and slides. Dr. Mary M. I. Daly of the Willard Parker Hospital for Communicable Diseases in New York City testified that her experience entirely confirmed Sister Kenny's claims. "If I were stricken with infantile paralysis, I'd rather have Sister Kenny treat me than any doctor I know," said Dr. Philip M. Stimson of New York, chairman of the American Medical Association's Section on Pediatrics.

In August Liza went to Memphis where the medical society gave her a dinner. "I wish to present the woman who has taught us all we medical men know about infantile paralysis," said Dr. E. M. Holder, president. The guest of honor rose and talked for almost an hour of her bush polio days, of her long "struggle." Well after the meeting ended, there was still a light in the banquet room, as Liza sat in a straight-backed chair answering the questions of the dozen doctors grouped around her.[6]

In New York, Duluth, Chicago, Toronto, New Orleans, Los Angeles, before the Michigan, West Virginia, Indiana, and Ontario medical societies, the American Academy of Pediatrics, and the Interstate Postgraduate Medical Assembly of North America, she conducted clinics and spoke. Several expert medical groups were now evaluating her method, and their reports were appearing. Chicago's supposedly hard-bitten Dr.

Philip Lewin prepared an article for the April 1942 *Illinois State Medical Journal* saying: "Miss Kenny's results speak for themselves. . . . [The method] should be made available as soon as possible to the whole country." And he closed fervidly with: "America gave General MacArthur to Australia. Australia gave Sister Kenny to America." Still a touch cautious, he sent the paper to his AMA editor-friend, Morris Fishbein, for review. Fishbein read the last few lines and said, "Strike them out." Lewin did, but nonetheless called Kenny treatment "one of the most outstanding advances in orthopedic surgery since the time of Hugh Owen Thomas and Sir Robert Jones."[7]

Dr. Mary Daly, Dr. Philip Stimson, and their colleagues at the Cornell University Medical College reported at length in the April 25 issue of the *Journal of the American Medical Association.* They had given forty-three patients the usual splinting treatment and twenty-eight the Kenny treatment. The Kenny patients were "better off in comfort, freedom from atrophy and deformity, rapidity of recovery, and possibly in extent of recovery." Stimson further said in July that her disputed symptom, spasm, was indeed among the factors which could aggravate disability, and it was owing to her lifework "that our attention has been attracted" to them.[8]

Dr. Earl Elkins of the Mayo Clinic, an associate of Dr. Krusen's, wrote an editorial for the June *Archives of Physical Therapy* saying: "All these facts make it urgent that the Kenny treatment be used in some form during the epidemics that may occur this year." At Rochester, Krusen addressed the staff. The tremendous enthusiasm for the new procedures seemed largely warranted, he said, although some claims were too enthusiastic. "Kenny protagonists have mentioned repeatedly that they have seen 'absolutely no deformities.' . . . Some patients do have flail extremities after the Kenny treatment and some walk with a Trendelenburg limp. . . . What the observers meant to say, I believe, is that they have seen absolutely no contractures, misalignments or spinal curvatures attributable to contractures. . . . In this observation, I am willing to concur."[9]

Chown in the *Canadian Public Health Journal*, Bingham of the New York Orthopedic Hospital in the *Journal of Bone and Joint Surgery*, Bennett and Cole, Pohl and Knapp in the *Archives of Physical Therapy* —in the space of a few years there appeared a flood of articles, almost all pro-Kenny and generally agreeing on several points:

Sister Kenny was right in urging early, aggressive treatment in the acute stage. "Every day is of importance," Cole said, "and a delay of 10 days or more can sometimes do irreparable harm."

"Spasm is constantly present in early poliomyelitis" (Stimson). If allowed to persist, it caused permanent contracture and further loss of function.

Her treatment rapidly relieved pain and sensitiveness, and maximum recovery and muscle power were achieved faster and more satisfactorily.

Her treatment also maintained what Pohl called "a remarkable state of health, tonus and vigor" in affected tissues. Blueness, coldness, skin thickening, chilblains, and skin ulcers, all formerly common, were not seen, and sticklike, atrophied limbs were usually avoided.

Paralysis caused by cell destruction was probably not influenced, but Cole said that when ideal treatment was given from the onset, the end result tended to be an individual with minimal or no deformity, no contractures, freely movable joints, and the ultimate in coordinated function that was possible with surviving muscles. By keeping limbs flexible and emphasizing normal muscle rhythm and coordination instead of strength, the treatment thus made "all the difference" in the ability to walk. "We can't halt paralysis when nerves are destroyed—no one can," Knapp added, but a healthy limb was immeasurably more useful than a deformed, atrophied one. "It is with increasing amazement," Bennett contributed, "that I see patients with very little muscle power carry out effective functional activity without the limping and lurching formerly seen."

For all these reasons, the Kenny treatment could now be considered "the treatment of choice."

"She has jarred the medical and allied professions out of their complacency," Lewin summed up, "into an immediate offensive attack on the local condition which she has so thoroughly proved exists." Knapp agreed: "Regardless of future developments . . . she has knocked us so completely out of our complacent groove of thought . . . that some worthwhile advance is bound to result from her revolutionary ideas and the frantic efforts of her opponents to refute them."[10]

Bennett wrote his former teacher Krusen: "After spending a great deal of time [in Minneapolis] with Miland [Knapp] and Pohl, as well as the Australian technician, it seemed that all of a sudden I understood what Kenny in her very mixed-up way was trying to put across. It was almost like getting religion—I felt like a purified convert."[11]

It was all exhilarating to her. She was the Queen of the May and the King of the Hill. She told one Australian that the university's first group of physicians in training included senior men from the Mayo Clinic, Stanford, Wisconsin, Missouri, Toronto, Chicago, and Harvard. "Are the Australian men as big and as willing?" she asked. She wrote to Charles Chuter and Health Minister Hanlon in Brisbane, to the Commonwealth health minister in Canberra, the Australian ambassador in Washington, the *Medical Journal of Australia*, and Australian newspapers. "My work has been very successful here owing to the just minds of the Americans," she stated. "It seems strange to think that the Royal Commission . . . kept quoting the American men as indisputable authorities. Well, those indisputable authorities have decided . . . that the 'revolutionary Kenny method' must be endorsed."[12] Yet she was beginning to berate the same authorities when they displeased her. And she often made the mild Dr. Knapp a scapegoat. Able to stand for the first time while Liza was away, one young woman patient was so happy she tried to take a dance step and fell. The doctors thought she might have hurt her affected knee, and Knapp had it immobilized temporarily, with a splint on each side. When Liza returned, she told him: "For all the good you did that knee, you might as well have spit on it."

One of Krusen's therapists, attending Kenny classes at the university, sent him a report. There were constant uproars, with Sister Kenny complaining that doctors elsewhere were mixing the Kenny and the unthinkable orthodox treatments. Sister Kenny thought Dr. Morris Fishbein's popular writings were encouraging this—the AMA editor wrote newspaper and magazine articles. She had promised Mr. O'Connor that she would ignore this, but now she must defend her treatment. "She doesn't like the [polio] foundation anyway, and the medical profession won't cooperate. Anyone not agreeing with her was asked to leave her class immediately."[13]

She walked out of a high-level meeting in the office of Dean Harold Diehl of the university's medical school. Basil O'Connor was present. Exasperated, he told the professors, "You'll never be able to deal with her. You're all gentlemen."

She was in such a black mood on the evening of a Minneapolis testimonial dinner in her honor. Four hundred guests—the mayor and aldermen, business, labor, and medical leaders—arrived at the grand ballroom of the Hotel Nicollet. One person was absent: Sister Kenny. Alderman Eric Hoyer, a Swedish-born painter and paperhanger risen to liberal politician, phoned her apartment. She refused to leave. Hoyer and Mayor Marvin Kline went to her rooms and found her in bed. Hoyer gave her what he remembers as "a good talking to."

"You don't want me," she said. "I'm not getting anyplace here."

"Lady," he said, in his melodious Swedish accent, "where is your underwear? I'll dress you if I have to."

"Leave the room!" she demanded. The stubborn Hoyer said he would be back if she weren't downstairs in fifteen minutes. She was down in twelve and walking into the ballroom in thirty.[14]

There was little time for such nonsense. Patients were arriving in Minneapolis from all parts of the country. Polio-stricken areas—Tennessee, North Carolina, Arkansas, Texas, Kansas, Seattle—were phoning for help. Straight from her classes went physical therapists and nurses. She and Minneapolis doctor-friends were swamped with letters, telegrams, and telephone calls. "PLEASE DO NOT COME TO MINNEAPOLIS NOW," the *American Weekly* admonished, "for there is no room to treat more patients adequately and the first job is to test, conclusively, the effectiveness of the method. If you write or telegraph DO NOT EXPECT AN ANSWER NOW, for replying to all the messages would keep the doctors doing nothing else."[15]

Patients came anyway. One was opera star Marjorie Lawrence, an Australian beauty. While honeymooning and singing Brünnhilde in Mexico City in 1941, she was suddenly afflicted with paralysis. She was treated at Hot Springs, Arkansas, for two months, then her husband, Dr. Thomas King, brought her to Minneapolis. Miss Lawrence wrote:

> I had been handled as though I would fall apart if any of my limbs were permitted to deviate to any extent from the rigidity in which the paralysis held them. Doctors and nurses were forever cautious not to "stretch" my muscles. But not Elizabeth Kenny. After she had finished with me, I lay on my bed unable even to speak, my only comforting thought being, well, if she doesn't kill me in the process she might cure me! To my profound relief the actual Kenny treatment proved a much gentler process.

It was established in Minneapolis that the singer did not have polio but, rather, a transverse myelitis, a spinal cord complication following a smallpox vaccination. Under Kenny treatment, her chest, abdominal, and shoulder muscles—her opera muscles—improved, but her legs remained paralyzed. On December 27, 1942, lying on a divan on the Metropolitan stage, she sang Venus in *Tannhaüser.* "It was an indomitable will, as much as any therapy, that enabled her to reappear," Liza wrote candidly. But the newspapers and public gave Sister Kenny credit and did the same later when singer Lawrence Tibbett's son came to her wearing braces and left without them, merely limping.[16]

"I have been besieged by people wanting to write my biography and film my life's history, so if you hear from me next in Hollywood don't be surprised," Liza told a friend. A few days later an Australian correspondent in Hollywood cabled his newspaper: "Producer Paul Kohner has just announced that he has acquired the screen rights to Sister Kenny's life."[17] Actually, no studio had decided yet to make a Kenny movie, but Liza, inspired, started writing her autobiography. In her apartment, beneath a lamp with tipped shade, she began filling pages. Night after night she wrote on, papers spread out on her dining table, a little bell at her side to summon Mary when she was needed.

Grand manner, thin purse. Her polio foundation allowance just housed and fed them. In addition, Liza was still getting her £8, 8 shilling Australian war pension every fortnight, about $20 a week. World War II was at its height, and Australian troops, as she was acutely aware, were fighting on every front. They had suffered catastrophically in Greece, Crete, and Singapore. In February 1942, Japanese aircraft based on New Guinea had bombed Darwin, the start of sporadic raids on northern towns, including Townsville. All combat troops were drained from the country; it feared invasion momentarily. The former war nurse got off a letter to Canberra in May. She wished to give up her war pension, she said, as her way of helping.[18] "I know the human race shall not fail to see that I get three meals and a bed," she blithely told friends.

The following year she succeeded in getting her National Foundation stipend increased to $900 a month for herself, Mary, Bill Bell, Valerie Harvey, and clerical help. But her irritation with the foundation was growing. The organization prepared an exhibit on Kenny methods for the June 1942 American Medical Association meeting in Atlantic City. More than 3,500 doctors, nurses, and physical therapists thronged to watch demonstrations. Two of Liza's therapists were on hand to demonstrate, but she was not invited. Her friend Dr. Pohl protested the slight, as well as a placard saying that Kenny training was being given at Warm Springs—no Warm Springs therapist had completed a Minneapolis course. Next the foundation sought Liza's cooperation in making a training film; she said none of her workers could take part without her personal supervision; Gudakunst, fearing the film would never be completed with her on hand, vetoed that. Bennett at Warm Springs tried to make amends by inviting her to visit him. She refused.[19]

Rochester's Henderson wrote O'Connor, supporting her: "She is quite inflexible in a way, but fundamentally she has the British sense of fairness, tinged perhaps by adherence to the principles for which she is fighting. Personally I have a good deal of admiration for her." Bennett disagreed. "I do believe it is about time Kenny's dictatorial attitude be shaken a bit. We are still practicing medicine in a democracy, and no patents have been granted as yet on medical routines."

This was the point. Her method was spreading, and this meant that no one could control it. Even revolutionary changes in medicine take place piecemeal, with some doctors changing radically and others clinging in part to old methods. Almost everyone was adopting heat and activity, but some continued to do some splinting or, more commonly, applied "Kenny" badly. She was unhappy, therefore, with the brief training for new Kenny therapists, even though the polio foundation pleaded that they were needed. She thought that all Kenny therapists should train for two years and was about ready to blow up publicly over this issue.

She was interrupted by honors. The American Nurses' Association asked her to address 3,000 nurses meeting in Chicago, and they made her an honorary member. In her response, she pleaded for more and better physical therapy for the wartime wounded. She had offered her services to the government to train medical corpsmen, she said, but "I have not yet been called."[20]

Doctors were still debating her unorthodox theory of "spasm." Did this condition really exist? Working with a group of polio patients at the University of Rochester in Rochester, New York, Drs. R. Plato Schwartz and Harry D. Bouman measured the electrical currents generated by muscle activity. Spasm, they concluded, was undeniably present.* Paralyzed muscles produced no current; those in spasm did. Spasm could be found both in muscles affected by polio and in some with no obvious symptoms. As voluntary muscle contraction improved with treatment or time, spasm decreased.

The condition was caused, these scientists thought, by partial blocking of nerve impulses where there was inflammation, rather than by complete paralysis of motor cells or brain centers. Roland Berg of the polio foundation, which financed the research, explained further that:

> Spasm and pain were not concomitant conditions as Miss Kenny had claimed [although] they occasionally were associated. . . . Spasm, furthermore, subsided voluntarily with or without treatment. Untreated muscles in spasm did not become paralyzed or deformed. The hot packs, so religiously applied in all cases, had as their main effect relief of pain. . . . [This] well bore out the preliminary opinion of physicians who "did not always agree with [Sister Kenny's] explanations, but did applaud her results."[21]

Schwartz did not have a large number of patients. Several authorities

* Schwartz chose to use the term "spasticity," meaning an increase in muscle tension.

remained convinced that untreated spasm could produce deformities; others remained uncertain. There was much still to be learned about the neuropathology of polio. Almost everyone agreed, however, that untreated pain could produce involuntary reflexes that crippled. Whether it was unrelieved spasm or unrelieved pain that was doing the damage seemed fairly unimportant to most Kenny adherents. For them, the most important thing this competent orthopedist had said was that something like her conception did exist.

Impressed, the American Congress of Physical Therapy (later the American Congress of Rehabilitation Medicine) gave Elizabeth Kenny its gold key, its first award to a woman and one of the few given to anyone but a doctor or a scientist.

Liza was invited to Hollywood to talk about a Sister Kenny movie. She was asked to take a polio-stricken boy back to Minneapolis. All air travel was controlled by military priority, so she managed to get space on an army transport plane. Finding the plane's cargo deck hard and bare, she commandeered a mattress from the ambulance that delivered the boy to the field. She told the driver that he would just have to buy another, and she sat on the deck alongside her patient for the ten- to twelve-hour flight.

Back in Minneapolis, she got ready to demonstrate before a group of doctors and therapists. The subject was to be a three-year-old girl, Sharon Carter. Sharon lay on her belly with her bare rump in the air. Tapping her with her forefinger, Liza said, "Pinch your buttocks together, Sharon." The child did not move. "Please," the nurse repeated.

"That ain't my buttocks, Sister," the child said. "That's my gluteus maximus." And she contracted it correctly and brought down the house.

A girl who had lost the use of a thigh muscle informed Liza that she had bawled out her quadriceps femoris for being lazy. A nine-year-old said he needed his tibialis anticus (in his lower leg) so he could kick a ward-mate in the gluteus maximus. Even six-year-olds were so well drilled that they could put their fingers on their hips if they were asked which muscle pulled their leg sideways and inside their thighs if asked which brought their knees together. It was all very cute, but Elizabeth Kenny seriously told classes: "We teach them the names of their muscles because it is really the patient who must reopen the nerve path between mind and muscle. It is easier if he has a speaking acquaintance with his anatomy."

Patients made progress. She took one boy out of a whole-body frame in which he had lain with all limbs splinted for nine months. He learned to get around with half-crutches, and his back became so supple he could flatten both hands on the floor without bending his knees. The girl with the lazy quadriceps and the boy who wanted to kick his roommate walked out of the hospital. A young man from Waterloo, Iowa, was admitted after sixteen months of immobilization; he could not sit, stand, walk, or feed himself. He began more than a year of treatment, after which he walked away to serve in the air corps.[22]

She or her therapists continued to take several patients from respirators, relax their muscles with heat, and teach them to breathe under their own power. Pointing to two new patients scheduled for respirators, she said once, "Give me the sicker one." Her patient lived, but the other died within twenty-four hours. By pulling on a patient's ribs, she argued, mechanical respiration aggravated the spasm in chest, neck, and jaw muscles. "This is all nonsense," she told Dr. Albert Bower as they walked through the respirator ward of Los Angeles County Hospital, where eighty-two patients were breathing with the aid of iron lungs.[23]

For a while her medical collaborators agreed. "The Kenny technique does not permit the use of respirators," Drs. Cole, Pohl, and Knapp said in an early pamphlet, and Stimson at Cornell wrote: "It is my sincere belief along with those who have been most closely associated with Sister Kenny that use of the respirator is now contraindicated in the routine treatment of acute poliomyelitis," though it might be used to keep a patient alive until he could get Kenny treatment. This proved to be too optimistic. Kenny centers before long had to use respirators to cut bulbar polio mortality, although well into the 1950s Kenny doctors insisted that too many people who didn't know polio very well still tended to put everyone with slight respiratory embarrassment into a respirator, causing unnecessary dependency on these machines and unnecessary crippling.[24]

A committee of skeptical orthopedists came to visit. One seemed mortified, she claimed later, because her patients weren't paralyzed. She angrily told him she could not paralyze people to suit him.

"Are those muscles paralyzed?" she asked, pointing to one patient she had never seen before.

"Yes," the group answered, the extensors of the leg were "completely" paralyzed.

She disagreed and within minutes had the patient holding the leg up. His problem was not paralysis, she announced, but muscle alienation. Some of the committee members walked away. Like others before them, they apparently were sure she had arranged to trick them with a subject who had been especially selected.

Some other sessions went better. Dr. Frank R. Ober of Harvard Medical School, the president of the American Orthopedic Association, arrived at John Pohl's invitation. Ober was called "the Bull" by his students. He promptly told Sister Kenny what he thought, and she told him what she thought. It was like two bulls ramming into each other, Pohl remembers. After a while they settled down to mere argument, and before the day was over they were getting along. Ober wrote an article for the *Journal of the American Medical Association*, calling Kenny treatment *the* correct treatment and adding that only a person skilled in it should use it. Then he contributed a glowing foreword to a new book that Pohl was writing with the tough nurse.[25]

But how many people really knew her technique, she was repeatedly asking. Impatient with what she called "half-baked" trainees, she declined to confer "proficiency" on the university's short-term Kenny graduates; their certificates said only that they had completed so many weeks of education. She told doctors, city officials, anyone who would listen that Minneapolis ought to provide a place for thorough training of therapists, and the city finally agreed. Its Board of Public Welfare, headed by Mayor Kline, voted to establish a permanent Kenny center.

A site? Her eyes settled on a half-hospital, half-school known as Lymanhurst, sparsely occupied by twenty-five to seventy-five children with rheumatic fever and by other child health clinics. "It's empty, it will do," she declared. "By God," sputtered Dr. Morse J. Shapiro, the rheumatic fever chief, "she's put me out." As it turned out, that led him to convince the Variety Club to help build a $2,500,000 University of Minnesota Heart Hospital, which helped the university become one of the first centers of open-heart surgery.

The precipitously vacated Lymanhurst was quickly remodeled, and in early December of 1942 her postacute cases were moved from the university and Minneapolis General Hospital. *Reader's Digest* scholarships helped a new set of therapy trainees start a two-year course. These young women wore new Kenny uniforms: trim dresses and Britishstyle organdy veils or headpieces in Liza's familiar "French" blue. Pohl was made the new polio hospital's medical supervisor; Knapp was to direct the university courses there. Her only titles were "honorary director" and "consultant." Whenever she chose, of course, she ran things. For example, everyone but she had assumed that all acute, as contrasted with continuing, polio care would still be given at the main hospitals rather than at her little place. At 5:30 one morning she abruptly phoned Mayor Kline: "This is Sister Kenny. I have no acute cases and there are some at General Hospital. What are you going to do about it?"

He was half-asleep. "Your hospital isn't set up for acute cases," he managed to answer. "You have no contagion wards."

"Build me some."

Kline reached his office at eight. She was on the phone waiting for him. "It's been hours since I talked to you," she said. "Can't you understand that this is urgent?"[26]

Within two days she had browbeaten a half-dozen General Hospital doctors into letting her move their acute patients into new rooms at her sixty-five bed institution. Twenty-seven polio patients made up the first group to occupy her beds. The number in some later epidemics would reach nearly 400.

On December 17, 1942, statuesque in a black coat and dress and black digger headgear, one brim jauntily up, the other down, she stood on a platform before the grimy but solid ex-school. Snow covered the ground. American flags, bright bunting, and a single Australian flag draped the platform. The flag with the Southern Cross was flanked by a New Zealand Air Force man, the closest kin to a digger that Minneapolis could muster. American sailors, soldiers, a WAC, and a WAVE stood among doctors and officials on the speakers' stand and on the freshly shoveled walk before it. A minister said, "Thank Thee, O Lord, for this messenger of mercy," as RKO and Pathé newsreel cameras whirred.

"She seems to be staring into space," a reporter wrote of Liza. "Her features are immobile." The mayor reached the end of his brief address. "And so," he concluded, "we dedicate Elizabeth Kenny Institute," and the wind whipped away a drape covering the new name, mounted over the entrance. Then she spoke. "The wind," the reporter wrote, "suddenly whips under the brim of her Aussie hat, and the faraway look vanishes. She clutches the brim with her hand, and from her throat comes a spontaneous laugh."[27]

The celebration continued into the evening, Liza appearing in a champagne-colored satin dress, grinning like a youngster. The next day she sat at a walnut kneehole desk in her new office. On the floor nearby rested three large pictures of her that were about to be hung in the lobby: one current photograph, one in her World War I sister's uniform, and a third made in 1911 in the silk-and-velvet-trimmed outfit that she had ordered in Guyra, New South Wales, when she had emerged as a nurse.

13

Phenomenon

FLAGPOLE SITTERS, English Channel swimmers, the Kinsey reports, and Masters and Johnson have at one time or another preoccupied us. Also Al Capone, Charles Lindbergh, Shirley Temple, Jonas Salk, and Elvis Presley. In the 1940s Elizabeth Kenny became such a phenomenon.

Her story hit the front pages and slick magazines with the impact of warm, simple drama: the lone underdog, the mere nurse, fighting the doctors and winning new life for the crippled. "There are few stranger and more romantic episodes in medicine," said Robert Potter in the *American Weekly*. "You have to go back to the work of Pasteur and Lister and their trials and tribulations to find a parallel." *PM*'s Albert Deutsch thought of both Pasteur, "who suffered the bitter attacks of medical conservatives," and a long line of nonmedical scientists: van Leeuwenhoek, Roentgen, the Curies, Metchnikoff, and Paul Ehrlich. "The Miracles of Sister Kenny," read the *New York Post* magazine. "That rainbow's end for doctors, the Sister Kenny treatment," gushed the *New York World-Telegram*, and Hearst columnist Inez Robb wrote: "They have weakened the villain of his power to twist and torture bodies into gross caricatures."[1]

In 1942, only twenty-one months after Liza Kenny's departure from Australia, the *New York Sun* named her the outstanding woman of the year. In the Gallup Poll the next year, she ranked just after Eleanor Roosevelt as the woman American women most admired; she kept that rank nine straight years. "She has become a national legend," said the *Minneapolis Star-Journal*, and the *Reader's Digest* reported: "Throughout Queensland a special blessing is asked for Sister Kenny and her work in the prayer with which all school children begin each day." That was inaccurate, but when Chicago's flamboyant health commissioner, Dr. Herman Bundesen, introduced her to a medical meeting he was just as effusive: "When the Saviour of Men was sought, He did not come from the palace of the great. And when a great medical reformer was chosen for this disease, the Divine Leader did not choose from the halls of science, but took a lowly worker from the bushland of Australia."[2]

Writers flocked to interview her. "A remarkable woman!" columnist Hedda Hopper found. "Steady as the Rock of Gibraltar, eyes clear and penetrating, unbounded, harnessed strength and a delightful sense of humor." Sigrid Arne wrote for Wide World that "Sister Kenny is no Hedy Lamarr. She's tall and solid, her eyes flash as she speaks, she doesn't sugarcoat." She was no lily-hand-on-fevered-brow brand of nurse, said the *New York Post*'s Eva Jolles. "There are power in her long arms, courage in her convictions and a tart edge to her tongue." *Newsweek* described her "innately shrewd mind and fierce pride."[3]

Little wonder then that crowds began mobbing her. At one New York affair, the police had to be called as a crowd slashed buttons from her frock and tried to get her hat. When the police rescued her, she grinned and said, "Thank goodness they left me with my underwear."

Such frenzy lasted five or six years. For the rest of her life, however, bellhops, airline stewardesses, and policemen asked for her autograph, and the lame began telephoning her in every city. In all, she reported, she was beseeched to cure every disease from palsy to blindness. Former polio victims and the crippled would wait in a hotel lobby fifteen or twenty strong; she often missed lunch or dinner examining or interviewing them one by one and in a very few cases suggesting a trip to her institute. She was also plagued by quacks, cranks, salesmen, and various varieties of doctors, mainly those on the fringes. "What kind of doctor is he?" she learned to ask and soon began shunning any but medical doctors. For years she could not take a walk without starting a procession. In a Fresno polio ward, a four-year-old boy once sang out: "Sister Kenny!" "How did you know it was Sister Kenny?" he was asked. "My Momma has a picture."[4]

She was at the peak, and she began acting and dressing accordingly. Her Brisbane bargains disappeared, to be replaced by elaborate gowns and dresses—a touch too elaborate. There was the black broadcloth and satin that she wore at the Kenny Institute dedication; it had a stiff, shirred waist and a bodice like medieval armor. She often added a velvet ribbon around her neck. And brocades, embroidery, a muskrat jacket, a white caracul cape, or a long, gray cape of Persian lamb that flowed like a magician's costume. She frequently overdecorated these with brooches, pins, three-strand pearl necklaces, and always a corsage—red roses or a spray of huge orchids. She also favored Australian opals and often kept a few loose in her handbag. The furs and jewels came only gradually, however, as she began to collect fees for her writing and, later, for a film.

Each of her costumes was topped with a fantasy of a hat. Open-lattice versions of Aussie digger headwear, straws with seven-inch brims and white-plumed galleons, all of them large. "Wouldn't I look awful in a little hat?" she would say. "It would look like a pimple on a pumpkin." In a black velvet hat with white ostrich feathers, she once walked into a Sydney café, and a reporter wrote, "Sister Kenny entered with a hat that would lay the ghost of Charles I." Grateful mothers of patients began making and sending her these glories, and Rex of Hollywood and John Frederick made her several. She looked more than ever like a figure out of the nineteenth century.[5]

Or like royalty. She mounted a platform or entered a limousine—she soon developed a taste for chauffeured limousines—with a ceremonious sweep that was part poise, part bravado. "She has the majestic force and bearing," Inez Robb wrote, "of the Queen Mother at a royal garden party." It was not all bravado, for, like a queen, she had dignity. She could remain immobile in public for long periods, all eyes on her. "Her repose," said one observer, "was more arresting than the march of a military band."[6]

Yet she could be as chilling as an iceberg. She often seemed incapable of relaxing, and her speech with strangers was frequently a defensive monotone. A few friends thought she had grown vain and was trying to make an impression. She was not, in truth, without vanity, and she did act. "But it was a damned good act," thinks an English doctor who liked her. "She would drive up and wait, like the Queen, for her chauffeur to open her door. She wore a hat you could see a mile away. But if you took it all in the right way, she was soon laughing."[7]

To her, her arrival any place was her arrival all over again in Brisbane or Sydney or Melbourne or America. She still half-expected rebuffs, so she tolerated none. As soon as someone winked or laughed, accepting her, she unbent. She became less prudish too, and even began applying a touch of lipstick now and then. "Sister!" Mary said in surprise the first time she saw it. "Well," Liza said defensively, "I photograph better." She learned to take a little sherry at a party. "After all," she explained, "in Adelaide they ask about your religion, in Melbourne your ancestry, in Sydney your bank account, and in Brisbane, where I come from, 'Will you have a drink?' " She usually nursed her drink all evening, however, or took tomato juice. She once said she had downed enough tomato juice to supply red corpuscles to the entire population of America.

More self-confident as success came, she began handling interviewers with a touch of wit. "How do I support myself? That's my private business," she told one reporter. "I'm not a kept woman, though. You can say that." Her ideal vacation? Going fishing two miles from any shore, "but medicine is such a jealous lover that lately the only exercise I get is putting my foot down." She sighed. "For social life, I climb into the front seats of taxicabs on my way to work and talk to the drivers. Very interesting fellows."[8]

She began more gallivanting. Her nearly solid two years in Minneapolis had been a long time for her. "My father was something of an Irish rover," she would sometimes explain and be off more and more.

A strong friendship with the willowy film star Rosalind Russell had started in 1941, shortly after some of the first publicity about Sister Kenny had caught the eye of a Hollywood writer named Mary McCarthy.* Miss McCarthy rushed to Minnesota to urge Sister Kenny, "Why not a movie about you?" After a first rebuff or two, the flattered Liza agreed to let her try. The film writer sought out Miss Russell, who was making hit after hit and who had helped form a Los Angeles Crippled Children's League. The actress agreed to meet Liza.

On an early winter day in 1941, then, Liza first arrived in Los Angeles while Miss Russell waited. Out from the plane stepped Sister Kenny—to the actress "a rather sad figure." But then she came down the ramp, "and she didn't walk, she marched, and behind her eyes you saw her intensity." Rosalind was hers. The leggy star asked her to lunch, where Liza, unfazed by a film celebrity, chided her: "Child, you have your skirt up."[9]

RKO Pictures hired Miss McCarthy to attempt a script, and Liza returned to California in mid-1942 to stay with her for a bit. The writer began asking Liza questions about her early life; some she answered, some she did not. But strolling around Miss McCarthy's country cottage

* Not the well-known novelist.

one morning, she saw a chicken choking. With a sharp knife, she unhesitatingly cut its throat and removed the obstacle. She then sewed the bird up with needle and thread, and soon it was strutting again. That told the screenwriter something.

Miss McCarthy also had her own seven-question psychological test. She tried it on Liza, ordering, "Answer immediately. Don't stop to think."

The first question was: "What do you like to do the most?"

"That's a toss-up between riding a horse or sailing a boat, and I'm too old to do either now."

"What do you hate to do most?"

"Go to teas with a lot of fat, overdressed, overbejewelled women who've never done one honest day's work in their lives."

"What do you consider the greatest crime in the world?"

"Any crime against children."

"What do you consider the worst thing a person can do, not a crime?"

"To betray a trust."

"What is your favorite quality in another person?"

"Frankness."

"What quality do you detest the most?"

"Any piece of low cunning!"

"What constitutes for you, in a phrase, happiness?"

Liza thought just an instant. "A clear conscience."

Miss McCarthy added two questions. "Would you ever consider committing suicide?" she asked and started to say, "Under what circumstances?" She never got to the second part, for Liza shot back: "Don't be a bloody fool!"

"What is your greatest fear?"

"To lose the use of my hands."

The movie project merely puttered along, but Liza and Rosalind Russell took to each other, and now—in January 1943—Liza and Mary stayed for a time with the actress and her husband of a year, Frederick Brisson.* Still slow in unbending, Liza at first called her "Miss Russell," but soon it was "Rosalind." Like Liza, she was mainly Irish and some Scotch by descent. She was Roman Catholic and religious, though she called her church "Our Lady of the Cadillacs." She was at this point thirty-five years old, experienced in the ways of Hollywood, and intelligent, and, to a nurse who had a hard time relaxing, a figure of abandoned fun who cheerfully sang or croaked away to amuse her guests. During her

* Then a theatrical agent, he was before long the Hollywood and Broadway producer of *Pajama Game* and other hits.

Broadway stardom in *Wonderful Town*, her singing was to be likened to the Ambrose lightship's calling its mate.

As for Elizabeth Kenny, the actress thought she was fascinating, and "the most fascinating thing was that she was a female, with any female's weaknesses. Vanity. Pride. And of course feminine giving of herself. She was a woman and she fought a woman's fight. But with anyone she liked, she was just longing for affection." Liza and the readily affectionate Rosalind walked in the Brissons' garden one night, and Liza was quiet. Then she said, in an odd tone, "Perhaps I should tell you about another part of my life."

"We're going to do all we can to represent your work faithfully," Rosalind assured her.

"I mean there was a man."

"Well! Now we're getting someplace!"

The actress recalls that "she said it very flatly. She told of this man who owned a station out in the bush, and how she met him. She said they often rode together and were to have been married, but then she got into her work. She talked about it very quietly and delicately, never flamboyantly. We talked for two and a half hours."

"Was he tall?" Rosalind asked.

"Well, wouldn't I look silly with a little man!"

Both women cried a little.

Hollywood lionized Liza. RKO Studios had a luncheon for her. The stars gave her their autographed pictures, and Liza reciprocated. Miss Russell was trying unsuccessfully meanwhile to get a real commitment from RKO or any studio to make a Kenny film. The executives applauded the nurse, but behind her back they asked Rosalind, "Who wants to see a movie about hot rags and massage?"

In New York, Liza was guest of honor at the 1943 President's Birthday Ball, the March of Dimes money-raiser. Cutting the birthday cake, she called President Roosevelt "the greatest conqueror in world history" for his conquest of his own polio and his role in starting the National Foundation for Infantile Paralysis.

On April 25, Anzac Day, the day that memorializes the Battle of Gallipoli, she was asked to broadcast from New York to Australia. She spoke of her seventeen nephews in the Australian forces. The war was still a desperate one for Australians: a division had surrendered at Singapore, another was decimated in Greece, but in the Libyan desert "the Tobruk rats" held for months against German attack. "I have been treated very wonderfully in America," Liza said on her broadcast. "But I am still an Australian."

In May the University of Rochester, site of Dr. R. Plato Schwartz's studies of polio spasm and pain, awarded her the honorary degree of Doctor of Science. "In the dark world of suffering you have lit a candle that will never be put out," said President Alan Valentine. When she returned to Minneapolis, she said only half-jokingly that the honor stemmed from Schwartz's attempting to disprove her concept and, instead, proving it.[10]

She went to Washington to have lunch at the White House. That was Basil O'Connor's doing, and, despite their differences, he was there too. The busy president took the time between a conference with General George C. Marshall and his first meeting with his new War Mobilization Board; Liza beamed as she received his hearty handshake. Seeing him sitting in his wheelchair—always a surprise to his visitors; he was never photographed in it—she was thoroughly moved. "I have often thought that God may have taken away President Roosevelt's power of locomotion to save him from a second-rate career," she wrote later. "One of my favorite phonograph records is 'The Blind Plowman' . . . 'God, who took away my eyes, that my soul might see.' "[11] When she got back to Minneapolis, however, and someone asked a little too ponderously if she had enjoyed the visit, she replied with a waggish, "Oh yes, but he *is* just another man."

She was due in New York City the evening of her White House visit but couldn't get a train seat; Basil O'Connor had a special rail car attached for her. She was feted at dinner that evening by the chancellor and faculty of New York University. On the next day, June 9, she was awarded another honorary degree.[12]

She strutted like a swagman. She was now a Doctor of Humane Letters as well as of Science. "I can now be addressed as Elizabeth Kenny, D.H.L.," she said, "but I do not consider it any advantage."

Competitors with inner devils are almost certain to clash.

Liza was still unsatisfied, restless, a perfectionist, proud Irish, still beneath her veneer the poor cousin, the daughter of Mick Kenny showing the world.

Basil O'Connor was born on the back side of the tracks in the factory town of Taunton, Massachusetts, the son of a tinsmith. One day he found his father crying; he had just been fired. The young O'Connor went to Dartmouth, Harvard Law School, made money, and co-founded the Wall Street law firm of Roosevelt & O'Connor—he was the member who produced most of the business. At Roosevelt's request, he got into the polio fight. He too was unsatisfied, restless, a perfectionist, and proud Irish, another end product of poverty and chagrin.

He was also educated and disciplined, and he wore sumptuously tailored clothes and a flower in his lapel. His enemies—he always had quite a few—called him sly, ruthless, even mean. His friends, and this included the people who worked for him, found him tough on the outside but sentimental inside, a boss who could almost never fire anyone and was almost fanatic about "making the world better." He was also brilliant, determined, logical, and a poisonous questioner. In the opinion of many scientists, such qualities in toto were to bring a polio vaccine into being about ten years ahead of the time when the world otherwise would have had one. O'Connor could easily have been a political figure; he was, starting in Albany, an original Roosevelt Brain Truster. After Roosevelt was elected president, he asked O'Connor what he wanted to do; O'Connor said he wanted to practice law. Actually he did so less and less, and before many years he hardly practiced at all; he was busy in the 1940s making the National Foundation a prototype for big health organizations. From 1944 to 1949, he also headed the Red Cross at FDR's request.

Liza's relations with O'Connor started bittersweetly on her arrival in 1940. He listened but found her no workplace. Still, he was interested and provided funds as soon as the Minnesota doctors asked for them. Now, however, running the new Kenny Institute was proving expensive for the city of Minneapolis, even though the foundation was giving the university an annual $33,000 to pay the medical teaching staff. Mayor Kline and fellow welfare board members went to New York in mid-1943 to ask O'Connor for another $139,000 a year.

O'Connor deferred his answer. By now he had decided that Elizabeth Kenny was too contentious to work with, although he realized that she was performing a service. In March 1943 he had even written her a conciliatory letter: "If I could [have] an autographed photograph of your good self, I should be very happy indeed." That spring he also tried sending her an assistant, Warren Coss—"to help you out," as O'Connor put the idea to her. He of course thought Coss might be a sort of manager or mediator for her. She had no use for anyone resembling a manager, Coss soon reported. "If I had wanted a manager," Liza told her staff, "I'd have married one."[13]

Coss told the following story. They were about to take a late train to Chicago, after a meeting in Hamilton, Ontario. Coss was informed that her passport had expired; he suggested staying to see the United States consul. Instead she boarded the train, saying, "Everyone knows who I am, I'll have no trouble." At 2:15 A.M. they reached the border, and she was asked to leave the train. "She refused to leave," Coss said. "She asked to be placed in custody and delivered to the British consulate in Chicago. The train was held up 70 minutes while we used every possible means of persuasion. . . . As a last resort we were going to buy a stretcher and remove her bodily, or set off the car and transfer all [the other] passengers to another car."

At last she yielded and "strode majestically" off. At the United States consulate next morning, the employees ordered her to be seated with other immigrants, "whereupon she demanded to be sent to a hospital and dashed out of the building." She finally was granted a temporary entrance permit. "Miss Kenny," the defeated Coss told O'Connor, "will not cooperate with any individual whom she cannot dominate, nor will she become associated with any organization in which she is not supreme."

Liza, on the other hand, had her own reasons for being disturbed. Mary Stewart-Kenny and a fellow therapist, Ethel Gardner, had just ended a two-month stay in Argentina; the polio foundation had reluctantly sent them there, at Liza's insistence, to train nurses to cope with an epidemic. This suggested to O'Connor a kind of possibly endless foreign aid that he did not want to begin. The therapists' time ran out, and the Argentinian government and the United States consul urged them to remain. But O'Connor believed they were treating patients and not just teaching, as originally planned. He also heard there was about to be a revolt (which there rapidly was, installing dictator Juan Perón as president). So Dr. Gudakunst wired Mary and Miss Gardner to return.

Liza was angered by the thought of leaving Argentinian or any other polio patients stranded. Her therapists stayed, but O'Connor quit paying them. In New York and again in Dean Diehl's office at the University of Minnesota, Liza and he met in anger. As far as he was concerned, he plainly said, the therapists had served their function abroad—and there also need be no Elizabeth Kenny Institute. He pointed out that the foundation had refused no university fund request; that now it was up to the university to decide how to disseminate Kenny methods in its part of the country; and that the foundation wanted to see the Kenny method become part of medical curriculums everywhere and "render the need for a Kenny Institute nonexistent." He also referred the fund-seeking Minneapolis city officials to the university.

Less formally, he told everyone that Liza had "a Jehovah complex." She shot back just as caustically: "When O'Connor sneezes, he wants everyone to jump. But not me." And she issued a statement: she was returning her last check from the foundation "in order to keep my self-respect."

The Kenny O'Connor confrontations made delicious theater: the controlled, brilliant O'Connor sucking calmly on a cigarette in a neat holder and Liza furious.[14] Their arguments involved more than two colliding personalities, however, and her case was not without logic. By now she was repeatedly calling the short courses financed by the foundation "shoddy," if better than nothing, for "it takes at least two years to learn my technique, and doctors and technicians here in the United States study it for nine weeks usually and then become experts."[15] If more training was required, it seemed obvious to her that she would have to control it. The foundation for its part, according to its historical notes, "was determined that the teaching and administration of the Kenny program were to be controlled by national headquarters. In the long run this was the most logical way. The foundation possessed the funds, the administrative experience and the support of the American people. . . . If they seemed somewhat heavy handed, their reaction was provoked by Miss Kenny." Yet this explanation, however well founded, does not come to grips with the two-year training issue.

"The National Foundation's marriage of convenience to Sister Kenny," says this record written later by a foundation historian, was "an uneasy coupling from the onset, the relationship was always stormy and the protracted separation proceedings were to be sensational." O'Connor in private told friends that "the madman always cuts the throat of his favorite daughter"—by which he meant that Sister Kenny could have accomplished far more had she been more tractable and maintained her relations with the powerful foundation. This was undoubtedly true. Had she been more tractable, however, she would not have been Sister Kenny.

"Jehovah complex indeed!" she flared back in these brouhahas. Then, often, she subsided, depressed. "Even faith needs a little backing now and then," she said. She called a Minneapolis newspaper one morning and said she was leaving the United States. After the statement was published, she retracted it.

She retreated again to solitude, with her new autobiography as her therapy. She sat at a table in her cramped apartment and covered it end-to-end with the scrawled pages. After a full day's work at her institute, she would fall into bed at 9 or 9:30. But she would wake at 2 A.M., often to work on the book until daybreak.

She looked back on "the twilight hours" when her mother taught the Kenny children. "My mother used to say, 'He who angers you, conquers you!' But my mother was a saint." She told of her discouragements and of bitter tears "shed in solitude." But now "justice" had prevailed and "a measure of victory has been won." "To the medical men of the United States of America," she concluded in a moment of optimism, "I pass the torch."

She sent parts of the voluminous manuscript to a few publishers and was turned down. She had met a well-known Minnesota novelist, Martha Ostenso, meanwhile, so she went to Dodd, Mead, Ostenso's publisher, and suggested her as collaborator. Dodd, Mead and Miss Ostenso agreed. A slender, pale blonde, deceptively frail-looking, she possessed her own inner fire. "Sister Kenny," she said at the start, "I know you've bowled over a number of doctors. But if there are any fights, I'll quit." Liza understood. Martha courageously trimmed Liza's manuscript nearly in half, otherwise reordered and rewrote, and added some segments from interviews. She would finish a section and wait while Liza read it. "What do you think of it?" Martha finally would ask somewhat uncertainly, and Liza would answer sharply, "You know it's ten times better than mine."

The Pohl-Kenny polio text was published before Miss Ostenso's was complete. That, too, had been a successful collaboration. "How did you manage it?" Ostenso wrote Pohl, and he later wrote her, "How did *you* accomplish it without being slain?" Miss Ostenso chose a title, *And They Shall Walk*, from Isaiah 40:15: "They shall mount up with wings as eagles; they shall run, and not be weary; and they shall walk, and not faint."[16]

Liza left her apartment when the city of Minneapolis bought her a roomy, two-story house on Park Avenue, a wide street of old residences and flour millers' mansions. The house had a lawn, flowering lilacs, and window boxes, just her style. But giving up her war pension and polio foundation stipend had again left her short of funds—she drew no Kenny Institute salary. She had just moved into the new home when she gave a speech to the local Exchange Club. A businessman named Jim Henry drove her home. "Can you keep a secret?" she asked him. "That lunch was the first real meal that I've had except tea and toast in five days." Even her stretcher patents were about to expire, she confided; in any case, war made it hard to get money out of Australia. Might the Exchange Clubs of America be willing to help her stay in the United States? He barely knew what to say at first, but the Minneapolis Exchange Club soon pledged her $416 a month for life.[17]

September 20, 1943, was her sixty-third birthday. "I celebrated my fifty-seventh birthday," she wrote, using her American count. "I rose, as always, at 5 o'clock, breakfasted, worked on a medical paper for two hours and then went to the Elizabeth Kenny Institute. . . . [I] went to bed at 10 P.M. It was a full day. But so are they all at the Institute, now just a little over a year old. They are days filled not only with work, but also with constant examples of the miracles wrought by patience, skill and faith."

Nine days later the Kenny Institute was incorporated as a nonprofit foundation with a board of directors of fifteen including Rosalind Russell. In the same month, *And They Shall Walk* was published, dedicated to "the mothers of mankind."

The date was November 12, 1943, the scene a cramped solarium atop Adelphi Hospital in Brooklyn. Packed around a treatment table, standing on tables and chairs, forty doctors and a number of nurses and therapists strained to watch. At the table stood the tall nurse, white hair brushed straight back. She was no fashion plate here; she wore a black dress, only a rhinestone pin and a lapel watch relieving its severity. All eyes were on her strong face and her long fingers, as they stretched to touch and explore fingertip by fingertip the muscles of an eight-year-old boy's deformed left leg. He had been unable to bend it for two years.

"Relax, son," she told him. Cautiously, she flexed his leg, while the ring of spectators watched. The boy seemed about to whimper, then stopped. "I never saw Kenny hurt a patient ever. I never saw a patient cry with her," one expert physical therapist reports. "That's more than I can say of us physios."

"This muscle is not denervated," Liza abruptly announced. "It is alienated because when he was taken sick it pained him, and so he stopped moving it. By the time the pain ceased, the muscle had been inactive so long it lost its sense. I will now restore that sense." She touched his leg. "Do nothing up here," she said, patting his thigh. "Get your brain down here if you can."

Then, sharply, "Jerry! Concentrate on your foot. Think of it. Move it!" The boy moved the leg himself. A nurse gasped, and the boy's father, standing behind him, said, "Thank God! This is the first time he has moved it in two years." Liza turned to tell the boy's physician what further attention he must have. "Sister Kenny Works 'Miracle,'" the headlines read the next day.

She moved from Jerry to another child, then another that day, pointing with outstretched index finger to untreated spasm, prodding, feeling, stroking, and lecturing. Over the motionless leg of a girl, ten: "Now this way, dear. Relax. You know what you do when you walk, don't you. No, don't you do it. I'll do it for you—like this. *Now* see if you can do it." Before the watching doctors and the bewildered eyes of a man and woman behind the girl, a muscle moved. Some doctors' eyes glistened, and the woman gasped loudly. Liza looked up. "Are you relatives?" she asked the woman, rather sharply.

"No," the woman said, "we're the parents."

Liza lectured on. "There *is* no paralysis in these muscles. They are not destroyed. If they were, I couldn't bring them back in 30 seconds, could I?"

More than a thousand doctors and parents telephoned after that day's demonstration, asking her to treat their patients or their children. She saw many. In Jersey City, she examined an eight-year-old patient of Dr. Nicholas Ransohoff, who had been under treatment for eight months but was unable to lift his head or sit up. Ransohoff planned to transplant a strip of fascia or muscle sheath from the boy's hip across his abdominal wall to enable him to sit up again. What about his crooked pelvis and shortened leg, Liza asked. When he was fourteen he would have more operations, the orthopedic surgeon replied. "I asked permission," she wrote, "to give him five minutes of true Kenny treatment. . . . In less than half an hour the patient was down walking. And all the deformities corrected."

Ransohoff himself went before the American Orthopedic Association and described this remarkable-seeming event from his standpoint:

> Sister Kenny demonstrated a patient whom the author thought had a pelvic obliquity and weak abdominal muscles. In less than two minutes, [she] showed that this apparent paralysis was due to the spasm of the quadratus lumborum [a back muscle that stabilizes the pelvis and trunk in walking]; she further demonstrated the inability of the abdominal muscles to work when stretched. She then "released" the spasm . . . bringing the abdominal

muscles back to their normal resting length, and overcame the incoordination. The patient thereafter was able to . . . hold himself in typical V position. . . . She also demonstrated satisfactorily the fact that incoordinated hamstrings could not flex the knee, and that, by restoring the "mental awareness" and coordination, the patient was able to flex the knee without difficulty.

Richard Metcalfe, a British orthopedic surgeon, later assessed a similar case: "The abdominal muscles, to all reasonable test, exhibited the muscle power 'zero,'" but she demonstrated that the lack of power was the result of tightness of the back muscles. "Under her skilled manipulation, the 'tightness' . . . was resolved, and within a matter of 10 minutes the abdominal muscles were contracting, and this in a case four months after original infection. I would never have believed it possible unless I had seen it with my own eyes."

What did she really *do* in these "miracle cases" that astonished medical and nonmedical observers alike? By her definitions, a key muscle was in spasm, and its shortness and tightness were pulling its opposing muscle out of place. The pull also caused pain, so the patient unknowingly learned *not* to employ the healthy muscle. This phenomenon, which she called "alienation," may have been well known by other terms. All muscles work in pairs or teams to maintain body balance; when one contracts, its opposite (or "antagonist") relaxes or stretches. Charles Scott Sherrington, an English physiologist, first showed in the 1890s that a muscle contraction is invariably accompanied by relaxation of its antagonist; he showed that this is an involuntary, reflex action, and that reflexes caused by pain block out all others, apparently to protect the body from harm.

Seeking to restore what she called mental awareness, Elizabeth Kenny would gently move an affected part in its normal arc and watch for a muscle tendon to stand out. If one did—often so slightly that it would be invisible to anyone without long experience—she knew that the muscle attached to it lived. What would have to follow in many cases was a long course of relaxing heat, stimulation, and reeducation. But in *some* patients—patients like those in Adelphi Hospital—she could feel so much tension or muscle tone that she knew that restoring some voluntary control might be quickly possible. So she would say, "Relax . . . think," as she moved the affected area, thus stimulating or exciting the involuntary proprioceptive nerve endings in the muscle and tendon. Then she would say, "Now you try," letting the patient, suddenly relaxed and free from pain, use his voluntary nerve pathways to move the crucial muscle.

Many polio therapists and even some doctors learned to perform the same feat. But doctors ordinarily lacked time to work with patients and develop the required skill. Some, not realizing this, scoffed at these "miracles." Dr. Ransohoff himself said: "Like all originators, [she] reports results which we have not yet been able to duplicate. She has been endowed with a great gift in the healing art. There is still a question as to whether or not she can impart this gift to her disciples."[18]

She did in fact impart it to many trainees and they to others. Before many years, the method would be described in physical therapy and rehabilitation manuals. She never failed to be irritated by the inappropriate use of the word "miracle," which she knew ruffled doctors. "All I did," she would say, "was straighten a pelvic obliquity, something I have done many times before."

But she was too seldom diplomatic. She had a tongue like a shillelagh, and she wielded it.

She had once seen an odd symptom in a girl in Australia, a contraction of the skin's tiny muscle network, giving the skin a thickened look. In a few days the girl had come down with polio. Liza now observed the same condition in some supposedly only "slightly ill" children who were brought to her institute. She decided that Dr. McQuarrie, the university pediatrics chief, must see one such child right away. She phoned him; he gave several reasons why he couldn't come then. She didn't think any were important enough to delay him, so she went on what she called a "sit-down strike."

A McQuarrie assistant desperately sent a car for his busy chief, who did come. Within forty-eight hours the patient had unmistakable poliomyelitis. "I had proved my point," Liza wrote. But at some cost. There was incident after such incident; in some she was wrong. Gradually sympathizers like McQuarrie were finding it harder to reply to persons who said, "Much of her treatment is fine, but she's impossible."[19]

She was bitter over the medical school's refusal to ask O'Connor for funds to run Kenny Institute. She argued over the National Foundation's printed claims, indeed exaggerated, that 900 persons to date had been "graduated" from the university with her "approval and certification." Hundreds had some training all right, but she was arguing that it was not enough; they were not university "graduates." A medical school professor may have furnished the careless statistics, it developed, but in the ensuing quarrel some of his colleagues accused her of "perjury" in denying her own part in the courses.

Dean Diehl vainly tried to smooth the waters. She turned up in New York and announced that she had run away from the University of Minnesota, which is "undoubtedly looking for me now." Does the university know of your feelings? she was asked. "They should," she answered. "I put it in the papers." She *must* leave the country now, she said, for lack of funds. Checks started pouring in. The *New York Journal-American* printed a foot-high photograph of a little girl, an ex-Kenny patient, skipping rope, beneath the caption: "Why Sister Kenny Should Not Go."[20]

She also charged Dr. Morris Fishbein, the powerful AMA editor, with "inviting" her to leave the country. An adversary seldom bested, he simply denied it. She continued to heap coals on him. A reporter visited him and found he had the air of a man who would be "glad to put his head sadly between his hands." A friend entered his office one day. "Morris was sitting on the telephone for the only time in his life saying an occasional 'Yes, yes, yes.' I said, 'Sister Kenny.' She was the only person who could carry the conversation when talking to Morris." Fishbein years later admitted: "Yes, I told her to go home. I told her she had done her work, and she should let it be put to the test and applied. I told her she couldn't do any more and that she was spoiling it."[21]

It was all more than she could take. Her clash with the polio foundation burst into the open. "The National Foundation is not supporting me," she proclaimed; her treatment could produce 88 percent recoveries compared with 13 percent for old ways; all so-called Kenny treatment except her institute's was a fraud. O'Connor had to start stumping the country to answer her. Since 1940, he assured the fund-giving public, the foundation had spent more than half a million dollars for the study and teaching of Kenny methods; $107,000 had gone to the University of Minnesota. In 1943, he said, "the third largest epidemic in the recorded history of the disease struck our country. Had it not been for the hundreds of doctors, nurses, and technicians trained with the public's money and ready to administer the Kenny method promptly, that epidemic might have resulted in a national disaster." It was "impossible" to educate enough technicians at one institute, hers or anyone else's. "In all the history of medicine few new theories have ever received such generous financial support."

She began charging that in April 1940, during their first interview, O'Connor had advised her to go home. Daughter Mary corroborates it, O'Connor denies it, and one of O'Connor's closest advisers, Dr. Thomas Rivers of Rockefeller University, himself anti-Kenny, said rather bitterly years afterward that O'Connor "bought" Sister Kenny at that first meeting. In her autobiographical manuscript, Liza was kind to O'Connor; she said that she did not doubt his foundation's sincerity.[22]

She was winning ever wider public backing. A New York newsman reminded her that she had struggled many years in Australia before winning recognition. "I intend to win here too," she answered. Another said: "She has leveled off on the National Foundation for Infantile Paralysis and the American Medical Association. These are no piker outfits. . . . She has cast herself for the role of David in a national David and Goliath affair." Albert Deutsch, one of the finest sociological and medical journalists of the time, wrote: "My bet is on Miss Kenny, a fighter if ever there was one."[23]

14

Controversy

BUT NOW SHE was plunged into new hell.

She had won over many orthopedists, yet these "bone doctors" remained her most severe opposition. Rather recent arrivals themselves as specialists of repute, they had widely abandoned or modified rigid immobilization; but a large number of them did not like to say so. In mid-1942 a committee of seven orthopedists had been named to evaluate Kenny treatment. The committee represented three orthopedists' groups, and a tall, blunt Mayo Clinic man, Dr. Ralph K. Ghormley, was appointed chairman; he had been assistant to the celebrated Robert Lovett in the early twenties. Ghormley was within a few years of succeeding the more temperate Dr. Melvin Henderson, a Kenny convert, as Mayo orthopedic head. Ghormley's committee visited sixteen clinics in six cities and examined 740 patients. They went to Minneapolis twice, and some members spent several days there, two and a half of them in the company of Sister Kenny. A good part of that time was spent in argument.

On June 15, 1944, in the first flush of what was to be the worst polio epidemic in twenty-five years, Dr. Ghormley presented the committee's conclusions at the annual American Medical Association meeting in Chicago, to the Section on Orthopedic Surgery. Ghormley made this ardent defense of pre-Kenny treatment:

There had been no one "orthodox" method but many, with "most"

United States cases treated along lines laid down by Lovett and others as early as 1916, including some heat and muscle training.

Her active and passive movements were acceptable; in fact, muscle reeducation had been "the basis" for orthopedic treatment for "many years." Her early handling, however, could be detrimental, and splinting benefited some patients.

"Muscle spasm" did exist in the early phases but usually disappeared spontaneously. Residual spasm might lead to deformity, but this was not a new discovery either; the effects of tenderness and stiffness had long been recognized. Hot packs "may relieve" pain and stiffness, but so would rest. Heat was no panacea, and its use should be guided by good medical judgment, not a rigid "method."

Her "mental alienation"? Again, not new. Her "incoordination"? Just another term for muscle substitution, long recognized.

Nerve cell destruction, not untreated spasm, was the most important cause of crippling. Nor could Kenny treatment prevent or minimize permanent paralysis. "We criticize severely the oft repeated statement of Miss Kenny to patients who have come to her after treatment elsewhere that had this case come to her early the disability would have been prevented."

Fifty to 80 percent of polio cases recovered spontaneously; she was taking credit for many. Her frequent contention that her method produced approximately 80 percent recoveries was not supported by accurate statistics in a significant number of cases. Her statement that only 13 percent recovered without paralysis under orthodox treatment was deliberate misrepresentation. "Miss Kenny has been told repeatedly that this is not a fair comparison," but she was still making it.

The committee finally condemned the wide publicity that had misled the public and many doctors but acknowledged that it had "stimulated the medical profession to reevaluate known methods" and treat patients more effectively.[1]

Liza was not in the meeting hall, but she was in Chicago. In a nonce she was using her own platform, the press. "Why I should be accused of perjury," she said, "I do not know." The report was a mass of misinformation, inaccuracy, prejudice, and nonsense. The committee did not know the disease and knew little or nothing of her method. They had seen only one acute case in Minneapolis. The group as a whole, she maintained, visited Kenny Institute only for three hours in June 1943 and for seven hours in 1944; it had "never" followed any cases through treatment.

She sent a telegram asking where the committee had traveled to see what they called the Kenny method. The reply said: "Committee agreed not to give out names of cities and hospitals visited." Outraged, she charged that not one practiced true Kenny technique, that their so-called modern treatment mixed Kenny and orthodoxy, and "to try my method without trained technicians is not a fair trial." She produced a letter from Dr. Henderson of the Mayo Clinic, written after he substituted for Ghormley on one Minneapolis visit: "The members of the committee were impressed by your earnestness and by your skill. I realize it is very difficult for you to appreciate the 'about face' the profession has to make. . . . So far as I am concerned, you have proved your point. It is quite evident that the disease . . . has more to it than the involvement of the anterior horn cells. Kindest regards."[2]

She had made some telling points, for the Ghormley committee was on weak ground on several scores. It included only orthopedists, thus slighting the views of physical therapists, pediatricians, and neurologists. Its statement that heat and muscle training had been "the basis" of treating most pre-Kenny cases conflicted with overwhelming testimony to the contrary. The bulk of its "Kenny" cases were almost certainly treated by a hodgepodge of adaptations. Most patients then arriving at Warm Springs, according to Dr. Robert Bennett, said they had had Kenny but most actually had received nothing but unrestricted activity and "hot towels a few times a day."[3] The committee had examined only ninety totally "non-Kenny method" patients, not many considering the variability of polio. Most were probably treated by expert hands, not at run-of-the-mill centers. The committee finally avoided saying whether previous treatment had been effective; it slid over the Kenny method's prevention of contractures and clung to the traditional, oversimplified view of paralysis; it both defended old methods and said hers "may" be good. The refusal to disclose the names of the centers that were visited was unscientific and irregular; it meant no other investigators could recheck the facts.

Liza's journalistic supporter Albert Deutsch called the report "a strangely unconvincing document, charged with emotional bias," though it grudgingly accepted her hot packs and muscle reeducation. Why was it so vituperative? He quoted one doctor: "How would you feel if your patient, after seeing Miss Kenny, bitterly accused you of having caused his crippled condition?" Such resentment, Deutsch wrote, made the report read more like a prosecutor's brief than a scientific document, and bias weakened its valid points.[4]

Dr. Ghormley maintained a discreet public silence during the controversy. In 1947 he published a short "History of the Treatment of

Poliomyelitis," a series of extracts from medical literature showing that various bits of Kenny treatment had been described by assorted doctors between 1911 and the 1920s. In it, he conceded that "much" of the old information had been overlooked or forgotten. A year later, he gave a talk strongly emphasizing the need for early movement and contrasting the glistening look of normal muscle with the dry, lackluster appearance of muscles that had been immobilized.

In 1953, after Elizabeth Kenny's death, Ghormley looked back on the fracas in a long interview:

> You know if she had come to this country and said, "I've got a treatment," without making extravagant and unjustified claims, there'd have been no trouble. Because her treatment was good—there's no doubt about that. Of course, to do without immobilization completely is, I think, wrong too. But she was a wonderful technician. And to indoctrinate a great number of people in her treatment was all right. But she came along and argued about the picture of the disease, on the basis of something she couldn't prove. If she'd set it up on the basis of a good treatment program alone, I'm sure 99 percent of doctors would never have crossed her on it.

What overall contribution, if any, had she made? "A vigorous program of physical therapy and reeducation of muscles," he readily acknowledged. "A great deal of this knowledge was in the literature—people just didn't read it. The average person *was* liable to treat them as she said, splint them and let them lie. But this was not true of many places." Still, "I don't think there's any question but that there is a difference in the treatment of polio because of her agitation."

It is hard to reconcile these statements with the harsh views of his committee in 1944. Despite the Ghormley report, the swing to new methods continued, though it may have been slowed. The report helped many doctors remain satisfied with spur-of-the-moment treatment, improvised when they suddenly faced epidemics. At the same time, heat and movement had become a rule; it was no longer possible for anyone to put patients in casts and forget about them.[5]

O'Connor announced that the controversy would not alter polio foundation policy. It would "continue to make available to the public such values as the Kenny method may possess by sponsoring and financing instruction." Medical director Gudakunst said: "Polio still kills and cripples, but those that aren't killed will get along lots better, thanks to the recent contributions of Miss Kenny and others." In the fall of 1947 his successor, Dr. Hart Van Riper, visited many areas suffering outbreaks and did not see orthodox immobilization used anywhere.[6]

The *Journal of the American Medical Association*, with unusual medical publishing speed, got the Ghormley report into its June 17, 1944, issue. The same issue carried a report on polio in Los Angeles County saying: "The Kenny concept of poliomyelitis has given us a new approach to diagnosis as well as treatment."[7]

♦♦

She demonstrated at Kenny Institute before a group of orthopedists and once more masterfully excited a muscle that the onlookers had agreed was paralyzed.

"Now what do you think?" she asked.

"We came to learn," they said.

"Too bad you didn't come before you started to write."

Could she stand these thickheaded doctors? Smoldering, she visited Buffalo, New York, where for too long pediatrician Marvin Israel had watched children screaming in splints. When both his sons contracted polio, he followed her precepts. He converted several colleagues and invited her to visit. One leading doctor agreed to show her his cases. "Well!" she said when they reached a stricken boy. "What plumber has been taking care of him?"

Chicago's Dr. Lewin, 90 percent pro-Kenny, asked her to read proof of a new book of his and see if there was anything she would like changed. She told him, "If you changed what I wanted, you'd have only two pages, the first flyleaf and the back one."[8]

Could the doctors stand *her*? Many had been becoming more hostile over her words and her ways. Many were questioning some newer claims. With Dr. John Pohl, she had begun calling polio a disturbance of the periphery (the skin and underlying tissues) and one that attacked muscles directly, rather than attacking the nerves first, thus producing other effects. A Harvard professor called this physiological nonsense; there would be more wrangling over it.

The Ghormley report, in short, was merely the official end to her medical honeymoon. And the main breaking point was her conviction that anything but her total approach and total concept was not only wrong but evil. She said in her autobiography, it is true, that "far from condemning" her skeptics, "I stoutly defend their right" to such challenge where patients' lives are concerned.[9] But she was seldom so tolerant; she could not really fathom the debate and slow change that greet any new medical thought; she considered all objections as either carping or stupidity.

She persisted in answering critics—she did it again just a few days after the Ghormley report—by parading her sturdy patient alongside the standard treatment's crippled one. "She gave the impression that deformities never occurred under her perfect treatment," testifies one doctor who worked at Kenny Institute. When they did appear, "she always said someone did something wrong." Even her backer, Dr. Knapp, wrote: "Miss Kenny has made inaccurate comparisons of patients treated by her methods and others."[10]

She insisted on calling the doctors' splints "archaic torture devices," their braces "medieval contraptions of leather and steel," and their iron lungs "torture chambers."[11] Seeing new patients, she would contemptuously order any existing splints removed. There was no consultation with the patient's own doctor and no tactful explanation. She treated the doctors in her classes like some medical men treated nurses. "Can you teach me to wiggle my ears?" one doctor once mockingly asked her. "It isn't necessary," she answered. "Any ass can do that."

Self-satisfied doctors, to be sure, provoked much of her wrath. Dr. John R. Paul in a 1971 history of polio assigns a share of the blame to some prominent orthopedists who tried to discredit her "almost, it would seem, out of professional jealousy." One University of Minnesota professor amused his students by putting on a wide hat and imitating her.[12]

Yet most quarreling doctors were sincere. Handled with tact, many of them might have come around. Instead, her name as a troublemaker began overshadowing her name as a healer. Dr. D. H. O'Donoghue, though he liked her method, said in the *Journal of the Oklahoma State Medical Association*: "Justifiably or not, Sister Kenny has antagonized a large group of the medical profession by a 'chip-on-the-shoulder' attitude, and she has the utmost contempt of any previous method of treatment. . . . She is completely intolerant of any opinion save her own." A book reviewer for the *Journal of the American Medical Association* thought her zeal bordered on religious fanaticism, and a University of Illinois sociologist agreed. The Kenny movement, he found, had many marks of a healing cult: her "legend" of humble origin and long struggle; her history of being set apart; her characterization of her opponents as criminal; her discovery of a new concept. She supplied all these critics with ammunition. "Personally," she said, "I consider that I have given the United States the greatest gift she has yet received from anywhere, and incidentally the world."[13]

More and more, her anger broke out uncontrolled. Sometimes it made her associates fear she might have a heart attack. Other times it was less real than calculated; she dominated some people by her fury. She often regretted her hard words, yet she could almost never apologize but only retire to her office or empty Park Avenue house and sink into a chair, chin in hand, or weep a bit. She well knew how much she was ridiculed. After some clashes she would say wryly, "After all, I'm only a lowly nurse." Even that status was shaky: she invented a "college" education for herself for *Who's Who in America*, and Martha Ostenso privately thought that "she was always scared something might break the bubble."

The atmosphere crackled. In irritation one day, Bennett at Warm Springs wrote Dr. Krusen: "After working with this so-called Kenny method of the past three years, I feel very strongly that any attempt to evaluate it statistically is an utter farce for the very simple reason that there is no Kenny method. Certainly the method approved by Miss Kenny today is not the method approved by her last week or last month or last year and will not be the method approved by her next month or next year. . . . Her present method is simply a modification of much that we have done in the past and will continue to change until she has absorbed everything that we have found."[14]

She was obviously still quietly willing to learn. She spent hours absorbing knowledge from John Pohl, Knapp, Cole, and others. "Her ideas were fluid. She simply reversed herself from time to time," say the doctors who worked with her. "Whenever anyone knocked her down, she came up with a new theory." But some alienated doctors, forgetting recent history and all the children in casts, had begun to assert that she had done nothing.

For this group, everything she said would henceforth be wrong. At the June 1944 AMA meeting, a Ghormley committee member said, "This report proves that what is good in the Kenny treatment is not new, and what is new is not good," a medical saw she was doomed to hear ten thousand times. Dr. O'Donoghue despaired that "at one of our largest national orthopedic meetings recently, we were treated to a debate on the Kenny method by well known and capable men, which progressed from discussion to argument and dispute, to actual recriminations, and finally degenerated to expostulation strangely reminiscent of the 'tis-'taint of our boyhood days." "I wonder what we have on trial," said another prominent doctor after the Ghormley report was read, "Sister Kenny's personality or the Kenny treatment."

As for Liza, one witness described her at her Chicago press conference on the Ghormley report as "a human tornado . . . with bristling white hair, flushed face and a grim, set mouth." Bitterly, she said:

"Whether I shall continue my work in America is for the people of America and the medical men of America to decide. . . . I have been asked to go to Hot Springs and Cold Springs and Lukewarm Springs and various other springs to have the honor of being on their directorates, and to share in their profits." The medical profession! She had asked only to be embraced by it, and now, spurned, she hated it. "They are infuriated because an outsider has done something they did not know." And, red with rage: "They have no mercy for the children of America. I have no mercy for them."[15]

July 1944. Minnesota lakes to gaze at again. The directors of the summer Aquatennial, a Minneapolis celebration, asked the famous Sister Kenny to ride in their parade. A little uncertain but willing, she joined the elaborate floats, bathing beauties, and royalty from every Alfalfa Festival and Livestock Show in six states. Down Nicollet Avenue, from the big, new sandstone post office, the parade started. Like a conquering heroine, she perched on top of an open car with the mayor and waved. She said it was like riding a hayrack.

"Everybody knew her, even the smallest children," a reporter wrote. "Mothers held their youngsters up in their arms to give them a better glimpse. . . . 'There's Sister Kenny,' someone would shout and . . . all around her name would be taken up. 'Sister Kenny, look over here. Take off your hat.'" Two Australian airmen jumped onto the running board of her car. A little boy selling American flags ran up and gave her one. She couldn't hide her pleasure. "I think they were glad to see me," she said.[16]

Early autumn. Polio at its peak, she went to Washington to address orthopedists and pediatricians at Gallinger Municipal Hospital. The meeting was advertised as closed to the public, but the audience numbered nearly 500, mainly anxious parents. For nearly two hours in a sweltering amphitheater, patient after patient was wheeled in, and she examined and probed and held the whole audience in attention.

At another Washington appearance, more than a thousand parents tried to crowd into a small lecture hall, "swept along," said the *Times-Herald*, "on a tidal wave of faith." Liza went home feeling much better. "I had a fine reception," she told friends. "I didn't know whether I was Al Capone or the Queen of England for a time." She was to return in October, she added, to attend a banquet with all the ambassadors from other nations. "This will be one of the most outstanding days in the history of Washington, so they say."[17]

Competition for the March of Dimes: the Elizabeth Kenny Institute in late 1943 had become part of a new Sister Elizabeth Kenny Foundation, taking over from the city. Mayor Kline, as its head, applied once more for a three-year, $840,000 National Foundation grant. O'Connor asked the National Academy of Sciences to advise him. It named a committee of well-known medical research men, which reported unfavorably; it said the institute lacked investigative staff and laboratory facilities. Looming in the background, though lightly mentioned, were Sister Kenny's "personal limitations." In early 1945 the new Kenny Foundation got O'Connor's definite "no." The divorce was now final.

The money to run the institute had to come from someplace, and neither Liza nor her loyal board of directors intended to bow in defeat. She had become the prime business of Mayor, and Board President, Kline's administration. Henry Haverstock, Sr., was a board member; she had put his son on his feet. Donald Dayton, a capable young department store executive, had a moderately withered left leg as a result of polio. There were also Jim Henry, her Exchange Club benefactor; I. S. Joseph of the welfare board; Alderman Al Bastis, 100 percent for Kenny; Mrs. C. C. Weber, who was financing the training of therapists; Dr. Pohl; Rosalind Russell. The Kenny Foundation launched its own national fund drive with Bing Crosby as honorary chairman.

She quickly involved the board in her fracases. As an early item, she wanted it to get an apology from the American Medical Association for her humiliation. She next wanted a trial for "perjury," to air the Ghormley report accusations. She began taking spastic children into the institute; she still considered, and rightly, that not enough was being done for cerebral palsy and thought she could get better results.

In March 1945 a spastic child, headed, so she thought, for her institute, was admitted first to General Hospital for an admission checkup. When she called to ask when he would be transferred, she was given a piece of stunning news. Weary of her battling, the university had decided to use the institute as a teaching center no longer, and the university's affiliated hospitals, like General Hospital, would cooperate only in polio cases. She admitted the child anyway, and a General Hospital department head called her and stormed, "If those spastic children aren't dismissed immediately, I'll come over and carry them out myself."

"The parents are over a thousand miles away," she replied. "Where will you put them, in the gutter?" But she disconsolately wrote the Kenny board, "I never undertake the treatment of any child without the supervision of a doctor," and she let the children be moved to another hospital.

She abruptly "resigned" from her new institute and foundation. She fled to New York again. "I am leaving the United States because it does not let the world know the value of my work," she said on this occasion. She would consider as a command, however, any suggestion from President Roosevelt that she stay. Would she return to Australia? "Nobody wants me there," she replied in a flat tone. "I may leave for Sweden at the invitation of the Swedish government." Now it was the *New York Journal-American* that printed a full page of jumbo photographs: six children being treated by Kenny therapists at Jersey City Medical Center, with the headline, "6 Good Reasons Why Sister Kenny Should Not Leave the U.S."

She just as abruptly returned to Minneapolis, arrived at the institute at 6:30 A.M. every day, and worked until noon on the polio patients. "I wish to express my deep appreciation and sincere gratitude" to the board members, she wrote, "in their action asking my reconsideration of my resignation." Just a week later *Time* reported: "For the umpteenth time, Sister Elizabeth Kenny . . . last week threatened to go home." She told the board she could not take all the aggravation—she had a bad heart. They had her examined; it was still fine.[18]

One day in April 1945 a lone young woman, Mary Stewart-Kenny, grasped a cold ship rail. It was a wet, dismal day on the North Atlantic, with waves that rolled like black dunes. Mary was twenty-eight, and despite the war was stubbornly on her way to Great Britain to marry a New Zealand flight lieutenant, Peter Jennings. She and Peter had met at the 1943 President's Birthday Ball in New York, and she soon told Liza, "We've clicked."

Mary until then had been Liza's assistant and daughter, but now she told friends that she had to break away. "Sister is wonderful, but she forgets us as people. She just thinks of the work." The only possible passage to Britain was on a Norwegian ammunition ship. Mary boarded it from a launch seven miles outside New York harbor, and through sixteen days of zigzagging, a submarine scare, and the muffled roar of depth charges, the young Australian dreamed of her "flight loo."[19]

The ship landed at Liverpool, and she phoned his base. "He can't come to the telephone," she was told at first, and finally, "The squadron leader is coming to Liverpool to meet you." Peter was missing. He had been pilot of a Lancaster bomber on the last mission of his tour; he had already dropped his bombs over Germany when his plane and another collided. Thirteen days after Mary's interview with the squadron leader, Hitler committed suicide; in another six days German armies began surrendering. Peter "just might" be in a prison camp, she was told.

On Mary's last night at home, Liza had laid out Mary's nightgown. She had been cheerless after Mary left. Now Mary cabled, and in June Liza flew to London; she and Mary were quickly in each other's arms, crying and laughing. It was not "Sister" now, Mary's usual name for her, but "Mother." Mary rested against her shoulder, they had their cry, then after a time Nurse Kenny announced, "Well, now, the work."

They went out to Queen Mary's Hospital at Carshalton, the site of Liza's London unit. A stick of fire bombs had straddled the hospital and damaged several buildings, but to Liza's surprise chief therapist Amy Lindsey and a crew of seven were still giving Kenny treatment. "I've fought for it," Miss Lindsey told them.

The Australian women looked in shock, however, at a London half in rubble. They strolled the dim streets—fuel was still short—and more happily heard "Waltzing Matilda" coming out of many pubs. An American serviceman spotted Liza's hat one night and said, "Aren't you Sister Kenny?" He took her to an Air Transport Command show, where she was cheered. Another day Liza and Mary walked into Queensland House, a Queenslanders' gathering site. There sat a skinny young antitank bombardier, just out of four years in German prison camps. He weighed a mere 100 pounds and was in London, he said, to put on some fat and get rid of some money. Introduced, he promptly asked Liza and Mary to lunch.

"You've got a lot of cheek," Liza said.

"Well, it isn't you I'm really interested in, it's her," he admitted, pointing to auburn-haired Mary.

Mary blushed, and the soldier, Stewart McCracken, son of a Queensland government official, became their constant escort. They liked his cheekiness; it was Australian and cheering. The war in the Pacific too was nearing its end when word came from Europe that the wreck of Peter's plane had been found and Peter's ring with it. The relationship between Mary and Stewart started changing, although Liza remained supremely unaware of it.

That was because she was still obsessed with Topic A: polio. They might all be sitting listening to the radio, when she would look up and say, "Let's shut that thing off and talk." Stewart would look at Mary and smile; they knew the subject. There was a poliomyelitis epidemic that summer in Belgium, and the Belgian National League against Infantile Paralysis asked Liza's help. She flew to Brussels with two Kenny technicians, treated patients, and taught for several days. She headed back to America around the first of September but left her technicians there for five months.

She returned to Minneapolis and an interview. "Sister Kenny announced soberly Monday night that she was happy," wrote a somewhat surprised newspaperman. She had dictated slowly and exactly: "Dr. DuPrague, president of the Belgian Red Cross, told me the work was 'magnifique.' Then he remarked that I had produced the atomic bomb in the world of medicine."[20]

She inwardly took note of her unannounced sixty-fifth birthday. She was heavy but still straight; her shoulders were square. The extra flesh made her jaw less overprominent. She was more self-possessed and calm much of the time, a woman who had stirred the world.

But she resigned once more during 1945 as a kind of little prod. "I have been notified by the Department of Justice that my term of residence in the United States has expired," she wrote the Kenny board, irritated at thickheaded government officials—who soon retreated.[21]

In Hollywood, Rosalind Russell was having her own troubles trying to sell the evanescent film *Sister Kenny*. She had visited Minneapolis several times, and each time Liza took her to Kenny Institute to show her how to give treatment. "Here," she would say, demonstrating, "you'll need to know this." The project remained so tenuous that the actress was unsure.[22]

In mid-1943 Miss Russell had given birth to a baby boy, Lance. In the spring of 1944, Liza went to California to speak to medical groups and to visit the Brissons. Lance was in the bath one day, when her gaze became sharper; then she said, "It's not a serious condition, but he has a spastic muscle in his right leg."

Brisson anxiously ran his home movies of the baby, slowing them for Liza's scrutiny. The infant should have expert attention, she declared; an orthopedist agreed, and the boy was sent to Kenny Institute under a false name. He was treated for eight or ten weeks, learned to walk while there, and left walking normally. The diagnosis remained uncertain. "He had been slow in developing, and did appear to have a mild spasticity when admitted," explains Dr. Pohl, who supervised his treatment. "He responded very quickly, however. What exactly was wrong is hard to say." The important fact was that Rosalind Russell's son went home walking properly. He grew up to play baseball and to ski, and his mother never looked at his leg without thinking of "Sister."

Determinedly the actress trudged from one studio friend to another to talk of a Kenny picture and to hear mainly, "We borrow money from banks, and they won't let us have any for something about a nurse." Without publicity, the Brissons financed a $40,000 Kenny medical documentary film. The idea was Freddie's. Liza had been tossing off so many directions about what "her" movie must show that he told her, "What you need is a technical film." Returning to Minnesota, she wasted no time before telephoning department-store executive Donald Dayton, the new president of the Kenny board, to say that she had to have $40,000 to make a movie. He said he would consult the board and see if the money could be found. She phoned again that afternoon.

"Mr. Dayton, have you done anything?"

"No, Sister, I've been busy."

"Well, never mind," she said, "I've got it." She had just learned that the Brissons would supply the money, though she had not asked them for it.

In Hollywood, Rosalind was at the peak of her long stardom; she had successfully played a troop of career women who scrapped with, but finally succumbed to, Gary Grant and a host of other male stars, and she was the country's third best box-office draw. Under contract to do three RKO pictures with the right of story approval, she told production head Charles Koerner, "If you want me to make *any* pictures here, you've got to make *Sister Kenny*."

Koerner gave in and glumly begged the brilliant Dudley Nichols to redo Mary McCarthy's unsuccessful script. A tall, wavy-haired Irish-descended idealist, Nichols had written *The Informer*; and his credits also included *For Whom the Bell Tolls* and *Stagecoach*. "Hell, I don't know anything about the woman," he said, but Rosalind begged him to go to Minneapolis and see her work. He went with a bias against her, he admitted; an Ohio physician's son, he was partial to doctors, not their foes. Handsome and dignified in a pin-striped suit, he arrived at Kenny Institute the week after the damaging mid-1944 Ghormley report was issued. An unyielding Liza was about to give a demonstration to twenty-five doctors.

A child lay on the table. "Will one of you come forward and examine this girl?" the nurse asked. The doctors sat quietly, so she turned to a senior orthopedist. "Will you kindly come forward, Doctor?" He did and said the patient exhibited a pelvic obliquity (twisted pelvis), a shortened leg, and an absence of plantar flexion (she could not flex her foot), all supposedly irreversible aftereffects of paralytic polio. Two other doctors confirmed the diagnosis.

Liza put the child over the foot of the table and, she explained later, "stretched her quadratus lumborum [in her back], corrected her pelvic obliquity, manipulated the foot, released the brake put upon the movement by the shortening, and the muscles responded." The medical visitors watched from chairs and tables as the guest expert acknowledged that his diagnosis had been wrong and that the muscle functions could be restored. The sophisticated screenwriter went back to California biased in Liza's favor.

Before 1944 was out, however, the slim Rosalind took sick, "overwork and everything else," she felt, causing a nervous breakdown. Liza anxiously advised her to eat more. The actress recovered rapidly but had to fulfill a commitment to Columbia Pictures. Liza meanwhile read and liked Nichols's script and gave him a copy of a laudatory letter from her Minnesota medical supporters to the Australian ambassador. "We cannot say that all medical men are boneheads," she told Nichols.

Preparations for shooting started in fall 1945. A Hollywood newsman asked Liza if Miss Russell resembled her as a young woman. "Yes, quite a bit, although I was even thinner than she in those days." Liza was on hand when the star was being fitted for early Nurse Kenny clothes. "What is her waist?" Liza asked. "Twenty-four," the fitter answered. "Hmmm!" Liza said. "Mine was twenty-three."

Nichols wrote, produced, and directed the film. He thought the aging therapist was a great woman, but he did not want her on the set. Australian Valerie Harvey, whom Liza considered to be her most capable therapist, was technical adviser. Liza visited the studio only once during the shooting. The picture was in its last stages; the wardrobe department had fitted the star with "symmetricals"—generous false calves under her stockings—as well as padding under her clothes to make her resemble Sister Kenny. Miss Russell, alerted, quickly whipped off all the pads; she was not at all sure of Liza's reaction.

The film was completed before the end of the year. Miss Russell was eager and pretty as the young nurse, and full of flip and vinegar as the old. In command of every movement, she stomped and thundered and moved the limbs of children just as Sister Kenny did. In Minneapolis,

Nichols had noticed that Sister Kenny, when she handled patients or lectured, "always used her right hand to be hard, to make tough gestures, to insist, emphasize. Her left hand always made gentle movements." He pointed this out to the star, and she acted it that way.

Liza squirmed at one point at her film self's slightly embroidered love-making with Dan, the shadowy love of her early nursing days, who for the screen became "Kevin." "Get them on the phone!" she ordered Mary. "A clinch! I will not have them making me a cheap little pantry girl." Her life, she told the studio, was no "maudlin love scene." The love scenes as filmed actually followed her own accounts fairly closely; she evidently did not find those maudlin.

The name "Dan" had been called an alias. But shortly before shooting began in late 1944 Liza came to the door of Valerie Harvey's room one morning, a room at Liza's house in Minneapolis, where Valerie was staying. "She was holding what I thought was a cable or telegram," Valerie remembers, and "she was crying, really crying." Dazed, Liza mumbled something about a friend dying. "A very dear friend," she sobbed. "Nobody would even believe I was interested, and now he is dead."[23]

Shortly afterward the following text of a "cable" from "Red Raven, New South Wales, Australia," got into the newspapers:* "Daniel Lewellyn Montgomery passed away at his home November first. Desired this message to be sent to you. 'Here in the silent hills you loved so well I wait for thee.' "[24]

The message closed: "Accept the sympathy of Craik and Gallager, Attorneys." However, there is no known place called Red River in Australia. There is no record of a New South Wales law firm named Craik and Gallager. This text, at least, might have been a studio publicity stunt.[25]

Who had died, then, when Valerie Harvey had seen Liza so upset? "Dan," she had told Rosalind Russell, had bought a house and station in Australia, hung up her picture, and told her the place was waiting for her, "and this went on for years. But I finally told him, 'I'm too old now, and I'm going on with my work.' " During her Townsville and tropical

*** And into Elizabeth Kenny's personal correspondence file at Kenny Institute, where the author found it years later, typed on a Western Union blank marked "COPY—CABLE."**

years, sisters Lydia and Doris Rollinson had believed that she visited Dan on her summer journeys south. "I visit him while the lilacs are in bloom," she once told them. However, when the movie, showing an aging "Kevin" in Australia, played on that continent, she told an interviewer, "They have put the man in the wrong country." Adopted daughter Mary believes "Dan" finally lived and was buried in South Africa.[26]

In the year 1945, in Liza's sixties, there were certainly no more Dans. The word began to get around, though, that "Danny Boy" was her favorite song, and orchestras played it for her at supper clubs. Not considering that too maudlin either, she often requested it, and Rosalind Russell often saw her cry as it was played.

Asked why she hadn't married, the nurse now usually said something lugubrious like: "I couldn't retire to a home of my own and have children, knowing that other children whom I could save were becoming cripples." Or, repeatedly: "Medicine is a jealous lover."

Once, however, she scornfully told the Rollinson sisters that the man they believed was "Dan" had a weak liver.

"What do you mean?" they asked.

"Because if he married, he'd die!"

What she was saying at least that once was that he wasn't really ready to be taken up on his offer. But she said it half-laughing.

"You can't trust any man," she would sometimes tell Mary, caustically.

"How about your father?" Mary once asked.

"Oh, that's different," Liza said, laughing again.

Blue-eyed Mary wanted Stewart and vice versa, and there was not much trouble about it on either side. Discharged from the army, McCracken was returned to Australia. Liza still thought of Mary as her successor. At first she opposed the marriage; she even offered Stewart a sum of money, something to "help" him in civilian life. He gave her a sharply Australian answer, unrecorded. Once she decided she was beaten Stewart says, she was "as kind as could be." Liza and Mary flew to Australia in April 1946, and Mary and Stewart were married in Brisbane in May.

After the honeymoon, Liza and Mary had many quiet talks. "You have a different look in your eyes," Liza would say.

"Well, I'm happy," Mary would answer.

"Well, weren't you happy with me?"

"Yes, but it's a different sort of happiness."

Liza glanced away just a little, with a strange look. Later she told Mary, "I have missed a lot by not having a family of my own." But just after the marriage—when a cousin asked, "Well, who did Mary marry?"—Liza scoffed: "Just a man!"

15

Turmoil

"CONTAGION, No Admittance," said a sign. Beyond it, beds and cribs jammed the corridors. On a litter, just carried in from an ambulance, a boy of ten cried; he was wheeled away to be hot packed. In a crib a little blonde girl stood and waved. She was getting well. In the next crib, another girl was asleep beneath her hot packs. Her sore and assaulted muscles were trying to pull her into an "S" shape; the Kenny therapists were trying to prevent it.

Everywhere nurses in white and therapists in blue carried hot packs that filled the rooms with their pungent smell of wet wool. Volunteers, many of them patients' mothers, helped place the hot packs, carried bed-pans, fed patients, and read to them. Other parents hovered nearby—one mother and father had four children in institute beds, several had two or three. One man leafed through a magazine held upside down; no one commented; his son was "critical." A husband and wife moved slowly toward the door. Their child had just died. This was Elizabeth Kenny Institute, Minneapolis, in the sweltering midsummer of 1946, in the grip of the greatest polio epidemic the United States had yet seen.

One hundred and eighty-seven patients at one point were crowded into the old gray building; its official bed complement was sixty-five. Dr. John Pohl's four-year-old daughter was a patient, her polio nonparalytic. A lean, anxious Pohl and a few medical assistants worked endless hours, making rounds, giving spinal taps to prospective admissions, hastily deciding whether a patient had to be placed in a respirator to maintain life, again and again doing a hurried tracheotomy (cutting an emergency opening in the throat for an air passage). Faced with a horrendously high bulbar polio incidence, a university group led by Drs. A. B. Baker and Robert Priest had successfully started the use of tracheotomies to get oxygen to starved brain cells. This cut the mortality rate in the respiratory form of the disease from 80 to 20 percent. Baker, chief of neurology, also broke down bulbar polio into subclasses, pinpointing the patients who most needed tracheotomies or a respirator to prevent death; he put the use of the awkward iron lung on a more scientific basis.

Kenny Institute filled, General Hospital filled, University Hospitals filled; a Sheltering Arms emergency polio hospital filled; another was set up at the army's Fort Snelling. Some of the teen-age Kenny patients asked for a piano. Sister Kenny told them that if there was room for a piano, there was room for another bed; they got the bed. An Emergency Polio Committee constantly had to make torturous decisions: which patients in the city should get the available respirators? which had no chance and must be left to die as peacefully as possible? which should the Kenny therapists—always too few—concentrate on? Kenny therapists gave the treatment in all these centers.

The therapist placed the first packs as the typical new patient tried to control his pain by lying rigid and immobilizing himself, frightened to move or let anyone move him. After relief of fright and pain, the therapist could begin some movement of limbs and joints. Meticulous attention to detail marked the work of these muscle technicians, and all shared Liza's positive attitude. This included no hasty resort to braces. A Swiss medical visitor, examining one woman, said of her right leg: "There is no control whatsoever there. It is completely flail." The other leg? "A little toe motion, that's all." The woman then got up and walked across the room with a pair of short Canadian crutches, just walking sticks. She had learned to rest her weight against the ligaments of her joints in a kind of skillful balancing, as well as using her hip and thigh muscles and the few remaining foot muscles.[1] Such results, more than any controversial theories, were Elizabeth Kenny contributions.

She was there in the midst of the maelstrom. She had rushed back from Australia in July and was again getting up at five in the morning and working all day, supervising, teaching, and taking a hand with the most vexing cases, getting home after midnight sometimes for another four or five hours of sleep. She also gaily tossed strewn toys back to tots in cribs—gloom would help no one—and, when she could, assured teenage girls, "You'll be dancing." She had evolved into "the keenest observer of the patient I had ever seen," another visiting doctor remarked. "Just by watching a child breathe, she could tell how much involvement there was in the chest wall, diaphragm, neck, and throat." She was not often wrong, and when she was, it was usually because she was overoptimistic. But sometimes it was the reverse: sometimes the human being's recuperative powers were greater than even she calculated.[2] She knew this, hence her conscious optimism. *Try* was her law.

She also worked like a coal heaver. She drank more cold tea. She walked through convalescent wards, and her eyes shone at seeing children sitting up and bouncing in their beds, or seeing the sturdier boys out of bed fighting, hot packs and all. Her eyes shone even brighter when she entered the rooms of the severely affected. They would need her kind of treatment—sometimes one or two years of the most skillful attention and maybe in the long run, she would at times concede, braces; but the concession was made only after great effort.

Dr. Pohl was able in late July 1946 to report that "in six years we have treated 500 Minneapolis polio victims, and not a single one is in a crippled children's school or hospital. That remarkable record is found in Minneapolis and nowhere else in the world." During 1940 to 1945, the number of youngsters with polio disabilities at the city's school for disabled children, Michael Dowling, dropped from 164 to 15, and no new patients crippled by polio were admitted. As of late July 1946, not a brace had been put on a Kenny patient in three years; none had needed surgery.[3] The cruel 1946 epidemic, however, was to put a few children in Michael Dowling and put braces on a larger number. The epidemic continued through late fall. Minneapolis had 763 cases; Minnesota, 2,881; the United States, 25,698, one out of every fourteen fatal and (in Minnesota) six out of ten paralytic. The Kenny staff treated 760 patients, 80 percent of them at Kenny Institute. As always, the institute generally got the worst patients, both from the Twin Cities and from far away.

Liza engaged in little acrimony that summer and autumn; there was no time for it. She did storm into one polio committee meeting, tongue-lashed the group for not notifying her, then stalked out. Her sister Julia came from Australia to stay at her home and help for a while. Julia's capable daughter Mary Farquharson was working at the institute. Educated as a Kenny technician in Brisbane, she had insisted on going on to full nurse's training. That made no big hit with Liza, but she still liked her.

Australian therapist Valerie Harvey was living with Liza too. At the Fort Snelling emergency hospital one day, she subjected Valerie—who was her right arm—to a typical tirade. "I know just how you feel," Dr. Pohl tried to tell Valerie later. "You want to go right home and pack. Don't do it. Everyone who works with her feels that way sometimes." Valerie went home at last at the end of the day, and Liza walked up to her with a glass of sherry. "Here," she said, "I think you need this. You've had a hard day."

"New York Honors Sister Kenny in Person Tonight," shone the lights over the RKO Palace in Times Square. It was the evening of September 27, 1946, and the world premiere of the new film *Sister Kenny*. Twenty thousand people jammed Times Square, filling the street and blocking traffic. Police tried to keep order. It was impossible.[4]

Liza had been the guest of honor at a pre-premiere party given by the Floyd Odlums—the industrialist and his aviatrix wife, Jacqueline Cochrane; not long before Liza had successfully treated the stubborn pain and spasms of arthritis in Odlum's arm. Limousines had to let the party group out a half block from the theater. Police made a path for Liza, who was dressed in a long evening gown, pearls, and a sequined bag, and laughing hard as if to say, "Isn't this ridiculous?" Holding her arm and running interference was Freddie Brisson. Rosalind had stayed away because she wanted it to be "all Sister's show." It was that: the crowd screamed as she neared the theater and climbed a platform to say a few words. As she started down, a barrier broke, and the crowd jolted the platform out of place. Liza teetered but grabbed Brisson's arm and, still aglow, entered the theater down a red plush carpet.

An hour late, the film started, with the title *Sister Kenny* deployed across a map of Australia. Soon a dour-looking Dr. Aeneas McDonnell was showing a young and compassionate Nurse Kenny some severely crippled infantile paralysis patients and saying in a low, mournful voice, "Eighty-eight out of every 100 cases finish this way"—a horrendous exaggeration. Her first bush polio patient, cured, was contrasted with a patient who had received orthodox treatment, a boy with crutches walking crabwise. Her Australian medical antagonists were made a composite "Dr. Brack," a paragon of sarcasm and know-it-all. Later in the film Miss Russell was a marvelous model of an older Sister Kenny, deep voiced, stiff and lofty in bearing, flip of tongue, often angry. "They can't hear the crying of children," she said of her medical foes.

The movie centered all of Liza's life around polio. Faced with the problem of making her a nurse, it graduated her from a nursing school in Toowoomba. That caused a little comment back home. Rosalind's Kennylike performance was the best part of the picture, prompting Liza's former Brisbane clinic director Dr. Fryberg to write: "Offer her the congratulations of one who knows you. . . . She out-tigers the tiger." Though it found the film "violently pro-Kenny," *Life* magazine titled it "Movie of the Week." But the story, for all of Dudley Nichols's artistry, was saccharine and one-sided, and the picture was considered a financial failure, though it eventually pulled out of the red to show a profit. "The propaganda was too heavy and spoilt an excellent character piece by Rosalind Russell," wrote Harry Summers, Liza's best Australian journalistic interpreter. "The film made Sister Kenny an infallible figure."[5]

That earned her more enmity among doctors. Bosley Crowther in the *New York Times* said, "The doubt that the film casts on doctors of conventional persuasion is cruel," and John McCarten of the *New Yorker* objected to the portrayal of Kenny clinics with a reverence that suggested Lourdes. Dudley Nichols never publicly defended his film, but he explained years later that he thought the important lesson of Elizabeth Kenny's story was that a revolutionary genius can sometimes know more than authority. "I tried to get at the basic truth of Kenny's life through a dramatic organization of actual or symbolic happenings. . . . The highest aim of fiction, as I see it, is to get at the real truth. . . . I had to condense, put the attitudes and actions of many doctors into one doctor, and thus the result to the literal mind seems to be fiction whereas it is the deeper truth."[6]

In essence, of course, he was correct, but that didn't help her with American doctors.

The movie put her even more in the limelight—the movie and the flamboyant ads for it, which proclaimed that "she was branded 'fake,' 'fool,' 'charlatan.' Yet the world learned to call her 'Angel.'" "One of the world's great stories of love, sacrifice and conflict." "She won FAME but lost LOVE." James Montgomery Flagg painted Rosalind Russell for the twenty-four-sheets, the big billboards. She wore a white nurse's uniform, held a child, and gestured sweepingly. In the background stood Australian eucalyptus trees. RKO Radio Pictures suggested "ballyhoo" or local publicity stunts to theater owners: "Nominate a nurse resembling Rosalind Russell"; "Celebrate Sister Kenny Week."

Liza loved it. In November the Kenny Foundation erected a fund-raising booth in Times Square, with a sign forty feet high. The staff played records to attract crowds, then had entertainers like Kate Smith sing and give the Kenny pitch. Liza showed up one Saturday night and, before anyone knew it, had the microphone. Within five minutes, 15,000 people were crowding Times Square. "She was a show gal," says Al Baum, a Kenny East Coast publicist who was present. "She began to be disappointed if there wasn't a crowd."[7]

And she flitted. "She didn't want to be stagnant," Baum reminisces. She would call him up and say, "I'd like to go out tonight, but I have no escort." He would get the car—"We always had a big car for her"—and pick her up. She usually insisted on riding up front with the chauffeur. The destination was often a nightclub. She had begun to relish night-clubs; she was almost invariably introduced for a bow, and people would come to her table and say, "God bless you, Sister." Watching a dance act at Earl Carroll's with daughter Mary, she made a medical observation: "You know, that exercise is very bad for the quadratus lumborum." When Baum took her to the circus, she pointed to the bareback riders and said, "You know, I could do that and stand up. If I put my hat over my horse's head, he'd rear while I was standing."

She regularly occupied a suite at New York's elegant Hotel Delmonico on Park Avenue. She overtipped the house staff, explaining, "They expect it from me." She made wealthy friends, whom she usually converted into Kenny Foundation campaign workers or benefactors. Finding her different and refreshing, tycoons like Floyd Odlum (Atlas Corporation) took her to dinner or lunch. Or Chester LaRoche, an advertising man (Young & Rubicam), who was married to Rosalind Russell's sister. Or young Orin Lehman of the investment and banking family, who had lost a leg as an army flyer and who founded Just One Break Inc.—JOB—for the handicapped. The Fox sisters, of the film family, often joined her for tea or a ride in her chauffeured car. Spotting her unmistakable hats, the police often stopped traffic for her. Her clothes became smarter and less ornate, and she wore fewer geegaws; but she still wore big hats, saying, "They wouldn't know me without them."

She began giving old-style Thanksgiving, Christmas, and Easter parties at her gracious new house in Minneapolis. She quoted Shakespeare and Shelley to her therapists and friends, told outback yarns, and laughed full-throated laughs, her head back and her shoulders shaking. Yet true intimacy still came hard. She worked and lived with Valerie Harvey for ten years before she called her anything but "Miss Harvey," and then it was "Valerie," not Val. The Dr. Pohls and the James Henrys were among the few friends who became close; Henry had arranged her Exchange Club living stipend. That monthly sum, her house, and her expense-paid living elsewhere provided a degree of financial security. She was able to improve on it, for she was still a good businesswoman and liked to say so. She collected $50,000 from RKO Pictures for *Sister Kenny*. Magazines called her for articles, and she volunteered others, for tidy payments. At the same time, she turned down innumerable profit-making schemes like Sister Kenny dolls, hats, or endorsements, and she frequently would pull fifty or sixty dollars from her purse and give it to a patient. Often people offered her gifts of cash; she had them write their checks to the Kenny Foundation. A staff member remembers one for $40,000. Another time, a well-fixed widow wanted to leave her her entire estate, as well as a lake home. Liza persuaded her, too, to make the gift to "the work" and had the home turned over later to the woman's grandniece.[8]

She continued to stay often with the Brissons at their airy French provincial home in Beverly Hills. Just back from someplace—New York, London, Pago Pago—she would stalk in, make for the library, and plump down in a big chair. She would take off her gloves, businesslike, open her old black calfskin handbag—no lipstick or powder puffs in it, only papers—dig out a ream or so of her latest polio documentation, and start to read aloud. Then she would say to Rosalind and Freddie, "Don't you think that I'm right?"

The newspapers would discover she was at Rosalind Russell's home and interview her about her latest forays. Their stories would inevitably start the phones ringing; the calls were mainly from parents trying to persuade her to see their unfortunate children. "Don't you get a terrific boot out of all this?" Rosalind once asked buoyantly. "Isn't it satisfying?" Liza said, "You don't know what it is to tell people you can't help them." When Rosalind and Freddie took her to a restaurant or a party, however, all the film stars would tell her how much they adored her, and she drank that in like old brandy.

In the afternoons, Liza would walk in the Brissons' garden and breathe in the aroma of a pair of Australian eucalyptus trees. In the evening, Rosalind would sometimes walk out to the guest house and sit on Liza's bed. "She was huge in a bed—I'd kid her, hug her and kiss her. We'd wrestle around, really have a brawl. I loved being around such a human being—she was a one-man show."

One night the actress said, "I'm afraid to die."

"Why?" Liza asked.

"I'd like to live forever."

Liza said, "I'd like to live every moment of my life, but not a moment after."

She would be up at six o'clock and on the telephone. Calling doctors. Complaining. Checking. How was the Kenny movement going in southern California? Calls to New York, Minneapolis, any city. She awoke sometimes at one, two, or three o'clock in the morning to reach for the phone and put in a long-distance call to some friend or foe. Her first reaction to any criticism was: "Get him on the phone!" She half-lived on the phone. At the Delmonico in New York, her secretary would leave her after dinner. Liza would tell her that she was going to have a quiet evening reading or listening to the radio—thrillers—and "get some sleep." Then the secretary would arrive and find she had spent her whole evening on the phone and had scheduled four new appointments, a press conference, and a visit to a hospital.

With Mary gone, she was alone more. At times she could endure it quietly for only a few hours, then she had to have someone to listen to her. So she would phone again—a Kenny Foundation functionary, a Kenny cousin in New York, Dr. Lewin in Chicago, or Freddie Brisson, her frequent New York escort—and say, "I'd like to go out," meaning a dinner club and music. But she could spoil the evening sometimes by not saying five words or by talking only of polio.

She was beginning to tell the same polio stories again and again, parrotlike; she flourished this document and that, though she knew them all to the letter. "This is it. . . . Here is the proof. . . . Isn't this right?" She was obsessed with the conviction that she was right. Yet, alone, she sometimes asked herself, "Am I wrong?" Her lonely room was soon filled with her ghosts: her failures, defeats, humiliations. The only answer was the phone. "Lonely? She was the loneliest person in the world," her sister Julia thought.

An old comrade-in-arms came by. Dr. Abe Fryberg of Brisbane clinic days, now Queensland's deputy director-general of health, and Dr. Thomas Victor Stubbs Brown had been named by the Queensland cabinet to inspect polio care in Britain and America. They arrived on the downslope of the 1946 epidemic with its thousands of cases to find "what was to all intents Kenny treatment everyplace in the United States," everyplace but at the Kendalls' in Baltimore, who were "getting results as good as Kenny's with the old splinting. But they were masters."

They observed several thorough demonstrations at the Kenny Institute, supervised by the "Tiger"; she grinned as Fryberg called her that. He found the treatment "very different" from what he had seen in 1936 and "not what was presented to the Queensland Royal Commission." He and Stubbs Brown issued an official report within a few months. They agreed with her about 75 percent. They acknowledged that in the older style treatment, which they still saw in some places, especially in Australia, any physiotherapy was most unusual before the third week, and this was much earlier than it had been in the past. They heard wide acknowledgment of advances made with Kenny methods and recommended that "treatment based on that of Sister Kenny," with modifications, be adopted in Australia.

Unfortunately, Liza's first word of the largely favorable document was a brief cable from Charles Chuter saying that it had called her concept "not proven." "Impossible for Brown Fryberg to give report on concept," she cabled back. "Took me 30 years to teach them immobilization was damaging. Will take another 30 years for them to understand what I am talking about." She cabled Fryberg in like vein but the next day addressed him again: "Take no notice of yesterday's cable. Have received Australian news summary. Approve of your report as presented." But when she read the full report later, she cabled Fryberg a third time: "Consider it weak, unscientific, contradictory and inaccurate." Mary and Stewart also confronted Fryberg on his return, and Mary told him his report wasn't worth much. He philosophically told her, "You have more spunk than you used to."

Between her nastier messages, Liza was writing Dr. Fryberg a pleasant congratulatory letter on his promotion to full director general of health, and in Australia later she tolerantly told him, "Old ideas are tough to get rid of, however there is no doubt that you made some very good observations." After Fryberg and Stubbs Brown went home she complained that "there's no one left for me to sharpen my wits on."[9]

That was not quite true. She still had Basil O'Connor. He, too, was now "ignoring the cries of crippled children," and during the 1946 epidemic, she complained, he had refused to support her treatment center. In rebuttal, the National Foundation photostated some of the checks paid to the Kenny Institute with March of Dimes funds; from May 1, 1946, to April 30, 1947, they totaled $136,467. But the polio foundation was merely paying for patient care on the same basis it made payments to any other hospital. All institute operations, including training and maintaining therapists and paying emergency workers, cost $423,891.

New York Daily News columnist Ed Sullivan, who would before long become a television star, embraced Liza. The Kenny Foundation had to ask the public for funds, he charged, "because Basil O'Connor's richly-endowed National Foundation won't let Sister Kenny have the money. . . . O'Connor, custodian of $20 million of public contributions, should render an accounting." O'Connor sent Sullivan an answer, and Sullivan conceded O'Connor's point that the National Foundation had invested $653,852 to disseminate Kenny methods. Sullivan nonetheless thought: "The issue is too grave, the time is too limited for the National Foundation to advise Sister Kenny to proceed through routine channels of application. . . . Everything else is dwarfed by the staggering revelation that the National Foundation has been proceeding in the completely erroneous belief that what it has been teaching is the Kenny method, when the woman who created the concept and the treatment points out that what is being taught is NOT the Kenny method. 'It is as if a Boy Scout's knowledge of first aid were opposed to the knowledge of a specialist,' she says."

The Sullivan affair was the "only time we got O'Connor to engage in direct controversy with her," the Kenny publicist Al Baum reports. "It was pretty rough but it was effective publicity." Liza began calling her rival money-raiser "the O'Connor Foundation," saying it was spending millions of dollars that belonged to the people to teach an obsolete theory. O'Connor's usual public reply to her personal attacks was "no comment." But between 1941 and the mid-1950s, the only year in which the annual March of Dimes raised less than it had raised the year before was 1946, a year when Kenny anti-National Foundation publicity was nearly at its brashest.[10]

Behind the scenes in that epidemic year, the polio foundation sent agents to Minneapolis, "and they literally wanted to take over management of the epidemic and push Kenny people out," says Donald Dayton, by then president of the Kenny board. "They applied tremendous pressure, including political pressure. O'Connor told the new mayor, Democrat Hubert Humphrey, 'My boss is your boss,' meaning Roosevelt. Humphrey rode with us."

By 1946 the polio foundation's main thrust was actually beginning to turn from interest in treatment toward interest in the polio virus. Polio research, long seemingly scattershot and unproductive, was beginning to hint at a possible result: a successful vaccine.

In 1945 the foundation had first hired a research director, Dr. Harry Weaver. Many scientists objected and said, "You can't direct research." Sometimes not, but in this case there were already enough clues so that a clever, aggressive man could start traveling to laboratories asking: What are the knowledge gaps? Who might fill them? In this way, Weaver interested a good many scientists in doing polio research and worked closely with the scientific advisory committees who were helping to allocate the research funds.

Weaver felt strongly that research in better treatment methods could no longer dominate and that foundation interest and spending had to be turned to prevention. Scientists at Yale and elsewhere had determined that polio virus was excreted from the stools of both polio patients and persons who had merely been in contact with patients and had no symptoms. This not only helped show how the virus was spread during epidemics; it also showed how thousands of people were exposed but not diseased, thereby becoming a population in which an epidemic was not likely to repeat itself for a while. Why then couldn't millions be purposely exposed and protected? If viruses could be grown and suitably modified in the laboratory, they might indeed be made into a safe vaccine.

In 1947 Weaver visited the University of Pittsburgh and asked a thirty-three-year-old researcher, Jonas Salk, to turn to the polio problem and help type the more than 100 known strains of polio virus to see how many broader types they fell into. The number turned out to be three, each a possible cause of the disease. The knowledge was essential to making an effective vaccine. Salk both spearheaded the typing effort and went on to try to develop the vaccine. He was only one of a growing corps of scientists who, with the foundation, Weaver, and O'Connor, increasingly saw prevention, and not a therapist's magic hands, as the way to fight the polio virus on its home ground.

There were still to be several years of polio epidemics, however, with devastating results. Therapist Kenny was in full sally now against anti-Kenny doctors and "modified Kenny," "semi-Kenny," and "modern" treatments. She visited such centers, she said, and saw patients with curved spines, arched backs, cupped shoulders, and hollow chests. Her meetings with doctors were becoming fewer, she complained, leaving their knowledge in a chaotic state.

She blamed almost everything on the polio foundation, saying that it was vital to have more training centers. She wrote innumerable reports, documents, multipage letters, and statements. They were clumsy, inept, and sometimes ridiculous, but they were also in part right.

Too many hospitals were haphazardly applying hot packs a few hours a day and calling it "Kenny," and too many doctors were attempting to treat the disease "without bothering to learn how," according to Gudakunst of the National Foundation. As late as the 1950s, the *Journal of the American Medical Association* would call for establishing "strategically located medical centers" throughout the country for polio treatment, and Bennett of Warm Springs would find that patients were commonly developing severe deformities because of "gross negligence and disregard."[11]

There was indeed a habitual shortage of qualified therapists. The sporadic nature of polio made it difficult to maintain such people everywhere, and physical therapy as a profession was just beginning to come into its own. Kenny treatment or anything like it also cost time and money, so some critics scoffed at wasting weeks treating the 50 or 60 percent of polio patients who were "nonparalytic" and seemed to recover without fancy treatment. Liza advocated treating nonparalytics at least twenty-three days to abolish spasm; she and Pohl argued that they often suffered stiff muscles that *would* leave curved spines, sway backs, twisted feet, and other deformities if untreated.

Many Kenny foes hooted, but by the 1950s this fact was being more commonly recognized. One study of seventy-five nonparalytics found that 38 percent showed at least minimal weakness in one or more muscle groups a year and a half to six years after their illness. Dr. Robert Bingham, a Riverside, California, orthopedist, examined World War II army "malingerers," some of them men threatened with court-martials and sent to psychiatric wards because of constant physical complaints. At least one army recruit in 100, he found, had muscle weakness or minor deformities almost certainly caused by mild, often unrecognized polio. Such deformities, it was learned, often got worse with age. Many "bad backs" might be the result of undiagnosed polio.[12]

One continuing difficulty was that there was never a scientifically valid test of Kenny versus other treatment, by selecting a large enough number of the afflicted in a single epidemic, putting half under Kenny care, half under some other, and following them for some years. Several people considered such a study, but within a few years of Liza's arrival, this kind of test on any scale became impossible. No one wanted to subject a large enough group to the unadulterated orthodox treatment.

There were a few small-scale comparisons. In 1943, Winnipeg Children's Hospital compared 100 cases treated before 1941 with 100 similar cases given Kenny treatment later. The conclusion was that Kenny was ten times better—Liza repeated that a thousand times. At New York Orthopedic Hospital between May 1941 and May 1942, investigators compared twenty-four patients given only Kenny treatment; twenty-four given conventional treatment, followed by Kenny treatment late in their illness; and twelve treated only by older methods. Again, the Kenny methods were clearly superior. In 1944–46 the navy examined eighty-eight patients at a center for polio-afflicted sailors who had already been treated for weeks or months in various parts of the world. Here, too, those treated early by Kenny methods were far better off.[13]

In 1945 Pohl reported that between 1940 and 1944 Kenny treatment had been given to 364 Minneapolis patients. Twenty-three died; of the rest, fifty-five—16 percent—were left with extensive residual paralysis; and thirty of these had to use crutches, braces, or canes. Kenny critics quickly said that similar statistics were being reported from centers like Boston Children's Hospital, where Kenny modifications were used. Indeed, some like figures had been reported before the Kenny era from major centers with skilled teams. The whole argument meant little in view of polio's huge variability from year to year and place to place (one reason, scientists were to learn, was that many of the so-called nonparalytic cases were caused by other viruses); and the fact that with Kenny or something close to it, patients with little muscle power ended up in better shape.

John Pohl maintained that a statistical comparison of Kenny cases with others was a practical impossibility. Paralysis affected each; but soft, flexible, and receptive muscles "can hardly be compared with those that are shortened, fibrosed and inelastic. . . . A paralyzed extremity [with] full range of joint motion can hardly be compared with one which is stiff and deformed." There were also, he added, the warmth and life maintained in affected areas, the effortless joint movement with smooth and coordinated muscle function, and the ability to walk without supports despite considerable weakness. For the same reasons, Bennett argued in late 1942 that even if treatment on Kenny principles offered no statistical advantage, it would still be the treatment of choice.[14]

The warfare over Kenny, the person, compounded confusion. By 1947 pro-Kenny doctors often had to remove any references at all to her name to get articles accepted by journals. And Liza was by now waving still another red flag at medicine. "I didn't bring a new treatment to America at all, but a new concept . . . the most important discovery made in this disease through all time." This was "the newer science of dermo-neuromuscular therapy" and "the peripheral disease of polio, which is not the disease taught in the medical world." The unseen polio virus, she maintained, attacked muscles first, *then* the nerves, not nerve tissue alone as science stated.

This was new since 1940. The Liza of 1940 was no pathologist. When she first told Minneapolis doctors of muscle spasm—and they smiled and asked, "What causes it? What makes these limbs so sore and painful?"—she had said, "I don't know. That's for you doctors to find out." She had begun to reach for ideas, however. In 1943 she told New Orleans doctors that spasm was caused by a zone of irritation in the spinal cord. She soon stopped saying that, though it well may have been the truth. She had been told that recovery of dead nerve, including spinal cord, tissue was impossible. Well, she was treating *muscles* and getting recovery; the damage she saw was surface and near-surface or "peripheral." The trouble must be there.[15]

Her friend John Pohl, pondering the same problem, had in fact suggested to her that the disease might be "primarily peripheral." In mid-1944 two University of Southern California researchers, Drs. Frederick J. Moore and John F. Kessel, also suggested that polio might primarily be a disease of peripheral tissue, from which the virus might spread. Dr. Herman Kabat, a University of Minnesota physiologist, said on the basis of experiments with mice that the virus seemed to interfere with cell metabolism. She read a headline about such reports in the *New York Herald Tribune*—"New Concept of Poliomyelitis; Seen as Disease of Muscle First and Nerve After"—and she sweepingly asserted, "I discovered that thirty years ago and they know it." She was soon saying regularly: "By treating disturbances in the periphery, previously not believed caused by the disease, I corrected the deformities."[16]

Pohl proceeded with scientific caution; he wrote only: "There is reason to suspect that the disease directly assaults the peripheral tissues, so devastating are the eventual changes in the peripheral structures and so damaging to locomotion." He was personally convinced this was probably the case, but was aware that anything like positive evidence was lacking. She hung back not at all and found constant "proofs." In some cases legitimate scientists either agreed or said they were thinking along similar lines—investigators in Brussels and at the famous Cajal Institute in Madrid, for example. Also, notably, Dr. Claus W. Jungeblut, professor of bacteriology at the Columbia University College of Physicians and Surgeons.

It had indeed long been firm scientific belief—quite wrong—that polio virus would grow "only" in nerve, that is, nonperipheral, tissue.

Jungeblut worked with Dr. M. A. (Mal) Stevens, Kenny Clinic orthopedist in Jersey City, and with Dr. Jesse Edwards of the Mayo Clinic, one of the country's leading pathologists. They supplied him autopsy material from fatal cases. He reported isolating polio virus both from skeletal (or ordinary, bone-pulling) muscle and from heart muscle, and maintaining it in laboratory animals. He wrote Sister Kenny that he considered this "direct evidence in favor of your concept. . . . I firmly believe that no intelligent approach to the control of poliomyelitis is thinkable without a clear understanding of these fundamental phenomena." Polio, he said, was probably a disease limited to peripheral structures in nine out of ten cases, with central nervous system involvement a rarer complication. Other scientists raised serious questions about Jungeblut's viruses: were those he studied in his research animals really human viruses? His work made no great mark.[17]

Beginning in 1948, however, Dr. John Enders and his associates at Boston Children's Hospital succeeded in growing polio virus in cultures of nonnervous tissue of many types—skin, muscle, and intestine. Enders, Thomas H. Weller, and Frederick C. Robbins won a Nobel Prize for this; it led directly to virus cultivation for vaccines. In 1951–52 both Dr. Dorothy Horstmann at Yale and Dr. David Bodian at Johns Hopkins learned that there is indeed an initial peripheral growth phase of polio virus; it appears in such areas as the alimentary tract, the food-carrying canal. It apparently multiplies there, then enters the bloodstream to cause a viremia or general virus infection, before it invades the nervous system.

In Enders's opinion, however, no one ever showed that the virus itself *attacked* the muscles or other peripheral tissues. It was *in* the bloodstream, yes. It was *not* strictly a neurotropic or nerve-invading virus as had long been believed. Liza Kenny's contention, however, was still not borne out, although some scientists continued to think that a major investigative program *might* reveal that at least some muscle changes occur before nerve changes. With the advent of the Salk and Sabin vaccines, polio research of this kind became virtually a dead issue, and most authorities still felt that "what happens of significance to the polio patient is that events in nerve cells are mirrored in the muscles."[18]

When Liza Kenny arrived in America, it was also widely and wrongly felt, however, that the effect on motor nerve cells was so devastating that there was little point in active treatment. She forced workers back to the laboratories and to older literature to realize that the virus could widely affect nerve cells in the spinal cord and the brain, not just the vulnerable anterior horn cells of the cord, the "classic" lesion; that fewer cells were left dead than was supposed; that damage to some could be temporary, making it critical to give prompt physical therapy to keep muscles in good condition during cell recovery; and that muscle fibers deprived of their nerve supply do not necessarily die immediately like cut flowers, but that active treatment can help keep them alive while nature makes repairs, sending out branching fibers to seek still live, still usable nerve connections to serve the damaged body.

Some of the most interesting research was started in 1943 by physiologist Herman Kabat and Liza's other early Minneapolis medical friend, Miland Knapp. Knapp had often told colleagues that he thought she was "getting at some reflex effect." Kabat and Knapp examined the spinal cords of polio victims and discovered the involvement of an often ignored group of nerve cells called the internuncial (or intermediary) neurons. These cells are part of the pathway by which the body automatically keeps millions of motor neurons in a ready yet inhibited, finely balanced state to maintain virtually the entire musculature in the condition of readiness called "muscle tone." Interrupt these paths, Kabat and Knapp postulated, and there could well be abnormal muscle shortness and tightness—her "spasm"—accompanied by crippling pain.

In short, they felt she was as she claimed "treating disturbances in the periphery not previously believed caused by the disease," even though the periphery was not the site where the virus attacked. The disease's *effects* were in truth "dermo-neuro-muscular." She did have a concept that was new and important, even though she grasped at too many straws and made too many claims in her frustrated efforts to prove it.*

She admitted no uncertainty. Enders's research, all research, was announced by her as "final proofs." "I am correct and the rest of the world is wrong," she said. "I cannot deny what my eyes see." She said again and again: "I have a message to give the world, and I shall not be thwarted. . . . I am engaged in a terrible struggle. . . . I have to have the bulldog courage to hear the cries of the afflicted children."

On some days, perhaps, she was a worn-down gladiator, saying, "I am getting older and weary of hardships . . . insults . . . disappointments . . . frustrations . . . heartbreak and humiliation." But soon she was again the prophet, convinced. "I want to get the whole world to use the Kenny treatment. I am going to campaign for that until I

* The Epilogue tells how Dr. Frederic J. Kottke in 1973 looked back at the research mentioned above and some done later.

die. . . . Don't think I am getting old. I have work to do and I shall finish it. Thirty years I fought, and I am beginning to win."[19]

Her accusers? She was ever more savage. "Anyone who stands between a child and his chance of a happy earthly existence is guilty of as great a crime as the torturers of the prison camps."

16

Flight

SHE HAD PROFOUNDLY affected polio treatment, she had been awarded a hundred honors. It was not enough. She demanded "recognition," "acceptance," "full medical approval"—she used the words again and again. "Why don't you settle back and rest?" her friends would ask. "I have not yet achieved acceptance!" she would insist, in a low, agonized voice.

What she wanted was the recognition of the enemy, the doctors, who would and could never agree to everything that she said. What she wanted was something almost no medical discoverer gets, and no one can give. Rarely are medical facts or opinions of any kind accepted unanimously; medical treatment, for better or worse, almost always differs widely with local judgment, custom, and competence; there is no central board to order doctors how to treat patients and no official seal. But she persisted in seeking "American Medical Association approval."

She was also dissatisfied with the progress of the Kenny Foundation. Kenny Institute was growing—polio kept it filled. Classes of Kenny technicians, all graduate nurses, were being given the two years of training she wanted them to receive. Kenny scholarships brought students from Argentina, Brazil, Canada, Chile, Colombia, Mexico, several other countries, and many states. But there were still not enough therapists; she wanted wide expansion, she could never stand slow, patient building. And years were passing; time was an enemy.

She had too many enemies. Her answer was ever more motion: she would take on the world. She had invitations to visit several European countries. She successfully sought others, and in April 1947 she was aboard the *Queen Elizabeth*, clutching a filigreed digger hat against the sea wind and staring into space; her main items of baggage were her documentary film with sound tracks in six languages and her capacious handbag crammed with documents, clippings, and the latest "proofs" of her theories.

Carrying both, she visited health centers and ministries in fourteen countries. In the Soviet Union she was asked about her politics. "I don't have any politics," she gibed, "but I don't like yours." She found much of European polio treatment similar to American pre-Kenny treatment. She planted Kenny seeds and took time for a private audience with Pope Pius XII. Her head covered with a mantilla, she and the pope were soon discussing polio. She sailed back in July and buoyantly told of her twenty-eight European medical conferences: "I would gladly do as much in New York."[1]

A letter came. Brother Bill was ill. She flew to Australia at the end of September 1947; the trip then involved many hops and little sleep for an aging lady. She devoured it. The globe whirled beneath her, all blue water, then Australian landfall, a black rim of coastline stretching for miles. Australian landfall from the air was always like a discovery, as the black rim gradually became white sand, with dark hills and gum trees standing against the bright blue sky and blue water. Her flight crossed Sydney harbor, with its hundreds of bays within bays. She flew on to Brisbane over dry, wrinkled landscape. To the west rose a jagged edge, the familiar Dividing Range.

She was a different Sister Kenny now in Australia, no longer a struggling, half-educated bush nurse, burning for notice. She could step off a plane smiling and confident. She made a formal report to her Australian medical sponsors and visited what was left of the Kenny clinics. She visited one with Dr. Thomas Stubbs Brown, the recent American visitor, fellow of the Royal College of Surgeons of Edinburgh, past president of the Queensland Branch of the British Medical Association, distinguished senior orthopedic surgeon at Brisbane General Hospital, and always a gentleman. Liza of course had her store of documents and instant statements. "Sister Kenny," Stubbs Brown asked, "will you trust me with your bag and its contents?" She turned to him with a gleam in her eye. "Dr. Stubbs Brown, I would trust you with anything except a case of polio."[2]

The Kenny clinic in Brisbane was only a shadow, she found. Most of the Australian Kenny clinics were still open, but they had few patients; they were still dependent on parents' "applications" for treatment. In Brisbane and Queensland, Kenny treatment or something close to it had become the norm, but throughout the rest of Australia, immobilization modified in varying degrees was more common. Some hospitals were developing excellent physical therapy departments with "a lot" of Kenny; some were still far in the past.

To goad them, she would passionately quote her American medical supporters to interviewers and took sweet pleasure in contrasting Australian medicine with American. "American doctors are very skeptical," she gloated, "but they just can't stand using one method of treatment when they know there's a better one available." Her countrymen did not have such inquiring minds, whereas "If you go to America with anything to offer, they make it their business to get it from you." She much preferred American doctors' blunt criticism to Australian doctors' tight-lipped hostility. "An Australian doctor will not say or do anything to upset the British Medical Association."* As for Australian nurses, she was proud of them wherever she found them, but they were too beaten down. "I have heard nurses tackle doctors in lectures in America and tear their theories to pieces." So much for the Australian medical establishment.

One of the members of the former Royal Commission, Dr. James V. "Jimmy" Duhig, a Brisbane pathologist, had undertaken a fierce personal crusade against her; he wrote the *Brisbane Courier-Mail*: "I take full responsibility for libel. . . . This crook must be exposed." She boldly phoned him, and he went to see her. He started reciting her sins before the commission: she had "deceived" crippled children. She raised her voice, and their meeting broke up.

Mostly, however, she was greeted with medical and official silence. Australia gave Elizabeth Kenny almost no banquets or medals and no honorary degrees. "Australia," she said acidly, "is not interested in me or my method." But Harry Summers wrote in the *Courier-Mail*: "It strikes me as interesting that a woman who rates a police motor escort in big American cities should come back home and be practically 'frozen out.' . . . The reason may be that she has failed to qualify for the one state to which we are too accustomed to reserve our lavish praise—she is not yet dead."

She admitted her disappointment to a few friends. "Personally," she told one, "I think it a sad thing that I had to leave my own country."

* Australian doctors then belonged to the British Medical Association, Queensland Branch, New South Wales Branch, etc. These branches later combined to form the Australian Medical Association.

Professor Wilkinson tried to console her: "You've always said you were only interested in happy children. You've achieved that here in Queensland. You've had a remarkable effect on the treatment." She denied caring. "Look!" said cousin Minnie Bell, "they've knighted a cricketer, and what recognition have they given you?" She just answered, "It doesn't matter."[3]

She entertained her former polio nurses and read them her documents. She visited Bill, now retired and living in Toowoomba. She saw much of Mary and Stewart. She saw all of her family and their families and dozens of cousins on these Australian visits; she had all her relatives card-indexed in her head. With the rest of the world, her own family called her "Sister" now, but some of the kinfolk were less respectful. One stern aunt had read some of the more exaggerated tales about her early nursing and bush romancing. "Why do you tell those awful tales?" she challenged. "Oh," Liza said, "nobody knows about those things in America. I've got to tell them something."

She came down with pneumonia. Dr. Noel Ure in Toowoomba found her difficult to treat, "really a hospital case," but she refused to go to the hospital. She also declined penicillin shots; he put her on sulfa tablets, which she took as long as it pleased her. Recovered, she was still a little breathless at times. Ure told her she was overweight. She made it clear that she would not reduce.[4]

She attended the Australian premiere of *Sister Kenny*, postponed almost a year so she could be there. The event was at the Regent Theatre in Brisbane. A Scottish band and 200 nurses in red and white uniforms marched down the street to the cinema house, where she stood in a pale green evening gown greeting the crowd. "It was very moving," she said, "and proved to me that I have won a great place in the hearts of the Australian people." There were no public functionaries there, however.[5]

She visited Charles Chuter, her Brisbane health official friend; he died not long after. He was almost the only Australian official who had been answering her letters. She looked very tired, Mary thought. She returned to America and nimbly explained the absence of an official reception: "I refused a fanfare and official welcome. I preferred the money be used for polio work." For Christmas she gave a smasher of a party. Twenty of her nurse-students came to her house on Park Avenue for what she called a real English Christmas dinner, with turkey and blazing plum pudding. "I love this," she sighed. "I love to call this a home I can call my own. I think I'll sleep for a week."[6] Shortly afterward she was off again.

Europe, Australia, America, London, Sydney, Brisbane, Toowoomba, New York, Minneapolis, an endless round. "Where will you live?" someone asked her. "I'm not going anywhere to live," she said. "My house is thatched when my hat's on." She went to Centralia, Illinois, to talk about a possible new Kenny clinic. She had to fly to St. Louis first, seventy miles away, to be met by a car. "I like to go fast," she told the driver. "By all means do not crawl along for my benefit."[7]

In Britain in the summer of 1948, she found a distinguished new medical friend, Richard Metcalfe, bone surgeon. As a World War II brigadier, he had been consultant orthopedic surgeon—chief orthopedist—to the British army; he left the army in 1948. He was chief orthopedic consultant to Queen Mary's Hospital at Carshalton. There had been a 1947 polio epidemic; the polio wards were still full, and Metcalfe on his first visit had found the Carshalton patients in surprisingly good condition.

"How did you do this?" he asked.

Physiotherapist Amy Lindsey almost whispered the answer: "It's Sister Kenny."

A dapper chap who always wore a flower in his buttonhole, Metcalfe on first meeting liked Liza's bravura and skill. He arranged visits to other hospitals; she discovered that though not as fully accepted as in America, Kenny methods had gradually made an impact. On a visit to a hospital at Woking, she found all the ambulances drawn up in military line in the courtyard and all the physical therapists at attention. She was very diplomatic when she inspected their patients.[8]

In New York in July of 1948, she turned up at a week-long First International Poliomyelitis Conference, with 2,000 experts from thirty-eight countries attending. The National Foundation was behind the assemblage; she had not been invited. Kenny Foundation director Kline asked for a place in the program for a Kenny spokesman; he was told that United States participation was restricted to National Foundation grantees. Her absence as a participant, commented journalist Albert Deutsch as the conference opened, was its "one big inexcusable flaw": "The National Foundation officials who deliberately ignored Sister Kenny in sending out invitations ought to be decorated with dunce-caps and put in the corner. . . . A foundation spokesman explained that Sister Kenny might have registered as a nurse or a physiotherapist. . . . This does not sound convincing."[9]

She was there, though. She represented the North American Newspaper Alliance as its correspondent; she carried a new, paid-up union card in the CIO American Newspaper Guild. She appeared in the pressroom in a royal purple dress and garden-party hat; her entourage included London therapist Lindsey, a press agent, a private detective, and a secretary who handed out Kenny literature, until she was stopped.

Correspondent Kenny sat quietly through the opening sessions of the conference. When she heard an attack on her theories, it was difficult for her to be silent; it grew harder still when a medical panel was asked about the cause of spinal deformities, and several doctors approached her and asked how she would answer. A number of delegates signed a request that she be allowed to speak; it was ignored. When Professor Herbert J. Seddon of Oxford University, a leading British orthopedist, said Kenny methods in Britain unfortunately cost three times as much as conventional ones, often making them too expensive, she forgot her reporter's role and demanded an opportunity to confront him at a press conference.

Seddon appeared with Dr. Nicholas Ransohoff, an American who had praised her treatment. A dozen reporters listened as she challenged Seddon. He replied by citing Ransohoff's published figures stating that Kenny care was perhaps five times as costly as immobilization. "I have to thank you heartily for methods that are advantageous to my patients," Seddon told the journalist-nurse. "You got rid of braces. But I do not agree with you on everything. I have to treat the very poor, and for them, when speaking on economic grounds, I cannot recommend the Kenny treatment on account of expense." Neither party gave ground. No one pointed out that a patient rehabilitated by active treatment may ultimately cost the community far less than one left lying untreated. As usual, Liza put her case poorly. "Frequently she left her subject entirely," *Newsweek* reported, "and launched into a stream of cutbacks into her history."[10]

As the reporters left, she was still talking but to an empty pressroom. Then, surprisingly, Seddon reappeared to shake her hand. He wanted her to know he admired her.

A new Kenny center had opened in January 1948 in the New York metropolitan area: two floors, 100 modern beds, and contagion, outpatient, and training areas at the 2,500-bed Jersey City Medical Center, one of the country's largest. The direct link to a general hospital made for high-quality care. Valerie Harvey was made head training therapist; the medical director was Dr. Mal Stevens, a first-class orthopedist even better known as a Yale All-American, a football coach, and doctor to the

New York Yankees. He liked Liza; he was accustomed to characters.[11]

Other Kenny units had been developing. The Jersey City staff maintained a small outpatient unit in New York City. There were now excellent Kenny centers with Kenny therapists in Buffalo, New York, and Pontiac, Michigan, outside Detroit. The Pontiac center, like Jersey City's, was in the city hospital. A Kenny movement had been started in California; in 1950 a 116-bed Kenny hospital was to be opened at El Monte in the Los Angeles area. A 65-bed Kenny clinic had opened at Centralia, Illinois, in 1947. Liza's nephew Bill Bell started a successful, if small, Kenny clinic at Wanganui, New Zealand, affiliated with a hospital in nearby Wellington. During epidemics Kenny therapists were dispatched to many cities and countries, and in Minneapolis they worked at six hospitals in addition to the Kenny Institute; many medical observers thought the city enjoyed the world's best polio care.

Unsatisfied, Elizabeth Kenny wanted to see her outposts operating in New York City, Chicago, Washington, all major cities, and training therapists by the hundreds. It might have happened: when polio was at its height, the need and emotional climate existed. In 1948 there were 27,726 polio cases in the United States, more than the record 25,698 cases of 1946; in 1949 there were 42,033 cases; 1950, 33,000; 1951, 25,386; and in 1952 a new awesome record of 57,879. The case load would not abate until 1956, the first year the new Salk vaccine was widely used. Hospitals in epidemic areas were painfully overcrowded. In the semirural, coal-mining area of Centralia before a Kenny center was started, one couple had to keep their acutely ill son at home for eleven days before a bed was found for him in Peoria. The boy was left with a permanent deformity of his left foot and ankle; the incident was far from unique. All the Kenny clinics were opened with deep feeling by officials and citizens caught in the grip of those frightening years. In the words of the *Centralia Evening Sentinel* when the Kenny unit opened there:

> It was the "blood, sweat and tears of local residents, the little people," who made the clinic possible. They were not the disciples of any treatment leader, they were not politicians, they merely wanted to insure proper, prompt treatment for the unfortunate victims of polio. . . . The Centralia Kenny Clinic is not a Chamber of Commerce project. It sprang from the need and suffering of 1946.[12]

The Kenny Foundation's response to such demand was limited by weak officials who always had to say "yes" to Sister Kenny. They themselves were hamstrung by uncertainty—they never knew whether she would back or blast them—as well as by the growing refusal of doctors to make Kenny ties. The foundation's executive director was the former mayor of Minneapolis, Marvin Kline, an engineer and architect by profession. As mayor, he had been one of the key figures in launching the organization and was its first president. He had been defeated as mayor in 1945 by the South Dakota–born pharmacist turned political science professor, Hubert H. Humphrey. A thin man with a pencil moustache, Kline had headed a toothless city administration; organized gambling and prostitution had flourished, as they had always flourished. Humphrey cleaned them up. It took Humphrey two tries to unseat Kline, however. Kline himself remained untouched by scandal, and the Kenny board asked him to become its full-time paid director.

Kline was neither a world-beater nor an incompetent in the job. He may have done as well as anyone could have with his limited authority. He did see to it that the Kenny Institute was well run; he also excelled at protecting his own flanks. In 1946 a group of board members led by Donald Dayton hired Booz, Allen & Hamilton, administrative consultants, to look at the organization; they recommended new blood, new medical ties, and a firm understanding with "Sister": she must stop flaying doctors and try working with them quietly. A former Chicago newspaperman, Will O'Neil, came to Minneapolis, organized a national medical advisory committee, and took other forward steps. A stronger chief executive was still needed; Dayton and his friends tried to fire Kline, but he had more votes than they did on the board of directors. Liza herself jettisoned the new medical advisers and in early 1948 called Kline from New York at six o'clock one morning. "Is that fellow O'Neil still there?" she asked. "I'm not going to come back as long as he's around." He was fired; the reform effort was ended.

The new Centralia clinic began having financial and licensing problems. It lacked a resident pediatrician and an orthopedist; one had to visit from Chicago, the other from St. Louis, and the Kenny Foundation was forced to announce that the clinic would be closed. Liza dashed to Centralia which was in an uproar over the prospective shutdown, and the town gave her an emotional parade. After a patient's mother ran up and kissed her hands—her four-year-old had just walked without aid for the first time—the nurse vowed that "so long as there is a breath of life within me, the clinic shall not close." She heaped abuse on Kline, met with the governor, won state approval, and kept the clinic alive for the moment.

Suddenly Kenny Institute in Minneapolis, the mother institute, was also in trouble. Doctors on the staff and in the community had tired of the brawling. Dissension, resignations, and threatened resignations began disrupting the medical staff, and even the friendliest doctors were refusing their cooperation. John Pohl, who had given the institute heart and soul, was deeply embroiled. He had become Elizabeth Kenny's main medical co-worker and mentor, but he could not run a hospital without medical help. Or Liza's support; she too had begun fighting him. He resigned.

A sobered Sister Kenny had to go to Board President Dayton and confess, "We have more than 100 children at the Institute, and there hasn't been a doctor there for three days." The alarmed Dayton immediately phoned Dr. E. J. Huenekens, a tough veteran pediatrician who was both Kenny-minded and a former county medical society president of high professional standing. Liza, Huenekens, and Pohl met in Dayton's office, and she herself asked Huenekens to take the job. A large and authoritative man, yet warm and disarming, he answered, "I'll take it only if we can fight polio and forget about fighting the March of Dimes. And if I'm going to be medical director, I have to be director in fact, not just name."

He turned toward Liza. "That means you, Sister."

She agreed. "You deserve a fair chance."

Huenekens in August 1948 thus became both chief of staff of the Kenny Institute and medical director of the Kenny Foundation. Liza's supporter Dr. Miland Knapp became chief of physical medicine in charge of treatment; relations with the University of Minnesota were reestablished and medical help was brought in. Kenny training would be made available to physical therapists as well as nurses; nurse-trainees would take a year of physical therapy training at the Mayo Clinic to fit them for broader work when polio epidemics waned.

An unhappy Pohl remained publicly silent. He inwardly felt Liza had allowed her treatment center to be taken over by doctors "who did not really understand her work and were unsympathetic toward it—she might better have closed the door."[13] Knapp naturally disagreed. She herself had momentary fits of changing her mind. "You're fired," she told Huenekens once. He was able to say now, "Sister, you have nothing to say about it," and she said no more. Over the next few years, Dayton and Kline made a new, again futile attempt to win National Foundation support. O'Connor said later that he would happily have supported the institute, but for Liza's presence. The Georgia Warm Springs Foundation was just such a National Foundation subsidiary.

The institute itself became a calmer, smoother-running place, but there were frequent squabbles between Kenny headquarters and its East and West Coast divisions. Again, Liza contributed. It was not merely her speaking out that helped trigger the quarrels. "She can never quite complete anything," Valerie Harvey thought sadly. "If she would just stay and work at the problems, she'd get things done. Somehow she leaves every time a real problem comes up."

In simple fact she was less and less able to cope with the daily problems of a polio movement and of a polio hospital in the grasp of the worst polio epidemics in history. She turned sixty-eight in September 1948, and her health was deteriorating. Marguerite Clark, medical editor of *Newsweek*, met her earlier in the year as she alighted from a plane for the dedication of the Jersey City Kenny Center, then wrote a sympathetic story in which she referred to her as granite-faced. Liza angrily phoned her. "When I was a girl," she said, "it was considered very improper to refer to a person's physical appearance. I am as God made me."

"Well, I'll talk about it to your press agent," said Mrs. Clark, startled.

"I have no press agent!" Liza flared, but at the end of the conversation she invited the writer to tea.

Actually her face was even more impassive than the stiff mask she had so often affected. The new masklike mien was in part a symptom of Parkinson's disease, shaking palsy, which was just beginning. She began to have trouble with an arm, another symptom. She told Mary she must have a touch of neuritis, but she knew better. The Kenny Foundation's Eastern division hired a new public relations man—the foundation had press agents if she did not. He had heard she was being treated for a "bad heart." "Oh, fiddlesticks," she said. "My heart is all right." She didn't mention the Parkinsonism.[14]

She was spending more time in New York. There she would call the inevitable press conference, but she was having a harder time attracting an audience, for editors were souring on her repetitive story. Journalists had sought her out over the years, though she had usually treated them autocratically. She would walk down a hospital corridor trailing reporters and say over her shoulder, "You can take that down"; "Don't print that"; "Take notes and get this right, because reporters always print such stupid things." Or: "If you're going to take a picture, take it now." A beaten *Minneapolis Tribune* photographer once scribbled on the back of his picture of her: "Photographer, Sister Kenny; assistant, Kam."

She never really wanted to be *interviewed*; she wanted to dictate the story, like an executive to a secretary. She often dictated in this manner at length, then drew a breath and told the poor reporter, especially one showing any trace of timidity, "Now read that back to me." She had also become known for giving telephone statements, then repudiating them. The Associated Press once ordered all its bureaus not to accept any statement of hers unless it was in writing over her signature. That policy lasted about a week; though skeptical reporters now asked, "What's new this time?" when she summoned them, most of the time they showed up.[15] She was even fussy about who attended. She would ask her latest New York public relations man, Peter Gazzola, to notify "only" the *New York Times* and the *Herald Tribune* because they "counted." He would ignore her and call everyone. One time the *Herald Tribune* was on hand but not the *Times*. She promptly got its city editor on the phone and told him: "The last story you ran about poliomyelitis was not factual, and now you are haphazard in your assignments. We notified you about this press conference yesterday, and the *Herald Tribune* is here waiting." "By God," Gazzola remembers, "they sent a reporter."[16]

When her interviewers finally appeared, however, she was gentler. She was mellowing; she was wiser, perhaps. She was also tired. She was saying more often that "I quite agree with the medical profession for their caution in not embracing new ideas, including my own, until they are satisfied they are effective." And: "They're wonderful men, most of them. I guess you have to fight them to appreciate them." And often: "I hope science will keep adding to the Kenny method until perfection is reached." Harry Summers in Brisbane said, "Now I feel the edge of her bitterness has turned," for she could even write lightly of the American tour of Drs. Fryberg and Stubbs Brown and how they "flitted in and flitted out" like a visitor to Australia who "lit his pipe in Sydney town and spat on the quay in Perth, and traveled back to England and wrote of the wide, wide earth."[17]

Her face softened, and her strong chin lost much of its pugnaciousness. Her silver white hair was done in soft waves; she could have modeled as Gold Star Mother. Her gait was slower and stiffer; she was having new leg trouble. But she still stood erect. Her look still had power. She could still look the dragon and, if she chose, cut you down with a phrase. In some ways mellow, in others she was more inflexible: the National Foundation was ever more villainous; she read and reread the same statements; she retreated even more into her own unsettled world.

She clung to her religion; she remained the daughter of a day when lives were ordered by it. Her practice was often highly informal, however. "Any church will do me when I want to go to church," she sometimes said. Or "I don't dust the seats of any church." A Presbyterian only of sorts with a lasting attachment to Catholicism, she explained that "When I feel the need to commune with God, I walk into any house of God." And "I believe in all religions." In New York, she occasionally dropped into the Episcopalian Cathedral of Saint John the Divine or the Roman Catholic Saint Patrick's Cathedral. In Brisbane she sometimes went to the Ann Street Presbyterian Church, where her cousin Percy Pearson, an Irish-Scotch cousin, presided. Asked why she was a Presbyterian, she sometimes said, "With my game knee, how could I be anything else. I can't kneel." In more serious moments, she said she liked it because it was the simplest faith. When asked why she felt so close to the Catholics, she replied: "Because they take care of the sick."

In Minneapolis, she went to Westminster Presbyterian Church at times, especially in her first years in the city. It was always the feeling of its wise pastor, the Reverend Arnold Lowe, that "she looked pretty much on her work as her religion." She confirmed this in her contribution to a newspaper series of "Lenten Guideposts":

> At a very early age my mother told me: "You are a child of God, and you will walk His path from cradle to grave."
>
> . . . My life is a prayer, day and night, given unreservedly to God. . . . And there is no profession that so closely follows in the footsteps of Christ than the work of healing—be that man or woman, a Christian, Jew, heathen or Oriental.[18]

One thing she did not get from religion and did not ask of it was peace.

She did not get it even in the last shreds of her role as "honorary director" of her foundation. She received an SOS from her Centralia, Illinois, friends: the foundation had finally decided that the clinic there must be closed. A volatile southern Illinois union official named John L. Matthews was just recovering from polio and was almost in shock at the decision. She was in Australia again; against medical advice, he signed himself out of the hospital and frantically flew there to see her. She flung cables at Centralia and Minneapolis and set out for the United States.

The clinic was closed in the meantime, and Dr. Huenekens, the new Kenny boss, hurried to San Francisco to meet her before she could issue any statements. He respectfully greeted her, and then he sat her down to talk. She quickly understood his message: there could no longer be two Kenny bosses. She returned with him to Minneapolis, and there on April 20, 1949, nine years and four days after her 1940 arrival from Australia, she formally announced her retirement from any direction of the Kenny Foundation.

It was inevitable; it was hard for her, but it was not a bitter quitting. It was Liza Kenny at her best. She saw clearly that her last official role but one had been played, so she appeared with Huenekens for that last role, making a statement before the press at her Park Avenue house. She walked down the sweeping staircase, stiff and travel-worn, yet with majesty. She sat in a wing chair, ever straight, shoulders back, and read: "My mission to the United States has been fulfilled in every possible way. . . . My contributions have been investigated, and evidence of scientists supports my clinical observations. . . . I have faithfully served the medical profession through good and ill, confident that the day would come when an outstanding member of the profession would take over the burden in the cause of humanity. That day has arrived." Her voice was a monotone, saying finis.

Dr. Huenekens also spoke. When needed, "Sister" had agreed to remain a teacher, technician, and consultant. But not at the moment.[19]

Earlier that year she had landed at Mascot, the Sydney airport, with what she darkly announced as a "secret" report. It had been prepared for the premier of Queensland, she said, "by professors at the University of Minnesota"—that meant her supporter Dr. Cole—and "will be a great surprise to Australians." She gave the document to Premier E. M. Hanlon, her former health minister benefactor, and awaited his answer. There was none. She said she would be back.

In the United States now in mid-May, she got word of her brother Bill's death of heart disease at age sixty-one. He had been her first girlhood "case." The Associated Press wanted a statement. "You must handle this very carefully," she told her public relations man, "because I loved him very dearly." From memory, she recited all his war citations.

Back in Australia to see his grave, she phoned Queensland's Health Ministry. What about her report to the premier? Was there any answer? She had also sent a copy to the health minister of New South Wales, Mr. Kelly. There was no answer from either. She departed in June, announcing that "I will return only if Australia calls for me. Mr. Kelly has refused three times to see me. I cannot waste my time."

Within weeks she was on the *Queen Mary* again, out of New York. She would establish a teaching center for Europe in Brussels "if facilities are available" and visit Rome and Athens "by special invitation." In Brussels she had a medical friend, Dr. Leon Laruelle, who was training therapists in her style. In Prague she was confronted as she got off her plane by "a woman as big as I" who "ran her hands over me, apologizing profusely that she had to search me for weapons." Satisfied that she was unarmed, the Czechoslovakian Health Ministry asked for a Kenny technician to give fifty nurses and physical therapists a four-month course.

"Sister," an official told Liza, "we will always leave a crack for you in the Iron Curtain."

She shot back in good spirits: "I will be happy to creep through whenever I am needed, so long as it's left open for me to creep out."

She returned to New York on the *Queen Mary*. It was still the day of shipboard reporters, and as the luxury liner docked, she alone was interviewed by the man from the *Times*. The director of the Bank of England, the new Rumanian minister to the United States, and Hedy Lamarr were just "other passengers."[20]

17

Peace

IN JANUARY 1950 a Joint Congressional Resolution, sponsored by Minnesota's new Senator Hubert H. Humphrey and Minnesota's Representative Walter Judd, gave Sister Elizabeth Kenny the first lifetime visa-free passage across United States borders granted any foreign visitor since the Marquis de Lafayette. All ports of entry were notified: Liza was to come and go as she wished.

She was pleased. She wrote a report from New York about the honor, with a terse addendum: she had just gone to the United Nations with Eleanor Roosevelt and Emily Post to be named the world's most influential women. She was not completely awed by such kudos. Congress had merely passed a bill, she explained, saying "I didn't need to get a visa or pay a head tax or promise not to shoot the president to enter this country."

She called another New York news conference, this time to announce that she would bequeath her "knowledge" to an international medical committee, including Dr. Stevens of her Jersey City and New York operation. That confused just about everyone, since there was already a national Kenny Foundation. She hurried back to Minneapolis, therefore, to state that she had full confidence in Dr. Huenekens, "a fine fellow," and Minneapolis must always be "the national and international headquarters." Once this was more or less resolved, the city of Minneapolis gave her a luncheon, where Governor Luther Youngdahl presented a scroll.[1]

More flights. London, Brussels, Amsterdam, Prague, Geneva, Dublin. More conferences, new affiliations, a meeting in Prague with fifty doctors, and assurances that her methods were being widely adopted. At a Dublin hospital, an Irish doctor about to visit America told her he got 90 percent recoveries in polio cases.

"If that's so," she said, "you're wasting your time going to America. America should be going to you."

"You saw my recoveries!"

"I saw many of your patients," said Kilkenny Kenny, "but there wasn't a recovery in the lot."

Minneapolis. Well-wishers gave her a music stand that had belonged to Florence Nightingale and Miss Nightingale's *Book of Common Prayer*; the great nurse had given the prayer book to a wounded British soldier in the Crimea in 1856. Photographed alongside the Nightingale memorabilia, standing like an old soldier, Liza announced that she was leaving for Australia for good, though "if the United States is in any stress at any time, I certainly shall come back."

February 1951. "Sister Kenny Comes Home," wrote a journalist in Melbourne. "Quietly, like a stranger almost, one of the nation's great daughters returns," but there were still no welcoming speeches, no smiling officials.[2]

In Brisbane, she had a namesake. Stewart and Mary had adopted a baby girl and christened her Elizabeth. Little Elizabeth was six months old. As the child grew, Stewart thought Sister would "bloody well take my head off" the first time he told the child to go to her and say "Grandma." But Sister did no such thing; she liked it.

She temporarily occupied a suite at Lennon's Hotel, General MacArthur's headquarters in World War II. Up the street—George Street with its British colonial architecture and American bustle—stood the old building with wooden verandas and its seventeen-year-old sign, "Elizabeth Kenny Clinic." Some long-term patients were still being cared for, but the foundations were crumbling and the boards needed paint. She made her visit there brief.

A few weeks later she stood on a high sloping lawn on the edge of Toowoomba, on the very rim of the Great Dividing Range, looking out into space. She had leased a fine house there, red brick and solid; the lawn was her lookout point, and the Range wind blew at her white hair as a far-off sparrow hawk rode the breeze. This was her old nursing beat. She could only look now—at chalky morning fog, blotting out everything but a few near hills and peaks; then, as the sun warmed, a view for miles of blunt peaks and blue slopes, heavily covered with pines in dark shade. Later, as the sun rose, she could see the same slopes turning a dazzling yellow green, as well as others that were bare and brown. Mount Lindsay, Mount Mitchell, Mount Barney, Spicer's Peak, Crow's Nest, down toward the hillocks like Gowrie Mountain with their hill-hugging farms, then roads and paddocks in the valleys and great fields of green, gold, and brown. She looked and said, "I've waited eleven years to come back."

Her illness was much worse. Her right hand trembled, and her right arm was almost useless; she walked stiffly and haltingly. She never complained. Dr. Noel Ure gave her some prescriptions to add to her store of pills and tablets. One day she shook them all down the sink. "That's the place for them, not in me," she told him.

She improved some. She went visiting, drinking tea, and talking about the old days. The Queensland health minister had thoughtfully provided her a secretary who doubled as driver of her modest new car. Her sister Julia was in Toowoomba, another sister was on a farm on the Downs, and another was in Southport, on the coast south of Brisbane. Every fair afternoon Liza rode off to visit relatives and country friends.

Nobby was still there with its scattered houses, stores, and a train chugging through the town alongside the main street, the rail line bordered by yellow wild flowers and a row of pepperina trees. The street was only dirt, but there were flowering vines and bushes in every yard, surrounding the Queensland houses on stilts. "M. Brodie, Nobby Store, Drapery—Grocery—Crockery—Ironmongery—Boots & Shoes" read a faded sign dated 1898. Michael Kenny had shopped there. In a remote field stood the red-roofed, onetime Kenny house, hardly a shed compared with Liza's Toowoomba dwelling. Pigs greeted her there, grunting. After a time, she said, "Let's go."

There were longer rides on some days and a motor trip with Julia to New South Wales and hilly New England, Sister's birthplace. They visited relatives in Guyra, where she had been a poor girl amidst better-off cousins. "Let's go see the old place," Julia said. "I don't want to go out there," Liza said abruptly. "I had enough of it then."

She would return to her crow's nest after these visits, rest, then call her secretary to open her mail from all over the world, so she could answer her critics and bombard enemies. She worked on a new book. Every so often she would stop, exhausted. A few minutes later she would start again and dictate for an hour. She found herself in demand in the neighboring towns to receive debutantes, open flower shows, and dedicate hospitals. Journalists regularly visited her. "I am proud," she told one, "that those who once scorned now come to learn."

"Who is that a quotation from?" he asked.

"That's a quotation from myself."

Every now and then she dictated a will. "She was wonderful for making wills," a friend says. But Topic A was still polio. "How can I rest when I get letters piled up that high?" she asked. "How can I rest when mothers come to my door to seek assistance for their children?" Queensland had a polio epidemic. She visited the Toowoomba General Hospital and was happily surprised; she praised the treatment as better than any she had seen outside her own institutes. She visited Brisbane General Hospital and made an equally laudatory statement. "The treatment seems rather familiar," she wryly told an orthopedic surgeon. He said with a grin, "We picked up some of it in the U.S."

Writer Harry Summers visited. Out came a pair of heavy-winged spectacles while she exhibited a document to him. Her movements slow, her speech deliberate, she talked in a deep-voiced monotone on "the one topic on which it is possible to engage her in sustained conversation—her work." He wanted her to talk about her life, but she just said, "What do my early years matter? It is the work that counts." He decided, "She is still restless. She has been a warrior all her life, and warriors do not rest until they die."[3]

Someone else asked if she intended to carry on polio treatment in Australia. "You ask Australia that, not me," she threw back. In Toowoomba Dr. Ure invited her to see some of his polio patients. It was with effort that she accompanied him. She would mainly sit in her lounge, he remembers, and look out her picture window at the shadows over the mountains, "and sit and watch them and talk and talk. About polio and polio."

On her better days, however, she managed to round up some new supporters: Toowoomba doctors and hospital representatives, a Queensland member of the Federal House of Representatives, His Worship the Mayor, and several clubwomen, including her ex-comrade in stretcher selling, Mrs. Sterne of Warwick, now Mrs. Sterne, O.B.E. The group established an International Organisation for Combatting Poliomyelitis. Mrs. Sterne was named secretary; Sister Kenny, patroness. "I have been deputized," announced Liza in Sydney two days later, to travel to the United States "to ask Mrs. Eleanor Roosevelt to be president."[4]

August 1951. It was to be her most dramatic American tour, for as she was leaving she surprised reporters by saying, "I am incurably unwell, and I have little time left in this world." They pressed her for the cause. Was it cancer? She would say only that it was not. "The only thing for it is absolute quiet, but I doubt if I can get it." Then she got on the plane, saying: "I might never arrive if I go by ship."[5]

Her illness and her purple pronouncement of doom thrust her back in the spotlight. Also, the press soon learned that a fellow passenger was a Pan American Airways pilot stricken with polio. Severely paralyzed, he had been told he might be able to walk with braces after a few years. He was aboard the plane on a litter; his wife brought Liza to him while they were over the Pacific. At her urging, he was admitted to the new Kenny hospital outside Los Angeles; in less than two years he was back in the air as a Pan American captain. His story, told now with hers, heightened the drama.[6]

While they were still en route, a Minneapolis newspaper published the first report that she had Parkinson's disease, "slowly progressive, finally fatal."[7] When her plane landed in Los Angeles in the middle of the night, some 300 press, radio, and television reporters and cameramen met her for an exchange that lasted four and a half hours. Did she really have Parkinson's disease? "Yes. There is no known cure. It grows steadily worse. I am slowly losing the use of my right arm and right leg." How long would she live? About two years, but "only God knows that. It may not be that long. I came over against medical advice. I still have much work to do."

"I HAVE ABOUT TWO YEARS TO LIVE—SISTER KENNY" the headlines read, and many doctors erupted. She was unnecessarily alarming thousands of patients, they charged; the onset of Parkinson's disease is slow, and many years may pass before a person can no longer get around; many patients succumb to other illnesses or infections, and the average patient may count on at least ten or fifteen years and be comfortable much of that time. The reporters tracked Liza down at the Brissons'. What about the doctors' statements? Instead of answering them, she wanted to read a polio treatise. The questioners persisted. "The doctors don't want to scare people," she said. "I'm not worrying about it—I don't worry about death ever." She said that she first learned that she had the disease in 1947, and a European specialist later "said my ailment was greatly brought on by the rigid hours I kept during the Minneapolis polio epidemic of 1946. I would do it all again, if I had a life to live over again." Why, she asked, was everyone so much more interested in writing about her than about her polio treatment? "After all, 20 years ago four doctors gave me four months to live because of my heart. They are all dead and I am still living." She winked. "It could be that the doctors are having their innings."[8]

She flew on to Copenhagen and the Second International Poliomyelitis Conference. This time she had an invitation from the Danish Infantile Paralysis Foundation; the well-known Danish entertainer Carl Brisson, Freddie Brisson's father, had a hand in that. There she heard Dr. Robert Bennett say, "Polio is a disease of tightness as well as of weakness, a disease of collagenous tissues as well as of the motor nervous system." "Well," she commented, "I can go back to Australia to die happy. After 40 years *some* of my theories, at least, have been accepted." She went to the official conference reception first. Basil O'Connor was in the receiving line. He refused to shake her hand; he thought she had crashed her way in.[9]

London: the Infantile Paralysis Fellowship gave her a scroll. New York: in her accustomed suite at the Delmonico, she sat for long spells and looked at her hands. She stirred herself for some interviews. "You mean go on living with *this*? Who would want to?" And "I notice that when I just start talking about my work, my hands begin to tremble." Then she said, as if to the four walls: "My work. Yes, that's the cause. God knows. It's all been worth it."

She was getting desperate. She tried alfalfa pills. She let an inventor try a leg exerciser on her. She disclosed that she was being treated with "ray transmissions," some ineffectual use of radioactive isotopes. She retained some humor, however. "I may go up in smoke or may live longer. I am willing to try an experiment in the interest of humanity."

Minneapolis once more. On a September afternoon, children with polio crowded around the windows of the Kenny Institute, as American and Australian flags waved, a police band played "Waltzing Matilda" and a new, cream-colored wing was dedicated as her "sixty-fifth" birthday present. (She was seventy-one that day.) The three-story, $606,000 wing was to house 75 patients, making the institute's official capacity 200 during nonepidemic periods, without beds in the corridors. A thousand people stood or sat on the lawn as Liza went to the speaker's stand and called the wing a far cry from a homemade table under an Australian gum tree.[10]

The clock was running down. Back in Australia, trying to rally support for a new Kenny clinic, she addressed delegates to a Women's Jubilee Convention in the national capital. She said that almost every country now had a Kenny center, and she asked, "What are *you* going to do?" Then, turning to a cabinet minister and a leader in Parliament, "What are you senators going to do?" There was silence, and she turned back to the audience and said, "What's the matter? Are they struck dumb?"[11]

A reader wrote the *Brisbane Courier-Mail* in January of the new year, 1952: "SISTER KENNY DESERVES TO BE INCLUDED IN HONOURS LIST. . . . No Australian has done more to keep Australia in the thoughts of the whole world." Other letter writers agreed. She read their letters and wrote the editor: "While I appreciate very much the kindly thought . . . I would be enforced to decline any honour . . . for I am known throughout the entire world as 'Sister Elizabeth Kenny,' and any alteration in that title, however honourable it would be, would cause confusion in the hearts of those to whom I have devoted my life."[12]

She looked out her picture window at the trees and shadows of the Dividing Range. She pulled herself in and out of her little black car, but she still could not relax. Because of numerous inquiries, she announced, "I am coming out of retirement briefly," and she set off on yet another American journey. She got off the trans-Pacific plane exhausted, after two nights of sitting up. New York, Jersey City, Buffalo, Minneapolis. It was like an obsession. She would say "Oh, they're killing me"—the people who were always wanting to see her.

"Why don't you put them off?" her traveling companion would say, puzzled.

"Oh, no, I've got to see them."[13]

She spent much time in these last few years with the Brissons. The night before the nurse's final return to Australia, Rosalind and Freddie took her out. Liza had Dubonnet and roast beef. They had to carve the beef for her. She was in low spirits, and she said, "Nothing has been done." "You have five medical centers now," they chided her. "How can you say that?" She left, saying little.

The year 1952 saw polio's most severe United States epidemic. Hospitals everywhere were deluged, including the Kenny Institute in Minneapolis, which was crowded with the severest cases, 373 of them at one point. Without publicity that summer, Dr. Jonas Salk was beginning his first vaccinations of 161 children, but his vaccine would not reach the general public for three years. Polio panic was more severe than ever; it was with high emotion that Americans had been reading the unfolding drama of Sister Elizabeth Kenny's illness. Polled by Gallup, American women voted her first in their admiration, ahead of Mrs. Roosevelt, their perennial favorite.[14]

In Toowoomba, Liza finished a little book, *My Battle and Victory*, then, almost pathetically, she wrote the *Australian Medical Journal* that it was time "something was done" to give the children of Australia a chance. "I am willing to help." She got some Labour party support; Dr. Herbert Vere Evatt, Commonwealth opposition leader, said a new effort should be made to bring Australia abreast in polio care. He had been the World War II foreign minister; he said President Roosevelt had told him how much was owed Sister Kenny. The government reply came in late October from Health Minister Sir Earle Page. He said Kenny treatment had "done very little" compared with other methods and cited the Royal Commission investigation.[15]

With her old fury, she summoned Toowoomba hospital officials to her house for a frantic, illogical conference and conspiratorially had her secretary take down everything they said. She wrote new letters to editors. Oddly, her malady seemed to recede. She was able to walk on her mildly sloping lawn. She wanted to buy a piece of land overlooking the Range and build her own house. She started planning a trip—to America, naturally. When Stewart and Mary visited in mid-November and Liza held out her arms and Elizabeth came running, she lifted her easily. Three mornings later, Wednesday, November 19, she was taken to see a piece of property on the Range. "A much better view," she said. "I'm going to buy it." That afternoon she had a paralytic stroke: the result of a burst blood vessel and blood clot in the brain, affecting her right side.

At first it seemed mild; she did not even want the doctor. Her sister Julia sat by her bedside, and the Irish in them produced a story.

"What are you thinking about?" Liza asked.

Julia laughed. "Remember the two Irishmen, one of them sick, and the sick one asked, 'What are you thinking about?' The other said, 'Oh, I was just wondering if they'd be able to get the coffin through that narrow door.' "

Liza laughed too. She became worse, however. Her speech became halting. Stewart and Mary arrived to find her upset. "I haven't finished my book," she told them—still another book. "I'll never see America again."

Her speech was getting thicker. She started crying. "Why are you crying?" Mary asked. "Is it because you can't speak?" Liza nodded. "You know about the Good Lord," Mary said. In 1940, when she had broken her arm, Mary had told her: "Well, maybe the Good Lord meant you to rest." Liza turned her face.

She was moved from her small bedroom to the large living room with its view of the Range. She summoned her solicitor and made a new revision of her will. She had accumulated £17,117 ($43,000), mainly earnings from the movie and her writings. She slowly dictated the meticulous, detailed testament of a bush woman who had accumulated a nest egg; she parceled out china, linen, glassware, vases, furniture, and her new automobile, item by item.

On Sunday, November 23, the doctor said all close relatives should be called; he thought she might not survive the day. The next day she tried to say something—she looked upward. There were some pictures from America on the walls, and one person thought she was trying to say, "America." Mary thought it was "Mother." Whatever the word, it was her last.

She was still conscious. The American consul from Brisbane visited. "Hearing Mr. Carson's American accent was a real tonic for her," her secretary told reporters. A *Time-Life* correspondent accompanied the consul. She lay quietly, staring straight ahead, he cabled, "her strong fighter's face in peaceful repose." A few days later she developed pneumonia. Still, cablegrams from America and Czechoslovakia were read to her—reports on polio. She flickered and smiled. She was rational for the last time on Friday, then became mostly comatose, and Dr. J. K. Ogden issued a statement: "No hope can be held for recovery. Sister Kenny has a very strong will to live, and until she lapsed into the coma fought hard for her life."[16]

There had to be a last melodrama. A father of a Newark polio victim cabled Ogden about an experimental drug, trypsin, being used to dissolve blood clots.[17] Ogden phoned Mount Sinai Hospital in New York, and a supply of crystalline trypsin was put on a British Commonwealth Pacific airliner. Tracked by world headlines, the plane fought headwinds but landed at Brisbane in nineteen hours, diverted from its usual landing at Sydney. It put down at 8:21 P.M. on Saturday at Eagle Farm Airport, and a car with police escort set out for the red-brick house. By 10 P.M. Dr. Ogden was administering the first dose, with no effect.

In Brisbane that night, Dr. Abe Fryberg dropped into the *Courier-Mail* office just to talk. "The truth is this," he told Harry Summers. "She was never done justice. She revolutionized the approach to polio. Look in any textbook and see what was previously said!" He paused, shaken, "And she made other claims that can't be justified."

She died quietly at 1:32 P.M. on Sunday, November 30, 1952.

The *Sydney Morning Herald* called her death "the loss of one of our great ones, perhaps of our 10 greatest," and the Australian Broadcasting Commission broadcast her funeral service overseas.[18] In almost every country her death was front-page news.

In Minneapolis, the city hall chimes rang out hymns, and the Reverend Arnold Lowe read a memorial service that included passages she had marked in her Bible, among them I Corinthians 15:55: "O death, where is thy sting? O grave, where is thy victory?"

On Allendale station in the tropical north on the day that she died, Doris Rollinson was out riding and mending a cattle fence. She knew Liza had always said she wanted to be buried under a gum tree. She found a big, glorious one and carved "Elizabeth Kenny" and the date on its trunk.

In Toowoomba, among purple jacaranda trees and red poincianas in magnificent bloom, Liza's cortege got under way, led by an old black hearse filled with flowers. The procession moved out of the city, onto the Downs. At roadside farms, wheat farmers stopped plowing, their slouch hats off and their heads bowed. At Nobby, the fifty-two children of the state school stood in two lines, heads down. "Nobby," a friend remembers, "thought it was a great honor to have her back."

She was buried in a patch of weed-choked graves well out in the country, surrounded by wheat fields and sunflowers. Her coffin was draped with a Union Jack and the Stars and Stripes, and in her hand rested a medal given her by the pope, placed there by one of her nurses. She was lowered into the earth between a pair of great gum trees that rose toward the sky in tall strength. The sun flashed on the gum leaves, and the day was still and quiet.

After a time a tall, slim headstone was placed over the grave. Like the stone on her mother's grave beside her, it read "In Loving Memory," and it bore a religious motto: "He giveth His beloved sleep."

Epilogue

A Nurse's Heritage

HER STORY was ended. But three questions may be worth looking at from a longer vantage point. What lasting movement did she leave after an almost immediate tragedy, a Kenny Foundation fund-raising scandal? What lasting effect did she have in medicine? Was she a great woman or a mere eccentric?

The headquarters of the Sister Elizabeth Kenny Foundation was on the twenty-fourth floor of the Foshay Tower, which was then the tallest building in Minneapolis. An improbable, thirty-two-story replica of the Washington Monument, it was built by a utilities king jailed shortly afterward for mail fraud; his name remains sandblasted in letters forty feet high on all four sides. Only a few stories beneath it was the office of Marvin L. Kline, executive director of the Kenny Foundation.

Kline was largely a yes man to Liza; he had to be. Through the 1940s he worked devotedly for her cause. Then in 1950—in an odd rehearsal of what would soon happen to him—he made a trip west to look into the dubious actions of Henry von Morpurgo, director of the foundation's autonomous northern California chapter. Von Morpurgo had raised

$187,000 for a proposed Kenny center but spent only $1,277 fighting polio, while paying himself, mainly as Henry von Morpurgo, Inc., public relations firm, $93,000. In early 1952 he was convicted and sent to jail for mail fraud; Kline testified at his trial.[1] So did Bing Crosby, who had innocently made Kenny radio appeals. Kline returned to Minneapolis saying little: he was already becoming involved in some mischief of his own.

Sister Kenny had been too ill to testify at the von Morpurgo trial, though she had gone to San Francisco in 1950 to give information. That had been among her last bits of Kenny Foundation business. In her last few years, she hovered only in the background. And she took her eye off the cashbox.

It was being well filled, however, by some new mail appeals by professional money-raisers, supplementing the volunteer doorbell-ringers. One John Carnell of Empire Industries of Chicago had first approached Kline in 1949, offering to start some test mailings free. Kline agreed. By 1951 Empire was mailing 16 million Kenny appeals, with a harvest of $1,272,000.[2]

Empire was owned by Abraham and David Koolish, father and son. Abraham Koolish has been described as the father of his variety of the modern charity promotion business: in 1943 he started the notorious direct-mail fund-raising for the Disabled American Veterans, by which millions of Americans each year received individual "idento-plates," miniature versions of their automobile license tags. Direct mailing is always the most expensive way of money-raising, for printing, postage, and handling can easily consume 50 percent of the take. In the Disabled American Veterans mailings, however, these "costs" sometimes ran to 90 percent. At the start, the Kenny Foundation did little better. Of that impressive 1951 million-dollar harvest, Kenny got a mere $265,000, a fifth of the total.

The Chicago operation grew at the same time that the Kenny board of directors was rapidly changing in composition from Liza's old backers to Kline's friends, mainly newly successful businessmen. Original board member Donald Dayton was now inactive; he finally resigned in 1953. Several others, including Dr. Pohl and Rosalind Russell, resigned or were dropped. One who was dropped was James Henry, whom Liza had named her "personal representative." A few years earlier Henry had begun to suspect that Kline was dishonest. He believed Kline had begun charging golf-club memberships, pleasure travel, and liquor to foundation "business." Neither Henry nor the board as a whole was even told of the massive new Chicago mailings, Henry later testified. In 1953, however, he came across a Kenny solicitation letter in Kansas. He quickly picked up more. He brought them to the next board meeting and, as he tells it:

> I said, "This was never approved by the board." Marv [Kline] hit the roof. He said, "I've got $350,000 in the treasury because of these letters. If Al Capone could raise that kind of money, I'd use him."
>
> They licked me. In June I was told I was no longer on the board.[3]

The foundation in fact was now only Kline and his publicity head and good friend, Fred Fadell. Hired in 1948, Fadell in 1950 had moved his own public relations firm, Fred Fadell & Associates, into Kenny offices, where he simultaneously was both the owner of the firm and the salaried promotion and information director of the foundation. In 1951 there began a series of interlocking transactions between the Chicagoans, Fadell, and Kline.

In a prosecutor's later words, there was "a fairly innocent start." Kline decorated his house with money borrowed from the Koolishes. Fadell wrote a $3,136 check to Empire for a piano, a gift to Kline. Empire paid Fadell $1,100, apparently for a piano and freezer. Empire's Carnell and various Koolish companies gave Kline and Fadell other gifts, and Fadell signed at least one unsecured note. Also in 1951, however, Empire and its successor, New Century Corporation, began sending Fadell direct payments for "promotional work": a first $5,000, then in 1952 a regular $2,500 a month that soon became $3,500. Between 1951 and 1959, Koolish enterprises paid Fadell some $359,000.

Fadell in turn was writing a series of equally cozy checks to "Marvin L. Kline, consulting engineer." Kline later told investigators that Fadell "wanted to pay me for the extra time and effort I put forth . . . in helping him to make good." Between 1952 and 1957 Fadell paid Kline $113,750, apparently splitting in half all his receipts from Chicago. And starting in 1956, go-getter Carnell (now president of New Century) collected $15,225 in kickbacks from the foundation as its "fund-raising consultant."

Abraham Koolish later denied knowing about the side payments to either Kline or Carnell. The Kenny board knew of none of these private payments; for a while it knew almost nothing about the whole money-raising operation. In 1951 the accounting firm of Arthur Andersen & Company was preparing a financial statement. Kline wanted to show only the net proceeds of the vast mailing without disclosing costs, but Andersen's senior partner, Alfred Nelson, refused to certify the statement unless mailing costs were included. He wanted a meeting with Kenny directors; Kline blocked it. The Andersen firm withdrew, and Nelson sent letters of explanation to the president, secretary, and treasurer of the Kenny board and some other members, but he informed no one else.

The foundation next hired Hanley, Zimmerman, & Moen, later Zimmerman & Moen, to make annual audits. Between 1952 and 1954, these reports concealed mailing costs completely; between 1955 and 1959, they combined them with other expenses (and included mail income with other income), again hiding the facts. Most of the mailing costs were buried under a Brobdingnagian category: "cost of therapist training operations; medical education and training programs; public education and information service; promotion and development of additional treatment facilities; grants for medical research; publicity and public relations." The theory, apparently, was that the cost of mailing letters that failed to bring in any cash was a cost of either "education" or "public relations." In 1953 a disturbed Luther J. Moen warned his accounting partner J. George Zimmerman that the Kenny board should be given all the facts including the payments to Fadell and Kline. Zimmerman disagreed. Moen thereafter kept away from the Kenny account but remained associated with Zimmerman.

Others too sniffed the wind but told no one, least of all the contributing public. This included some agencies that are supposed to be watchdogs. The National Better Business Bureau repeatedly asked the foundation to furnish mailing costs; Kline and Fadell evaded or ignored its requests, and in 1952 Kline brazenly wrote the bureau that: "The Kenny Foundation does not employ an outside fund-raising agency or paid solicitor, nor does it pay fees or commissions. Fund appeals are done by volunteers, directed by a moderately paid but small campaign staff." The National Information Bureau, National Budget and Consultation Committee, and Minnesota Community Research Council were other agencies that investigated and "accredited" or "disaccredited" fund appeals; all denied the Kenny Foundation their approval in some years, but none told the public.

Four Kenny board members did object. Joseph R. Jones, vice-president of the Security First Bank of Los Angeles, submitted a resolution requiring Kline to give the board regular and detailed audits. It was passed; Kline ignored it. Jones kept seeking details but seldom received them. He finally got the 1952 and 1953 figures and read them to his fellow directors. Jim Henry, Jones, Lawrence Draper, Jr. (San Francisco attorney), and A. S. Van Denburgh (president of a Los Angeles investment management firm) voted to cease doing business with the Chicagoans. They were badly outvoted; Jones and Draper resigned, Henry and Van Denburgh were not reelected, and the remaining directors showed only occasional signs of interest in finances.

In 1955, however, the Koolishes were indicted for federal mail fraud in connection with other charities, and some previously satisfied Kenny board members objected to doing business with them. The Koolishes' Empire firm promptly faded away, and a new Kenny arrangement was made with New Century Corporation. Its main officers had been Empire employees; its work was really done by LaMarge Mailing Service Company, managed by David Koolish. According to Kenny board members, Kline and Fadell assured them that New Century was unrelated to Empire or the Koolishes.

The new Kenny board in fact trusted Kline completely. Since 1952 his salary had been $25,000 a year, good but not exorbitant; in 1955 the board sweetened it by starting to buy him five $50,000 annuities, cashable at any time, though labeled "deferred retirement." The first was given to him right away; he got one more each year. In 1957 the Internal Revenue Service told him they were taxable; he cashed one to pay the tax. The IRS also discussed his checks from Fred Fadell. Kline had paid his tax, but these payments from Fadell were now prudently halted. At about the same time, however, Kline's salary was increased to $48,000. The authorities for this were an executive committee resolution and a treasurer's memorandum. No executive committee member could later remember either document, though a set of minutes bore what appeared to be the signature of secretary Phil G. Kraft and stated that the pay resolution was brought by Kraft and approved by president R. Bruce Reinecker and treasurer Robert D. Onan, and the pay memorandum bore what seemed to be Onan's signature.

New Century–LaMarge was waxing fat, meanwhile. It gave Kline no cost accountings, though one 1956 mailing brought in $1,542,000 from which the Chicagoans deducted $1,485,000 before handing on the balance. By 1960 New Century also had some 3,500,000 names on its Kenny list, which it rented out. On this reuse of Kenny mailing lists alone, the government later said, the Koolishes took more than $3,000,000 in unlawful profits. In all, the foundation received some $30,674,000 in public gifts from 1952 through 1959, $19,451,971 of this amount in response to the Chicago mailings. The Chicago fees and expenses were $11,497,704, leaving the foundation $7,954,267 or 40.9 percent. In round numbers, the Koolishes charged Kenny $11.5 million in fees and expenses for raising $19.5 million. In truth, as a prosecutor later said, the Kenny Foundation was like a subsidiary of Koolish enterprises.

An uncomfortable man finally blew the whistle. Harvey M. Dean, war veteran, Shriner and grower of roses, was the foundation's director of finances. An expert accountant, his Kenny job was to count the money, not raise it; but he fretted about the Koolish operation and about Kline's luxuries, and he told Kline (he said later) that either foundation auditors or some other reliable auditors should examine all the Chicago records. Kline shrugged Dean off, and Dean began putting detailed memorandums about the shady transactions in his desk.

At least four times, so he told Dayton later, he went to the ninth floor of the Dayton Company—Minneapolis's largest department store—and approached President Dayton's office. Each time he got cold feet and turned around. He knew the financial operations were wrong; he kept honest books. But he also knew a scandal could mark many innocents, and so he delayed. In December 1959 he at last told the story, both to Dayton and to friends who knew Minnesota Attorney General Miles Lord. Dean asked his friends to tell Lord, who started inquiries. Lord also uncovered an IRS report on Kline's annuities, taxes, and kickbacks. With an accountant friend and two assistants, Lord soon went to the twenty-fourth floor of the Foshay Tower and said, "As attorney general I'm responsible for enforcing trusts administered by charitable corporations. I'm taking over."[4]

He did not find Kline present. The now-wan ex-mayor had gone to the hospital with "heart trouble." But, Lord recalls: "His son was grabbing the old man's records and running out with them. I warned him that this could land him in jail. I also told him, 'Have your father say hello to his nurse. She's my niece.' Kline was out of the hospital in an hour." Lord enlisted volunteer accounting help—nineteen people were soon auditing Kenny records—and salvaged $230,000 in mail contributions by ordering them impounded instead of being mailed to Chicago for "processing." He also prompted the frightened Kline to return his three remaining $50,000 annuities to the Kenny treasury. Lord resigned in midinvestigation to become United States district attorney, and the state inquiry was continued by thirty-two-year-old Attorney General Walter Mondale.* Despite great pressure from some of the more influential Kenny directors, Mondale on June 27, 1960, released a report telling the whole story. The irregularities, he emphasized, did "not relate in any way to the medical staff." But his tale of the management was a horror:

> Prior to 1950, the foundation appears to have been managed in a sound, reasonable and businesslike manner. . . . In the early 1950s, certain important actions were taken without approval of the board of directors or executive committee, at least so far as the corporate minute book disclosed. . . . There is no mention of the relationship with Empire Industries and the

* Mondale soon became a United States senator and Lord, a federal judge.

direct mail campaign until November of 1952, although well over a million dollars had been involved by that time. The minute book reflected only a discussion of the nature of the operation and not of the receipts and costs. . . .

Although Arthur Andersen & Co. had informed the board of directors of their refusal to certify the foundation's financial statements without disclosing costs of the mail campaign, the minutes recite only that the correspondence was referred by the executive committee to a sub-committee. . . .

In 1954, the board of directors passed resolutions requiring the executive director to furnish an annual budget . . . [for] approval each year. . . . Annual budgets were not in fact . . . submitted . . . or approved. Detailed audit reports as required by the resolution of the board of directors were not in fact submitted. . . . Minutes of certain meetings of the executive committee, particularly those involving sensitive subjects, were not disseminated. . . .

Matters that should have been brought to the attention of the board of directors were not disclosed to them or disclosed in a misleading manner. . . . Approval or ratification of the board of directors on certain matters was obtained without full knowledge or understanding of all directors. . . . It appears, in summary, that Mr. Kline dominated and controlled the management of the affairs of the foundation to an extent that he was enabled to derive unconscionable personal profit from his position.

One member of the executive committee stated that Kline in fact exercised all of the powers of the board of directors with practically no opposition or control. . . . Another officer stated that he didn't believe it was his function or responsibility to be concerned with the finances. . . .

None of the directors that were questioned knew the cost of mail campaign or the cost of fund raising, though expenditures for these items amounted to over 1½ million dollars annually. The president of the foundation [Reinecker, head of National School Studios] stated that he was unaware that the "Special Events Committee" [a purely paper committee] conducted the mail campaign, though he was its original chairman, appeared on the bank resolution as an authorized signature, and signed checks totaling hundreds of thousands of dollars to Empire Industries, Inc., in payment of mail campaign costs.[5]

Harvey Dean, a man of conscience if not dispatch, turned over all his memorandums and information. He suffered a heart attack within a few weeks and died six weeks after Mondale's report was published. This meant his memorandums could not be admitted as evidence in court, though they still provided the prosecutors with an invaluable guide. In the atmosphere of public shock and indignation over the scandal, the benign, grandfatherly accountant was laid to rest by his family without a public funeral. This account of his role was never told.

In July a Hennepin County grand jury indicted Kline for grand larceny in the matter of his pay increase; the signature of treasurer Robert Onan had been either forged or obtained by fraud and deceit, the jury decided.

It also recommended that all Kenny board members resign as having been "neglectful." In October, J. George Zimmerman lost his CPA certificate because of professional misconduct. In early 1961 Kline was convicted of grand larceny and sentenced to up to ten years in prison. In December 1961 a federal grand jury indicted Kline, Fadell, Zimmerman, and four Chicago money-raisers—Abraham and David Koolish, John Carnell, and Philip Rettig—on several counts of mail fraud and conspiracy.

The case did not go to trial until March 1963. United States Attorney Miles Lord had lost a trump card—Harvey Dean's memorandums and testimony. He needed another. He believed there was one vulnerable defendant, publicist Fred Fadell. Fadell had maintained throughout questioning that all he had done was "legally and morally" right. He told Lord that he was a good Catholic who attended daily mass and took regular confession. A tireless talker, Lord talked to him for hours. Fadell's moral exactitude, it became apparent, was his only shield; if it could be broken, he would be without defenses. Lord convinced him that they should visit a priest.

> We saw the priest and Fadell kept rationalizing, saying he had been an independent public relations man, taking fees.
>
> Finally the priest told him, "Fred, I think you're rationalizing."
>
> And finally Fadell said to me: "I think you've got yourself a witness."[6]

The trial opened on March 19, 1963. On April 10 Fadell pleaded guilty to a single mail-fraud charge, the mailing of one fraudulent letter, which was but a part of the whole scheme. The trial continued. By taking Koolish monies, Lord charged, Kline and Fadell had been "double agents and betrayed the trust of the foundation, the polio victims and the public." The defense called all the so-called kickbacks legitimate payments, but on May 29 the jury found Kline, the Koolishes, and Zimmerman guilty of thirty-seven of a possible sixty counts. Defendant Philip Rettig had become ill; his case was later dismissed. But Kline and each of the Koolishes were sentenced to prison terms of up to ten years. The Koolishes were each fined $17,000, the legal maximum. Carnell's sentence was five years in prison; Zimmerman's, five years of probation; Fadell's, a year and a day of imprisonment. All the defendants were described by the judge as unscrupulous and greedy conspirators, who "stole the dimes and dollars donated with sacrifice by so many" and "deprived crippled children and adults of needful physical rehabilitation." He added: "The unfortunate Sister Kenny case teaches us many things, principally that avarice is a pernicious human vice."

On April 15, 1964, a thin and graying Kline, age sixty, was booked and fingerprinted at the Hennepin County jail, in the same courthouse–city hall where he had spent five years as mayor. He was taken to Stillwater State Prison to be assigned work as an orderly or janitor.

Kline served his federal and state sentences concurrently. After three years he was paroled. Fadell served six months, Carnell a year. The Koolishes were imprisoned for seventeen months at the federal penitentiary at Terre Haute, Indiana. In 1966 they agreed to pay the Kenny organization $1 million as the result of a Kenny lawsuit seeking $3.8 million, which was settled out of court.

Elizabeth Kenny's role in this fund tragedy? Only that she permitted weak men to surround her. The chicanery did not begin until her last few, feeble years, when she was too often absent and too ill to detect it. In her prime, it would not have happened. Yet she had known these men and tolerated them.

The members of the Kenny Foundation's 1960 board of directors were the main targets of judicial and public bitterness. Three judges commented harshly on their neglect and indifference. "Seldom is encountered greater collective naïveté among a large group of successful businessmen," said Judge Levi M. Hall in sentencing Kline for grand larceny, and one newspaper letter writer asked: "Are board members not misleading the contributing public when they allow their names to appear as directors of charity trusts, yet exercise none of the duties incumbent upon them?" As investigator Lord summed it up, "The whole problem in the Kenny case was that the board members let the professionals take over. The lessons are that directors should direct. Auditors should audit. Contributors should inquire. And public agents should be more adamant about their requests for information."

Years after the Kenny scandal, reliable public watchdogs over public money-raising are still lacking. In 1974 more than 500,000 national and local health, welfare, cultural, educational, civic, and religious agencies raised $25 billion. Health and welfare agencies alone raised $6.2 billion, compared with $188 million in 1940.[7] Repeated studies show waste, high costs, unrevealing financial reports, huge duplication of effort, and many promises of problem-solving medical research, with, far too often, little money spent on it, although "research" is the key slogan of many groups. Too many spend the largest share of their money on administration, money-raising, and "public education," public education too often meaning publicity and fund-raising.

Some money-raisers believe that true fund-raising costs should seldom exceed 15 percent. Others say a more reasonable limit is 25 percent. Whatever the limit should be (and this is impossible to set, without weighing each group's size and problems), the Los Angeles Board of Social Service Commissioners, a zealous public watchdog, has reported that the real money-raising costs of various Los Angeles health campaigns run from 12 to 36 percent, at the same time that some of the same agencies' national headquarters announce costs of only 7 to 15 percent, mainly by assigning part to "public education."

The Minnesota Legislature responded to the Kenny scandal by requiring charities to make full annual reports to the attorney general. By the 1970s, most states and several cities had similar licensing or registration laws. The Social Service Board of Los Angeles, for example, can bar no fund-raisers but can deny endorsement to any whose costs exceed 15 percent or who fail to meet other standards. But the administration and effectiveness of government regulatory programs is "quite uneven," a Rockefeller Citizens' Committee on Voluntary Health and Welfare Agencies found. "In all but a few cases [they are] limited in scope and merely exclude the obviously fraudulent agencies." The study director added: "Most attorney generals' reports mean very little. Nobody standardizes the reports they get, and nobody evaluates them." And few effective controls have been devised to stop out-of-staters from mail soliciting.[8]

The Rockefeller committee unsuccessfully urged establishment of a National Commission on Voluntary Health and Welfare Agencies to help regulate drives and draft better laws and regulatory methods. The idea of such regulation is unpopular among even the most reputable money-raisers. For example, the National Foundation and the American Cancer Society complained bitterly of "unfair" denial of approval in some years by the Los Angeles board. The National Foundation's Basil O'Connor (who died in 1972) considered both the existing National Information Bureau and the proposed new commission as "elite vigilantes," who would tell givers what to do, though knowing little about health agencies and health needs.[9]

O'Connor without question was a man who spent money to get money, much of which was well spent.* However, the facts the public still needs

* *Give! Who Gets Your Charity Dollar?* (Garden City, N.Y.: Anchor Press/Doubleday, 1974) by Harvey Katz maintains that National Foundation fund-raising consumed more than 40 percent of receipts during 1938–55 and 30 percent in 1971. There is a good deal of truth in Katz's book; but his evidence for assignment of the fund-raising costs is either weak or missing. The National Foundation says

and deserves to have about any fund drive are (1) how much money is coming in? (2) how much does it cost to raise it? (3) what is done with it? If every agency had to undergo uniform accounting by independent accountants and the results were publicized in understandable form, the public could know these things.

The Rockefeller committee recommended uniform accounting with outside review and full disclosure. Led by the National Health Council (an organization of major health fund-raisers), the National Social Welfare Assembly, and some of the best agencies, a uniform accounting system has been developed, and many groups are using it. But 1973 was the first year in which the National Health Council and the National Assembly for Social Policy and Development (the former National Social Welfare Assembly) expected that all their member organizations would use these uniform standards.

If a cause is unworthy, there is still no watchdog dedicated to telling the *public* about it. The best informed body is probably the nonprofit National Information Bureau, with headquarters in New York City, which does analyze fund-raisers' finances. To avoid lawsuits, however, "confidential" reports are made only to its members, mainly corporations and united funds. An individual may join and ask for reports on specific charities for a "minimum" contribution of $15 a year. Few but the most sophisticated givers, however, know this. Some newspapers and television stations refuse time or space to disapproved organizations, but the uninformed public often continues giving millions of dollars.

If we can accept the National Information Bureau's word, most charitable organizations are "reasonably sound," but some are not; a few are "downright frauds"; "others are guilty of mismanagement or irresponsible use of contributed funds." Many groups have begun making fuller public reports, but some blatantly ignore public inquiries. In early 1974 Senator Walter Mondale—prosecutor in the Kenny scandal—chaired congressional hearings in which witnesses testified that a charity called the Asthmatic Children's Foundation, mailing an annual Christmas appeal to 5 million persons, had raised $9,910,075 over the past eleven years, of which 86 percent was consumed by fund-raising or overhead.

that audits by the firm of Haskins & Sell show that between 1938 and 1958, 12.6 cents on the dollar was spent on fund-raising and 16.5 cents on fund-raising and administration. In 1972 this foundation reported a 23.4 percent fund-raising cost and 8 percent for management.

On the polio foundation, 1938–55, see Richard Carter, *The Gentle Legions* (New York: Doubleday, 1961) pp. 91–138.

A strong federal law may be the only way to force all charities to disclose their true finances as part of their appeals. Years after the Kenny scandal, the public is still getting almost no guidance on where it may or may not give with confidence.

The man who rescued the Kenny Foundation was the eminent Dr. Frank Krusen of the Mayo Clinic, who had warily greeted Liza there in 1940.

Almost immediately after the scandal broke, the medical director, E. J. Huenekens, and his Kenny Institute colleagues told the board of directors that every doctor would quit unless they stepped down. On August 30, 1960, two months after the attorney general's scalding report, the entire board resigned.[10]

In September Krusen agreed to leave Rochester, where he had three years to serve until retirement, to head the tarnished foundation. At sixty-two, he already possessed almost every honor medicine could give, more than forty altogether. He had started the first physical medicine department in a United States medical school (at Temple in 1929); he headed the noted Baruch Committee that helped universities upgrade these departments and train specialists to care for the thousands of amputees, paraplegics, and other victims of World War II. He was often called the "father" of physical medicine. He was affable, white-haired, a skilled medical diplomat, also portly. He was, in addition, a Pennsylvania Dutchman and a fighter, and he believed the Kenny movement was "something worth saving." Kenny Institute, he said, was a place "too good to die" and was desperately needed as "a national reservoir of rehabilitation knowledge and staff."

For months Krusen lived in a nine-by-nine room at the institute and worked sixteen hours a day. He drove several thousand miles through five states, speaking to group after group, catnapping in the back seat of his car, summoning fund-raising volunteers back to work, and winning places in united funds and chests. Drawing on friendships in government, foundations, and medicine, he saw the organization through a period of deficits, retrenchments, and bitterness. Fortunately, doctors kept sending their stricken patients to Kenny Institute, and the preponderant medical and public reaction, Krusen reported, was, "What can we do to help keep it open?" Its doors never closed, and the number of referrals from doctors in several states never dropped.

In December 1961 Kenny won another vote of confidence: the United States Office of Vocational Rehabilitation chose its first two centers for rehabilitation research and training, with a half a million dollars a year in federal funds allocated to each. One was to be Dr. Howard Rusk's celebrated Institute of Physical Medicine and Rehabilitation at New York University, the other, Kenny Institute and the University of Minnesota, working together. Krusen saw this as "the first step toward federal support of research and training in rehabilitation comparable to the support given heart disease, cancer and other diseases through the National Institutes of Health." Polio, under control by vaccines, was now a disease that would appear only where vaccination lagged. The first business of the Kenny Institute and the Kenny Foundation had already become the rehabilitation of victims of all illnesses and crippling accidents.*

Dr. William J. Mayo had said in 1925 that "Rehabilitation is to be a master word in medicine," but few had listened. It remained for Rusk, with the aid of Krusen and others, to seize World War II and its aftermath as an opportunity to show the public how "rehab" could put the injured back on their feet, or at least give them hope, and could do the same for most disabled persons. Rehabilitation, says Rusk, is "what happens after the stitches are out and the fever is down, the program that trains the individual to live with what he has left." Rehabilitation's message is that for most victims of accidents, strokes, arthritis, spinal cord injuries, heart disease, lung ailments, multiple sclerosis, cerebral palsy, epilepsy, and scores of other disorders, helplessness is not necessary.

Unfortunately, rehabilitation remains a hard concept for the average person to grasp, compared with the simple idea of a polio vaccine or a cancer cure. It is a long and unwieldy word and a time-consuming and expensive process (though the cost of rehabilitating a disabled person is less than the cost of maintaining him on public aid for a year). Most hospitals and doctors still give it more lip service than time, staff, and space, while at least 10 million disabled Americans need rehabilitation but are not getting it, according to Rusk, and "throughout the world, millions of handicapped people lying helpless . . . could be up and about."[11]

Krusen committed Kenny deeply to this cause. When he left at age sixty-five, again to become a professor at Temple, his successor was Dr. Paul Ellwood. Ellwood had worked at Kenny most of the time since

* Donald Dayton (who assembled and temporarily headed a new "Interim Caretakers' Committee" after the scandal) found that Marvin Kline had begun to do a capable, even "unbelievable" job of converting the institute into a general rehabilitation center.

1952; as Krusen's assistant, he was largely responsible for the operational job of building the former polio hospital into a comprehensive rehabilitation institute.

The two also began to make the institute a training and study center, or think tank, for the rehabilitation field. This soon led Ellwood down another path, and the Kenny Foundation for a time evolved into an American Rehabilitation Foundation that operated both Kenny Institute and a national health policy center.*

Ellwood's successor as head of the renewed Kenny Institute was Dr. Loren R. Leslie. Under him, it became a part of a new Minneapolis Medical Center joining three hospitals and Kenny. Kenny began operating advanced physical medicine and rehabilitation departments at Northwestern and Children's hospitals, with a new relocated institute building becoming part of the new complex. To Leslie, this marked "a coming of age for rehabilitation," one showing it had "gained credibility as a member of the health community."

The institute's twofold role—patient care and "worldwide outreach"—included:

Research in new rehabilitation techniques—for example, biomedical engineering and bioelectronics, such as implanted electronic systems to restore body functions. "It is no longer enough to say we should 'accept' disability," Leslie argued. "We need to start trying to conquer it."

Education of doctors, nurses, therapists, psychologists, social workers, counselors, and other health workers in rehabilitation methods, with some 400 Kenny courses yearly at hospitals, nursing homes, and other sites throughout the country.

Publication of textbooks and training materials for rehabilitation workers.

Sister Kenny Institute, in short, had become one of the world's respected rehabilitation centers and one still pursuing what its workers called "the Sister Kenny approach": dedication to the worth of the individual.

* In 1973 the latter became an independent, nonprofit corporation named InterStudy. Ellwood and his Kenny-based group had originated the important "Health Maintenance Organization" idea, adopted by the Nixon administration and Congress as a future health-care direction. An "HMO" is a group of doctors giving a body of consumers prepaid care, with an emphasis on prevention. This had existed before, but Ellwood inspired the government to make it one option for those covered by health insurance and otherwise to encourage the HMO movement.

In her last years, controversy swamped both Elizabeth Kenny and any unemotional view of her contributions. When all was said and done, what were they, in polio and beyond it?

In poliomyelitis:

Dr. John R. Paul of Yale University wrote in 1971 that, "in retrospect, there is no denying that Sister Kenny's ideas and techniques marked a turning point, even an about-face. . . . By determination and sheer will-power, she helped to raise the treatment of paralyzed patients out of the slough into which it had sunk."[12]

She forced doctors to halt arbitrary, long-term splinting and casting. "The abandonment of rigid fixation of the paralyzed part, long a sacred tenet . . . is a great step forward, and for this we are indebted to this shrewd and forceful lady," Professor Herbert J. Seddon, a noted British orthopedist, said shortly after her death.[13]

She contributed both early, intensive physical therapy and constant treatment, in generous amounts. Together with relief from pain and relief from tightness, they lessened muscle contracture and reduced deformity. For example, they cut the incidence of scoliosis or spinal curvature, grim and unsightly, and virtually emptied children's orthopedic hospitals.

She introduced hot packs. They relieved pain and made early physical treatment possible. They kept skin and tissues healthier. True, a hundred doctors and others had advocated hot packs or heat earlier. But few had been using them to any significant degree. Later electrical studies of muscle activity showed that both heat and motion can help keep muscle fibers capable of recovery.

She advocated and helped develop a system of muscle reeducation that made the most of the muscles that were left intact. She successfully taught her methods of joint movement, passive stimulation, and the reestablishment of reflexes, mental awareness, muscle function, and coordination.

She called to doctors' attention a whole set of symptoms, including some previously missed or ignored. The exact role of some is still uncertain. Perhaps her greatest villain was spasm. Several research findings have supported its existence, though conclusions on its role vary. Many keen observers believe it is important, and any examination of medical papers written in the late polio years will find spasm and the need to treat it an almost universal topic. "It definitely does exist, and hadn't previously been recognized and described as clearly," Krusen said in 1954. Seddon thought her observation showed "remarkable insight"; spasm was often either absent or temporary, he said, but if severe or persistent, it helped cause contracture and deformity, as she insisted.[14]

Her collaborator Dr. John Pohl describes this observation of hers in simple terms: "I think she deserves credit for making an original discovery, which was that these kids when sick with polio become sore and stiff, and that soreness and stiffness can lead to deformity. I think it's given to very few people to make such an important medical discovery, and I don't think anyone should detract from that."[15]

As she worked with her medical collaborators, she—and they—also became more sophisticated and referred not just to "spasm" but more and more to "shortening" and "tightness" as simpler and, in common medical parlance, better understood descriptions of the same phenomenon.

"Much of Kenny is Pohl," some knowledgeable doctors around her said in the 1940s. Some indeed was. Some too was the increasing sophistication of doctors and medical scientists at the University of Minnesota and its affiliated hospitals, seeing much polio in those years, being prodded by her thinking, and prodding her. In the summer of 1973 one of this group—Dr. Frederic J. Kottke, a young doctor in training when she arrived in the United States and one strongly influenced by the polio era—spoke at a recognition day for another collaborator of hers, Dr. Miland Knapp. Kottke, head of physical medicine and rehabilitation at the university, looked back at Kenny's "concepts" in the cumulative light of physiological, anatomical, and clinical or bedside research—much of it research that she had triggered.

She had seemingly erred, and aroused opponents' ire, by downgrading the importance in poliomyelitis of true paralysis: neuron or nerve cell death and accompanying muscle shriveling. She knew these existed, of course. But she stubbornly insisted that the supposedly classic nerve cell lesion, destruction of the anterior horn cells in the spinal cord, *could not exist*, except as a secondary result of some primary muscle damage, in case after case where she was able to restore muscle function. Her detractors stubbornly defended the classic concept like gospel in what seemed at the time to be an insoluble impasse. The more complex explanation, Kottke believes, depends on the work of a famous neuroanatomist, Ramon Lorente de No, at the Rockefeller Institute in the 1930s, on the Minnesota research of Kabat and Knapp in the 1940s, and on many observations since.[16] Kottke explains that: "We used to think of our central nervous system as an on-off system. Instead, it is on all the time, highly active, fast running but delicately controlled and balanced between activation and inhibition." It is the vital *anterior horn cells*—the motor neurons in the forward horns or protrusions of the spinal cord—that *stimulate muscles*. But as part of the same circuitry there is also a pool of *internuncial* or *intermediary* neurons or interneurons—all names for the same cells—that simultaneously *moderate or inhibit* the anterior horn cells.

Whether or not an anterior horn cell fires depends on how many activating impulses and inhibiting impulses reach it. One impulse is not enough to discharge it. "There must be hundreds of activating impulses in excess of inhibiting ones." Though many of both may survive the polio virus, there may still be severe loss of central nervous system inhibition.

The result is abnormal reflex activity. This includes release of the sympathetic or autonomic nervous system (the nerves that automatically serve our internal organs) from central control. The sympathetic system thus overreacts to stimuli like cold. Blood vessels constrict and react more slowly to heat.

The skin is the first organ to feel the unwelcome cold—Liza Kenny as a young bush nurse spoke of seeing a reaction like gooseflesh on the skin of a girl who within days would exhibit obvious polio symptoms.

Like any irritating mechanism, the skin cooling activates motor nerve cells. The inhibiting role of the remaining internuncials has now been weakened, however. Complex nerve and reflex pathways or control circuits are interrupted, in particular, the "gamma loop," a feedback system involving small gamma motor neurons in the spinal cord. This circuit normally tunes or plays our muscle fibers like harp strings to smooth and control muscle contraction.

The cataclysmic effect of this entire chain of events—hypersensitive sympathetic nerves, abnormal blood vessel constriction, cold extremities, alarm signals flashed to the brain and nerve centers, poorly controlled or inappropriate reflexes—is abnormal muscle shortening. The prolonged shortening soon builds up metabolites in the muscles to create a polio victim's pain.

Kottke thinks that this scenario might very well explain the muscle effect that Liza Kenny called "spasm," an effect so profound that it could fool even the best clinicians, pre-Kenny, into thinking it was the same as permanent, irreversible paralysis. Whether or not this reconstruction is entirely right—circuits and print-outs of the nervous system are far from being wholly understood—scientists are certain today that anterior horn cell damage is far from the whole polio story. They know other nerve cells in the brain and spinal cord may be involved.

As one research step, Kottke, Keith Stillwell, William Kubicek, and Mildred Olson showed that polio patients with painfully cold, swollen feet—a typical symptom—do have excess sympathetic nervous system activity. With Kottke and Olson, Dr. Glenn Gullickson, Jr., showed that the polio victim's exaggerated response to cold and exaggerated blood vessel constriction also impair circulation to the epiphyses, the knobby, cartilage-coated ends of the long bones. And this impaired circulation can impair epiphyseal growth. The polio patient may commonly end up with one leg shorter than the other, unlèss, by Liza's heat or other means, there is reduction of excess sympathetic activity and normal blood flow.[17]

What of the "alienation" or pseudoparalysis that Elizabeth Kenny could so often begin to relieve, apparently within minutes? In 1942 Dr. Mary Daly wrote that during the recovery period patients frequently showed "what Sister Kenny calls 'mental alienation.' Although able at the end of one day's exercises to perform a coordinated action with a given muscle or muscle group, the patient would completely forget on the following day how that action was performed. However, after several passive motions the patient would again remember." In 1957 Dr. Donald Covalt of New York University was demonstrating a hemiplegic patient whose arm had been paralyzed for four years and then came back to life. "Is this the alienation that Sister Kenny talked about?" he asked. "I don't know. But it must be something with a neuro-muscular connection."[18]

Kottke recalls that in the mid-1940s Knapp and Kabat pointed out that "when internuncial neuron involvement destroyed some of the pathways through the anterior horn cells, the patient would also lose coordination." And with retraining, it was demonstrated again and again, the patient could learn to use muscles which appeared to be paralyzed. "When Sister Kenny called this mental alienation and Dr. Knapp called it reversible paralysis, everybody rose up in arms," Kottke remembers. "But it looks as though our present picture of the neuromuscular system helps tell us how this occurs."

What is most important long after Sister Kenny's death, Kottke concludes, is that "her concept of polio and therefore the kind of treatment that was needed" were new and different, that "she made us focus on how the neuromuscular system really functions," and that "our experience with Sister Kenny and with polio have impacted on physical medicine and rehabilitation as they are practiced today. They have given us ideas for research—on neuromuscular physiology, on kinesiology or the whole science of motion, and on walking and balance. They have given us models for patient care, and affected the way we educate doctors and therapists."

In short, Elizabeth Kenny helped shape the attack on all disability: modern rehabilitation. She preached restoring usefulness and self-care in Australia in the early 1930s, when she was laughed at. In the United States in the early 1940s, said Dr. Philip Lewin, "physical therapy was almost dead among orthopedists. She created so much interest in it that she saved it." This exaggerates: physical therapy was a spirited if still small profession, and rehabilitation, led by Rusk, was about to burst forth anyway in response to the demands of World War II. Still, Dr. John Coulter of Northwestern University agreed with Lewin that she had made a "great" contribution.[19]

Central to her contribution, Kottke adds, is the fact that

> her care of the polio patient was programming by objective. Government and industry have only in the past few years been talking about management or programming "by objective," but she did it. She said that when a child gets over his polio, he should be able to stand up again. Therefore, as we relieved muscle shortening, we had to reestablish full range of motion for normal standing and balancing. If the patient was to stand later, we had to maintain him in his bed in a proper "standing in bed" posture. So she added her own kind of footboard and a mattress blocked away from the footboard to position the foot and instep. Today's "rehabilitation" or "physiatric bed" is an outgrowth of her "Kenny bed." These are just a few facets. The point is that when you truly keep the patient's outcome in view, you have an entirely different and better outcome.

Also, her step-by-step methodology—stimulation, restoration of muscle awareness, restoration of muscle function—is a sequence now followed widely in muscle reeducation.

> When she had her patient concentrate on one motion at a time and repeat it many times, she was, we know now, programming what we call the extra-pyramidal nervous system.* In training the cerebral cortex to consciously control muscle function, which she unknowingly did and we still do, she was also training this system. And most of our easy, coordinated activity is extra-pyramidal rather than pyramidal. We can pay attention through the cerebral cortex, we've learned, to only one thing at a time. We say, "I can do many things at a time," but we can actually pay attention to no more than three activities at a time, and we do that by switching attention from one to another. Most of the things that we do multiply are done by our extra-pyramidal programming. She taught it by teaching the patient to concentrate, by working in a quiet place with no diversion, and by emphasizing the repeated use of one muscle at a time.
>
> The patient, we have also learned, has to have some sensor to tell him

* Most of the fibers that lead from the motor area of the cerebral cortex of the brain to the spinal cord form a nerve path, the pyramidal tract, named for a layer of large pyramid-shaped cells in the cortex. This tract controls the motion of the skeletal muscles that move our arms, legs, and bodies. But there is also an extra-pyramidal system involved in control of motion; its fibers originate in the subcortical area of the brain including the cerebellum. Among other functions, it is responsible for most of the motion we don't consciously think about and for adjusting new motions to motor activity elsewhere. Both systems contribute to an integrated result.

when he is contracting a muscle. Again she anticipated us. She used joint motion. We have since found that most of our perception of muscles indeed occurs by joint motion rather than because of any muscle sensors. She also used what she called "cutaneous stimulation"—moving a neglected muscle quickly or stroking or stimulating the area over it to produce a contraction to make the patient aware of the muscle. She said this not only helped the patient feel the contraction but also strengthened the contraction. Everyone scoffed at her, but in 1952 Hagbarth at the Karolinska Institute showed that if you stimulate the skin over a dog's gastrocnemius muscle, you do increase its contraction. We too then found that in a patient with weakness, whether from polio or stroke or multiple sclerosis or other causes, stimulation of the skin overlying the belly of a muscle *will* cause facilitation and increase its contraction.

Her hot packs too have been widely incorporated into physical therapy to relieve pain and tightness. But beyond any tools or technique and beyond even the foresight that Kottke describes, she contributed something else—her therapeutic aggressiveness. Seeing polio patients in bed in casts, she not only knew this was wrong, but also knew it was defeatist. In discrediting such immobilization, she helped discredit all excessive rest. One post-Kenny experiment found that healthy young volunteers immobilized for weeks in plaster casts become weak; their muscles become flabby; they feel giddy when they stand; their bones are depleted of calcium. These things happened to astronauts when they failed to exercise during space flights. They happen to anyone kept in bed long without activity. Dr. Sedgwick Mead wrote in 1962 that Sister Kenny severely jostled the advocates of the "rest cure" for polio, strokes, fractures, multiple sclerosis, peripheral nerve disorders, and other disorders. In his phrase, she helped end "a century of the abuse of rest."

Resting too long, giving up, taking refuge in immobilization of the body or mind were all an abomination to her. "What she taught," says Dr. Paul Ellwood, "is what is widely believed today. You can do a great deal with what you have left." A large part of her contribution, in other words, was sheer stubbornness: her refusal to accept the inevitability of crippling at a time when it was generally accepted.[20]

A Minneapolis minister summed this up by saying that she made men and women in dire need feel that "tomorrow I shall walk again. Tomorrow is still mine."[21]

Did Elizabeth Kenny finally achieve greatness or any measure of it? One doctor said after her death, "Frankly, I couldn't help but feel annoyed that she got so much acclaim, while so many truly important scientists stay unknown."

She was no scientist; she was a crusader. One friend saw her accompany a group of doctors to examine some corpses in the anatomy laboratory—"To her, all dead limbs and explanations. She looked but disdainfully, as if to say, 'How boring. Let me observe a living body.'" She did observe in living bodies some phenomena that others had missed. She did have in this sense what William James defined as genius: "the faculty of perceiving in an unhabitual way." And original or not, she did more than any other person to revolutionize polio treatment and made an impact far beyond polio.

One person who assessed her life, Professor Herbert J. Seddon, praised her accomplishments but thought she lacked two "qualities of greatness": "She was never content to let the idea sink in [but] hammered everybody with the whole powerful apparatus of modern propaganda. . . . If her story is strictly accurate, she never made a mistake."[22] He could have said worse. She sometimes lied. She exaggerated. She made claims that she could not fulfill. She was probably both paranoid and megalomaniacal to some degree. Unusual traits in the great? Think of Isaac Newton, "a neurotic of the most advanced sort," a scholar says. Pasteur, full of self-praise, brutally outspoken. Joan of Arc, driven. "How 'normal' a rating would the psychologist accord to any ardent reformer—to one who will pound doors until they open?" asked a National Foundation historian discussing Miss Kenny.

Clara Barton, the Civil War nurse who founded the American Red Cross, constantly courted dignitaries, sought out newspaper reporters, bedecked herself in medals, and struck dramatic poses—all to fight apathy. Even Florence Nightingale, cast in myth as the gentle lady with the lamp, was actually stubborn, sharp-tongued, and a skilled intriguer, "no sweet, shy, delicate flower of Victorian womanhood," a student notes. In her younger years she was sickly and depressed, frustrated because her family considered nursing on a level with prostitution. Feeling (much like Liza) that "God spoke to me and called me to his service," she finally defied them, also (like Liza) turning down a marriage proposal from a man she adored. When she and her nurses descended uninvited on the filthy army hospitals in the Crimea, the British ambassador called her "bad-tempered, heartless, pompous and lazy." She herself wrote: "No man, not even a doctor, ever gives any definition of what a nurse should be than this—'devoted and obedient.' This definition would do just as well for a porter. It might even do for a horse. It will not do [for a nurse]."

Does this sound a little like Liza Kenny? Such people have always aroused the deepest hatred and enmity in their contemporaries. They have the uncommon spark. "There is no great genius," said the ancients, "without some touch of madness." Yet Elizabeth Kenny, when all was said and done, leavened the madness, for she proved herself right on simple principles. She battled, accepted her defeats, and changed her ideas when she had to, but hung on. When she was depressed, she sat in her solitary gloom until she recovered, then she opened her door for a fresh start until she won.

Acknowledgments

TRUTH IS HARD to recapture an instant after an event, let alone ten or twenty or eighty years later. The facts about some events in Elizabeth Kenny's life remain cloudy. For most, I have set down the version that I believe to be true. In important cases I have taken note of other possibilities.

Conversations quoted in this book are as people remember them, as Sister Kenny recorded them, or in some cases as I heard her say them. Nothing has been "fictionalized," although a biographer can only seek corroboration wherever possible and try to be right. In the words of an inscription on one Dead Sea Scroll, "No man there is who can tell the whole tale."

The more technical sections on polio have been reviewed in full or in main part by Drs. Miland Knapp, John Pohl, and Frederic Kottke, and by Vivian Hannan, former chief teaching therapist at Kenny Institute, now at the University of Minnesota. I am in debt for her help in vividly describing Kenny therapy. The sections on the long-misunderstood poliomyelitis virus have been read by Drs. John F. Enders and Gilbert Dalldorf. But on these matters too, I have sometimes had to choose between conflicting opinions, and any errors are mine.

I began work on this biography in 1955 after making an initial trip to Australia in 1953, a few months after Elizabeth Kenny's death, to write a series of biographical articles for the *Minneapolis Tribune* and other newspapers. I completed the work during leaves and vacations from that newspaper and, later, from the *Washington Post.* Some of the research and writing was supported by study grants from the Kenny Foundation, the National Foundation, and the Elmer L. and Eleanor J. Andersen Foundation.* Except to check facts on a few pages, no one from any of these organizations has seen or asked to see the manuscript, in which my views often differ from the views of the two former polio groups.

My conclusions often differ too from those of Sister Kenny's family. Yet I am greatly indebted to many of them for help, in particular, to one of her sisters, Mrs. Julia Farquharson; two other sisters who survived her, Mrs. Margaret (Maggie) Scotney and Mrs. Mary Scotney; her adopted daughter Mary Stewart-Kenny McCracken; her niece Mary Farquharson Fredlund; and her nephew Jack Kenny, most recently an editor of the *Sydney Morning Herald.* I owe special thanks for help or encouragement to three former editors, William P. Steven, Bower Hawthorne, and Daryle Feldmeir; to Harry Summers, Australian journalist; Dr. Saul Benison, University of Cincinnati medical historian†; Drs. Frank Krusen, long of the Mayo Clinic, Jarvis Nye of Brisbane, and Wesley Spink of the University of Minnesota; Martha Ostenso, novelist and collaborator on the Kenny biography; Carolyn Willyoung Stagg; Rosalind Russell, a bright and gracious person—and more than 200 others I interviewed: old settlers in Australia, Kenny friends and relatives, doctors, scientists, polio workers, Kenny enthusiasts, and Kenny detractors. I interviewed Elizabeth Kenny often in the late 1940s and the early 1950s.

* The Sister Elizabeth Kenny Foundation later became, corporately, Sister Kenny Institute and the American Rehabilitation Foundation, then merged in 1975 with Abbott-Northwestern Hospital as a part of the Minneapolis Medical Center, but retained its own identity. The National Foundation for Infantile Paralysis became the National Foundation.

† His forthcoming history of polio and the National Foundation for Infantile Paralysis promises to be definitive.

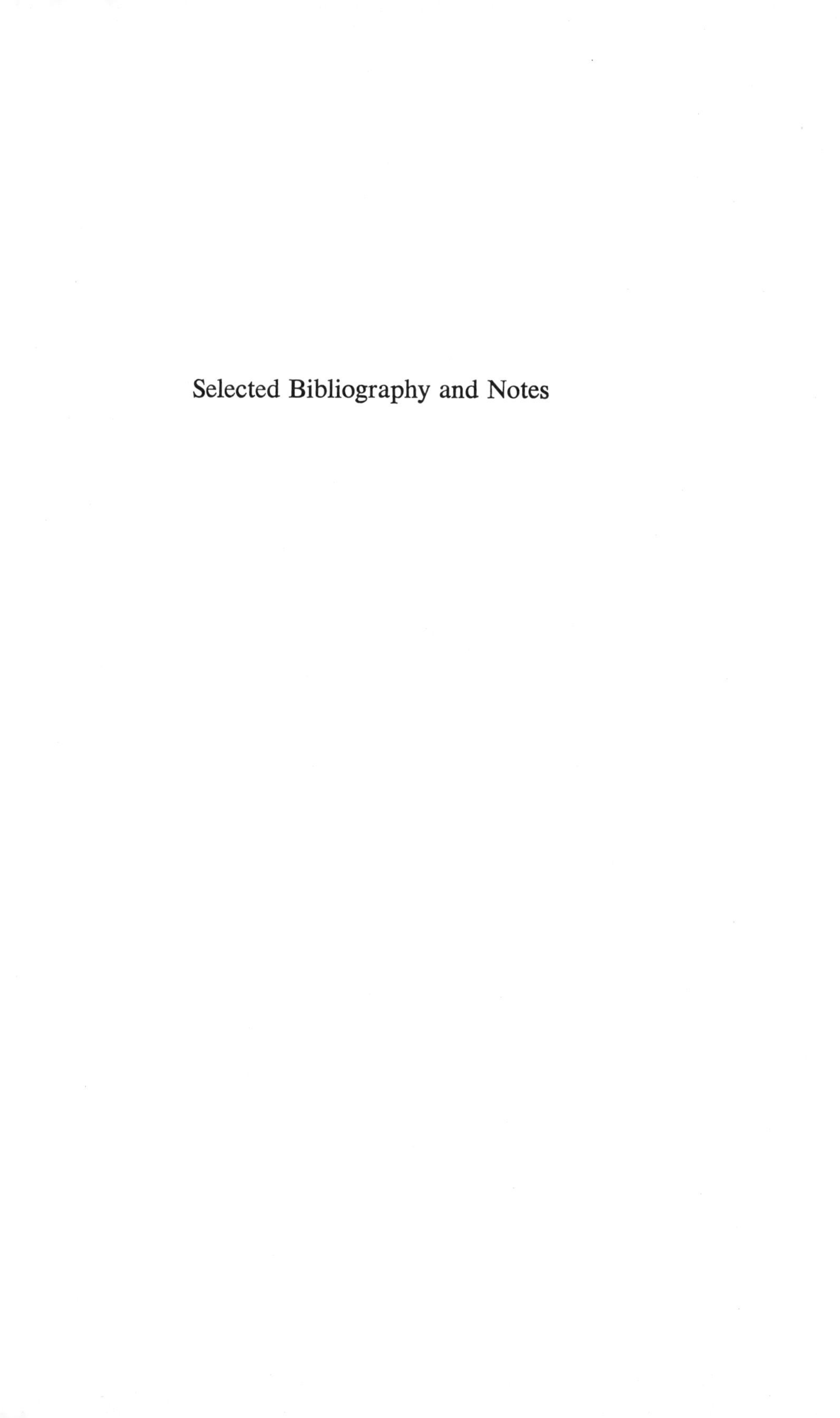

Selected Bibliography and Notes

Selected Bibliography

Publications by Sister Elizabeth Kenny

And They Shall Walk: The Life Story of Sister Elizabeth Kenny, written in collaboration with Martha Ostenso. New York: Dodd, Mead, 1943.

Cause and Prevention of Deformities in Poliomyelitis. El Monte, Calif.: Sister Kenny Polio Hospital, May 20, 1952. (Pamphlet)

Concerning the Disease Poliomyelitis. Minneapolis and Jersey City: Elizabeth Kenny Polio Institutes, 1948. (Pamphlet)

" 'Doctors, I Salute You,' " *American Weekly*, March 2, 1952.

"Evidence Presented to Luther Youngdahl, Governor of Minnesota, and Doctor Wallace Cole, University of Minnesota, Covering the End Results of Ten Years' Research Concerning Poliomyelitis." New York: distributed by the author, April 1950. (Mimeographed)

" 'God Is My Doctor': The Real Story of Her Battle against Infantile Paralysis," *American Weekly*, March 26, April 2, 9, 16, and 23, 1944.

Infantile Paralysis and Cerebral Diplegia. Sydney: Angus & Robertson, 1937.

"Infantile Paralysis: Its Description and Treatment," *New Orleans Medical and Surgical Journal*, October 1943.

Kenny Concept of Infantile Paralysis and Its Treatment, The, by John F. Pohl in collaboration with Elizabeth Kenny. St. Paul: Bruce Publishing Co., 1943.

My Battle and Victory. London: Robert Hale, 1954.

Paper presented by Elizabeth Kenny at a medical conference held under the auspices of the Sister Elizabeth Kenny Foundation. Minneapolis: distributed by the author, October 1949. (Mimeographed)

Physical Medicine: The Science of Dermo-Neuro-Muscular Therapy as Applied to Infantile Paralysis. Minneapolis: published by the author, 1943. (Pamphlet)

"Poliomyelitis." Minneapolis: Sister Elizabeth Kenny Foundation, 1950. (A mimeographed set of questions and answers)

Poliomyelitis: A Systemic Disease. Buffalo, N.Y.: Sister Kenny Treatment Center, July 14, 1952. (Pamphlet)

Poliomyelitis: Findings in Investigations of Evidence Concerning Poliomyelitis. Minneapolis: Elizabeth Kenny, 1947. (Pamphlet)

"Report to Dr. Wallace Cole." Minneapolis: distributed by the author, undated, probably about March 1950. (Mimeographed)

"Sister Kenny Tells 'Why I Left America,'" *Woman's Home Companion*, March 1951.

Treatment of Infantile Paralysis in the Acute Stage. St. Paul: Bruce Publishing Co., 1941.

"Truth Is the Daughter of Time." Address on receiving an honorary degree, University of Rochester, Rochester, N.Y., May 2, 1943. (Unpublished)

Publications on Polio and on Sister Kenny

Aaron, Harold. "The Kenny Treatment," *Consumer Reports*, February 1949.

———. "Poliomyelitis," *Consumer Reports*, February 1949.

Berg, Roland H. *Polio and Its Problems.* Philadelphia: Lippincott, 1948.

Bower, Albert G. (Ed.). *Diagnosis and Treatment of the Acute Phase of Poliomyelitis and Its Complications.* Baltimore: Williams & Wilkins, 1954.

Brand, Jeanne L., E. T. Sweeney, and L. Williams. "The History of the National Foundation for Infantile Paralysis through 1953—Vol. IV: Medical Services." New York: National Foundation for Infantile Paralysis Historical Division, 1955. (Unpublished)

Cohn, Victor. "Angry Angel: The Real Story of Sister Kenny," *Minneapolis Tribune*, October 29–November 18, 1953.

———. *Four Billion Dimes.* New York: National Foundation for Infantile Paralysis, 1955. (Reprint of a series of articles on the history of the Salk vaccine and the polio movement that appeared in the *Minneapolis Tribune*, April 1955)

Cole, Wallace H., John F. Pohl, and Miland E. Knapp. *The Kenny Method of Treatment for Infantile Paralysis.* New York: National Foundation for Infantile Paralysis, 1942. (Pamphlet)

Committee on Interstate and Foreign Commerce, House of Representatives. *Health Inquiry (Poliomyelitis).* Washington: U.S. Government Printing Office, 1953.

Davis, Audrey B. *Triumph over Disability: The Development of Rehabilitation Medicine in the U.S.A.* Washington: Smithsonian Institution, 1973. (Catalog for an exhibition at the National Museum of History and Technology)

Deutsch, Albert. "The Truth about Sister Kenny," *American Mercury*, November 1944.

Horder, Lord, (Ed.). *British Encyclopedia of Medical Practice.* 2d edition. Vol. 10. London: Butterworth, 1952.

International Poliomyelitis Congress. *Poliomyelitis: Papers and Discussions Presented at the First, Second, Third, Fourth, and Fifth International Poliomyelitis Conferences.* Philadelphia: Lippincott, 1949, 1952, 1955, 1958, and 1961.

Jolles, Naomi. "The Miracles of Sister Kenny," *New York Post*, February 6, 1943.

Jones, Robert, and Robert W. Lovett. *Orthopedic Surgery.* New York: William Wood, 1929.

Kline, Marvin L. "The Most Unforgettable Character I've Met," *Reader's Digest*, August 1959.

Krusen, Frank H., F. J. Kottke, and P. M. Ellwood Jr. (Eds.). *Handbook of Physical Medicine and Rehabilitation.* Philadelphia: W. B. Saunders, 1965.

Levine, Herbert J. *I Knew Sister Kenny.* Boston: Christopher Publishing House, 1954.

Levinson, S. O., and Philip Lewin. *Infantile Paralysis: Physician's Manual.* Springfield: Illinois Department of Public Health, 1942.

London County Council, Honorary Advisory Committee. "Report on Infantile

Paralysis Clinic at Queen Mary's Hospital, Carshalton." November 10, 1938. (Mimeographed)

Lovett, Robert W. *The Treatment of Infantile Paralysis.* Philadelphia: Blakiston, 1916.

Miller, Lois Mattox. "Sister Kenny vs. Infantile Paralysis," *Reader's Digest,* December 1941.

______. "Sister Kenny Wins Her Fight," *Reader's Digest,* October 1942.

______. "Sister Kenny vs. the Medical Old Guard," *Reader's Digest,* October 1944.

National Foundation for Infantile Paralysis. *Principles of the Kenny Method of Treatment of Infantile Paralysis.* New York: National Foundation for Infantile Paralysis, about 1943. (Pamphlet)

______. *The Story of the Kenny Method.* New York: National Foundation for Infantile Paralysis, April 1944. (Pamphlet)

Paul, John R. *A History of Poliomyelitis.* New Haven and London: Yale University Press, 1971.

Peabody, Francis W., George Draper, and A. R. Dochez. *A Clinical Study of Acute Poliomyelitis.* New York: Rockefeller Institute for Medical Research, 1912.

Potter, Robert D. "Sister Kenny's Treatment for Infantile Paralysis," *American Weekly,* August 17, 1941.

Reiten, Grace. "Our Daughter Had Polio," *Saturday Evening Post,* August 21, 1954. (Kenny Institute during an epidemic)

Stubbs Brown, Thomas Victor, and Abraham Fryberg. "Report on Concepts and Treatments of Poliomyelitis." Brisbane: December 6, 1948. (Unpublished)

Thelander, C. A. (Chairman), J. V. Duhig, Jarvis Nye, Alec E. Patterson, and R. S. Lahz. "Report of the Royal Commission on the Investigation of Infantile Paralysis." Brisbane: 1937. (Mimeographed) Also, *Medical Journal of Australia,* February 29, 1938.

Tubby, A. H., and Robert Jones. *Modern Methods in Surgery of Paralysis.* London: Macmillan, 1903.

Wickman, Ivan. *Acute Poliomyelitis (Heine-Medin's Disease).* Translated by J. Wm. Maloney. New York: Journal of Nervous and Mental Disease Publishing Co., 1913.

Yoder, Robert M. "Healer from the Outback," *Saturday Evening Post,* January 17, 1942.

NOTE: The author also had access to the files of the Sister Kenny Institute and Foundation, the archives of the Queensland Government Premier's Office and Ministry for Health and Home Affairs, the papers of Dr. Frank H. Krusen, and the files of the *New York Times,* the *Minneapolis Star,* the *Minneapolis Tribune,* the *Brisbane Courier-Mail,* and the *Sydney Morning Herald.*

Medical Articles on Polio and on Sister Kenny

Agassiz, C. D. S., R. H. Metcalfe, M. Mitman, and A. Topping. Quoted in "Poliomyelitis," a report of the Society of Medical Officers of Health, *Lancet,* 24:113 (June 17, 1950).

Bennett, Robert L. "The Influence of the Kenny Concept of Acute Poliomyelitis on Physical Treatment through All Stages of the Disease," *Archives of Physical Therapy,* 24:453 (August 1943).

______. "Physical Medicine in Poliomyelitis," *Poliomyelitis: Papers and Discussions Presented at the Second International Poliomyelitis Conference.* Philadelphia: Lippincott, 1952.

______. "The Role of the Physician in Prevention of Musculoskeletal Deformity after Poliomyelitis," *Journal of the American Medical Association,* 153:79 (September 12, 1953).

———. "Evaluation of the End Results of Acute Anterior Poliomyelitis," *Journal of the American Medical Association*, 162:851 (October 27, 1956).

Bingham, Robert. "Kenny Treatment for Infantile Paralysis," *Journal of Bone and Joint Surgery*, 25:647 (July 1943).

———. "Muscular Fibrodystrophy," *Journal of Bone and Joint Surgery*, 29:85 (January 1947).

———. "Muscular Fibrodystrophy in Children," *Western Journal of Surgery, Obstetrics and Gynecology*, 58:288 (June 1950).

Bundesen, Herman N., and M. M. Peet. "Medical Committee's Statement on Kenny Method," *National Foundation News*, 1:5 (December 1941).

Chown, Bruce. "Newer Knowledge of the Pathology of Poliomyelitis," *Canadian Public Health Journal*, 33:276 (June 1942).

Cole, Wallace H. "The Kenny Concept of Infantile Paralysis," *Wisconsin Medical Journal*, 42:778 (August 1943).

———, and Miland E. Knapp. "The Kenny Treatment of Infantile Paralysis: A Preliminary Report," *Journal of the American Medical Association*, 116:2577 (June 7, 1941).

———, John F. Pohl, and Miland E. Knapp. "The Kenny Method of Treatment for Infantile Paralysis," *Archives of Physical Therapy*, 23:399 (July 1942).

Daly, Mary M. I., Jerome Greenbaum, Edward T. Reilly, Alvah M. Weiss, and Philip M. Stimson. "The Early Treatment of Poliomyelitis, with an Evaluation of the Sister Kenny Treatment," *Journal of the American Medical Association*, 118:1433 (April 25, 1942).

[Elkins, Earl C.] "Kenny Treatment for Poliomyelitis," unsigned editorial, *Archives of Physical Therapy*, 23:364 (June 1942).

———. "The Treatment of Poliomyelitis," *Kentucky Medical Journal*, March 1950.

Ghormley, Ralph K. "History of the Treatment of Poliomyelitis," in American Academy of Orthopedics, *Lectures on Regional Orthopedic Surgery and Fundamental Orthopedic Problems*. Ann Arbor: Edwards, 1947.

——— (Chairman), Edward L. Compere, J. A. Dickson, R. V. Funsten, J. Albert Key, H. R. McCarroll, and Herman C. Schumm (Committee for Investigation of the Kenny Treatment of Poliomyelitis). "Evaluation of the Kenny Treatment for Infantile Paralysis," *Journal of the American Medical Association*, 125:466 (June 17, 1944).

Hansson, Kristian G. "The After-Treatment of Poliomyelitis," *Journal of the American Medical Association*, 113:32 (July 1, 1939).

Huenekens, Edgar J. "The Diagnosis and Treatment of Infantile Paralysis," *Postgraduate Medicine*, 7:100 (February 1950).

Hulett, J. E. "The Kenny Healing Cult: A Preliminary Analysis of Leadership and Patterns of Interaction," *American Sociological Review*, 10:364 (June 1945).

Jones, Robert. "Contributions to Orthopedic Surgery," *Medical Annual*, 1893, 1895.

———. "An Address on Certain Operative Features in Paralysis of Children, with Special Reference to Poliomyelitis," *British Medical Journal*, 2:1520 (December 9, 1911).

Kabat, Herman, and Miland E. Knapp. "The Mechanism of Muscle Spasm in Poliomyelitis," *Journal of Pediatrics*, 24:123 (February 1944).

Kendall, Henry O., and Florence P. Kendall. "Care during the Recovery Period in Paralytic Poliomyelitis," *U.S. Public Health Service Bulletin*, No. 421, April 1938.

———, and Florence P. Kendall. "Report to the National Foundation for Infantile Paralysis on the Sister Kenny Method of Treatment in Anterior Poliomyelitis." March 1941. (Unpublished)

Knapp, Miland E. "Kenny Treatment for Infantile Paralysis," *Archives of Physical Therapy*, 23:668 (November 1942).

———. "A Hypothesis to Explain the Muscular After-Effects of Poliomyelitis," *Archives of Physical Medicine*, 29:334 (June 1948).

———. "The Contribution of Sister Elizabeth Kenny to the Treatment of Poliomyelitis," *Archives of Physical Medicine and Rehabilitation*, 36:510 (August 1955).

———. "Lower Motor Neuron Disease," *Postgraduate Medicine*, 46:203 (October 1969).

———, Lewis Sher, and S. Smith. "The Results of Kenny Treatment of Acute Poliomyelitis: The Present Status of 391 Patients Treated between 1940–1945," *Journal of the American Medical Association*, 115:117 (January 10, 1953).

Kottke, Frederic J. "The Role of Poliomyelitis in the Development of Physical Medicine and Rehabilitation." Address given on Dr. Miland Knapp Recognition Day, Minneapolis, May 26, 1973.

Krusen, Frank H. "Observations on the Kenny Treatment of Poliomyelitis," *Proceedings of the Staff Meetings of the Mayo Clinic*, 17:449 (August 12, 1942).

Laruelle, Leon. "The Brussels Poliomyelitis Center—Report of the Activity of the Kenny Section." August 10, 1949. (Unpublished report to the Sister Elizabeth Kenny Foundation)

Lewin, Philip. "The Kenny Treatment of Infantile Paralysis during the Acute Stage," *Illinois Medical Journal*, 81:281 (April 1942).

Lovett, Robert W. "The Principles of the Treatment of Infantile Paralysis," *Journal of the American Medical Association*, 62:251 (January 24, 1914).

———. "A Plan of Treatment in Infantile Paralysis," *Journal of the American Medical Association*, 67:421 (August 5, 1916).

———. "The After-Care of Infantile Paralysis," *Journal of the American Medical Association*, 68:1018 (April 7, 1917).

———. "The Diagnosis, Prognosis and Early Treatment of Poliomyelitis," *Journal of the American Medical Association*, 78:1607 (May 27, 1922).

———, and W. P. Lucas. "Infantile Paralysis: A Study of 635 Cases from Children's Hospital, Boston," *Journal of the American Medical Association*, 51:1677 (November 14, 1908).

Lowman, Edward W. "Preventable Deformities in Poliomyelitis," *Archives of Physical Medicine*, 28:455 (July 1947).

McKinley, J. C., Irvine McQuarrie, William A. O'Brien, and Maurice B. Visscher. "The Present Status of Poliomyelitis Management," *Journal-Lancet*, 44:249 (July 1944).

Mead, Sedgwick. "Practical Rehabilitation in Poliomyelitis," *Poliomyelitis: Papers and Discussions Presented at the Third International Poliomyelitis Conference*. Philadelphia: Lippincott, 1955.

———. "A Century of the Abuse of Rest," *Journal of the American Medical Association*, 182:344 (October 27, 1962).

Metcalfe, R. H. "A Critical Evaluation of the Kenny Treatment," *Medical Press*, 454 (November 17, 1954).

———. "The Place of Orthopedics in the Treatment of Poliomyelitis," *Medical Press*, 477 (November 17, 1954).

Moldaver, Joseph. "The Physiopathological Aspect of Disorders of Muscles in Infantile Paralysis," *Journal of the American Medical Association*, 123:74 (September 11, 1943).

———. "An Analysis of Neuromuscular Disorders in Poliomyelitis," *Journal of Bone and Joint Surgery*, 26:103 (January 1944).

Muenster, Joseph J., Frederic J. Kottke, and T. W. Gucker. "Symposium on Poliomyelitis," *Journal of the Missouri Medical Association*, 44:209 (March 1952).

Ober, Frank R. "Pain and Tenderness during the Acute Stage of Poliomyelitis," *Journal of the American Medical Association*, 120:514 (October 17, 1942).

———. "Early Management of Poliomyelitis and the Kenny Treatment," *Connecticut Medical Journal*, 7:16 (January 1943).

Plastridge, Alice Lou. "Report in Re: Trip to Observe Work of Sister Kenny." March 15, 1941. (Unpublished report to the National Foundation for Infantile Paralysis)

Pohl, John F. "Kenny Treatment of Anterior Poliomyelitis: Report of the First Cases Treated in America," *Journal of the American Medical Association*, 118:1428 (April 25, 1942).

———. "The Kenny Concept and Treatment of Infantile Paralysis," *Journal-Lancet*, 45:265 (August 1945).

———. "Early Diagnosis of Poliomyelitis," *Journal of the American Medical Association*, 134:13 (July 26, 1947).

———. "The Peripheral Disease of Poliomyelitis," *Journal of Bone and Joint Surgery*, 29:1027 (October 1947).

Ransohoff, Nicholas S. "Experiences with the Kenny Treatment for Acute Poliomyelitis in the Epidemic of 1942, Monmouth and Ocean Counties, New Jersey," *Journal of Bone and Joint Surgery*, 26:99 (January 1944).

Roth, Bernard. "The Surgical and Orthopedic Treatment of Infantile Paralysis," *British Medical Journal*, 2:459 (September 6, 1884).

Seddon, H. J. Review, *British Medical Journal*, 4762:802 (April 12, 1952).

———. "Sister Kenny," obituary, *British Medical Journal*, 4796:1262 (December 6, 1952).

"Sister Kenny," editorial (unsigned), *Minnesota Medicine*, 23:375 (May 1942).

"Sister Kenny," editorial (unsigned), *Minnesota Medicine*, 36:67 (January 1953).

Stimson, Philip M. "Minimizing the After-Effects of Poliomyelitis," *Journal of the American Medical Association*, 119:990 (July 25, 1942).

Treanor, W. J., and Frank H. Krusen. "Poliomyelitis: Modern Treatment and Rehabilitation," *Irish Journal of Medical Science*, 294(6th series):257 (June 1950).

Visscher, Maurice B., and Jay A. Myers. "Sister Kenny—Five Years After," editorial, *Journal-Lancet*, 65:309 (August 1945).

Notes

Introduction: A Nurse's Revolution

1. Interviews with Drs. Frank Krusen and Miland Knapp.
2. Interview with Dr. John Pohl.
3. Robert M. Yoder, "Healer from the Outback," *Saturday Evening Post*, January 17, 1942.
4. Interviews with Henry Haverstock, Jr. and Dr. John Pohl.
5. H. N. Bundesen and M. M. Peet, "Medical Committee's Statement on Kenny Method," *National Foundation News*, December 1941. Editorial, *Journal of the American Medical Association*, 117:1980 (December 6, 1941); 117:2171 (December 20, 1941).
6. Dr. John Coulter, quoted by Dr. Frank Krusen. Dr. Edward L. Compere in the *Minneapolis Star-Journal*, September 9, 1943. Dr. Philip Lewin, quoted in an article by Lois Mattox Miller, "Sister Kenny Wins Her Fight," *Reader's Digest*, October 1942.
7. *Washington Times-Herald*, February 3, 1944.
8. *Minneapolis Star-Journal*, September 28, 1946.
9. Dr. Wallace H. Cole, "The Kenny Concept of Infantile Paralysis," *Wisconsin Medical Journal*, 42:778 (August 1943).
10. Article by Janet M. Geister (J. M. G.) in *Trained Nurse and Hospital Review*, July 1942. Dr. Frank Krusen, "Observations on the Kenny Treatment of Poliomyelitis," *Proceedings of the Staff Meetings of the Mayo Clinic*, 17:449 (August 12, 1942).
11. *Minneapolis Star-Journal*, September 10, 1943.
12. Interview with Sister Kenny, March 20, 1950.

Chapter 1: Australia

1. James Carty, *Ireland: From Grattan's Parliament to the Great Famine* (Dublin: C. J. Fallon, 1952). Other sources on Ireland are: T. Corcoran, S.J., *Some*

Lists of Catholic Lay Teachers and Their Illegal Schools (Dublin: Gill, 1932); R. D. Edwards and T. D. Williams (Eds.), *The Great Famine* (New York: New York University Press, 1957); National Tourist Publicity Organization, *Official Guide, Kilkenny* (Dublin: undated); Rev. T. O'Herlihy, *The Famine* (Drogheda: Drogheda Independent, undated); A. M. Sullivan, *The Story of Ireland* (Dublin: Gill, undated).

2. Carty, *Ireland*, pp. 16 and 41.

3. Family history: Sister Elizabeth Kenny, with Martha Ostenso, *And They Shall Walk* (New York: Dodd, Mead, 1943), pp. 1–2, 37–38; Kenny Foundation biographical files; interviews in Australia and Ireland with Julia Farquharson, Rev. P. W. Pearson, Mrs. James (Minnie) Bell, Anne Bell, and Michael Kenny (a Dublin cousin). Kenny and Pearson were keen family historians. Richard Pearson was the son of John Pearson, a Scotch medical man, possibly a recognized doctor. By Sister Kenny's account, "Big Jim" Moore sailed on the *Orestes* in 1844; P. W. Pearson says it was on the *Cadet* in 1841. She wrote that Moore was born in Scotland; the other accounts agree that he was "northern Irish and all Irish."

4. Carty, *Ireland*, pp. xvii–xviii, 42–43.

5. Arnold L. Haskell, *Waltzing Matilda: Background to Australia* (London: Black, 1948), pp. 12–14.

6. Anthony Trollope, *Australia and New Zealand*, Vol. I (London: Chapman & Hall, 1873), pp. 207–210.

The background on nineteenth- and early twentieth-century Australia in chapters 1–5 is also from Marjorie Barnard, *Australian Outline* (Sydney: Ure Smith, 1943); R. M. Crawford, *Australia* (London: Hutchinson's University Library, 1952); C. Hartley Grattan, *Introducing Australia* (Sydney: Angus & Robertson, 1949); Haskell, *Waltzing Matilda*; Paul McGuire, *Australia: Her Heritage, Her Future* (New York: Stokes, 1939); Marcie Muire, *Anthony Trollope in Australia* (Adelaide: Wakefield, 1949); Irma Pearl (Ed.), *Our Yesterdays: Australian Life since 1853 in Photographs* (Sydney: Angus & Robertson, 1954); Steele Rudd, *On Our Selection and Our New Selection* (Sydney: Angus & Robertson, 1954), humorous fiction on the Darling Downs; Bill Wannan, *The Australian: Yarns, Ballads, Legends, Traditions* (Melbourne: Australasian Book Society, 1954).

7. The history of Sister Kenny's Australian forebears in this and later sections: interviews with the three sisters who survived her (Julia Farquharson, Margaret Scotney, and Mary Scotney), and with Rev. P. W. Pearson and other New South Wales cousins.

8. Sister Kenny for several years of her life gave her birth year as 1886; this is the year usually listed. I found the correct date in the baptismal register of the Church of England at Warialda and confirmed it in local birth records and with the registrar general of New South Wales.

Chapter 2: Elizabeth

1. Information about Sister Kenny, the Kenny family, and the region in chapters 2–4 is mainly from her sisters Julia, Margaret, and Mary, from Mary Farquharson Fredlund, Jack Kenny, Mary Stewart-Kenny, and Kenny Foundation biographical files. In addition, information on New South Wales was provided by Sister Kenny's cousins James and Minnie Bell, Anne Bell, Thomas Kirk, Anne Waters, Catherine Whan, Alicent Woodward, and Rev. P. W. Pearson; and on Queensland by old settlers and friends, Nell and Mrs. Fred Buckle, Cecil Bishop, Malcolm Brodie, Grace Earle, H. W. Hinrickson, Harry Langsdorf, Mary Kessler Pauli, and Sam Rooney.

2. Interview with Mrs. Frank Free.

3. Interview with Sister Kenny.
4. *Ibid.*
5. *Ibid.*
6. John Manifold, *Selected Verse* (London: Dennis Dobson, 1948).
7. McGuire, *Australia*, p. 67.
8. The winter of 1892–93 is my estimate. She was about twelve, though years later she wrote that she was then ten.
9. Letter from Mother Mary Ursula to author, May 27, 1953. Interviews with Mother Mary Ursula and Mother Patrick at the Ursuline convent in Armidale in 1955. I found a copy of Sister Kenny's *Who's Who in America* entry in the Kenny Foundation files. Her sister Julia in 1953, then a highly alert seventy-four, could recall for me only the bits of schooling described. Julia wrote me later: "She attended school from the age of six until fifteen, nine years in all." In interviews conducted in 1955 Julia could not be more specific: "Her schooling lasted nine years, because sometimes we missed school"—the periods when Michael Kenny moved his family.
10. Sister Kenny, " 'God Is My Doctor': The Real Story of Her Battle against Infantile Paralysis," *American Weekly*, March 26, April 2, 9, 16, and 23, 1944. Kenny Foundation biographical files. Kenny, *And They Shall Walk*, pp. 10–11.
11. Sister Kenny told this story to screenwriter Mary McCarthy in one of their many long talks in 1942.
12. Interviews with Mary Stewart-Kenny, Julia Farquharson, Mary Scotney, Mary McCarthy, and Chressy Kenny (William's widow). Kenny, *And They Shall Walk*, pp. 12–13. Kenny, " 'God Is My Doctor.' " Naomi Jolles, "The Miracles of Sister Kenny," *New York Post*, February 6, 1943. Yoder, "Healer from the Outback." Sister Kenny wrote in the 1940s that when Willie's muscle training started she was fourteen, he eleven. It is more likely that she was eighteen; she and Willie were seven years apart.
13. Kenny Foundation biographical files; Kenny, *And They Shall Walk*, p. 17.

Chapter 3: Womanhood

1. Kenny, *And They Shall Walk*, p. 15. Interview with Mary McCarthy. For this chapter generally, see chapter 2, note 1.
2. Interviews with Minnie and James Bell.
3. *Ibid.*; Kenny, *And They Shall Walk*, pp. 15–17.
4. Kenny Foundation biographical files. Jolles, "The Miracles of Sister Kenny."
5. Information on Sister Kenny's career choice is from Kenny Foundation biographical files; Kenny, " 'God Is My Doctor' "; *New York Herald Tribune*, June 31, 1943; and interviews with Mary Stewart-Kenny, Mary McCarthy, and Alicent Woodward.
6. Information about "Dan" is from Kenny Foundation biographical files; Kenny, " 'God Is My Doctor' "; Kenny, *And They Shall Walk*, pp. 18–21; Associated Press, January 21, 1946; and interviews with Mary Stewart-Kenny, Rosalind Russell, Martha Ostenso, Mary McCarthy, and Alice Perrott, all confidantes of Sister Kenny.
7. The two brief autobiographical quotations in this section are from Kenny, *And They Shall Walk*. Valuable information was obtained from journalist Harry Summers, Catherine Caskey, and Alicent Woodward; *Brisbane Courier-Mail*, March 17, 1951; interviews with Mrs. M. B. Harper, Australasian Trained Nurses Association; and letters to the author from the Australasian Trained Nurses Association, New South Wales Branch, the New South Wales Nurses' Registration Board, and the Queensland Nurses and Masseurs Registration Board, all in 1953.

Chapter 4: Bush Nurse

1. Sources for this section are chapter 2, note 1; Miller, "Sister Kenny Wins Her Fight"; Yoder, "Healer from the Outback"; and anecdotes Sister Kenny told Nurse Ella Morphett Olsen, Alice Perrott, Mr. and Mrs. Jock Jones, New York cousin Charles Newton, and writers Dudley Nichols and Mary McCarthy. The Sister Kenny quotations are from " 'God Is My Doctor' " and J. M. G. in *Trained Nurse and Hospital Review*, July 1942.

2. The sources for descriptions of her first polio treatments and the role of Dr. Aeneas McDonnell are Kenny, " 'God Is My Doctor' "; Kenny Foundation biographical files; Miller, "Sister Kenny Wins Her Fight"; Robert D. Potter, "Sister Kenny's Treatment for Infantile Paralysis," *American Weekly*, August 17, 1941; *Time*, December 8, 1942; Kenny, "Truth Is the Daughter of Time," unpublished address given at the University of Rochester, Rochester, New York, May 2, 1943; Kenny, *And They Shall Walk*, pp. 21–32; Yoder, "Healer from the Outback"; and Sister Kenny's conversations with Alice Perrott, Mrs. H. Sterne, Mary McCarthy, Rosalind Russell, Dudley Nichols, Peter Gazzola, and the author.

The year she saw these patients was almost certainly 1911, but in later life she was careless about dates, sometimes consciously so in order to drop years from her age. Various calculations and her own statements put the year as 1909, 1910, 1911, 1912, or 1913. In her autobiography she wrote, "I was 23," which is impossible. Between 1940 and 1952, she said it was 1911 (when she was actually thirty-one) in the majority of the accounts that seem to be the most reliable.

She referred to her first patient as Amy, Amy McNeil, and, once, as Ruth. She more often did not identify her at all, and once she wrote of a "little bush boy." All the names were certainly pseudonyms. It seems safe to believe that the patient was a two-year-old girl.

3. Kenny, " 'God Is My Doctor.' "

4. *Toowoomba Chronicle*, August 11, 1939.

5. Bernard Roth, "Surgical and Orthopedic Treatment of Infantile Paralysis," *British Medical Journal*, 2:459 (September 6, 1884). Ivan Wickman, *Acute Poliomyelitis (Heine-Medin's Disease)*, translated by J. William Maloney (New York: Journal of Nervous and Mental Disease Publishing Co., 1913).

6. Robert W. Lovett, "Principles of Treatment of Infantile Paralysis," *Journal of the American Medical Association*, 62:251 (January 24, 1914); Lovett, *The Treatment of Infantile Paralysis* (Philadelphia: Blakiston, 1916); Lovett and W. P. Lucas, "Infantile Paralysis: A Study of 635 Cases from Children's Hospital, Boston," *Journal of the American Medical Association*, 51:1677 (November 14, 1908). Robert Jones, "Contributions to Orthopedic Surgery," *Medical Annual*, London, 1893, 1895; Jones, "An Address on Certain Operative Features in the Paralysis of Children, with Special Reference to Polio," *British Medical Journal*, 2:1520 (December 9, 1911). Francis W. Peabody, George Draper, and A. R. Dochez, *A Clinical Study of Acute Poliomyelitis* (New York: Rockefeller Institute for Medical Research, 1912). A. H. Tubby and Robert Jones, *Modern Methods in the Surgery of Paralysis* (London: Macmillan, 1903).

7. Herbert J. Levine, *I Knew Sister Kenny* (Boston: Christopher Publishing House, 1954).

8. Interview with Dr. Alexander Horn. Sir Alexander Ogston was both a noted orthopedist and the discoverer of the Staphylococcus germ.

9. Sources for this section and those immediately following are Kenny, " 'God Is My Doctor' " and interviews with Sister Kenny, Margaret and Mary Scotney, Mary Stewart-Kenny, Jack Kenny, Catherine Caskey, H. W. Hinrickson, Eileen Donahue Hutchinson, Mary Pauli, Mrs. J. V. Wilesmith, Roy and Una (Clairingbould) Pickering, and Dudley Nichols.

Chapter 5: War Nurse

1. Grattan, *Introducing Australia*, p. 206. Labour party leader Andrew Fisher made the pledge.

2. C. J. Dennis, *Selected Verse of C. J. Dennis* (Sydney: Angus & Robertson, 1950). Dennis used blanks instead of "bloody"; Grattan, *Introducing Australia*, fills in the blanks.

3. Authorities say the name "digger" may also have had its beginnings in Australia's gold fields.

4. *Toowoomba Chronicle*, July 1, 1916.

5. In Brisbane in 1953 and 1955 I had long talks with Alice Perrott, then in her seventies, a lovely person with fine features, who had a firm memory of her 1915 shipboard meeting with Elizabeth Kenny and a long friendship with her during the war and for nearly three decades following the war.

Additional sources for this chapter: those who saw Sister Kenny during World War I—Michael Kenny, Roy Pickering, Mrs. H. Sterne, Australian Army nurses Pattie Kirton Alcorn and Ella Morphett Olsen; those whom Sister Kenny told of the war—James and Minnie Bell, Catherine Caskey, Doris Rollinson, Lydia R. Culley, Mrs. Jock Jones, Dr. James Guinane, George Keyatta, Charles Newton, nurse Mary Lynch Patterson, Dr. Aubrey Pye, Alicent Woodward, Mary Stewart-Kenny, Stewart McCracken, and the author; also, Kenny, " 'God Is My Doctor' "; Kenny, *And They Shall Walk*, pp. 33–65; *Sydney Morning Herald*, October 14, 1926, and February 28, 1935; Jolles, "The Miracles of Sister Kenny," and undated newspaper cuttings in Mrs. H. Sterne's scrapbook.

6. Sister Kenny's Australian Army Nursing Service appointment certificate lists her "effective" appointment date as May 30, 1915; she actually enlisted later that year, but the certificate was not issued until December 1918.

Sources of information about Sister Kenny's army records are letter to the author from W. Vinicome, deputy commissioner of the Repatriation Department, Commonwealth of Australia, April 17, 1956; letter to the author from F. R. Sinclair, secretary of the Department of the Army, October 2, 1953. Sinclair reported that there was no record of her place of enlistment, that there was uncertainty about her enlistment date, and that there were many other gaps in her records.

7. *Sydney Morning Herald*, February 8, 1935, a biographical sketch of Sister Kenny (one of the first) written by her friend Eleanor McKinnon, world founder of the Junior Red Cross.

8. Interview with Mrs. H. Sterne, Warwick, a staunch friend of Sister Kenny's who had become Elizabeth Sterne, O.B.E., for service to several organizations and, she said, "general handyman for the down and out."

9. Interview with Dr. James Guinane.

10. Wannan, *The Australian*, p. 32.

11. Kenny, " 'God Is My Doctor,' " April 9, 1944.

Chapter 6: Inventor

1. Sources of information on her postwar flu hospital and her illness: interviews with her sisters Julia, Margaret, and Mary, and with Nell Buckle and Catherine Caskey; Kenny, *And They Shall Walk*, pp. 65–69; and McKinnon in the *Sydney Morning Herald*, February 28, 1935.

2. Sources of information on country nursing and Daphne: Kenny, " 'God Is My Doctor' "; *Townsville Daily Bulletin*, October 6, 1936; Kenny, *And They Shall Walk*, pp. 70–74; very valuable for this chapter and later are the oral and written recollections of Jack Kenny, her brother Henry's son, then a young newspaperman. Other information is from interviews with Mary Stewart-Kenny, Sister Kenny's

sisters Julia, Margaret, and Mary, James and Minnie Bell, Mrs. Fred Buckle, Catherine Caskey, Mrs. Frank Free, Dr. Glen Hickey, Stanley Kuhn, Harry Langsdorf, Mary Pauli, Sam Rooney, Mrs. H. Sterne, Mother Patrick and Mother Mary Ursula of Ursuline convent and school, Armidale, and a letter from William Cregan, Daphne's father, to the author, May 18, 1956. Nell Buckle of Toowoomba and Nobby proved a spirited and an invaluable guide to the area and its people.

3. Letter from Msgr. John P. O'Connor to the author, April 2, 1956. One cousin insisted: "I went to the opening of the Catholic church in Guyra with her. She bowed down and crossed herself and went all through the ceremony. She was baptized by the bishop in Armidale, but when she got back to Queensland she turned back to Protestant again." Her sister Julia called the story false. Sister Kenny did flirt with Catholicism, but she never became a practicing Catholic.

4. The May 14, 1926 *Brisbane Daily Mail* reported: "Sister Kenny (Nobby) played no small part. Her helpfully terse remarks cleared several somewhat cloudy situations, and restored the sunshine of good fellowship."

5. The records of Queensland's registrar general show that Mary was legally adopted by Sister Kenny (a point sometimes disputed by Kenny's detractors) on April 28, 1926.

6. Sources of information on the Sylvia stretcher: sources named in note 2; the Kuhn family (Stanley, Sylvia Kuhn Stenzel, and their mother, Mrs. August Spieker); ex-war nurses Pattie Alcorn, Ella Olsen, and Beryl Henson; Alice Perrott; Dr. Aubrey Pye; Marjorie A. Higgins, general secretary, St. John Ambulance Association, Sydney; Edward Everson, J. N. Fletcher, William Miles, and C. Noble of Drug Houses of Australia; Kenny, " 'God Is My Doctor' "; Kenny, *And They Shall Walk*, pp. 74–77; Yoder, "Healer from the Outback"; the *Brisbane Courier-Mail* and *Sydney Morning Herald* files; and Mrs. H. Sterne's undated clippings.

7. *Brisbane Daily Mail*, August 26, 1926. *Sydney Morning Herald*, October 14, 1926. The first manufacturer was Laycock and Littledyke, Brisbane, followed by Elliott Bros. (later Drug Houses of Australia).

8. *Sydney Morning Herald*, April 24 and 26, 1930.

Chapter 7: Polio

1. Sources of information for her northern Queensland meanderings and her treatment of polio: the Queensland files; *Townsville Daily Bulletin* files; Jolles, "The Miracles of Sister Kenny"; the following publications by Sister Kenny—" 'God Is My Doctor' "; "Doctors, I Salute You," *American Weekly*, March 2, 1952; *Infantile Paralysis and Cerebral Diplegia*; *My Battle and Victory*, pp. 107–108; and *And They Shall Walk*, pp. 77–110, 115–122; interviews with Reg McAllister (ex-secretary to Queensland Premier William Forgan Smith), Allen Sewell (ex-first assistant to Undersecretary for Health and Home Affairs Charles Chuter), Kenny nurses Leila Cooper Hall, Mary Lynch Patterson, attendant Greg Healy, secretary Mary McCrae, waiter Herbert Steele, Sister Mary Dorothea (Mater Hospital), MPs Thomas Aikens and George Keyatta, Drs. James Guinane, Glen Hickey, Henry J. Taylor, V. F. O'Neill, Fabian Pincus, Aubrey Pye, Sir Raphael Cilento, *Townsville Daily Bulletin* reporter Austin Donnelly, ex-patient Alexander Rainnie; and Sister Kenny's recollections to Dudley Nichols and Mary McCarthy.

Information on Maude's treatment is from interviews with Doris Rollinson and Lydia R. Culley and a letter from Maude Rollinson Wharley to the author, December 1, 1955.

2. Sources on the history and treatment of polio and on virology are John R. Paul, *A History of Poliomyelitis* (New Haven: Yale University Press, 1971), especially chapter 32 on Sister Kenny; Roland H. Berg, *Polio and Its Problems*

(Philadelphia: Lippincott, 1948); F. Macfarlane Burnet and Wendell M. Stanley (Eds.), *The Viruses: General Virology*, Vol. I (New York: Academic Press, 1959); F. Horsfall and I. Tamm, *Viral and Rickettsial Diseases of Man* (Philadelphia: Lippincott, 1965); my own observations of treatment in the late 1940s and early 1950s; and interviews with many doctors and scientists then and since. Additional sources on virology are interviews with Drs. Gilbert Dalldorf, John F. Enders, and John R. Paul, and recent reviews of my material by Dalldorf and Enders.

3. Ida May Hazenhyer, "History of the American Physiotherapy Association," *Physiotherapy Review*, 26:1, 2, 3, 4 (1946). Howard A. Rusk, *A World to Care For* (New York: Random House, 1972). Interviews with Drs. Howard Rusk, Miland Knapp, and Frank Krusen.

4. Interview with Mary Stewart-Kenny.

5. John Kobler, *The Reluctant Surgeon* (Garden City, N.J.: Doubleday, 1960), pp. 250–251.

6. Mary Stewart-Kenny, who began working with her as a polio therapist in 1938, denies that Sister Kenny ever moved polio patients' limbs under water. Contrary evidence is stated by Sister Kenny in her *Infantile Paralysis and Cerebral Diplegia* (Sydney: Angus & Robertson, 1937), p. 7, as well as by other testimony.

7. Interview with Sir Raphael Cilento, an official observer, then critic, then opponent.

8. Medical reports, letters, and government orders of various dates in the Queensland files. She was already known to health officials at this point; she had persuaded them to give her a rail pass for her work "for the disabled."

9. Sister Kenny in various accounts. Interview with Dr. Pye.

10. Jack Kenny, recollections, June 11, 1953.

11. Kenny, *Infantile Paralysis and Cerebral Diplegia*, pp. 3–4.

12. Interview with Dr. Rae W. Dungan.

13. Cilento's reports in the Queensland files and quoted in C. A. Thelander, J. V. Duhig, Jarvis Nye, Alec E. Patterson, and R. S. Lahz (Eds.), "Report of the Royal Commission on the Investigation of Infantile Paralysis," *Medical Journal of Australia*, 1:187 (February 29, 1938).

14. Interviews with Leila Cooper Hall and Sir Raphael Cilento.

15. Sister Kenny later denied that *she* had ever said that any of her patients had been "cured." But in *Infantile Paralysis and Cerebral Diplegia* she quoted Guinane, without protest, as saying so. Cilento used the word "cure" equally loosely in Report to Minister, quoted in Thelander et al., "Report of the Royal Commission on the Investigation of Infantile Paralysis."

Chapter 8: Crusader

1. *Sydney Morning Herald*, February 16, 1935. Sources for information on Sister Kenny's progress in chapters 8 and 9 are Queensland files; *Brisbane Courier-Mail* and *Sydney Morning Herald* files; Kenny publications, *Cause and Prevention of Deformities in Polio* (El Monte, Calif.: Sister Kenny Polio Hospital, 1952), " 'God Is My Doctor,' " *My Battle and Victory* (London: Robert Hale, 1954), *Poliomyelitis: Findings in Investigations of Evidence Concerning Poliomyelitis* (Minneapolis: Elizabeth Kenny, 1947), *And They Shall Walk*, pp. 111–203; Sister Kenny's recollections to Dudley Nichols, Martha Ostenso, and Mary McCarthy; interviews with Mary Stewart-Kenny, Julia Farquharson, Jack Kenny, Mary Farquharson Fredlund, Valerie Harvey, Mary Luddy, Mollie O'Hara Chapman, Marjorie Bridle, Betty Shuter, Leila Cooper Hall, Mary Lynch Patterson, Mary McCrae, Mr. and Mrs. Jock Jones, Beryl Long, Reg McAllister, Allen Sewell, Drs. Raphael Cilento, J. V. D. Duhig, Abraham Fryberg, James Guinane, Jarvis Nye, Aubrey Pye, H. J.

Wilkinson, Philip Addison, Henley Harrison, Norman Little, Kenneth Starr, and those cited in chapter 7, note 1; and letters to the author from Drs. Addison, Nye, and Pye.

2. *Sydney Daily Telegraph*, March 22, 1935; *Brisbane Courier-Mail*, March 25, 1935; *Brisbane Telegraph*, March 27, 1935; *Labour Daily*, March 27, 1935.

3. Quoted by Eleanor McKinnon in the *Sydney Morning Herald*, February 16, 1935.

4. Queensland files and interviews with Allen Sewell, Leila Cooper Hall, and Harry Summers.

5. Sir Raphael wrote me on September 8, 1972, that my accounts of his role were misleading. He said that without his assistance "Sister Kenny would never have received a hearing in Queensland at all," and that not he but she made the statement cited on the limited "objective" of treatment. Cilento is so quoted in a report to Health Minister Hanlon, dated August 9, 1934, summarized in Thelander et al., "Report of the Royal Commission," pp. 6–7.

6. Kenny, *Infantile Paralysis and Cerebral Diplegia*, pp. 113–114, 120.

7. Undated clipping, Mrs. H. Sterne's scrapbook.

8. Sister Kenny's statements to Mrs. Frank Free and Mrs. Jock Jones.

9. Headline, *Smith's Weekly*, June 28, 1934. Doctors quoted here are Jarvis Nye and Aubrey Pye, but many others testified similarly.

10. Regarding McDonnell's sometime ambivalence about Sister Kenny, his lasting admiration for her nonetheless, and his last days: interviews with Roy Connolly, Kate Knapp (ex-nurse at McDonnell's St. Vincent's Hospital), Duncan McInnes (secretary and general manager, Toowoomba General Hospital), Olive David Robinson (ex-matron at Toowoomba General Hospital), H. T. Symington, Drs. Glen Hickey, Jarvis Nye, and A. W. L. Row (McDonnell's partner). The information was generally confirmed by McDonnell's son John.

11. These particular statements were made to Jack Kenny and Mary Stewart-Kenny. She made many similar statements.

12. Queensland files.

13. Professor H. J. Wilkinson in his foreword to Kenny's *Infantile Paralysis and Cerebral Diplegia.*

14. Many doctors in Australia and the United States testify to Sister Kenny's ability to learn over the years. Quotations here are from Drs. Norman Little, Aubrey Pye, and Jarvis Nye, and from Mary McCrae.

15. *Townsville Daily Bulletin*, October 6, 1936.

16. Interview with Tony Rail, Brisbane businessman.

17. Sources for this and later trips to Britain: Richard Metcalfe, *Medical Press*; interviews with Metcalfe, Mary Farquharson Fredlund, Michael Kenny, Sister Kenny's friend and landlady Ann Ellison, therapists Amy Lindsey, Margaret Reardon, and nurse Helen Grant.

18. Quoted in *And They Shall Walk*, pp. 148–149.

Chapter 9: Defeat

1. Thelander, et al., "Report of the Royal Commission." For other sources on this chapter, see chapter 8, note 1.

2. *Brisbane Courier-Mail*, January 6 and 12, 1938.

3. Sources for the preceding section are *Brisbane Courier-Mail*, January 7 and 12, 1938, *Truth*, January 12, 1938, and the Queensland files.

Kenny clinics or wards (see following paragraphs) were then operating in Queensland at Brisbane, Cairns, Rockhampton, Toowoomba (St. Vincent's Hospital), and Townsville; in New South Wales at Newcastle and Sydney; and in Victoria at Melbourne (Children's Hospital).

4. London County Council, Honorary Advisory Committee Report, November 10, 1938.

5. Kenny, "Truth Is the Daughter of Time."

6. Queensland files.

7. *Sydney Morning Herald,* July 4, 1939.

8. The most important sources for this crucial period are Queensland files; Kenny's *Cause and Prevention of Deformities,* " 'God Is My Doctor,' " *My Battle and Victory, Poliomyelitis: Findings,* and *And They Shall Walk*; interviews with Allen Sewell, Mary Stewart-Kenny, Jack Kenny, Drs. Abraham Fryberg, Norman Little, Jarvis Nye, Aubrey Pye, and H. J. Wilkinson, nurses Mary Luddy and Leila Cooper Hall; and Sister Kenny's detailed verbal account to Dudley Nichols.

9. She told part of this Myers story in *And They Shall Walk,* related his running away in *My Battle and Victory,* and gave more details in her 1947 and 1952 medical pamphlets.

10. This and following paragraphs are from the Queensland files, the *Brisbane Courier-Mail,* March 15, 1940, and the *Sydney Morning Herald,* March 29, 1940.

11. Letter from Dr. H. J. Wilkinson to Dr. M. Henderson, March 8, 1940. Letter from Forgan Smith to Basil O'Connor, March 4, 1940.

12. Alicent Woodward was the perceptive cousin.

13. Forgan Smith told O'Connor that the Queensland government alone had spent more than £50,000 on Kenny clinics. Sir Raphael Cilento told the author in late 1972 that it was £82,000 or $800,000 to $850,000 "at a minimum nowadays."

Chapter 10: America

1. Sources on Franklin Roosevelt and the polio movement: Berg, *Polio and Its Problems,* pp. 26–31; Cohn, *Four Billion Dimes* (New York: National Foundation for Infantile Paralysis, 1955); Paul, *History of Polio,* pp. 301–323, 432; large sections of Lela Stiles, *The Man behind Roosevelt: The Story of Louis Howe* (Cleveland: World, 1954); Turnley Walker, *Roosevelt and the Warm Springs Story* (New York: Wyn, 1953); and interviews with Basil O'Connor and many other figures of the early and later National Foundation for Infantile Paralysis days, including Roland Berg, Dorothy Ducas, Paul de Kruif, Joseph Savage, Thomas Wrigley, Drs. Morris Fishbein, Philip Lewin, Jonas Salk, Thomas Rivers, William Shannon, Hart Van Riper, and Harry Weaver.

2. J. D. Kershaw and K. W. N. Palmer, "Treatment of Polio in Early Stages," *Medical Press,* 451 (November 17, 1954). Dr. H. Rusk, *New York Times,* February 5, 1950. *Life,* August 15, 1949. Grace Reiten, "Our Daughter Had Polio," *Saturday Evening Post,* August 21, 1954. Paul, *History of Polio,* p. 216.

On the United States polio panic: Berg, *Polio and Its Problems,* pp. 1–25; and Paul, *History of Polio,* pp. 148–160, 212–224, and 304. Berg and Paul tell of New York City's amazing 1916 travel bans.

3. *New York Times,* April 18, 1940.

Chapters 10–17, Sister Kenny's American and late years, are based on the following: many of Sister Kenny's own writings, especially *Cause and Prevention of Deformities, My Battle and Victory, Poliomyelitis: Findings,* "Doctors, I Salute You," "Sister Kenny Tells 'Why I Left America,' " *Woman's Home Companion,* March 1951, "Truth Is the Daughter of Time," " 'God Is My Doctor,' " and *And They Shall Walk,* pp. 203–272; Kenny Foundation files; Jeanne L. Brand, E. T. Sweeney, and L. Williams, "The History of the National Foundation for Infantile Paralysis through 1953—Vol. IV: Medical Services," unpublished report (New York: National Foundation for Infantile Paralysis Historical Division, 1955); John F. Pohl in collaboration with Elizabeth Kenny, *The Kenny Concept of Infantile Paralysis and Its Treatment* (St. Paul: Bruce Publishing Co., 1943); interviews with Mary Stewart-Kenny, Stewart McCracken, Julia Farquharson, Drs. Miland Knapp, John Pohl, and Frank Krusen, therapists Mary Farquharson Fredlund, Vivian Hannan, and Valerie Harvey, Donald Dayton, James Henry, Marvin Kline, Dudley Nichols, Martha Ostenso, Rosalind Russell, all close confidants of Sister Kenny; also interviews with Drs. Harvey Billig, Robert Bingham, Albert Bower, Wesley Burnham, Wallace H. Cole, Gilbert Dalldorf, Harold Diehl, Earl Elkins, Paul Ellwood, John F. Enders, David Fingerman, Morris Fishbein, Ralph Ghormley, E. J. Huenekens, Claus Jungeblut, Frederic Kottke, Philip Lewin, Irvine McQuarrie, John Paul, Hart Van Riper, Lewis Sher, Marvin A. Stevens, and Harry Weaver; therapists Rita Eck, Ethel Gardner, and Amy Lindsey; Drs. Saul Benison and Jeanne Brand, polio historians; June Barron Berman, Roland Berg, Freddie Brisson, Marguerite Clark, Henry Haverstock, Jr., ex-Minneapolis mayors Eric Hoyer and Senator Hubert H. Humphrey, Lloyd Johnson, Orin Lehman, Chester LaRoche, Frank Mayer, Mary McCarthy, Lois Mattox Miller, Charles Newton, Basil O'Connor, Betty (Mrs. John) Pohl, Robert D. Potter, Florence Rowe (longtime secretary for Sister Kenny), Larry Salter, Mildred Spencer; Kenny publicists Al Baum, Fred Fadell, Peter Gazzola, and Will O'Neil; and correspondence with Floyd Odlum, Ed Sullivan, and many of the people cited above.

4. Dr. Sedgwick Mead, "A Century of the Abuse of Rest," *Journal of the American Medical Association*, 182:344 (October 27, 1962).

5. Kristian G. Hansson, "The After-Treatment of Poliomyelitis," *Journal of the American Medical Association*, 113:32 (July 1, 1939).

6. Brand et al., "History of the National Foundation."

7. Berg, *Polio and Its Problems*, p. 125.

8. Brand et al., "History of the National Foundation."

9. Descriptions of Sister Kenny's polio treatment are from her writings and those of others, supplemented by Vivian Hannan, Dr. John Pohl, and Dr. Miland Knapp.

10. Kenny, *And They Shall Walk*, pp. 261–262. Kenny, "Sister Kenny Tells 'Why I Left America.' "

11. Drs. Philip Lewin and Karl F. Meyer.

12. Yoder, "Healer from the Outback."

13. Interview with June Barron Berman.

Chapter 11: Victory

1. Sources for the first section are Dr. Wayne McFarland's report to Dr. Krusen; Brand et al., "History of the National Foundation"; and Wallace H. Cole and Miland E. Knapp, "The Kenny Treatment of Infantile Paralysis: A Preliminary Report," *Journal of the American Medical Association*, 116:2577 (June 7, 1941), appearing after a normal lag for expert review and editing.

2. *Minneapolis Star-Journal*, September 15, 1940.

3. Interview with Dr. Jay Davis.

4. Henry O. Kendall and Florence P. Kendall, "Care during the Recovery Period in Paralytic Polio," *United States Public Health Service Bulletin*, April 1938. Sister Kenny believed that muscle testing aggravated spasm and that many muscles were incorrectly rated at zero, leading doctors to write them off.

5. Kenny, *And They Shall Walk*, pp. 223–224, 235. Interviews with Mary Stewart-Kenny and Valerie Harvey.

6. Alice Lou Plastridge's report to the National Foundation March 15, 1941, on a trip to observe the work of Sister Kenny.

7. Sources here on her respirator treatments are interview with June Berman; Kenny, "Sister Kenny Tells 'Why I Left America' "; and Jolles, "The Miracles of Sister Kenny."

8. Interview with Dr. John Pohl.

9. Interview with Dr. Miland Knapp.

10. Brand et al., "History of the National Foundation." Kenny, *Treatment of Infantile Paralysis.*

11. *Minneapolis Tribune,* December 21, 1941. Interviews with Ethel Gardner and Vivian Hannan.

12. Letters from O'Connor to Krusen, February 3, 1941; Krusen to O'Connor, February 6, 1941; O'Connor to Krusen, February 10, 1941.

13. Interviews with Drs. Irvine McQuarrie, Frank Krusen, and Philip Lewin, and with Basil O'Connor and Lawrence Salter (associate public relations director for the American Medical Association). Brand et al., "History of the National Foundation."

14. Brand et al., "History of the National Foundation." Editorial, *Journal of the American Medical Association,* 117:1980 (December 6, 1941). H. N. Bundesen and M. M. Peet, "Medical Committee's Statement on the Kenny Method." The Solandt, Hines, and Steindler findings are in Berg, *Polio and Its Problems,* pp. 140–141. *New York Times* and *PM,* December 5, 1941. A. Steindler, "Contributory Clinical Observations on Infantile Paralysis and Their Therapeutic Implications," *Journal of Bone and Joint Surgery,* 24:912 (October 1942); and "Recent Changes in Concept of Treatment of Poliomyelitis," *Archives of Physical Therapy,* 23:325 (June 1942).

15. *Minneapolis Star-Journal,* December 4, 1941.

16. *Minneapolis Tribune,* December 5 and 21, 1941.

17. *New York Times* and *PM,* December 5, 1941. *Newsweek,* December 15, 1941. Dr. Don W. Gudakunst, National Foundation for Infantile Paralysis, to Salter in Brand et al., "History of the National Foundation."

18. Kenny, " 'God Is My Doctor' " and *And They Shall Walk,* pp. 246–247.

Chapter 12: Revolution

1. Interview with Joseph Savage.

2. *PM,* April 30, 1942.

3. Harold S. Diehl, "Summary of the Relationship of the Medical School of the University of Minnesota to the Work of Sister Elizabeth Kenny," March 29, 1944.

4. Brand et al., "History of the National Foundation."

5. *PM* and *New York Herald-Tribune,* April 30, 1942.

6. *Memphis Press Scimitar,* August 19, 1942.

7. Kenny, "Infantile Paralysis: Its Description and Treatment," *New Orleans Medical and Surgical Journal,* 96:134 (October 1943). Philip Lewin, "Kenny Treatment of Infantile Paralysis during the Acute Stage," *Illinois Medical Journal,* 81:281 (April 1942). Interviews with Drs. Lewin and Fishbein.

8. Mary M. I. Daly, Jerome Greenbaum, Edward T. Reilly, Alvah M. Weiss, and Philip M. Stimson, "The Early Treatment of Poliomyelitis, with an Evaluation of the Sister Kenny Treatment," *Journal of the American Medical Association,* 118:1433 (April 25, 1942). Philip M. Stimson, "Minimizing After-Effects of Poliomyelitis," *Journal of the American Medical Association,* 119:990 (July 25, 1942).

9. [Earl C. Elkins], unsigned editorial, *Archives of Physical Therapy,* 23:364 (June 1942). Krusen, "Observations on the Kenny Treatment."

10. Bruce Chown, "Newer Knowledge of the Pathology of Poliomyelitis," *Canadian Public Health Journal,* June 1942. Robert Bingham, "Kenny Treatment for Infantile Paralysis," *Journal of Bone and Joint Surgery,* 25:647 (July 1943). Robert L. Bennett, "The Influence of the Kenny Concept of Acute Poliomyelitis," *Archives of Physical Therapy,* 24:453 (August 1943). Wallace H. Cole, John F. Pohl, and Miland E. Knapp, "The Kenny Method of Treatment for Infantile Paralysis," *Archives of Physical Therapy,* 23:399 (July 1942). Miland E. Knapp, "Kenny

Treatment for Infantile Paralysis," *Archives of Physical Therapy*, 23:668 (November 1942), and quoted in Miller, "Sister Kenny Wins Her Fight."

11. Letter from Bennett to Krusen, June 26, 1942.
12. Queensland files.
13. Krusen papers.
14. Interviews with Diehl, O'Connor, and Eric Hoyer. George Grim, *Minneapolis Tribune*, September 15, 1953.
15. Robert D. Potter, "Sister Kenny's Treatment for Infantile Paralysis," *American Weekly*, August 17, 1941.
16. Marjorie Lawrence, *Interrupted Melody* (New York: Appleton-Century-Crofts, 1949), pp. 185–201. Kenny, " 'God Is My Doctor.' " Interview with Vivian Hannan. *New York Journal American*, November 11, 1943.
17. *Sydney Morning Herald*, March 9, 1942.
18. Sister Kenny to the Commissioner of Repatriation, March 13, 1942.
19. Interviews with Drs. Pohl and Krusen. Letter from Bennett to Gudakunst, June 13, 1942.
20. Brand et al., "History of the National Foundation."
21. Berg, *Polio and Its Problems*, pp. 136–140. R. P. Schwartz and H. D. Bouman, "Muscle Spasm in the Acute Stage of Infantile Paralysis as Indicated by Recorded Action Current Potentials," *Journal of the American Medical Association*, 119:923 (July 18, 1942). Schwartz, Bouman, and W. K. Smith, "The Significance of Muscle Spasm in the Acute Stage of Infantile Paralysis Based on Action Current Records," *Journal of the American Medical Association*, 126:695 (November 11, 1944).
22. Interview with Rosalind Russell. Miller, "Sister Kenny Wins Her Fight." Marvin L. Kline, "The Most Unforgettable Character I've Met," *Reader's Digest*, August 1959. Kenny, *Cause and Prevention of Deformities.*
23. Interview with Dr. Albert Bower.
24. Cole, Pohl, and Knapp, *The Kenny Method of Treatment.* Stimson, "Minimizing After-Effects." Interviews with Drs. Robert Bingham, Wesley Burnham, and E. J. Huenekens.
25. Interviews with Drs. Knapp and Pohl. Frank R. Ober, "Pain and Tenderness during Acute Stages of Polio," *Journal of the American Medical Association*, 120:514 (October 17, 1942). Pohl with Kenny, foreword to *The Kenny Concept.*
26. *New York Times*, December 17, 1948. Brand et al., "History of the National Foundation." Interviews with Marvin Kline and Dr. M. J. Shapiro. Kline, "The Most Unforgettable Character."
27. *Minneapolis Star-Journal*, December 13, 17, 18, and 19, 1942. Abe Altrowitz in the *Minneapolis Times*, December 18, 1942.

Chapter 13: Phenomenon

1. Robert D. Potter, "Sister Kenny's Treatment." *PM*, October 2, 1946. Jolles, "The Miracles of Sister Kenny." *New York World Telegram*, October 26, 1942. Inez Robb, International News Service, November 23 to November 26, 1943.
2. *Minneapolis Star-Journal*, December 4, 1941. Miller, "Sister Kenny vs. Infantile Paralysis." Bundesen quoted in Kenny, " 'God Is My Doctor.' "
3. Hedda Hopper, *New York Daily News*, July 24, 1943. Wide World, October 17, 1942. *Newsweek*, June 26, 1944.
4. Interview with Mary Stewart-Kenny. *People*, June 1951. *Fresno Bee*, April 1, 1944.
5. Interviews with Mary Scotney and Lydia Rollinson Culley.
6. Inez Robb, International News Service, November 23 to November 26, 1943. J. M. G. in *Trained Nurse and Hospital Review*, July 1942.

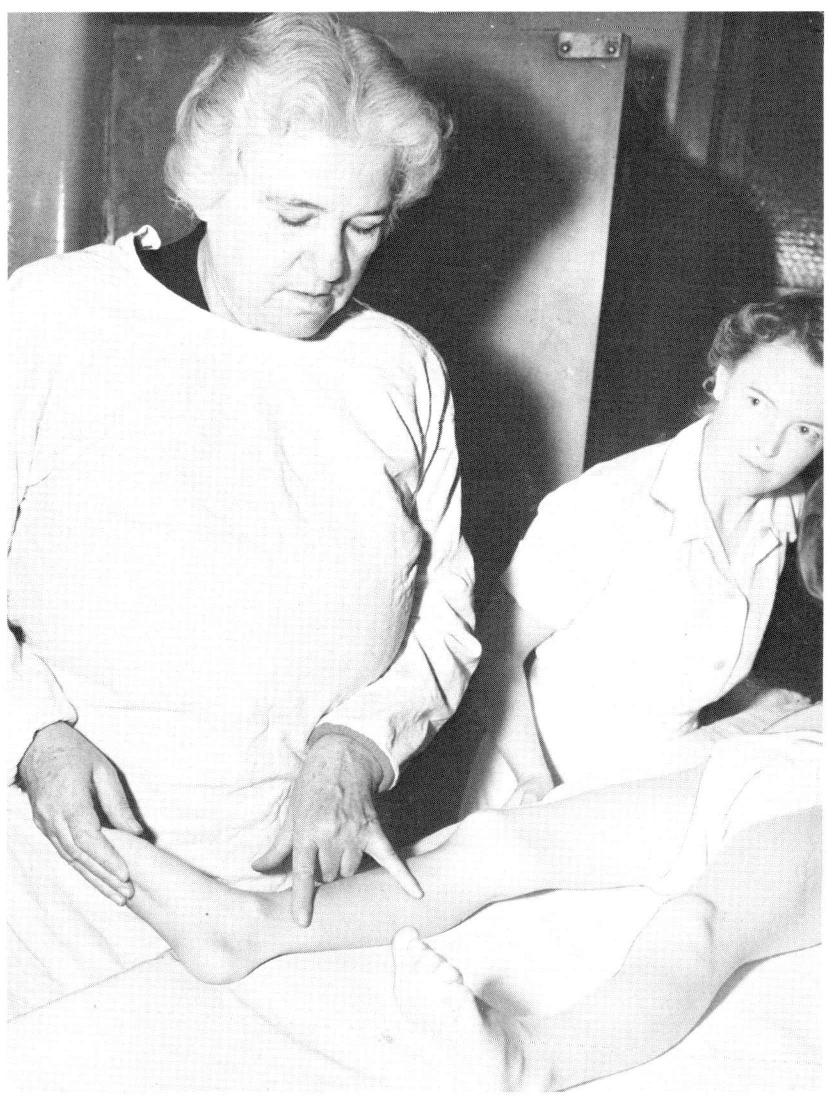

She bent over a patient like a gardener over a plant. Her hands and wrists slightly arched, she ran a finger delicately over a stricken limb or moved the limb in smooth patterns. (*Minneapolis Tribune*)

Honored at a banquet, she sat with Dr. John Pohl, a new friend who knew the old polio treatment "was just no damned good." (*Minneapolis Star*)

She used a doll to teach three-year-old Sharon Carter, for "it is really the patient who must reopen the nerve path." (*Minneapolis Tribune*)

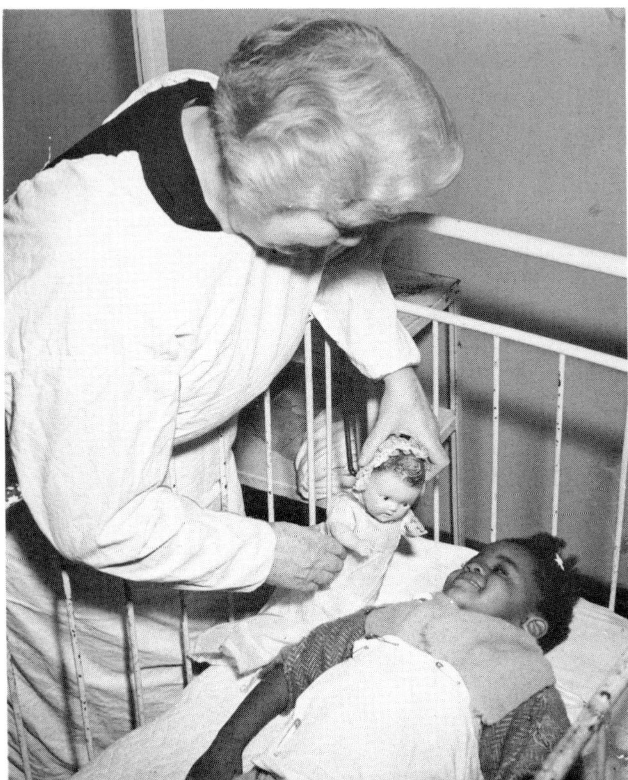

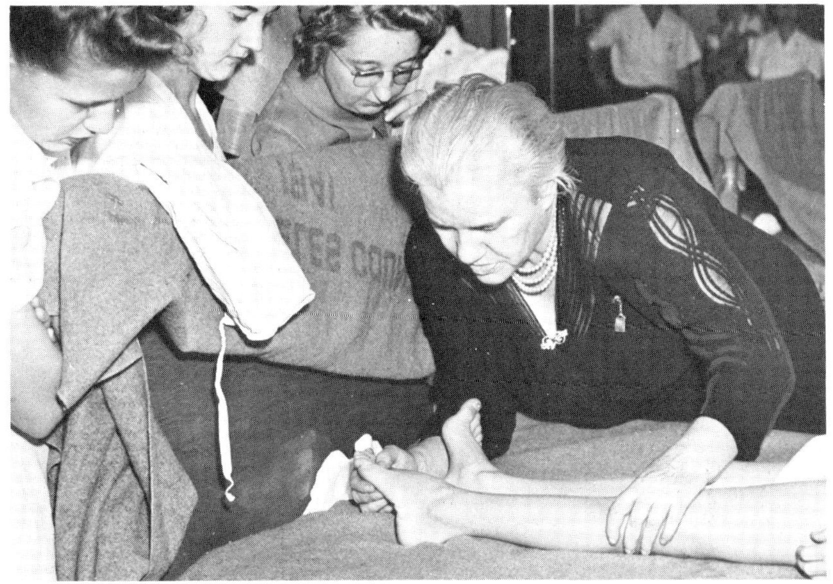

She demonstrated on a child at Los Angeles County Hospital, as the nation discovered what writers called her "miracles." (National Archives)

December 17, 1942: Kenny Institute is dedicated. From left, Vivian Hannan, daughter Mary, Sister Kenny, Valerie Harvey. (Sister Kenny Institute)

June 1943: White House lunch with Franklin D. Roosevelt and his friend Basil O'Connor of the March of Dimes, who, she soon said, was "ignoring the cries of crippled children." (Office of War Information)

7. Interview with Dr. Richard Metcalfe.

8. Interviews with Mary Stewart-Kenny and Mary McCarthy. Jolles, "The Miracles of Sister Kenny."

9. Sources for this section are interviews with Rosalind Russell and Mary McCarthy.

10. *New York Times,* January 24 and May 4, 1943. *New York Herald-Tribune,* January 26 and 31, and April 26, 1943. *Minneapolis Star-Journal,* June 8 and 9, 1943.

11. Kenny, "Sister Kenny Tells 'Why I Left America.' "

12. Interview with Basil O'Connor.

She received honorary degrees from three universities (Rutgers, New York University, and the University of Rochester), the Variety Club's Humanitarian Plaque, and many other honors.

13. Letter from O'Connor to Sister Kenny, March 9, 1943. Sister Kenny's reaction to Coss was obtained in an interview with Vivian Hannan. Coss's written report was submitted to O'Connor on August 12, 1943 (he reported verbally much earlier).

14. On O'Connor's personality: interviews with O'Connor and many others; Cohn, *Four Billion Dimes.* Information about Sister Kenny's quarrels with the National Foundation and with O'Connor here and in later chapters: Kenny Foundation files; interviews with Sister Kenny, Mary Stewart-Kenny, Ethel Gardner, Donald Dayton, Marvin Kline, Basil O'Connor, Roland Berg, Drs. John Pohl, Harold Diehl, Morris Fishbein, and Thomas Rivers, and historians Saul Benison and Jeanne Brand.

15. *Minneapolis Star-Journal,* July 15, 1943. *New York Herald-Tribune,* October 9, 1943.

16. Interviews with Mary Stewart-Kenny and Martha Ostenso. Kenny, *And They Shall Walk,* pp. x and 271. Pohl with Kenny, *The Kenny Concept.*

17. Kenny, " 'God Is My Doctor.' " The Exchange Club pledge was reported in the *Minneapolis Star-Journal,* August 19, 1943. Interview with James Henry. In later years, according to Henry, the sum was paid to the club's Sister Kenny Education Fund by the Kenny Foundation, but it was raised in a campaign by club members.

18. These "miracle" cases were described by Kenny, "Sister Kenny Tells 'Why I Left America' "; Kenny, *Cause and Prevention of Deformities in Poliomyelitis;* Jay Nelson Tuck in the *New York World-Telegram,* November 12, 1943; the *New York Times,* November 13, 1943; Gerold Frank in the *New York Journal-American,* November 14, 1943; Nicholas Ransohoff, "Experiences with the Kenny Treatment for Acute Poliomyelitis in the Epidemic of 1942, Monmouth and Ocean Counties, New Jersey," *Journal of Bone and Joint Surgery,* 26:99 (January 1944); and R. H. Metcalfe, "A Critical Evaluation of the Kenny Treatment," *Medical Press,* November 17, 1954.

19. Kenny, " 'God Is My Doctor.' " Interview with Dr. McQuarrie.

20. *New York Times,* February 4, 1944. *New York Journal-American,* March 26, 1944.

21. *New York Times,* February 4, 1944. *Detroit Free-Press,* April 1, 1945. Interviews with Sister Kenny, Will O'Neil, and Dr. Morris Fishbein.

22. Howard W. Blakeslee, Associated Press, in the *Minneapolis Tribune,* April 16, 1944. Numerous speeches and radio talks by Basil O'Connor, 1943–44. Thomas Rivers quoted in *Tom Rivers: Reflections on a Life in Medicine,* by Saul Benison (Cambridge, Mass.: M.I.T. Press, 1967), p. 282.

Paul de Kruif, bacteriologist turned medical writer (and an early polio drive official who split with O'Connor), wrote in *Life among the Doctors* (New York: Harcourt, 1949), pp. 306–310: "My undercover agents have even told me that an effort was made to deport the fighting sister." In an interview, he said it was O'Connor who tried it. O'Connor's answer: "Not true! We knew we'd be found out if we tried. And I didn't give a damn whether she went back to Australia or any-place else."

23. *New York Journal-American*, February 3, 1944. *Detroit Free Press*, March 28, 1945. *PM*, September 1, 1943.

Chapter 14: Controversy

1. Ghormley et al., "Evaluation of the Kenny Treatment for Infantile Paralysis," *Journal of the American Medical Association*, 125:466 (June 17, 1944). The committee was named by the Section on Orthopedic Surgery of the American Medical Association, the American Academy of Orthopedic Surgeons, and the American Orthopedic Association.

2. Brand et al., "History of the National Foundation." *Minneapolis Star-Journal*, June 15 and 20, 1944. *Minneapolis Tribune*, June 15 and 16, 1944. *New York Post*, June 15, 1944. Letter from Dr. Henderson to Sister Kenny, November 30, 1942.

3. Bennett quoted in Lois Mattox Miller, "Sister Kenny vs. the Medical Old Guard," *Reader's Digest*, October 1944.

4. Deutsch, *PM*, June 20, 1944. *American Mercury*, November 1944.

5. Ghormley, in *Lectures on Regional Orthopedic Surgery and Fundamental Orthopedic Problems* (1947), and an interview with him.

6. Brand et al., "History of the National Foundation." Van Riper testimony on June 1, 1948 to the House Committee on Interstate and Foreign Commerce.

7. H. O. Swartout and W. P. Frank, "Multiple Familial Cases of Poliomyelitis," *Journal of the American Medical Association*, 125:499 (June 17, 1944).

8. Jolles, "The Miracles of Sister Kenny." Interviews with Mildred Spencer of the *Buffalo Evening News* and with Mary McCarthy.

9. Kenny, *And They Shall Walk*, p. viii.

10. Interview with Dr. Wesley Burnham. Miland Knapp, John Moe, A. V. Stoesser, and J. C. Michael, "Report on Poliomyelitis Studies Made at Minneapolis General Hospital," *Journal-Lancet*, January 1945.

11. Kenny, " 'God Is My Doctor.' "

12. Interview with Valerie Harvey. Paul, *History of Polio*, pp. 340–343.

13. O'Donoghue quoted in Lois Mattox Miller, "Sister Kenny vs. the Medical Old Guard." Anonymous review in the *Journal of the American Medical Association*, 118:179 (January 10, 1942), of Kenny's *Treatment of Infantile Paralysis*. J. E. Hulett, Jr., "The Kenny Healing Cult: Preliminary Analysis of Leadership and Patterns of Interactions," *American Sociological Review*, June 1945. Interview with Dr. Philip Lewin on the "greatest gift."

14. Letter from Bennett to Krusen, July 6, 1943.

15. *Newsweek*, June 26, 1944. *Minneapolis Star-Journal*, June 20, 1944.

16. *Minneapolis Star-Journal*, July 23, 1944.

17. *Washington Times-Herald*, September 2 and 3 and October 23, 1944.

18. Information in this section is from the Kenny Foundation files; Brand et al., "History of the National Foundation"; letters from Sister Kenny to the Kenny Foundation board, March 16 and 22, 1945; and *Time*, April 2, 1945.

19. Interviews with Mary Stewart-Kenny and Stewart McCracken.

20. *Minneapolis Tribune*, September 13, 1945.

21. Report from Sister Kenny to the Kenny Foundation board, October 1, 1945.

22. Sources for this section are interviews with Rosalind Russell, Freddie Brisson, Donald Dayton, Valerie Harvey, Mary McCarthy, Dudley Nichols, Mary Stewart-Kenny, and Stewart McCracken, and many newspaper and magazine articles.

23. Sources for this section are interviews with Mary Stewart-Kenny, Valerie Harvey, and the Rollinson sisters.

24. An Associated Press story in the *Minneapolis Tribune*, May 21, 1946, repeated by Earl Wilson in the *New York Mirror*, January 5, 1951.

25. Letter to the author from J. B. Brewer, assistant to the secretary of the New South Wales Law Society.

26. *Brisbane Courier-Mail*, April 16, 1946.

Chapter 15: Turmoil

1. Interview with Will O'Neil. Other sources for this period are files of the *Minneapolis Star-Journal*, the *Minneapolis Tribune*, and the Kenny Foundation; interviews with Valerie Harvey, Mary Farquharson Fredlund, Julia Farquharson, and Drs. John Pohl and E. J. Huenekens; and the author's memories.

2. Interview with Dr. Robert Bingham.

3. Berg, *Polio and Its Problems*, pp. 131–132. *Minneapolis Star-Journal*, July 28, 1946.

4. *Minneapolis Star-Journal* and *Minneapolis Tribune*, September 28, 1946.

5. Letter from Dr. Fryberg to Sister Kenny, October 19, 1946. *Life*, September 16, 1946. *Brisbane Courier-Mail*, November 18, 1947.

6. *New York Times*, October 6, 1946. McCarten quoted in the *Australian Woman's Weekly*, March 1951. Letter from Nichols to the author.

7. Sources for this section are interviews with Al Baum, Mary Stewart-Kenny, Valerie Harvey, Charles Newton, Florence Rowe, Chester LaRoche, Orin Lehman, John Pohl, James Henry, Rosalind Russell, Freddie Brisson, and Julia Farquharson.

8. On payment for film: interview with Rosalind Russell. On gifts: interviews with Sister Kenny, Mary Stewart-Kenny, Marvin Kline, and Lloyd Johnson. The widow was Mrs. Emil Oberhoffer, whose husband was the first conductor of the Minneapolis Symphony Orchestra.

9. T. V. Stubbs Brown and A. Fryberg, "Report on Concepts and Treatments of Polio," December 6, 1948. Interviews with Drs. Fryberg, Stubbs Brown, and Mary Stewart-Kenny. Letters and cables in the Kenny Foundation and Queensland files, December 1946 to March 1947.

10. The position of Sister Kenny and the Kenny Foundation in this controversy was recapitulated in Kenny Foundation publicity documents ("The Sister Elizabeth Kenny Foundation and the National Foundation for Infantile Paralysis," October 9, 1947; "Story of the Sister Elizabeth Kenny Foundation in the Fight against Polio"); "For the Record" (National Foundation for Infantile Paralysis brochure, 1947); Kenny, "The Polio Controversy," an open letter to the *San Fernando Sun*, October 15, 1948; "Little Old New York" by Ed Sullivan, *New York Daily News*, October 17 and 31, 1946; "Answer of the National Foundation for Infantile Paralysis to Ed Sullivan Column of October 17, 1946," October 25, 1946; and interviews with Al Baum, Donald Dayton, and Basil O'Connor. The National Foundation for Infantile Paralysis said in 1948 that by then it had spent more than $2 million to teach and investigate Kenny methods, with more than 1,000 doctors, nurses, and therapists given some training at the University of Minnesota alone.

11. Sources for this section: Sister Kenny's report to the Kenny Foundation board, January 9, 1946; Kenny, *Cause and Prevention of Deformities in Polio*; Kenny Foundation files; letter from Dr. Don W. Gudakunst to Basil O'Connor, September 9, 1945; editorial in the *Journal of the American Medical Association*, 149:840 (June 28, 1952); Robert L. Bennett, "The Role of the Physician in Prevention of Musculoskeletal Deformity after Poliomyelitis," *Journal of the American Medical Association*, 153:79 (September 12, 1953).

12. Robert Bingham, "Muscular Fibrodystrophy," *Journal of Bone and Joint*

Surgery, 29:85 (January 1947). Bingham, "Muscular Fibrodystrophy in Children," *Western Journal of Surgery, Obstetrics and Gynecology*, June 1950. E. Moskowitz and L. I. Kaplan, "Follow-Up Study in 75 Cases of Nonparalytic Poliomyelitis," *Journal of the American Medical Association*, 152:505 (August 15, 1953).

13. Letter from Dr. A. E. Deacon, Winnipeg, to Sister Kenny, September 28, 1949. Robert Bingham, "Kenny Treatment for Infantile Paralysis," *Journal of Bone and Joint Surgery*, 25:647 (July 1943). Edward W. Lowman, "Preventable Deformities in Poliomyelitis," *Archives of Physical Medicine*, 28:455 (July 1947).

14. Pohl, "The Kenny Concept and Treatment." Bennett, "The Influence of the Kenny Concept."

15. Interviews with Sister Kenny. Numerous Kenny speeches and writings including "Infantile Paralysis: Its Description and Treatment." *New York Herald-Tribune*, August 6, 1944.

16. Herman Kabat and Miland E. Knapp, "The Mechanism of Muscle Spasm in Poliomyelitis," *Journal of Pediatrics*, February 1944. Kabat, "Studies on Neuromuscular Dysfunction: XV, Role of Central Facilitation and Restoration of Motor Function in Paralysis," *Archives of Physical Medicine and Rehabilitation*, September 1952. *New York Herald-Tribune*, August 6, 1944. Interviews with Dudley Nichols and Dr. John Pohl. John Pohl, "Early Diagnosis of Poliomyelitis," *Journal of the American Medical Association*, 134:13 (July 26, 1947).

17. Claus W. Jungeblut, "Newer Knowledge on Pathogenesis of Poliomyelitis," *Journal of Pediatrics*, July 1950. Jungeblut, "Studies on Viremia in Poliomyelitis," *Journal of Pediatrics*, January 1954. Jungeblut and M. A. Stevens, "Attempts to Isolate Polio Virus from Paralyzed Muscle of Patients during the Acute Stage," *American Journal of Clinical Pathology*, August 1950. Jungeblut and Jesse E. Edwards, "Isolation of Polio Virus from the Heart in Fatal Cases," *American Journal of Clinical Pathology*, July 1951. Jungeblut and E. J. Huenekens, "Studies on Viremia of Poliomyelitis: Isolation of Polio Virus from the Blood of a Fatal Case," *Journal of Pediatrics*, January 1954. Letter from Jungeblut to Sister Kenny, December 21, 1949. John R. Paul, *A History of Poliomyelitis* (New Haven: Yale University Press, 1971), pp. 267–269 and 382–389. Interviews with Dr. Jungeblut.

18. Interviews with Drs. John Enders and John R. Paul. Letter from Dr. Enders to the author, April 3, 1972.

19. Interviews with Sister Kenny. Kenny, " 'God Is My Doctor,' " "Truth Is the Daughter of Time," *My Battle and Victory*, *And They Shall Walk*, "Sister Kenny Tells 'Why I Left America,' " and quotations in many newspaper stories.

Chapter 16: Flight

1. Kenny Foundation files. *New York Times*, April 27, 1947. Kenny, "Sister Kenny Tells 'Why I Left America.' " *New York Herald-Tribune*, July 31, 1947.

2. Interview with Dr. Aubrey Pye.

3. *Brisbane Courier-Mail*, May 8, 1946 and November 18, 1947. *Woman's Day*, March 1951. Interviews with Drs. J. V. Duhig, Philip Addison, H. J. Wilkinson, and with Minnie Bell. The knighted cricketer was Sir Donald Bradman.

4. Interview with Dr. Noel Ure.

5. Sister Kenny quoted in the *Minneapolis Star*, December 28, 1947.

6. Interviews with Mary Stewart-Kenny and Sister Kenny.

7. Herbert J. Levine, *I Knew Sister Kenny* (Boston: Christopher Publishing House, 1954) pp. 44–45.

8. Interviews with Richard Metcalfe, Amy Lindsey, and Margaret Reardon.

9. Albert Deutsch, *New York Star*, reprinted in the *Minneapolis Tribune*, July 23, 1948.

10. *Newsweek*, July 26, 1948. Interviews with Richard Metcalfe and Amy Lindsey.

11. Primary sources for this section are Kenny Foundation files; interviews with Sister Kenny, Donald Dayton, Hubert H. Humphrey, Marvin Kline, Valerie Harvey, Will O'Neil, and Drs. E. J. Huenekens, John Pohl, and M. A. Stevens; Levine, *I Knew Sister Kenny*, pp. 15–20; *Minneapolis Tribune*, August 4 and 15, 1948; and *Minneapolis Star*, November 6 and December 6, 1948.

12. Quoted in a letter from Dr. Herbert J. Levine to the author, September 23, 1972.

13. Letter from Dr. Pohl to the author, July 29, 1967.

14. *Newsweek*, March 15, 1948. Interviews with Marguerite Clark, Mary Stewart-Kenny, and Peter Gazzola.

15. Dr. Don Gudakunst's "confidential" memorandum of early 1944 in Brand et al., "History of the National Foundation."

16. Experiences of Wendell Weed, Will Jones, Florence Rowe, Wally Kamman, Peter Gazzola, and the author, among many.

17. Interviews with Sister Kenny. Many Kenny quotations, including those in the *New York Times* and the *Minneapolis Tribune*, July 13, 1948. Summers, *Brisbane Courier-Mail*, November 18, 1947.

18. "Lenten Guideposts," *Minneapolis Tribune*, March 24, 1952. Interview with Rev. Arnold Lowe.

19. Levine, *I Knew Sister Kenny*. *Minneapolis Tribune*, March 9 and 15, 1949. *Minneapolis Star*, April 20, 1949.

20. Sources for this section are *Sydney Morning Herald*, January 25 and June 4, 1949. *New York Times*, July 8 and August 25, 1949. Interview with Peter Gazzola. Kenny, "Sister Kenny Tells 'Why I Left America.' "

Chapter 17: Peace

1. Kenny Foundation files. Tex McCrary and Jinx Falkenburg, *New York Herald-Tribune*, August 31, 1951. *Minneapolis Tribune*, February 12 and March 3, 1950.

Witnesses of events in this chapter are Mary Stewart-Kenny, Stewart McCracken, Elizabeth Kenny's sisters (Julia, Margaret, and Mary), Chressy Kenny, Pearl Baldock, nurse Marjorie Bridle, Carl Brisson, Freddie Brisson, Rosalind Russell, Nell Buckle, Fred Hubbard (*Time-Life*), Mollie Shortt (Sister Kenny's last traveling companion, the daughter of Alice Perrott), Harry Summers, Alicent Woodward, and Drs. Noel Ure and J. K. Ogden.

2. Interview with Sister Kenny. *Minneapolis Tribune*, December 3, 1950. *Women's Day and Home*, March 5, 1951.

3. *Brisbane Courier-Mail* and the *Toowoomba Chronicle*, March 17, 1951. *People*, June 20, 1951.

4. *People*, June 20, 1951. *Toowoomba Chronicle*, June 13, 1951. *Sydney Morning Herald*, August 16, 1951.

5. *Minneapolis Star*, August 16, 1951.

6. Letter from Mrs. Jack Hall to Sister Kenny, October 25, 1951. Letter from Pascal Cowan, Pan American Airways, to the author, April 2, 1956.

7. *Minneapolis Tribune*, August 14, 1951.

8. Interview with Sister Kenny. *New York Herald-Tribune*, August 31, 1951.

9. Robert L. Bennett, "Physical Medicine in Poliomyelitis," *Poliomyelitis: Papers and Discussions Presented at the Second International Poliomyelitis Conference* (Philadelphia: Lippincott, 1952), p. 261. Interviews with Carl Brisson and Basil O'Connor.

10. Tex McCrary and Jinx Falkenburg, *New York Herald-Tribune*, August 31, 1951. *Minneapolis Tribune*, September 20, 1951.

11. *Sydney Morning Herald*, October 15, 1951. *Toowoomba Daily Bulletin*, November 2, 1951.

12. *Brisbane Courier-Mail*, January 14 and 17, 1952.

13. *New York Times*, March 23, 1952. Interview with Mollie Shortt.

14. Gallup Poll, *New York World-Telegram*, January 14, 1952.

15. Interview with Dr. Philip Addison. Queensland files.

16. The United States consul was Charles Carson.

17. The father of the Newark polio victim was Simon Bloom of the *Newark Jewish Ledger*.

18. *Sydney Morning Herald*, December 1, 1952.

Epilogue: A Nurse's Heritage

1. Files of the Kenny Foundation, the *Minneapolis Star*, *Minneapolis Tribune*, the *San Francisco Chronicle*, and the *San Francisco Examiner*, 1950 and after.

2. Report of the attorney general on the investigation of the Sister Kenny Foundation, Inc., State Capitol, St. Paul, June 1960. Indictment, the United States versus Marvin L. Kline, Fred Fadell, Abraham L. Koolish, David F. Koolish, John B. Carnell, Philip G. Rettig, J. George Zimmerman, United States District Court, Minneapolis, December 1961. Interviews with Donald Dayton, James Henry, Miles Lord, and Dr. E. J. Huenekens. Files of the *Minneapolis Star*, *Minneapolis Tribune*, 1960 through 1964.

3. Interview with James Henry.

4. Interviews with Donald Dayton and Miles Lord.

5. Report of the attorney general on the investigation of the Sister Elizabeth Kenny Foundation.

6. Interview with Miles Lord.

7. Interview with Helen O'Rourke, director, Philanthropy Advisory Department, Council of Better Business Bureaus. Other sources consulted for this section were Harvey Katz, consultant to the 1974 Mondale Subcommittee Investigation; Peter G. Meek, executive director, National Health Council; Melvin Van de Workeen, executive director, D. Paul Reed, late executive director, and Pamela Brooks, of the National Information Bureau. Ad Hoc Citizens Committee, *Voluntary Health and Welfare Agencies in the United States* (New York: Schoolmasters Press, 1961). Richard Carter, *The Gentle Legions* (New York: Doubleday, 1961), pp. 84–87; 91–138; 295–299.

8. Ad Hoc Citizens Committee, *Voluntary Health and Welfare Agencies*, and interview with Robert Hamlin, study director.

9. "Government by Elite Vigilantes," an address given by Basil O'Connor in 1961.

10. Interviews with Drs. Frank Krusen, E. J. Huenekens, Paul Ellwood, Loren Leslie, and Howard Rusk.

11. Dr. Howard Rusk's autobiography, *A World to Care For* (New York: Random House, 1972), pp. 289, 295–296.

12. Paul, *A History of Poliomyelitis*, p. 394.

13. H. J. Seddon, "Sister Kenny" (obituary), *British Medical Journal*, 4796:1262 (December 6, 1952).

14. Interview with Dr. Krusen. Seddon, "Sister Kenny."

15. Interview with Dr. Pohl.

16. Frederic Kottke, "The Role of Poliomyelitis in the Development of Physical Medicine and Rehabilitation," address given on Miland Knapp Recognition Day, Minneapolis, May 26, 1973.

Kottke based this view in part on Ernst Gellhorn, "Patterns of Muscular Activity in Man," *Archives of Physical Medicine and Rehabilitation*, September 1967; K. E. Hagbarth, *Acta Physiologica Scandinavica*, Volume 26, Supplement 94, 1952; Frances Hellebrandt, unpublished communication to Kottke; H. Kabat, "Studies on Neuromuscular Dysfunction," *Archives of Physical Medicine and Rehabilitation*, September 1952; Kabat and Knapp, "The Mechanism of Muscle Spasm in Poliomyelitis," *Journal of Pediatrics*, February 1944; Knapp, "The Contribution of Sister Elizabeth Kenny to the Treatment of Poliomyelitis," *Archives of Physical Medicine and Rehabilitation*, August 1955; J. Minckler, "Pathologic Alterations in Surface Relations and Morphology of the Human Synapse," *American Journal of Pathology*, July-September-November 1942; H. J. Ralston, "Recent Advances in Neuromuscular Physiology," *American Journal of Physical Medicine*, April 1957; T. G. Simard and J. V. Basmajian, "Methods in Training the Conscious Control of Motor Units," *Archives of Physical Medicine and Rehabilitation*, January 1967.

Also: F. J. Kottke and G. K. Stillwell, "Studies on Increased Vasomotor Tone in the Lower Extremities Following Anterior Poliomyelitis," *Archives of Physical Medicine*, June 1951; Kottke, W. G. Kubicek, and Mildred E. Olson, *Proceedings of the International Congress of Physical Medicine* (London: Headley Bros. Ltd., 1952), p. 116; Kottke, Glenn Gullickson, and Mildred E. Olson, "Effect of the Sympathetic Nervous System on Longitudinal Bone Growth after Acute Anterior Poliomyelitis," *Archives of Physical Medicine and Rehabilitation*, December 1958.

17. Kottke works cited in note 16.

18. Mary M. I. Daly et al., "The Early Treatment of Poliomyelitis, with an Evaluation of the Sister Kenny Treatment," *Journal of the American Medical Association*, 118:1433 (April 25, 1942).

19. Interview with Dr. Lewin. Coulter is quoted by Krusen in the *Proceedings of the Mayo Clinic*.

20. Dr. Sedgwick Mead, "A Century of the Abuse of Rest," *Journal of the American Medical Association*, 182:344 (October 27, 1962). Frederic Kottke, "Effects of Limitation of Activity upon the Human Body," and G. M. Martin, editorial, *Journal of the American Medical Association*, 196:909 (June 6, 1966).

21. Rev. Arnold Lowe, in a memorial service for Sister Kenny at Westminster Presbyterian Church, Minneapolis, December 4, 1952.

22. Seddon, "Sister Kenny." Brand et al., "History of the National Foundation."

Index

Index